Project Management Institute

COLLABORATIVE PROJECT
PROCUREMENT ARRANGEMENTS

Derek H.T. Walker, PhD, MSc, Grad Dip (Mgt Sys)
Professor of Project Management
School of Property, Construction and
Project Management, RMIT University
Melbourne, Australia

**Beverley M. Lloyd–Walker, PhD, Grad Cert (Change Mgt
AGSM), Grad Dip Info Mgt, Grad Dip Post Sec Ed, BBus**
Centre for Integrated Project Solutions (CIPS),
RMIT University,
Melbourne, Australia

Library of Congress Cataloging-in-Publication Data

Walker, Derek H. T.
  Collaborative project procurement arrangements / Derek H.T. Walker, PhD, MSc, Grad Dip (Mgt Sys), Professor of Project Management, School of Property, Construction and Project Management, RMIT University, Melbourne, Australia, Beverley M. Lloyd-Walker, PhD, Grad Cert (Change Mgt AGSM), Grad Dip Info Mgt, Grad Dip Post Sec Ed, BBus, Senior Lecturer, Victoria University, Melbourne, Australia.
      pages cm
  Includes bibliographical references.
  ISBN 978-1-62825-067-1 (pbk. : alk. paper) -- ISBN 1-62825-067-4 (pbk. : alk. paper) 1. Project management. 2. Industrial management. 3. Personnel management. I. Lloyd-Walker, Beverley M. II. Title.
  HD69.P75W345 2015
  658.4'04--dc23
                          2014048227

ISBN: 978-1-62825-067-1

Published by: Project Management Institute, Inc.
                   14 Campus Boulevard
                   Newtown Square, Pennsylvania 19073-3299 USA
                   Phone: +610-356-4600
                   Fax: +610-356-4647
                   Email: customercare@pmi.org
                   Internet: www.PMI.org

PMI Publications welcomes corrections and comments on its books. Please feel free to send comments on typographical, formatting, or other errors. Simply make a copy of the relevant page of the book, mark the error, and send it to: Book Editor, PMI Publications, 14 Campus Boulevard, Newtown Square, PA 19073-3299 USA.

To inquire about discounts for resale or educational purposes, please contact the PMI Book Service Center.

        PMI Book Service Center
        P.O. Box 932683, Atlanta, GA 31193-2683 USA
        Phone: 1-866-276-4764 (within the U.S. or Canada) or +1-770-280-4129 (globally)
        Fax: +1-770-280-4113
        Email: info@bookorders.pmi.org

The paper used in this book complies with the Permanent Paper Standard issued by the National Information Standards Organization (Z39.48—1984).

10 9 8 7 6 5 4 3 2 1

Table of Contents

Acknowledgments

We would like to thank and acknowledge the Project Management Institute (PMI) for generously funding the grant "Understanding Relationship-Based Procurement" for part of our research. We would also like to thank and acknowledge the Australian Research Council (ARC) for funding part of this research under the ARC Linkage Grant LP110200110 to gather data in parallel with the PMI grant, and to thank the Alliancing Association of Australasia (AAA) for their funding of the study "Profiling Professional Excellence in Alliance Management in 2010." This book draws upon the AAA original work in the light of the PMI and ARC research studies.

We also would like to acknowledge and thank Mr. Alain Mignot who was CEO of the AAA until its amalgamation with Infrastructure Partnerships Australia (IPA). He was an original industry research collaborator of ours whose intellect, insights, and support, as well as his inspiration has been a significant driving force for much of the research into alliancing in Australasia.

We also acknowledge and thank all academic and practitioner subject matter expert participants who generously gave their time. We would especially like to thank Dr. Mattias Jacobsson and Dr. James Harley who participated as part of our team in data gathering and analysis as part of the ARC grant and provided insights that contributed to this book. Dr. Jacobsson also provided valuable specific feedback on the draft. Without the contribution of our research collaborators for this book and the practitioner participants who generously gave us on average an hour of their valuable time, this research would not have been possible.

Contents

Abbreviations

Abbreviations are provided for terms used frequently throughout this book. Not all abbreviated words appear here, as those words may be used only within a few pages of first being used.

3BL	Triple bottom line – financial, environmental and social bottom lines	KPI	Key performance indicator
AAA	Alliancing Association of Australasia	KRA	Key results area
ALT	Alliance leadership team – the high-level board of alliance participant sponsors	KSAE	Knowledge, skills, attributes and experience
AM	Alliance manager	MC	Management contracting
AMT	Alliance management team – the operational-level participant executive team	NCTP	Novelty, complexity, technology, pace
		NMA	National Museum of Australia
		NOP	Non-owner participants in an alliance
BAA	British Airports Authority	OL	Organizational learning
BAU	Business as usual	P/PA	Project and program alliancing
BIM	Building information modeling	PA	Project alliance
BOO	Build-own-operate	PFI	Private financing initiative
BOOT	Build own operate transfer	PM	Project management
BOT	Build-own-transfer	PMBOK®	*A Guide to the Project Management Body of Knowledge*
CD	Competitive dialogue		
CMM	Capability maturity model	PMI	Project Management Institute
CoP	Community of practice	PO	Project owner
CSR	Corporate social responsibility	POR	Project owner representative
D&C	Design and construct	PPP	Public-private partnership
DA	Design alliance	RBP	Relationship-based procurement
DBB	Design bid build	SA	Program service alliance
ECI	Early contractor involvement	SCM	Supply chain management
HR	Human resource	SD-Logic	Service delivery logic
HRM	Human resource management	SME	Subject matter expert
ICT	Information communication technology	T5	Terminal 5 Heathrow - the BAA Terminal Five Heathrow contract agreement
IPA	Infrastructure Partnerships Australia		
IPD	Integrated project delivery	TOC	Target outturn cost – the expect cost that a project will eventually cost
IT	Information technology		
JV	Joint venture	VfM	Value for money
KM	Knowledge management	WLB	Work-life balance

Executive Summary

The research question

Clients choosing a specific category of relationship-based procurement (RBP) would benefit from a clearer definition of not only the characteristics of these forms of project procurement but also the knowledge, skills, attributes, and experience (KSAE) required of project managers delivering these projects. Several research questions naturally flow from this research problem:

Q1 – What are the fundamental characteristics of emerging relationship-based forms of project procurement?

Q2 – Do these forms vary in different parts of the world and, if so, in what way?

Q3 – What specific KSAEs that are required to deliver such projects are currently underdeveloped or missing from traditional project managers' knowledge and skills sets?

Q4 – How may any identified gaps be bridged?

Context of the research

This research is undertaken within the context of the global construction industry sector. More specifically, it deals with a form of relationship-based project procurement and delivery for large-scale building and engineering infrastructure works. It undertakes analysis of data gathered from subject experts from Australia, the U.S., Hong Kong, the U.K. and several European countries.

Brief overview of the methodology

We adhere to the paradigm of project management (PM) and forms of project procurement being a socially constructed concept. These forms did not exist before people started to do what we describe as project work. We believe that *PM* and project *procurement* exists in the sense that we find it convenient to interpret activity we can observe. People do *PM* work when they transform an idea of some kind of beneficial change (such as creating a software tool to perform a set of functions, or building a new transport facility for people and goods to be moved around a city, or transforming a business's administration system to comply with certain needed standards) into a project output. The process of obtaining the required resources to perform this transformation is what we perceive the major role of a project procurement process. Our perspective of what we assumed to exist drives us to believe that PM and a procurement choice for a project owner representative (POR) exists as a social construct. Therefore, we argue that attempting to conceptualize the phenomenon of a project procurement system must be based on trying to understand the descriptions and stories of project managers engaged in a project procurement process. We view PM as a learning and transformational co-generated learning process.

We undertook a research approach of interviews with 50 subject matter experts, 14 of whom were academics and 36 were practitioners. We first reviewed the literature, both from a scanning the environment sense to gain an appreciation of the state of the art but to also hone in on particular case study work that could reveal additional insights that could inform our research. Often authors of case studies and other studies are obliged to edit out important insights to focus their paper for a particular audience. Additionally, authors may be able to reflect on their results as time has elapsed and current context changes since the materials and evidence were published. We initially relied primarily on the published literature and our reflection on our research to identify 14 subject matter experts (SMEs) who we could interview. We also reflected upon and re-examined several previous related research studies that we had completed. We interviewed a total of 36 subject matter experts from several countries. And our interviews were recorded and transcribed to provide over 500 pages of transcription that we analyzed using a grounded theory sensemaking approach with the aid of the NVivo10 tool. Findings were validated through a series of presentations to academics at international conferences in Australia, the U.K., the U.S., and in several European cities. We also presented findings for review and comment to two separate sets of subject matter experts from those we interviewed in the U.K. in October 2013, one at Oxford University in the U.K. and the other at the Cabinet Office Westminster, the U.K. Details of the methodology, the description of those interviewed and the validation process is contained in the monograph.

Brief Overview of the Findings and Application for Practice

We believe that the value that this monograph contributes to the PM literature can be summarized with reference to the monograph as follows:

- A substantial discussion and presentation in Chapter 2 of PM theory that underpins the study and linked it within a project procurement context;
- A substantial discussion and presentation in Chapter 3 of business theory aspects of RBP that sets the study in context and underpins the study within a project procurement context;
- A substantial discussion and presentation in Chapter 4 of human behavior aspects of RBP that sets the study in context and underpins the study within a project procurement context;
- Table 6 that updates and presents findings from our Alliancing Association of Australasia (AAA) study of profiling Alliance Manager Excellence. The table presents a model that incorporates feedback from practitioners that enthusiastically supported its applicability to both alliance managers and high performing project managers working on complex projects;
- Table 9 that presents a current definition of RBP forms as understood in a set of countries in the world. This provides a significant attempt to explain the terms and how the approaches are applied globally;
- Figure 25 that provides a model for categorizing collaboration forms linked to RBP terms, generally used globally together with Table 10, that explains the degree of relationship intensity characteristics to supplement the understanding that readers can gain from Figure 25;
- Figure 27, the Wittgenstein's Idea of Family Resemblance model that identifies 16 "petals" or elements that has been grouped into platform foundational, behavioral factors and processes, routines, and means drivers of RBP forms. This, together with Table 11, Table 12 and Table13 explains in detail what each element and sub-element/ theme means and how the element may be measured. This provides an RBP taxonomy visualization model that can be developed through a color-coded table (an example of this is presented in Table 14, with a sample analysis presented in Table 15) or a radar chart diagram for any given RBP configuration, as illustrated in Figure 28. This facilitates better understanding of each element's characteristics. KSAEs and benchmark standards can be determined by using the associated table in Appendix 2, enabling best use of each element's characteristics to deliver value through the project.

This contribution addresses the research aim to present a body of research work that helps people better understand the various emerging forms of RBP and how to identify what KSAE may be required for any particular RBP form.

The principal practical value delivered by this monograph includes presentation of a visualization tool for understanding forms of project procurement so that as they evolve over time and are interpreted across the world, a more explicit and clearer explanation of how they fit upon a relationship-based procurement continuum might be used. This should help academics, practitioners and policy makers become more confident that they are "speaking the same language." The second main contribution made is the development of the relationship-based procurement taxonomy that is presented in Chapter 6 of Section 1 of the book and elaborated upon in Appendix two of Section 2.

CHAPTER 1

Introduction and Scope of this Book

Chapter 1 Introduction

This chapter reports on research undertaken for, and sponsored by, a Project Management Institute (PMI) globally competitive research grant. This chapter introduces the purpose of the research by initially stating the research problem to be addressed. This is followed by a brief explanation of our research approach, which is governed by our worldview that in turn helped us to identify both the research questions to be addressed and our research design. We follow with a brief outline of the sources of literature that are justified to be used in this study. This then leads to the introduction chapter conclusion.

The Purpose of the Research

We began this research project with a focus on collaborative project procurement arrangements, mainly in the construction and infrastructure industry sector. We originally envisaged these arrangements as a continuum with design and construct (D&C) at one end and project and program alliancing (P/PA) at the other. P/PAs are increasingly becoming a popular collaborative project arrangement form. These arrangements are often referred to as relationship-based procurement (RBP) within the Australasian and the U.K. context (Davis & Love, 2011; Mills & Harley, 2010; Wood & Duffield, 2009). There is also an increasingly emerging interest in P/PAs in other countries (see, for example, Howell, Windahl, & Seidel, 2010; Laan, Voordijk, & Dewulf, 2011; Manchester Business School, 2009c). However, the shape and form that RBP in general, and project alliancing in particular, takes around the world differs. Until recently, interpretation of European Union procurement regulations were thought to rule out P/PA choices by project owners; however, that mood is gradually changing and project alliances (PAs) in forms similar to those delivered in Australia are being undertaken (Laan et al., 2011). Moreover, in Europe, an interesting form of close integration between project owner and contractors during the project tendering procurement stage has emerged. It is called the competitive dialogue (CD) process (Hoezen, 2012). Another form collaboration between project owner (PO), designer, and delivery contractor called integrated project delivery (IPD) emerged in the U.S. during the early part of this century (Mathews & Howell, 2005). Lahdenperä (2012) maps these trends of flowing influence that have direct implications for the requirement of skills development for project owners (clients), project architects, and design teams as well as for project delivery contractors. It would be in the interests of project owners, PMI members, project management (PM) academics and practitioners to have a better understanding of this emerging trend.

PMI's *A Guide to the Project Management Body of Knowledge (PMBOK® Guide)* (PMI, 2008) currently has gaps in its coverage of collaborative project procurement arrangements, even though we have known for several decades that they have been shown to be an effective way to deliver better value for money than do many more traditional project procurement approaches (Egan, 1998; Latham, 1994). We were successful in a research grant to undertake a global study of P/PA practices with a focus on alliances and similar forms of supply-chain integration that are being adopted and adapted globally.

We aim to help narrow the project procurement knowledge gap in the *PMBOK® Guide* for collaborative approaches to project procurement through publications flowing from our current work and the research work undertaken to write this book. This research outcome will improve our ability to compare and contrast RBP forms around the globe; more specifically, how P/PA compares with other identified RBP forms. The impact of this new form of RBP on the knowledge, skills, attributes, and experience (KSAE) profiles of successful project managers could then be identified. By contrasting these new KSAEs against current PM competencies, changes to country-specific and/or worldwide PM KSAEs could be recommended. This would then potentially influence any future development of the PM competency framework (PMI, 2007).

The Research Approach

The research problem as stated above is that the shape and form of RBP, and in particular project alliancing, around the world does differ, and this triggered us to contemplate developing a taxonomy of RBP approaches so that we can see P/PAs in a wider global context and be more confident that it possible to develop such a taxonomy.

Mingers (2003, p. 559) describes a paradigm as "particular combinations of assumptions" or more plainly, the assumed truth until proven otherwise. It is important for researchers to be clear about what they assume to be true. He further explains the term paradigm as "… a construct that specifies a general set of philosophical assumptions covering, for example, *ontology* (what is assumed to exist), *epistemology* (the nature of valid knowledge), ethics or *axiology* (what is valued or considered right), and methodology" (Mingers, 2003, p. 559).

We adhere to the paradigm of PM and forms of project procurement being a socially constructed concept. They did not exist before people started to do what we describe as project work. We believe that *PM* and project *procurement* exist in the sense that we find it convenient to interpret activity we can observe. People do *PM* work when they transform an idea of some kind of beneficial change (such as creating a software tool to perform a set of functions, or building a new transport facility for people and goods to be moved around a city, or transforming a business's administration system to comply with certain needed standards) into a project output. The process of obtaining the required resources to perform this transformation is what we perceive the major role of a project procurement process.

Our ontological position (our perspective of what we assumed to exist) drives us to believe that PM and a procurement choice for a project owner representative (POR) exists as a social construct. Therefore, we argue that attempting to conceptualize the phenomenon of a project procurement system must be based on trying to understand the descriptions and stories of project managers engaged in a project procurement process. If project procurement is a social construct then literature about it and normative guides to be found in, for example, the *PMBOK® Guide* are contestable. Further, as Koskinen (2012) argues, much of PM entails process thinking and he sees projects as learning episodes. Much of traditional PM thinking as presented in the *PMBOK® Guide* assumes a project as a product or product plus a service, even though it also describes PM as a set of processes. We view PM as a learning and transformational co-generated learning process.

We see a project-based organization in particular as a learn**ing** and not a learn**ed** organization. An organization that undertakes projects can continuously absorb knowledge and learn from experiences. This learning is also facilitated from the KSAE and social capital assets that other project team members bring to a project through the collaboration process. Project-oriented organizations undertake specific projects as a normal part of their operations, usually using internal PM resources supplemented with some external PM consultant resources (Gareis & Hueman, 2007; Turner, Huemann & Keegan, 2008); therefore, they also have the capacity to absorb knowledge through the collaboration process. This worldview naturally skews our perspective of what KSAE should be expected of proficient project managers.

Essentially, our epistemological stance (our perspective of the nature of valid knowledge) and our axiological position (the evidence that we most highly value) relies on analyzing the accounts of those engaged in those processes. The acceptability of evidence is, in our view, based on a rigorous account of their lived reality. Case studies provide a useful way to research phenomena from this epistemological perspective (Yin, 1994). While we have undertaken case studies as significant research in this area (Davis & Walker, 2008; Lloyd-Walker, Lingard, & Walker, 2008;

Walker & Hampson, 2003b; Walker & Hampson, 2003c; Walker & Lloyd-Walker, 2011a; 2011b; 2011c; Walker & Rowlinson, 2008a), we also value the numerous case studies and research of a wide range of others.

Our principal axiological stance is that we value a pragmatic and transparently reflective practitioner-oriented research approach where case studies have been undertaken that reveal the untidy and messy real lived experience of those engaged in these projects. We value the insights that many published case studies reveal in the literature because these surface a rich context that underpins our understanding of this area.

As active researchers, we have experienced the frustrating process of writing and publishing research results. Often, much valuable material and research insights are excluded from a final published paper for many valid reasons. Word count may be a severe limitation, as may be the focus of a particular publisher. This led us to consider that rather than duplicate studies already documented, we could conduct a form of meta-study where we rely on a combination of published literature, our reflections on our own relevant case study research, and to extending our fieldwork research by inviting a number of the authors that have conducted important work in this field to share further insights on their work with us. We are fortunate in that we have a wide network of colleagues who have shared our interest in this area, and indeed from time to time we have collaborated with some of these on research projects and writing other papers. We, therefore, believe that we can undertake a peer review of the area as collegial facilitators.

Our research approach to work that we discuss in this chapter is to first review the literature, both from a more standard stance of scanning the environment to gain an appreciation of the state of the art but to also hone in on particular case study work that we consider could reveal additional insights. These opportunities may occur because an author was obliged to edit out important insights to focus his or her paper to a particular audience, or the case study authors may be able to reflect on their results as time has elapsed and current context has changed since the materials and evidence were published. We therefore propose to rely primarily on the published literature and our reflection on our research to identify a number of subject matter experts (SMEs) who we could interview. This extends the concept of a literature review in a valuable and insightful way. We also undertook several case studies in the application of RBP to bridge gaps in our knowledge.

We decided to collate evidence from published case study findings and other authoritative sources to establish a series of propositions about how an RBP approach might be categorized with associated KSAEs. This model could then be tested, consistent with our ontological and epistemological stance, by presenting findings to be revealed, questioned, and improved through several workshops with SMEs with both an academic and practitioner background. We chose academic experts because they have a potential skill to extract and synthesise tacit knowledge from experts through interviews and for their rigorous comparison with theory to synthesis and make sense of knowledge gained from practitioner SME stories and revelations. We chose to workshop findings with SMEs so that we could test our findings from sourced experts. This results in our findings being tested to be valid. Shalin (1992, p. 260) expresses pragmatic validation in terms of results being workable, understandable, and useful. We argue that rigor is maintained from a pragmatic perspective (Lovitt, 1997; Morgan, 2007; Shalin, 1992).

We also believe that to understand the process of project sponsors developing a way to convert the idea/concept to deliver a beneficial change into actual delivery of that beneficial change as a *project procurement process*. We need to differentiate between a purely transactional and the relational approach to this procurement process. Similarly, the procurement of a project is also a process of routines where known approaches and routines learned previously can be modified, adapted, and applied, such as was reported on the Heathrow Terminal 5 (T5) project (Davies, Gann, & Douglas, 2009).

A transactional approach implies that the project owner (PO) or their representative presents a substantially *status quo* position, a design that has been developed to a point of tender. In this more traditional approach, much criticized in, for example, U.K. government reports (Murray & Langford, 2003) for being inflexible and dismissing the early input of those that would actually deliver the project, the environment is established for a great deal of game playing and adversarial and opportunistic behavior (Masterman, 2002; Walker & Hampson, 2003c). This approach can be contrasted with an RBP approach where integration of the PO or most likely the POR, with those who advise the POR, and the entity that eventually is contracted to deliver the project. In RBP approaches, these entities collaborate to develop a coherent and pragmatic project delivery strategy. There are a number of forms of RBP and they are described in the literature in a dazzling array of terms and epithets.

Clients choosing a specific category of RBP would benefit from clearer definition of not only the characteristics of these forms of project procurement but also the knowledge, skills, attributes, and experience (KSAE) required of project managers delivering these projects.

Several research questions naturally flow from this research problem in the light of our stated research approach orientation as discussed above:

Q1 – What are the fundamental characteristics of emerging relationship-based forms of project procurement?
Q2 – Do these forms vary in different parts of the world and, if so, in what way?
Q3 – What specific KSAEs that are required to deliver such projects are currently underdeveloped or missing from traditional project managers' knowledge and skills sets?
Q4 – How may any identified gaps be bridged?

We argue that our research approach can contribute new knowledge through the RBP taxonomy and associated KSAE capability maturity model (CMM). We acknowledge that this is a first step and we are confident that the taxonomy and KSAE CMM presented in this book will be improved upon over time as others extend the insights from case studies and as the whole approach evolves. We respectfully request those who develop these tools and concepts based on our work will cite this seminal work appropriately.

Fundamental Introductory Project Procurement Concepts

Projects vary considerably in their purpose and objectives. They all begin with an identified need and benefit that the project outcome is designed to provide (Bradley, 2010). The focus of this research is the point at which a project is procured, that is when an entity (internally or externally commissioned) commences the project delivery phase. The concept of project phases is fundamental to the PM worldview (PMI, 2008). In theory, a project arises out of a strategic need to do something or obtain something that defines a project goal and objectives (Artto, Kujala, Dietrich, & Martinsuo, 2008). Traditional PM theory holds that projects begin with an initial project concept and definitional phase, where benefit outputs from a proposed project are identified. This is followed by an intermediary phase in which the project is designed, a business case is presented to a high-level sanctioning entity (Klakegg, Williams, & Magnussen, 2009) that links the project brief and its outcome with the triggering strategy, and that this project concept is sanctioned if it is to proceed to the next phase (Bentley, 2010; Morris & Jamieson, 2004; Office of Government Commerce, 2007b). The next phase is a design development from the brief to a working solution; then resources are procured to deliver that project. Once the project is delivered, it is handed over to operational entities to deliver the outcomes facilitated by the project outputs (PMI, 2008).

More sophisticated approaches to the management of projects (and programs of projects) involve a stage gate system. This system provides for a series of checks and balances where the alignment of the project outputs and outcomes is tested against the strategic purpose of the project (Cooper, 2005; Cooper, Edgett, & Kleinschmidt, 1997; Klakegg, Williams, Walker, Andersen, & Magnussen, 2010; Office of Government Commerce, 2007c). In theory projects can be terminated if their *raison d'être*, their purpose, is not being fulfilled. For most projects, once they are sanctioned, they are very difficult to stop or substantially amend. This presents a serious limitation to PM and results in many project failures due to the weakness and vulnerability of sanctioning a project that cannot be stopped or substantially changed while being delivered (Klakegg, 2010). This insight lends weight to perceiving greater value in RBP approaches offering greater strategic flexibility over the delivery of projects and how scope, scale, and an ability to negotiate possible project termination if it becomes a strategic liability.

Morris and Geraldi (2011) describe three levels of PM. Level 1 relates to technical operational delivery-oriented and instrumental PM at an activity level. The strategic Level 2 perceives PM as being holistic within an organization and encompasses front-end development and moving from concerns over efficiency to effectiveness. Level 3 is about managing the institutional context and generating value to the broader enterprise by achieving a communities and institutions value proposition. This level considers the "parent" environment as well as the external environment.

Many projects delivered for external project "clients" (rather than project oriented for internal organizational "clients") need this kind of consideration. This is because the project teams that deliver a project are drawn from numerous independent organizations that come together to deliver that project but they have a separate "parent organization" agenda and needs—as do many of the communities and institutions that are affected by the projects delivery and existence.

This study naturally had to be constrained and limited in scope. Projects can be seen to comprise of many types with very different characteristics. We will discuss that later in this book.

Literature Supporting RBP Analysis

We will discuss a number of concepts from the literature with which we will use to either help us shape our understanding of the research problem stated earlier and to make sense of available literature, or to help us frame questions to ask selected literature authorities we interviewed and as a basis of supporting our SME workshops.

Project procurement choice may be influenced by a number of factors. Many of these need to be set in context. The literature that we chose to use to underpin our study is illustrated in Table 1 and explained in terms of rationale or purpose for its use. Three broad areas of literature were explored in this book.

First, we needed to place this firmly in a PM context because the study is about project and program procurement. We now need to explain project types and how they may affect a procurement choice as well as how the project life cycle defines our study focus. We will draw upon existing extensive project procurement literature to identify a taxonomy that can be used to more effectively categorize procurement choices that can be accepted globally.

Second, we need to place the study firmly in an organizational business context because PM is about delivering benefits to commercial, government, or not-for-profit organizations. We adopt the Artto and Wikström (2005) view of business, and project business in particular, as comprising a set of activities that seek to further the strategic direction of that organization and that both for-profit and not-for-profit organizations engage in project business. We explain that project work is outsourcing because our project procurement taxonomy is based on an organization-external delivery of projects after the project sanction phase of the project life cycle has been reached. Design of

Literature	Literature Chapters and Their Relevance
Project management theory aspects	**Project types**: Because one size does not fit all project types in terms of recommended procurement approach. **Project life cycle**: Because some forms of procurement can link into the early phase better than others. **Project procurement forms**: Because there are different forms of procurement for traditional, partially integrated arrangements, consortia, and completely collaborative arrangements. **Iron triangle implications**: Because non-traditional procurement forms extend performance beyond the "iron triangle."
Business theory aspects	**Business justification for outsourcing**: Because the logic for adopting various procurement forms is dependent upon the project's rationale for being. **Governance fundamentals**: Because the form of governance chosen to be applied to the project procurement and delivery process affects behaviors and likely performance outcomes. **Complexity implications**: Because choice of project procurement is affected by the perceived level of complexity of the environment within which the project is developed and delivered.
Human behavior theory aspects	**Trust and commitment**: Because some forms of project procurement require different approaches that enable collaboration through team trust and commitment to the project outcome. **Collaboration frameworks**: Because the effectiveness of collaboration is impacted by the way that project team members co-learn, are able to understand each other's perspective and to build social capital as a project asset to improve project delivery outcomes. **Competence classifications**: Because one of the important aims of this research was to understand how the PMI Competency Development Framework (PMI, 2007) and other competency frameworks may be used to inform recommended improvements in the PMI Competency Development Framework.

Table 1. Relevant literature

an appropriate procurement approach is linked to project governance, which relates to business governance, so we need to include discussion on that aspect. Much of the outsourcing undertaken today is influenced by global markets and complexity issues associated with turbulent and volatile economic conditions. Also, organizations these days are more aware of stakeholder engagement and this has triggered interest in triple bottom line (financial, environmental, social) issues.

Third, projects are delivered by people. We, therefore, need to include discussion on human behavior (people) aspects of PM and project procurement and how their KSAE influence a project procurement choice decision. We focus on strategic human resource management (HRM) issues and KSAE issues in terms of capability maturity models (CMM), because these can provide a useful link to competence concepts, which in turn have an impact on project procurement approach choice.

Chapter 1 Summary

The purpose of this chapter was to introduce the study and its rationale. It was important for us to first explain the problem to be addressed. We also needed to clarify our position in terms of our worldview; what we perceive as being a valid ontological, epistemological, and axiological stance to take in researching this topic. We presented the research questions that logically flow from our worldview of the research problem, given our research perspective. Lastly, we indicated the literature that we felt was relevant to explore and to support conclusions made from this study.

This leads us to the three literature review chapters which explain the relevance of theory to the research questions and how they are useful in making sense of the findings.

Project Management Theory Aspects

Chapter 2 Introduction

This chapter presents the theoretical background and context required to underpin the study. The concepts discussed in this chapter frame literature that we found supports development of the RBP approach taxonomy and are useful in explaining the rationale for that taxonomy. As explained in Chapter 1, we accessed three broad streams of literature: project management theory aspects, business theory aspects, and human behavior aspects. Each of these three streams forms a separate chapter in this book. Figure 1 illustrates this chapter's work breakdown structure.

In this section we will discuss project type theory, project lifecycle theory and discuss some of the project procurement categories advanced and largely accepted globally, followed by a section on the implications of the iron triangle view of project performance measurement on project procurement choice. The chapter is then summarized.

Project Characteristics

The Shenhar et al. Diamond Perspective: NCTP

Shenhar (2001) argues that it would be a mistake to consider that there is a "one-size fits all" approach that is applicable to managing projects. This is relevant because we agree that project type has an impact on a series of strategic management factors, not least being procurement options. Shenhar departed from contingency theory developed by Lawrence and Lorsch (1967) to propose viewing project types based on scales of project scope and technological uncertainty. He later developed that perspective further with Dov Dvir to propose a project typology that they termed the *Uncertainty, Complexity, Pace* model (Shenhar & Dvir, 2004: p. 1267; Shenhar & Dvir, 2007). The uncertainty dimension was seen as a combination of novelty and technology and this was then developed into their *Novelty, Complexity, Technology and Pace* (NCTP) framework to illustrate a particular PM perspective. The framework has four dimensions.

Novelty is measured as being derivative, platform, or breakthrough. This dimension describes the extent to which methods are well defined. Derivatives are extensions of existing products or methods. Platforms are new generations and refinements in existing families of products or methods. Breakthroughs are paradigm shifts going beyond innovation to invention or significant reframing that develops a totally new way of looking at a problem.

Complexity is measured as being assembly, system, and array. Complexity refers to moving from an assembly to a system and array. An assembly involves creating a collective of elements into a component. A system, by contrast, involves a complex collective of entities into a new form, a reconfiguration or reframing of parts into a new whole with different characteristics from those of the pre-existing system. An array-type project radically shifts the paradigm. An array defense project may turn a set of physical network relationships into virtual ones where a radical new technology is introduced as the change agent.

Technology is classified as being low tech that relies on well-established technologies, medium tech that uses an existing technology base and incrementally extends it, high tech involves new technologies that may have been

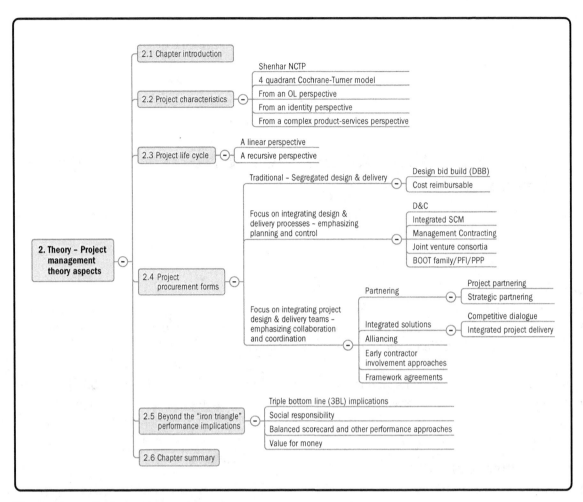

Figure 1. Project management theory aspects

experimented with and tested in other contexts. It may be "new" in the context being applied, but at least there is a reasonable body of knowledge about its impact and influences in other contexts; super high tech projects are based upon new paradigms when the project was initiated.

Pace is perhaps the new concept in this project typology. Regular refers to an evolution as it happens with little sense of forced urgency. Fast/competitive projects are motivated by a sense of urgency, so they do not follow a natural rhythm but are accelerated by force. Blitz/critical, as the tag implies, is driven by an acute sense of urgency and turbulence. The implication that these typologies present revolves, in procurement terms, around how to best encourage performance, accept and trade risks, and develop a rewards and penalty structure that matches a project type to what can otherwise be developed by other PM teams. Project sponsors need to recognize the project context and match a risk and reward strategy, as well as recognize the value generated by intellectual input of teams in different types of projects.

Selecting an appropriate project procurement strategy involves assessing the nature of the project-external environment, including available internal and external resources to deliver the project, stakeholder expectations, etc.; deciding upon the nature and characteristics of the end-product (deliverable); and the details of the task to be accomplished. These are represented by the "shape" of the NCTP model emerging from these influences. The response to the identified NCTP risk profile should inform the project procurement approach. The selected approach considers interactions between the project management team and its supporting supply chain, the structure of the project delivery team and the way that they are integrated and coordinated, the governance tools that can be used to manage the project, and the type of people and the capabilities, skills, and motivations that the team will bring to the project.

The Turner and Cochrane Four-quadrant Perspective

One of the other seminal literature sources that defines project types comes to us from Turner and Cochrane (1993). They identify four types of projects based upon a four-cell model of methods being well-defined and goals being well-defined (yes-no). Their typology is as follows:

1. *Engineering projects* or "earth" projects have both goals and methods solidly defined. Early published project case studies typically cite construction, shipbuilding, aerospace, and manufacturing project examples because they attract a "scientific" view of operations management influence;
2. *Project development projects* or "water" projects have poorly developed methods but well-developed goals. These are characterized as being somewhat fluid but structured in the way that a river, stream, lake, or ocean naturally creates a boundary;
3. *Applications software development* or "fire" projects have a well-defined methodology but poorly defined goals. The procurement emphasis may be directed toward requiring a particular methodological approach that is known (or reasonably assumed) to be successful while holding the end goal more fluid; and
4. *Research and organizational change projects* or "air" projects have poorly defined methods and poorly specified goals. These are characterized as being illusive and generally invisible though these project can be redefined by including intangible goal elements through a process of linking intangible to tangible outcomes. The key to making these projects less difficult to deal with is to either separate the outcomes into several phased projects, or to fully link the tangible and intangible outcomes.

Naturally, the above are idealized and conceptual. Most engineering and construction projects, for example, are tendered under a design, then bid, then build (DBB,) approach but they still only have about 80–90% goal certainty documented and methods solidly defined. Any remaining detailed project specification is managed through contract variations.

Projects from an Organizational Learning Process Perspective

Koskinen (2012) provides us with the perspective of projects as being learning laboratories in which groups and teams of people come together to achieve a common goal, and in doing so, co-create new knowledge used in problem solving and use of knowledge-in-action. The previous two views of projects take as an assumption that there are best practices "out there." Best practices do come from somewhere and they evolve; however, the previous two perceptions of a PM typology are highly instrumental, positivist, and product-oriented. Koskinen (2012) calls for a PM typology perspective that recognizes patterns of processes beyond those identified by the PMI's *PMBOK® Guide* (PMI, 2013). The implication for this perspective is that it takes a very human view of PM (Koskinen, 2008; Koskinen, 2010; Koskinen & Aramo-Immonen, 2008; Koskinen & Pihlanto, 2006; Koskinen, Pihlanto, & Vanharanta, 2003) in which the way that people create, share, and use knowledge inside a "project system" has great bearing upon how we should design project procurement to capitalize upon knowledge being built as a project outcome, along with whatever physical artifact or service that is intended to be delivered. Organizations are seen as organic entities that create their own distinctiveness. They draw upon their internal energy to drive growth and dynamically (including replacing its own components when necessary) produce outputs and outcomes from interacting with external boundaries, drawing upon understanding through making sense of these and feeding off them in a biological sense to become a living autopoietic organization (Maturana, 1999). We see from Small's (Small, 2009; Small & Walker, 2011, p. 397) learning organization perspective that "Autopoietic theory includes descriptions about complex behaviors and relationships which autonomous organisms have both internally and externally through structural coupling of their systems with environments in which dynamic relationships underpin a multitude of interactions." This brings to us the concept of projects being complex adaptive systems (CAS) that helps us to make sense of the Shenhar and Dvir (2007) and Turner and Cochrane (1993) views of project types from viewing a project as both a "thing" and (learning) process.

Snowden (2002) complements the above organizational learning PM perspective and has developed a useful model of the way that activities and approaches interact in relation to problem solving, leadership and the management of co-learning. Snowden (2002; Kurtz & Snowden, 2003) developed the "Cynefin" framework to explain various domains in which knowledge is developed and used to cope with states of the ordered known, the ordered knowable, the un-ordered complex and the un-ordered chaotic domains. *Known* domains are simple, where stability and predictability allows bodies of knowledge, information, and best practice to be categorized and directly applied. He describes the *knowable* as being within a complicated domain and within "the domain of experts, whose expertise enables us to manage by delegation without the need for problem and solution categorization. There is a human imposition of order but it is more fluid than in the space of the known. A major issue in the space of the knowable is entrainment of thinking" (2002, p. 106). *Complex* domains require of PM teams an ability for pattern matching to understand the situation context and to apply an array of routine scripts or to adapt these (as perceived to be appropriate) based on the nature of complexity which could stem from structural complexity of interlinking systems and elements (human, technical, or cognitive) that affect action. *Chaotic* domains defy analysis, and so this is a place where experts with a very wide range of experience of complex situations can experiment by rapidly trying out responses. Having the experience and resilience to be able to rapidly gauge reactions to the intervention, they can adjust and react accordingly, and through an appreciation of the value of the feedback provided by others over the years, they are well prepared to reduce apparent chaos to something closer to complexity or knowable (see Appendix 2, Table 6, Skill 5). These four domains represent states of order with a core state of disorder that impinges upon the other domains that can shift their context and be shifted as circumstances and situations fluidly change. Individuals show a preference and predisposition toward how they steer away from disorder to one of the four domains and steer toward the domain direction they best cope under—thus, they turn areas of disorder into order or "un-order." An important distinction that Snowden makes is that these four domains are not neatly boxed into quadrants but rather they represent cultures. Cynefin roughly translates from the Welsh word for habitat, place, or home community, and is somewhat akin to the cultural or intellectual space in which knowledge is created and shared in Nonaka's concept of *ba* (Nonaka & Konno, 1998). The framework is used in ways that takes this place metaphor to map such characteristics as the permeability of boundaries in knowledge transfer, access to action and decision making, as well as how movement from one domain to another may be undertaken and what consequences may ensue.

Drawing upon concepts articulated by Koskinen and Snowden helps provide an explanation of, and guidance for, working at the more extreme edge of project work where turbulence, uncertainty, ambiguity, and rapid response is required to be deployed in managing and working in projects.

The important point that we make here is that the project type literature, and this chapter only has a focus on two significantly renowned authorities in this area, indicates that any procurement approach (internally or externally commissioned) needs to consider procurement choice based on optimizing or satisficing across a number of complexity dimensions. The Shenhar and Dvir (2007) perspective suggests that procurement choice should consider complexity dimensions associated with design novelty, technology or context complexity and time/pace uncertainty. The Turner and Cochrane (1993) project typology suggests design certainty, project strategy and tactical methods uncertainty, scope uncertainty and general appetite for flexibility or rigidity in process that support line control or allow small group/individual self-organizational freedom. The Snowden and Koskinen views suggest to us that we should consider learning as an important and often neglected perspective of PM that needs to be "designed into" a projects' procurement path.

Projects from an Identity Perspective

Why should we be concerned about a project's image or identity? A project often has an identity but rarely is this identity made clear. Exceptions often occur post-completion when an identity emerges, for example with iconic projects such as the Sydney Opera House. It was initially planned as a cultural centre but while the project architect Utzon was clear about what it was to represent, other stakeholders were not so sure until much later (Murray, 2004). Sometimes an iconic project has its identity well-articulated as part of the project vision, but often the identity is left mute or largely ignored. This is unfortunate because people do identify with their projects. We have seen this phenomenon appear in all our research over many decades. Our research respondents stated that when they felt a sense of purpose about the project they were working, it reinforced a strong sense of engagement experience and this, in turn, highly motivated them.

Identity lies at the core of culture; the shared assumptions and core values that shape the culture of an individual, organization or sense of nationhood (Schein, 2004) inspires loyalty or contempt (Alvesson, 2000; Schön, 1983). We are well aware of the power of brand image and branding and reputation (Alsop, 2004), but frequently this is forgotten in relation to creating a project identity for the purpose of gaining commitment from stakeholders, particularly when trying to attract the best talent to work on a project (Younger, Smallwood, & Ulrich, 2007). Johannes (2004), for example, found that reputation was a prime motivation for the formation of numerous joint ventures (JVs) in Hong Kong, and was considered a valued asset. This motivation can become an expected outcome for companies participating in project design and delivery as these organizations seek to build credibility and expertise. Image was specifically considered as one of the key selection criteria for the National Museum of Australia (NMA) project alliance. One selection criteria in particular was demonstration of:

> Successful public relations (PR) and industry recognition. At least three examples of successful PR and industry recognition from previous projects such as proactive community involvement, previous track record of managing community expectations and credible stakeholder involvement. Examples of where a potential PR disaster may have been turned around. (Walker, Hampson, & Peters, 2002, p. 88).

This criteria was in place because of a fatal accident involving the death of a teenage girl from flying debris when the old Acton Peninsular Hospital was demolished on site now occupied by the NMA, the site was feared have bad karma and so the old "image" of the site had to be supplanted with a new positive one (Walker & Hampson, 2003d). Therefore, reputation, brand enhancement, and positive image can be a consideration in project procurement. One could ask the question "How can we best place this project in a positive light so that it gains support from both direct stakeholders as well as shadow stakeholders who may exert influence but are not readily identifiable?"

Vision is linked to the project identity concept: what is the project's purpose and overriding impression meant to convey about the project. Christenson (2007) studied the role of vision in project success, and in a paper from that work he identified in a case study of a difficult and challenging project how the project vision played a critical part in its delivery by turning several failed attempts to deliver a complex IT project into its final successful delivery (Christenson & Walker, 2004). Drawing upon and adapting to a PM context the work of Lynn and Akgün (2001) that was based on product innovation context, Christenson and Walker (2004, p. 42) use four vision effectiveness measures for analysis:

1. It must be understood: It must capture the core purpose, preferred future state and essence of the project objectives, its *raison d'être*
2. It must be motivational: It must make a convincing case for following the project vision concept that can be internalized by project stakeholders and that provides a compelling value proposition
3. It must be credible: It must be consistent with stakeholder cultures or sub-cultures to appeal at the assumptions and values level so that the vision statement artifact resonates with them;
4. It must be demanding and challenging: It should be proactive to facilitate teams to work smarter and more effectively, perhaps identifying stretch goals.

This provides useful guidance in presenting the vision of a project so that it maximizes its chance of gaining the necessary support from stakeholders and, in particular, builds motivation and presents stretching targets for those actively engaged in project design and delivery. Vision provides a sense of future perfect—what could be—and it can transform the lowliest-sounding project into an exciting and enticing challenge. Pitsis, Clegg, Marosszeky, and Rura-Polley (2003) provide a project case study example of this. The project's aim was to construct a deep underground storage of storm water runoff to avoid animal feces and rubbish polluting Sydney Harbour after torrential rain downpours. The vision was transformed into a project that critically supported the 2000 Olympic Games by enhancing the image of Sydney's harbor to the world. This project vision was able to transform the attitudes of otherwise hostile resident stakeholders so that the project was accomplished with exemplary success in stakeholder engagement and achieved acknowledged remarkable overall project management and project success (Pitsis et al., 2003). This does, however, beg another question: How do we best develop and express such a project vision?

Metaphor provides us with an effective way to convey complex concepts in a convenient short-hand way that is readily accepted. Though as Holyoak and Thagard (1997) point out, this should be within the constraints of similarity, structure and purpose. The metaphor used must represent shared understanding of that image and its purpose must be consistent within the context it is applied. Winter and Szczepanek (2009) provide us with interesting and useful images of project types that help us understand their aims and objectives. They present seven core images of projects as:

1. A social process, with fluctuating impact of events that involve people and their perceptions and how they make sense of events and how they respond;
2. Political processes—people have agendas, aims and accountabilities to various constituants and this shapes the way they believe that the project should unfold. Not all people share the same agenda;
3. Intervention processes, diagnosing some problem or need to enact a transformation and then put in place and manage the required actions to fulfil the intervention objectives;
4. A development process, creating some new or refurbishing existing infrastructure as an input into a productive outcome, for example in IT, engineering/construction, training and education, etc.;
5. Value creation, a process to create value for a specific group of stakeholders, be it tangible or intangible;
6. A temporary organization may exist as a separate entity or operate independently within a larger organization. In both instances this temporary organization has been created for a specific purpose and only exists to fulfill that purpose. Upon fulfilment of its purpose, or handover of the deliverable item (project outcome), it will be closed down and the people who worked within it will be demobilized. The temporary organization will then no longer exist; and
7. A change process, planned and executed plans to make a feasible and desirable change the *status quo* in some particular way;

Henderson (2005, p. 12) used another Olympic metaphor to stereotype work performance attributes of team members, using Greek gods as "archetypal, that is universal images, symbols and patterns that represent ways of being and behaving—ways we recognize from our shared, collective unconscious." Her paper provides useful insights into how team members represented by the metaphor of these gods might work together, but it does assume knowledge of the characteristics of those gods and so some knowledge of Greek mythology is needed.

Another more accessible use of metaphor is the behavioral attributes of animals as a metaphor for human behaviors. Needing to drain a swamp before dealing with the crocodiles is one phrase widely used in PM circles as is being surrounded by sharks. Shelley (2007; 2011; 2012) developed a series of animal behavior metaphors from A to Z that he tested rigorously and found to be a useful way of identifying stakeholder behaviors as well as in PM team selection and engagement. Two examples of animals from Shelly's book are summarized to illustrate the metaphor:

- "Owls can survive well enough as independent individuals, but they prefer to take others under their wing and protect them by developing their skills. They have a great knowledge and a fine sense of the environment and the behaviors of the animals within their immediate environment. (2007, p. 82)
- Eagles are at the top of the food chain in their environment, despite much larger and physically stronger animals being present. Their capabilities and behaviors enable them to avoid any dangers these larger creatures may pose, so they do not have to compete directly with them. They remain above the other powerful animals in the environment because they have the ability to soar above them. From their great height and with their vision they are more aware of the potential opportunities and risks, and capable of reacting to them faster and more effectively" (2007, p. 40).

This metaphorical tool could be applied to project types, by using an animal metaphor to project the image of a project. In this way, a project procurement path can be shaped somewhat by providing an easily understood guiding project image.

Projects from a Complex Product-Services Perspective

This form of project characteristic is more prevalent in projects where engineering solutions include both a product such as a ship, an aircraft or other engineered product, together with a service to supply maintenance, upgrades, training and development of how to best use the deliverable, and other aspects of service delivery. This is what is called complex products and systems (Brady, Davies, & Gann, 2005) where systems integration is a necessary feature (Davies & Hobday, 2005; Davies, Hobday, & Prencipe, 2005). This complex products and systems perspective is useful, as it recognizes the added value and intangible value needs of such projects because while the product side of the procurement process and transaction may be more easy to specify through collaboration and joint sensemaking between the project owner and project deliverer, the service elements are generally very difficult to set rules and explicit protocols for. The process, like the competitive dialogue (CD) process explained later, is one of joint sensemaking and knowledge exploration of the context and parties. This perspective suggests better tools that can be used to analyze underlying mechanisms that support negotiated understanding such as trust and commitment and governance arrangements that are discussed in more detail in Chapter 3, and also helps to understand the supply chain management approach variations that resulted in the T5 Agreement that is also discussed in more depth later. The product-service concept has also been applied as a way of understanding RBP in shipbuilding and the delivery of nuclear plants (Ahola, 2009; Ahola, Laitinen, Kujala, & Wikström, 2008; Martinsuo & Ahola, 2010; Ruuska, Artto, Aaltonen, & Lehtonen, 2009; Ruuska, Ahola, Artto, Locatelli, & Mancini, 2011).

The service-dominated logic (SD-Logic) perspective was proposed by Vargo and Lusch (2004; 2008) as an inevitable new form gaining competitive advantage and delivering superior value through co-creation of value. They argue that value can only be truly delivered when the receiving party and delivering party engage in a genuine dialogue about expectations and desired outcomes in a way that both parties understand each other's value proposition, in an environment in which concepts and concrete examples of value can be mutually explored. They developed what the call foundational principles (FPs), several of the most salient of these are FP9, which is that "All social and economic actors are resource integrators . . . (this) Implies the context of value creation is networks of networks (resource integrators);" and FP10—Value is always uniquely and phenomenologically determined by the beneficiary . . . (this implies that). . .value is idiosyncratic, experiential, contextual, and meaning laden. The SD-Logic firmly places value as being co-produced through an intelligent interaction between parties.

Prahalad and Ramaswamy (2004a; 2004b; 2004c) also see the two parties (supplier and receiver) as central to a process of presenting building blocks of co-generation of value through what they call DART to describe the elements of this relationship. The D in DART stands for Dialogue, conversations about value where each party's concept of value is articulated, explored, and understood. A stands for Access, and this access challenges the notion that consumers can only experience value through ownership. A wider set of opportunities can emerge by providing access to insights, feelings, emotions, as well as technical data and explicit information. R stands for Risk assessment. This moves beyond what may go wrong but includes understanding perceptions of harm and ramifications for actions whose unintended consequences can cause harm. Finally, T stands for Transparency. This complements dialogue and risk assessment when open communication and true access to understanding is provided. By probing value propositions openly, transparency of assumption, expectation, and capacity to deliver can be delivered. This SD-Logic perspective makes a fundamental shift in approaches to the perspective taken under this type of project delivery.

The above project classifications, while useful for describing project types as systems, do not indicate how human aspects of complexity manifest themselves or what KSAE are needed for each project type.

Project Life Cycle Theory
A Linear Perspective

The *PMBOK® Guide* (PMI, 2008, p. 19) identifies a four-phase project life cycle with several sub-phases: initial, starting the process with an output of a project charter; intermediate 1, organizing and preparing with an output of a project management plan; intermediate 2, executing, carrying out the work with an output of acceptable deliverables; and final, closing out the project with an output of producing all project close-out documents.

The initiating phase involves identifying and clarifying an idea that proposes to deliver a specified benefit that subsequently requires a transformation of some kind to produce the benefit deliverable. The project is the transformation process, and it moves through various steps and phases. An identified benefit idea becomes the input to the project management process that allows the transformation to take place to deliver that benefit output. In theory, according to the *PMBOK® Guide*, the initial phase also includes development of a project charter for the idea. The second phase involves a project proposal being scoped; resources estimated and input assumptions of commitment requirements of various kinds being documented in the form of a business case. This may be called the project concept and it should be subject to a rigorous stage gate approval process where the business case is reviewed, challenged and refined in its projection of commitments and assumptions (Klakegg, 2010; Williams, Samset, & Sunnevåg, 2009). The *PMBOK® Guide* does not mention specific stage gate review processes, but it does encourage approvals to ensure that a project proposal fits and aligns with the business's strategic intent. This is an important consideration for other authoritative sources on this aspect (Department of Treasury and Finance Victoria, 2010; Office of Government Commerce, 2007b; 2007c; Victorian Auditor-General's Office, 2008). The decision stage gate approach is explained in Chapter 3 of Klakegg *et al.* (2010) as a generic decision stage gate process. Their study was based on numerous case studies drawn from the U.K., Norway and Australia.

Figure 2 extends their reference model that helps fill the gap that is evident in some imprecise elements of the PMI life cycle model. The model is based on Klakegg et al. (2010, p. 38) from a synthesis of case studies and several government models including one from the National Audit Office (2001, p. 7). Figure 2 places an additional front-end phase to the Klakegg et al. (2010, p. 38) model which occurs as a business development phase undertaken internally where benefits are mooted as potential project ideas. Also, we show a use and disposal phase because we are encouraged (based on sustainability ideals) to consider the implications of the impact of the use and disposal of the project's end product or process.

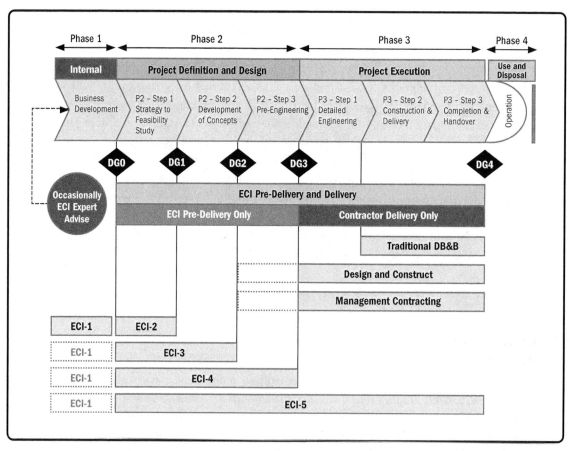

Figure 2.   Decision stage gate reference model (Source: Walker and Lloyd-Walker, 2012b, p. 3) Decision gates: DG0 = formally recognized idea, DG1 = acceptable initiative to investigate, DG2 = choice of concept, DG3 = go/no go, D4 = accept outputs for the operation phase. ECI = early contractor involvement.

The Figure 2 business exploration phase indicates the initial project life cycle phase as the point at which a project idea is explored and a business development proposal is tested at a decision stage gate (DG0). The idea would be a strategic response to an identified need or benefit requirement arising out of the preceding business development Phase 1. If this is accepted (usually at board level) and promoted by a project champion or sponsor, it is approved to move forward to project definition and design (Phase 2).

The idea is further developed with a strategy to feasibility stage study being conducted. Scope is better defined with a range of alternative solutions suggested and assumptions for each option are made more specific and tangible. This idea is then tested at the end of P2 Step 1 through decision gate 1 (DG1) by the board level decision makers and moves from feasible idea to concept option development phase. Options may be narrowed at that stage so that further development may result in a robust business case that defines the concept sufficiently, along with estimated resources and commitments required enabling a decision to be made at decision gate DG2. Pre-engineering (project design) is approved to continue to the stage where a decision can be made to sanction the project at DG3. This is the 'go or no-go' point. At this point (in theory), the business case should be accepted and a decision made about project procurement.

This stage gate approach is perceived as broadly applicable across most project types. It was initially developed with innovation project delivery projects in mind (Cooper, 2005) but has been adapted for IT projects (Office of Government Commerce, 2007b; Victorian Auditor-General's Office, 2008). Within a construction and engineering project stage gate application context, if the traditional design then bid then build option is accepted, detailed design will be commissioned (either internally or externally), and when that design is substantially complete, the project is put out to the market for tender and subsequent appointment of a contractor to build the facility. This construction delivery phase continues to completion and at that point, when the PO or POR accepts the completed facility, the decision stage gate DG4, which is acceptance of project handover at completion, is reached. Figure 2 also illustrates how early contractor involvement (ECI) can occur in the gateway process and how other project procurement choices link into this model. This will be explained in more detail in the following chapter section.

The *PMBOK® Guide* views the project execution phase as a planning and organizing phase (PMI, 2008) followed by an actual execution final project phase where the deliverables of the project are handed over and close-out documentation is produced and delivered.

A Recursive Perspective

PM authorities such as PMI and IPMA see the project life cycle process as being mainly linear, though the *PMBOK® Guide* – Fourth Edition (PMI, 2008, p. 19) illustrates the planning and executing phase processes as exhibiting some iteration. In practice, however, we observe a highly recursive element of PM activity involved in most projects. As stated earlier, it is highly unlikely that requirements are 100% defined, that these if defined are not subject to change as time moves on and context and circumstances change with inherent implications for procurement and project delivery. Traditionally procured projects deal with this level of recursiveness by building in provisions for contract administration of the work to involve a change order management process whereby changes to the contract can be negotiated without undue disruption to the main work taking place. In terms of construction projects, it is normal for substantial changes to be needed post-contract award due to interpretation of local bylaws, building regulations, and client-demanded changes. Similar arrangements are accommodated in other industry sectors. The Chaos information technology (IT) project reports (Standish, 1994; 2003), for example, reveals widespread perceptions of project management failure as unacceptable cost and time blowouts frequently occur through scope creep and poor risk and uncertainty management.

Many IT projects these days are adopting a highly recursive approach to viewing the project design and delivery parts of the project life cycle by adopting an agile project management approach (Augustine, Payne, Sencindiver, & Woodcock, 2005; Cobb, 2011; Highsmith, 2004). The agile approach involves flexibility in adjusting specifications and requirements by delivering outputs in a series of rapid time boxes. These micro-stage deliverables are then presented to POs for instructions on where next to proceed in moving forward, or to make recursive changes by undertaking re-work to respond to the turbulent and rapidly changing technological market. This is also true of new product development projects where time to market is vital (Conforto & Amaral, 2009).

If we look at the field of innovation, we see early examples of suggested effectiveness of recursive trial-and-error approaches to taking an idea to delivery of a product/service (Eisenhardt & Tabrizi, 1995; Wheelwright & Sasser Jr., 1989). The germ of an idea is formed and a series of experiments are devised to shape a benefit against its value proposition and test opportunities for delivering the benefit, as well as test the idea against a range of benefit recipient perspectives. In this way, the idea is semi-frozen after a series of experimental iterations to gain reactions from potential beneficiaries. Prototypes and beta-versions can be launched, moving toward a broadly distributable model that can then be fully launched. The recursive process allows ideas to be dropped or modified and morphed into other ideas that can mature into a final delivery version (Tuulenmäki & Välikangas, 2011).

Clearly not only does project type (characteristics), as discussed in the previous section impact upon procurement choices, but also does the way that the POs wish to manage the project life cycle. This has a strong impact on procurement choice. The Snowden Cynefin framework discussed earlier is also useful in looking at phases of projects as forms of boundaries and how those boundaries may or may not be crossed.

Forms of Project Procurement

Figure 3 illustrates three broad project procurement approaches and forms discussed in this chapter section. They are focused on the construction and engineering project sector but in our experience we see similar variants of these appearing in many other applications of PM principles in a wide range of businesses.

Numerous authors have explained the range of procurement forms in the construction management literature. For example, Walker (1993) provided an exposé on procurement forms while others later documented a range of

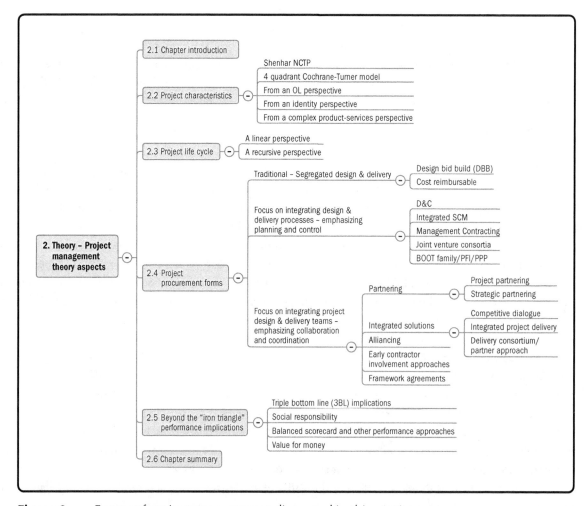

Figure 3. Forms of project procurement discussed in this section

diverse choices that construction clients and POs can make (Barnett, 1998/9; Masterman, 1992; Masterman, 2002; Rowlinson & McDermott, 1999; Walker & Hampson, 2003c; Winch, 2003; Walker & Rowlinson, 2008b). In this section, we focus mainly on construction project procurement options. This is mainly because they appear more uniformly accepted as a typology, have been in existence and tested and validated for several decades, and because we are more familiar with these. We use these as a baseline for developing a project procurement taxonomy.

1. Traditional—Segregated Design and Delivery Procurement Forms

Figure 3 outlines the traditional procurement form that tends to separate the design and delivery while the remainder reflect more closely an integrated design and delivery approach.

1A – Design Bid Build (DBB) is one traditional procurement form that is very much the dominant procurement form operating in most countries. In this procurement approach, it is assumed that the project design is complete enough to enable a bidding process to establish the cheapest and/or the quickest tender cost. It also assumes that the price of design variations encountered throughout the delivery process will not be excessive (Masterman, 1992, p. 170). Tender requirements also include a stipulated completion time, often accompanied by a timeline schedule to fix the completion time and to indicate major milestone events for parts of the project. The tender specification document also fixes the quality expectations and often determines exact materials to be used and standards to be achieved. The resources necessary for undertaking the project design may be internally sourced or outsourced.

Masterman (1992, p. 54–59) describes Design Bid Build (DBB) approaches as a *separated procurement system*. A key feature of this procurement approach is that the level of detailed design specification is generally very high at the time of calling for bids by project delivery organizations. Contract terms are rigid, with bidders usually submitting a fixed-price and fixed-time tender, often with a submitted schedule of milestones for project stage output delivery. Changes inevitably result from the tendered specification during the project delivery phase. Most construction and engineering projects are multi-year projects, and while the overall project objective rarely changes radically, many small changes are required and requested by the POR and these are accommodated and administratively dealt with through a change order (sometimes called contracts variation) administrative system. This leads to a great deal of negotiation, even though it is normal for construction and engineering projects that bidders submit a schedule of unit rates for tasks that make up the tender sum. A great deal of energy and resources can be tied up in settling claims for contract variations. This has been a source of much criticism in the construction industry for several decades, as evidenced by numerous major government commissioned reports in the U.K. (see, for example, Murray & Langford, 2003: such as the Latham 1994: and Egan 1998) reports that criticized the traditional project procurement approach and the litigious "claims mentality" that it engenders.

The advantage of the traditional approach theoretically lies with its market contestability for "the lowest" bid cost and/or shortest time combination. However, this is predicated upon:

- very high levels of design specificity at the time of tender;
- low uncertainty about events requiring substantive subsequent design change;
- contractors that are highly effective in carrying out the work as planned; and
- contractors having a sound relationship with the POR to be able to foster mutual adjustment on side-issues rather than get into a confrontational mindset where every proposed design or task sequence change leads to claims for "extras."

The disadvantage (as has been observed by many construction industry experts and from numerous reports in the U.K. (see, e.g., Murray & Langford, 2003) and, in Australia, NBCC (1989)) is that most project designs are not sufficiently defined at bid stage to avoid many contract extras being claimed, often using schedule of rates that favor the contractor. The result is often poor value for money (VfM), wasted energy by both the POR and contractor that could have been more constructively applied (Hutchinson & Gallagher, 2003), and therefore the lowest bid price is seldom the "cheapest end price" (MacDonald, 2011).

An additional and often hidden disadvantage is that frequently the projects are tendered in an open tender system with no pre-qualification process to filter out potentially poor performers based on past track record or lack of qualification based on capacity to deliver. Frequently, we hear that estimators believe that under this procurement choice the bidder that has "forgotten or left out the most" wins the bid. Also, with many tenders being submitted even using a pre-qualification system, it is not uncommon for 10 or more tenders to be submitted. The cost of tendering for the unsuccessful bidders is retrieved indirectly through profit margins having to include bidding costs for both successful and failed bids. This cost was highlighted by both Latham (1994) and Egan (1998) as being a waste to society at large.

1B – Cost reimbursement (Cost-Plus): variants of the DBB provide an alternative form used when either the design is far from complete or when the design team and POR decide that they need the flexibility to change the design without worrying about claims for extension of time and cost implications for doing so. A 'cost plus' approach is a procurement form that can therefore be adopted when the design specificity is very low or subject to frequent and extensive change. It may be appropriate for high-tech projects, highly regulatory-sensitive projects where permits or authorization may be lengthy, ambiguous, complicated, or otherwise uncertain and risky. It may also be appropriate where the PO wants to be flexible about accelerating work in order to gain first-to-market advantage. The project may also be a vanguard project where there is a strategic desire in procuring the project is to learn as much about and from the project as is feasible (Brady & Davies, 2004; Davies & Hobday, 2005; Frederiksen & Davies, 2008; Lenfle, 2008; Lenfle & Loch, 2010).

In cost-plus projects, the designers usually direct the project deliverer (contractor) to undertake work as directed, and this is driven by an evolving and changing set of design details as the project proceeds. Often the POR will seek advice on an estimate of the project as a target cost which (in theory) is approved with a business case having been submitted to the PO with a realistic contingency to anticipate the final end cost. Masterman (1992, p. 60) describes a number of variants to a cost plus approach. A pure cost-plus is used when the design and delivery method may be highly uncertain with a very low level of initial project design specificity and a project deliverer receives a fee based on the final cost of the project and has an input into the design and delivery varying from "doing what they are told," or being an integral part of the design adaptation and project delivery phases. The contractor selection may be based on a combination of their fee as a percentage of final cost, and this is based on a series of "schedule of rates" that are submitted for undertaking work completed on the project. This includes tasks that may be completed, but it also includes tasks that are required to be re-worked due to the PO changing plans about what is needed.

Cost-plus variants highlighted by Masterman (1992, p60) includes cost reimbursement with a variable fee, where target-cost contracts have either incentives built in to reduce scope creep or have a more reasonable fees structure arrangement where the scope changes substantially.

There are also variants where the contractor's fee is a management fee that includes providing advice on the practical delivery of the design, advice input into the design, and coordinating much of the work which is undertaken as tendered work packages by sub-contractors using a traditional DBB format for these work packages. The skill level required of this project procurement form is high and it is often termed direct or agency construction management (Barnett, 1998/9; Walker & Hampson, 2003b) because the construction management contractor needs to take on the role of professional advisor and needs to have well-developed relationship maintenance and coordination skills. A project procurement approach of on-call contracting may be adopted for small contracts or a series of small contracts where similar arrangements are made (Walker & Hampson, 2003b, p. 21–23). In the U.K., for example, an approach similar to this has been used adopting what are called framework agreements (Green, Fernie, & Weller, 2005; Khalfan & McDermot, 2006). These have also been used for IT projects (National Audit Office, 2009).

In essence, the PO is buying the option to make substantial changes as the project design unfolds, with the cost reimbursable variants using the traditional procurement approach. This can be an advantage but a costly one. The advantages of flexibility and time are often offset by high costs and high transaction costs involved in negotiation, client-side and contractor-side sets of administrators who negotiate the costs based upon schedules of rates from a tender document, or assessments of "reasonable" unscheduled costs. The disadvantages are that in the more traditional approach, the designer has a greater power and authority level than the contractor. This sets up the situation for opportunistic behaviors creeping in to undermine trust and collaboration. A further disadvantage is price uncertainty. The more collaborative forms of cost reimbursement such as agency construction management and framework agreements foster greater collaboration and less opportunistic behavior, but this is not guaranteed by the governance system that these forms introduce.

2. Focus on Integrated Design and Delivery Procurement Arrangements—Emphasising Planning and Control

These forms are at least partially either contractually or physically integrated. A key feature of this cluster of forms of project procurement is that there is a planning and control logic driving the project and a belief that integration is primarily achieved through planning and control systems. Naturally, this does not imply that the people management and collaboration aspects are not important but that the emphasis is on systems integration through planning and control. We include in this cluster:

2A design and construct (D&C);
2B integrated supply chain management (SCM);
2C management contracting (MC);
2D consortia of joint venture (JV) contractors; and
2E the build-own-operate-transfer (BOOT) family of infrastructure approaches that has morphed over the last two decades into public private partnerships (PPPs) or private financing initiatives (PFIs).

2A - Design and construct (D&C) integrates the design and delivery functions either through an integrated firm mechanism which has an in-house design team, as well as a delivery team or by the delivery organization out-sourcing the design to another team that becomes its design services provider. Alternatively, the situation may arise that a design practice is the main contractor, with the delivery being outsourced to a delivery service provider. It is rare that all design services are provided by one design firm, as there are a host of specializations required in construction and engineering projects. These may include a range of outsourced specializations such as interior design, landscape design, building services design, hydraulics, safety systems, etc. D&C integrates the majority of the project supply chain so that design and delivery are more closely linked.

D&C is used significantly in many countries. For example, page 161 of the country reports of Manchester Business School (2009c) states that D&C entered the market in the U.K. in the 1960s and that at around 2004 it comprised about 40% of the commercial building market. The common thread is greater but not whole integration of the design and delivery teams in an integrated team.

For D&C, a concept design (which varies in design specificity) forms the basis of an integrated design and construction procurement form (i.e., delivery for non-construction projects). Several (usually three or more) consortia of designer/builder groups tender to undertake the project and to integrate their efforts and collaborate. The design in such cases is usually specified in functional performance terms e.g., "a school for 1,000 students to conform to Department of Education standards." It is also often developed from conceptual design drawings that indicate style and ambience of the facility to be built.

There are several variants on a D&C procurement form (Masterman, 2002, Chapter 2; Walker & Hampson, 2003b, p. 16–19). *Novated* D&C is a system where design is developed to a point where the project "feel" and "look" and function are very clear, and then it is put out for bidding on a D&C basis to further develop the design with the original designers and construct the facility. Sometimes the design to be novated was determined by a design competition, and other times it may be a PO design team or commissioned design group that developed the design prior to bid. The Melbourne Cricket Ground (MCG) Southern Stand Re-development was an example of this form of novated D&B (Walker & Hampson, 2003b, p. 18). The range of D&B possibilities span from a situation where a PO brief is used for a D&C bid on purely functional performance specifications to partial design details provided as a guide to a novated D&B form.

The advantage of the D&B approach is closer cooperation and (hopefully) collaboration between the design and delivery teams. This closer collaboration is aimed at reducing the cost of potential disputes and contract administration negotiations throughout the delivery process because there is a single entity that is responsible for delivery to the bid performance rather than detail design documentation.

The disadvantage is that the client loses much of the flexibility to change the design and to retain detailed control over the final product. Opportunistic behavior may still take place in the interpretation of the functional performance criteria. The PO may feel that quality may be compromised because the "devil is in the details" and the D&C contractor may hold the view that a client is intruding unnecessarily if the PO becomes assertive about quality and is trying to live "a champagne life on a beer budget."

The last form discussed as a D&C variant is the 'turnkey' approach. This is similar to the other D&C forms described, except that the D&C contractor exercises initiative and responsibility and the PO negotiates with the turnkey contractor on what was needed and then leaves the task including interim financing to the contractor. The transaction for payment is made literally when the facility is occupied by the PO through being given the key. Masterman (2002, p. 82) states that this system originated in the U.S. during the early 1900s and has been used extensively since. This approach has been largely overtaken by other procurement form under the Build Own Operate Transfer (BOOT) "family" and Private Finance Initiative (PFI) and Public Private Partnership (PPP) forms of project procurement described later in this section.

2B - Integrated supply chain management (SCM) is a procurement arrangement that has gained great traction in use in the U.K. in particular as a result of recommendations arising out of the Egan (1998) report. SCM places greater reliance on how the supply chain from PO to contract worker is integrated in terms of hierarchical and reciprocal relationships and how they integrate to create value—rather than act as separate subcontractor and supplier entities that are merely slotted in when and where circumstances demand.

The first phase of this SCM development, borrowed from the automotive and aerospace industries, manifested itself in a "just-in-time" approach to integration of activities. Added to this was the concept of the project management team as a systems integrator. This concept came from these industries as well as from new product development.

One aim of the SCM approach is to reduce the number of subcontractors that any contractor uses regularly to a core that can truly add value to the end result while retaining competition through choice. The logic is that if a small number of subcontractors or suppliers develop strong bonds of trust and commitment through collaboration, that it is easier to reduce transaction costs (see the section on transaction cost economics later in this chapter) and to enhance the chances of generating innovation that benefits all parties. Companies such as Toyota have pioneered supply chain integration and innovation (Dyer, Cho, & Chu, 1998; Dyer & Nobeoka, 2000; Sobek, Liker, & Ward, 1998; Spear, 2004; Spear & Bowen, 1999), but other manufacturers have also adopted this approach as seen in the 1990s by Dell computers (Treacy & Wiersema, 1993). The aim is to not confine the supply chain to a just-in-time mindset (Womack, Jones, & Roos, 1990) where the main contactor "calls the shots" and obedient suppliers fall in line by delivering the quantity requested exactly when requested. Just-in-time may enhance efficiency from the contractor's perspective, but it still misses many opportunities that collaboration can accrue. The paradigm shift from just-in-time and "lean" to integrated SCM brought with it added collaborative features. These include clustering of isolated small subcontractors and suppliers into larger entities that can be responsible for integrated component manufacture that the system integrator can more effectively coordinate—including introducing innovation and business process reengineering. The parties get to work together and share insights, learn more precisely what barriers and constraints to effectiveness and productivity exists, and then seek to remove as many impediments to effective production as possible. Davenport and Glaser (2002) argue this development to be a knowledge management initiative where the component assembling entity is a critical part of the knowledge chain. Hobday and his colleagues (Hobday, Davies, & Prencipe, 2005; Hobday, Rush, & Tidd, 2000;) move beyond an SCM perspective to perceive the project management role as being one of an integrator of a complex mix of products and services. However, the guiding logic appears to be a belief that the emphasis should be on things, resources, and systems in a way that they can be planned and monitored, and thus performance can be controlled.

Zhang and Gregory (2011, p. 740), in their discussion of SCM for global engineering product delivery, refer to *innovation value chains* and make the important point that "In order to improve their ability to generate, develop and disseminate new ideas, companies need to take an end-to-end view of their innovation efforts, pinpoint their particular weaknesses and tailor innovation best practices as appropriate to address the deficiencies." A salient point raised by Hansen and Birkinshaw (2007, p. 122) is that the purpose of a value chain is for a producer of products (or projects) to best capitalize on inherent value offered by each link and integrate the outcomes from a chain of suppliers to maximize value from the entire chain. The integrating organization can analyze the practices, innovation record, and other information of the project supply chain to assess which links in the chain are strongest and weakest and how the end-to-end set of relationships between chain links can best be configured. This may involve either fine-tuning the chain by adding, removing, or substituting links, or taking action to improve the capacity of lower value contributing links so that they may add value through their inclusion. This presents an interesting obligation on value chain integrators (as opposed to supply chain managers) because it assumes greater analytical power of the integrators to be able to identify and measure value contribution performance and able to facilitate links in the chain to improve their value contribution performance.

Zhang and Gregory (2011, p. 740) suggest ways in which global engineering companies can use a value chain model that illustrates elements of idea generation and selection, design and development, production and delivery, service, and support and disposal and re-cycling activities that add value from an end-to-end perspective. They suggest a framework (p. 745, Table III) to map value contributions with the engineering value chain elements against value creating mechanisms of *efficiency, effectiveness* and *flexibility* (and any other identified mechanisms relevant to the project benefit outcome) and network configuration mechanisms such as network structure, operations processes, governance systems, support structure, and external relationships (we could also add to this internal relationships). This application of SCM value analysis can provide a useful tool for configuring supply chains in a highly effective manner.

2C - Management contracting (MC) allows for early contractor involvement in the design development process with the benefit of allowing contractor expertise to be made readily available to the design team. This approach features extensive use of buildability or constructability advice that maintains value in terms of the quality of product as well as providing elegant solutions to production problems. The term "management contracting" used in the U.K. is synonymous with the term construction management used in Australia or the U.S. (Sidwell & Ireland, 1989). Under the MC method, the contractor acts as consultant builder providing significant advice on the practicality of the design and expected construction methods to be employed. The MC will also provide systems integration services for a fee, such as construction planning, cost control, and coordination and supervision of those who have direct contracts with the owner to carry out operational work, and in doing so applies many SCM principles. Trade or work package specialists physically undertake the work under separate contracts with the client and these are integrated and managed by the MC team. An alternative within this option allows for the MC team to take responsibility for the construction works as head contractor. Either way, the MC team provides design development advice and supervises and manages the construction process (Walker & Hampson, 2003b).

Advantages of using the MC approach are consistent with D&C in that it allows:

- reduced confrontation between the design teams and the team responsible for supervising construction activities;
- early involvement of construction management expertise;
- overlap of design and construction;
- increased competition for construction work on large projects due to work packaging;
- greater development of documentation;
- fewer contract variations; and
- public accountability.

2D - Joint venture consortia

Two forms of consortia are discussed here, Joint ventures (JVs) and strategic alliances. According to Manchester Business School (2009c, p7-8)

> ". . . construction consortia occurs where a group of supply interests come to an agreement to develop and market services jointly. The study consortium distinguished between consortia formed specifically to tender for a particular project, which were considered to be 'normal business practice', and those intended to have a longer period of existence, during which the firms developed new construction services or tendered jointly for a number of projects. This form of collaboration, in contrast to the others, does not involve the client."

JVs are often marriages of convenience. One party in the JV needs the skills, local knowledge, financial stability, or other resources or access to resources. In this sense, a JV has an emphasis on integrating resources and subsystems with a view to better controlling outcomes. Other JVs may be more strategic in nature and be active across many projects, and may primarily be a means by which one JV party seeks a synergistic association with other JV parners to ramp up skills and knowledge (Bleeke & Ernst, 1993; Doz & Hamel, 1998) or to gain access in local markets (Arroyo, 2009; Arroyo & Walker, 2008).

While JVs or strategic business alliances may be concerned primarily to achieve business advantage through an empahsis on planning and control of resource inputs, there is also in that organizational form an added emphasis on collaboration to make effective decisions and take efficient action. Johannes (2004) conducted an in-depth study of construction JVs in Hong Kong. The first phase involved him interviewing nine senior-level executives at length from French, Japanese, part-British, the People's Republic of China, and a Hong Kong-owned contracting and engineering organizations involved in major infrastructure projects in Hong Kong. The second phase of his study involved a detailed survey of 40 administrative, managerial and executive personnel involved in the implementation of four project-based construction JVs. This study indicated substantial knowledge-sharing motives as well as JVs forming arrangements to share scale and scope risk, build relationships for the future, and build "brand" image with more experienced JV partners. The need for culture was found to have significant impact upon relationships, and the need for both national and organizational cultural norms and practices was shown to be critical. This aspect will be discussed in terms of RBP later. His thesis findings are illustrated in Figure 4.

Two key aspects of this study that are relevant to this book are that cultural filters and skills in perspective taking were vitally important in JVs. Parker, Atkins, and Axtell (2008) identified the motivational influences of perspective taking as a person's beliefs and role orientations; affect, mood, and emotion; social processes; task and work design, and a cooperative and relational work context. These require a person to be motivated to understand the other person's point of view rather than assume that they automatically share the same understanding. Others have argued from empirical research results that a JV form of collaboration can only work effectively where a range of complementary organizational technical, business, political, and cultural capabilities, etc., are present (Kogut, 1988; Bing,

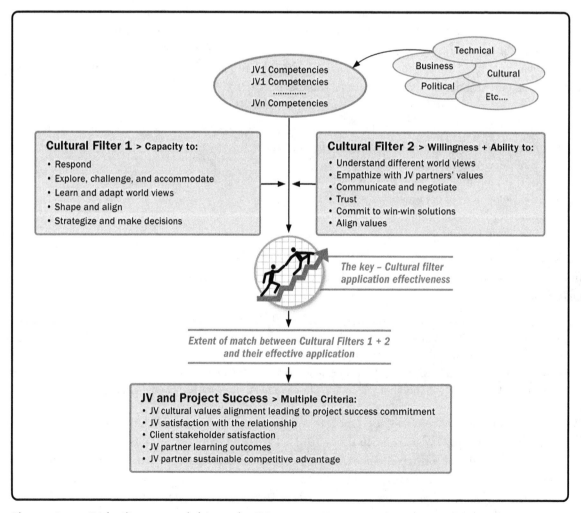

Figure 4.   JV facilitators and drivers for JV success (Source: Johannes, 2004, p. 179)

Tiong, Fan, & Chew, 1999; Thorsdottir, 2001). Figure 4 clearly illustrates the importance of both a capacity or and a willingness to collaborate for mutual benefit.

2E – BOOT family procurement approaches evolved from the turnkey projects concept. Turnkey is a form of D&C project where all project costs are fully financed by the turnkey developer until final delivery to the PO. The PO then pays the turnkey developer the full contracted sum upon "turning the key" over to opening the fully operational facility. This form of arrangement has evolved to emerge into a highly popular project procurement option for many government and for-profit PO organizations. The build-own-operate-transfer BOOT "family" of project procurement options emerged globally during the late 1980s into the 1990s as a widely adopted concept.

The advantages of D&C and turnkey to a PO are naturally extended in the BOOT approach. Under this family of forms of project procurement, a PO will write an extensive briefing document that outlines in extensive detail what the project aims are and what functional points are required with key performance indicators (KPIs) specified to satisfy expected delivery quality not as a product but as a service. The various forms of the BOOT family are more fully explained as follows:

Build-own-transfer (BOT) was an immediate successor to the turnkey approach. It operates in a similar manner in that the PO specifies a detailed brief and it is tendered to a small number of BOT entities, groups of organizations with a range of capabilities in design, delivery, finance, and operations to provide the project infrastructure. This may, for example, be a hospital, prison, or head office facility. The entity finances the project up to the point of hand-over, similar to the turnkey approach. The financing and legal costs can be high and so this approach is not feasible for small projects. One major difference to this approach in contrast to a turnkey approach is that often there is an anticipated greater focus on project life cycle so that there is a balance between long-term operating costs and short term capital costs (Walker & Smith, 1995). That anticipated advantage, however, is not tested, as the PO takes over the project upon completion.

The next member of the BOOT family is Build-own-operate (BOO). Under this arrangement, a client develops a brief and tenders for a service rather than a facility. The service is to provide a facility and to also operate it indefinitely. At a more simplistic level, this may be to build an office building, for example, and to provide it to the client at an agreed cost with all running costs and maintenance included in that cost arrangement. The approach has advantages when a client's existing facility is transferred to a BOO party with a need for extensive renovation or rebuild or substantial modification to be made, with an option that the facility be transferred to the PO. In this case, the risk and uncertainty associated with the project delivery for a risky venture is passed to the BOT entity. This may make sense if the client has little knowledge of facilities management and renovation and upgrade of existing (perhaps dilapidated) premises. This approach shares similarities to an extensively used procurement option adopted during the 1970s and 1980s in North America under the concept of "lease-back." The client would develop the brief in the same way that was described for turnkey and BOT, and instead of paying a lump sum at the point of delivery, a lease-back deal would be negotiated with the eventual PO. There would usually be an option to re-lease at the expiry of the lease period, as well as for the entity to transfer ownership. The expected advantages are that the project has life-cycle considerations built into the project design because the project deliverer has to finance the capital and operational costs and amortize these in a cost-competitive matter to win the bid.

A variant of the above form of BOO is where the operation extends to a full service. In a hospital, for example, the BOO entity taking over responsibility for medical services would be subject to a quite different pricing strategy to a simple lease-back form. The former would be linked to a complicated set of medical output KPIs rather than charges per square meter of occupied facility.

The final BOOT family form is the full design, deliver, operate, and—after an agreed period—transfer the asset to the PO. Both BOOT and BOO approaches can pose a considerable challenge in assuring that KPI definitions of service provision represent true value for money (VfM). It must be remembered that the sophistication on both the PO and complex and highly multi-disciplinary entity that formed in order to present a unified BOOT bid is considerable and formidable. These forms of procurement require very high levels of expertise from all parties. The development of a brief that can be easily understood by the BOOT entity bidders is of itself a considerable challenge. The BOOT entity needs to meld a group of highly disparate professionals from legal, design, operation, and construction into a coherent team so that they understand each other enough to collaborate effectively.

The BOOT concept has over the past two decades been rebadged somewhat. The term public finance initiative (PFI) became popular in government circles, particularly in the U.K. when Prime Minister Thatcher promoted more direct private-sector involvement in service provision such as running hospitals, prisons, and other formerly public-only provided community services. Owen & Merna (1997, p. 164) explain that "The private sector will provide the funding for the capital projects and operate a facility for the public benefit. They will receive revenue from operating this service and hence make a profit. Having a private provider of a capital asset can enable public bodies to purchase services without the need for the initial capital investment." They add in their paper that a "Public Private Partnership Program Ltd (4Ps)" was established in the U.K. "in April 1996 enjoying all party support" (Owen and Merna, 1997, p167). The terms PFI and PPP have become synonymous over the ensuing years. Most of the literature concerning this area now seems to refer to PPPs. Readers may consider PPP, BOOT and PFI to be concerned with similar if not near identical forms of project procurement. PPP is being used extensively as a procurement choice. Regan, Smith, and Love, for example, state that (2011, p. 7) "in Australia, PPPs account for around 10% of state capital spending in Victoria, around 7% in Queensland, and lesser proportions in the other States and the Commonwealth."

The fundamental characteristics that all these forms share are that in part:

1. The cost of facilities (project and service delivery) is shifted from the public to the private purse;
2. That assets are shifted off-balance sheet, thus potentially freeing up available financial resources for other purposes, which may include tax reduction with a user-pays policy for use of assets and services;
3. The sudden realization that potentially vast amounts of expensive infrastructure targeted at the public good may be financed through the public sector can result in excessive demands upon highly skilled and limited human resources because of an over-eagerness to rectify decades of neglect by the public sector to maintain and develop infrastructure;
4. In theory, better VfM is derived from a more holistic perspective of the project design so that operating costs and capital costs are balanced because the PPP/PFI/BOOT entity is required to fund the facility on a long-term basis, and so minimizing operational costs over that period encourages a life-cycle-costing mentality when developing the project design;
5. There has been severe criticism about the way that the cost benefit or business case has been presented. The cost comparator interest rate used for a discounted cash flow calculation can be manipulated to make many of these projects appear to present VfM when this is questionable (Fitzgerald, 2004; Flyvbjerg, 2009; Grimsey & Graham, 1997; Hodge, 2004; Williams, 2010);
6. That the skills required of all parties involved, PO and project delivery team, are formidable and represent a quantum leap from that expected of deliverers of traditional projects (Ezulike, Perry, & Hawwash, 1997; Grimsey & Graham, 1997); and
7. The cost of mounting a BOOT/PFI/PPP bid is very expensive and highly risky for the bidding consortia in terms of cost versus likely reward when there may be only two bidders. Even when the government or PO offer to compensate unsuccessful bidders for part of their bid costs, this is rarely sufficient to ameliorate the risk of several serial highly expensive unsuccessful bids. Added to this is the opportunity cost of tying up highly skilled talent for protracted bid periods.

In summary, the BOOT/PFI/PPP project delivery approach is a complex choice, and there needs to be a high level of PO consideration of both upside and downside impacts.

3. Focus on Integrated Project Teams—Emphasizing Collaboration and Coordination

Five forms of collaborative arrangements will be focused upon in this subsection:

3A partnering (both strategic [3A-1] and project [3A-2]);
3B integrated solutions (competitive dialogue (CD) [3B-1], integrated project delivery (IDP) [3B-2] and delivery consortia/partner) [3B-3]
3C alliancing (project alliances (PA) [3C-1], design alliances (DA) [3C-2] and program service alliances (SA) [3C-3]);
3D early contractor involvement; and
3E framework agreements.

3A – Partnering is not a procurement choice *per se;* rather it is an enacted philosophy or cultural state that can be applied to other procurement forms. It has features, characteristics, and cultural artifacts that define its presence. Two forms of partnering are discussed here—strategic and project partnering.

3A-1 - Strategic partnering occurs across projects in a similar way to project partnering, but it usually applies to a single supply-chain team member who works with a client on a continuing basis across a range of projects and over time with goals to provide continuous improvement and, more usually, continuous innovation, so that the client and contractors (or designer for design strategic partnerships) gain advantage of learning from one project being applied to the next project. This learning could be technical where one project is similar to the next, or it may be administrative where permits, processes, etc., are similar from one project to the next, or there may be benefit derived from the ongoing partnering through parties getting to know each other intimately and how the working relationship may be enhanced through being, in essence, an "integrated" team. One of the more historically lengthy and well reported strategic partnering arrangements that spanned several decades is that between the U.K. chain Marks & Spencer and the building contractor Bovis, now Bovis-Lend Lease (BLL). Bovis was a pioneer in management contracting (MC) in the 1970s and extended MC arrangements with its subcontractors to feature innovation, organizational learning, and collaboration (Bennett & Jayes, 1995; Matthews, Pellew, Phua, & Rowlinson, 2000).

One highly innovative form of strategic partnering is reported upon from a case study of a German organization *Baufairbund* (BFB) (Lönngren, Rosenkranz, & Kolbe, 2010). In this strategic alliance, a range of construction project delivery teams formed a strategic partnership. The case study authors described the partnership role as follows:

> "The close cooperation among the parties involved provides a comprehensive service for building and tenancy that is intended to offer the entire spectrum of life cycle and value creation in the construction industry, from the original consultation through to the planning and realization of the building project up to and including subsequent services surrounding financing and facility management, e.g. maintenance and operation. The main difference between BFB and a general contractor is that the BFB is not limited to the building project, but is committed to long-term collaboration. In this way a learning process can take place during the cooperation of the various trades. . . .
>
> During the actual construction phase, the main responsibility of the BFB is project management. This comprises the supervision of project progress in terms of deadlines, but also quality standards. At the same time, detailed planning and the exact coordination of the various trades is being elaborated, in order to guarantee the seamless flow of work at the construction site. (Lönngren et al., 2010, p. 408). . ."

This is an interesting form of partnering that is akin to alliance forms to be discussed later in this section. Key elements that were reported as being vital for the alliance are trust between partners and a common IT platform that helps to coordinate and focus them on projects.

3A-2 Project partnering occurs at the project level when applied to a range of parties within a project in which they form part of the project supply chain.

Naoum (2003, p. 71) opens his paper by stating that "Partnering is a concept which provides a framework for the establishment of mutual objectives among the building team with an attempt to reach an agreed dispute resolution procedure as well as encouraging the principle of continuous improvement. This framework enthuses trust, cooperation and teamwork into a fragmented process which enables the combined effort of the participants of the industry to focus upon project objectives." This view is shared by many scholars who have written on the topic (Bresnen & Marshall, 2000; CII, 1996; Eriksson, 2010b; Lenard, Bowen-James, Thompson, & Anderson, 1996; Ogunlana, 1999; Smyth, 1999; Thompson & Sanders, 1998; Walker & Hampson, 2003a; Wood & Ellis, 2005). Nyström (2005a) takes an interesting view of partnering through the lens of searching for family resemblances in a group of people. He undertook a broad literature review to determine a commonly attributed set of characteristics of partnering and then, based on the Wittgenstein family resemblance concept, developed a typology of partnership. His research work provides a useful meta-study of numerous case studies and other empirical research. The main characteristics he extracted within this family was with an analogy of a flower with a core element and petals. The (partnering) core contained trust and mutual understanding as core features, with the following as adjunct components (petals) of which a variety can be seen as present in the case studies he reviewed: relationship building activities; predetermined dispute resolution methods and provisions; economic incentive contracts; provision of a facilitator; a culture of openness and transparency; continuous structured meetings to build and maintain relationships; and a well-developed method of selecting partners.

Table 2 critically examines partnering and helps us understand what partnering may look like. Green (1999a; 1999b) cautions us about the rhetoric-reality gap in partnering and points to the many ways that it can be used coercively and in ways that provide advantages for "strong" players within a partnered group, and how it may exploit the weak or naive. Bresnen (2003) discussed seven deadly sins of partnering in a similar vein. These criticisms expose the potential for abuse that a partnering agreement can impose upon unwary participants.

A partnering arrangement can impose some generally valuable processes. For example, the development of a common vision that can be supported by parties is known to be a strong factor that can sustain projects through adversity, as Christenson's (2007) research demonstrates. Facilitated workshops that result in a partnering charter can achieve such a strong shared vision. Similarly, the development of an agreed dispute resolution system that unearths potential matters or issues that could lead to disputes provides an agreed way of dealing with disputes in an open and respectful way. It provides parties with a means to escalate unresolved issues to higher authority levels in a way that takes the emotional heat out of differences in interpretation of issues and resolution of alleged unhelpful behaviors. This has significant value in reducing transaction costs associated with dispute resolution. Developing a collegial and shared problem-solving environment and co-creation of learning and sharing knowledge is also highly valuable. However, as Green (1999a; 1999b) and Bresnen (2003) argue, these virtues can be undermined by Machiavellian participants and the purpose of partnering can be undermined.

Partnering can remain aspirational and does need not only strong relationship-building skills of its participants, but also considerable support and energy and a different paradigm from the highly commercial winner-takes-all and aggressive leadership styles that are often seen among project managers. It also needs an accompanying governance system that supports its ideals for it to be viable. While it can provide credible results in situations of uncertainty, risk, and shared decision making, it is less demonstrably valuable where there is a perceived stability of objectives, perspectives, and methods to be deployed, because a business-as-usual approach requires less energy and resources to achieve a similar result than may be achieved by partnering in these simpler situations.

Partnering Characteristic	Comments
Trust and mutual understanding	This is a core essential ingredient. We later discuss theory on trust. A central part of this is an ability to see other party's perspective.
Relationship building activities	Necessary to maintain trust and commitment and to initiate new team members being initiated to the project. This involves demonstrating authentic behaviors and building realistic expectations of each other.
Predetermined dispute resolution methods	Necessary to establish ground rules and governance. A ladder of issue escalation is agreed to so that problems are dealt with efficiently and effectively.
Incentives	Necessary to meet partner's value proposition for both economic and non-economic intangible benefits. Pain/gain sharing is expected. Other incentives and sanctions may compliment or better fit the value proposition.
Provision of a facilitator	Necessary for a responsible third party to coordinate how the partnership is established and maintained. Quality of facilitation is also important.
Culture of openness and transparency	Necessary for trust and commitment to be seen as fairly and justly applied.
Structure to build and maintain relationships	Necessary to manage the relationship as a subproject. Partnering recognizes the primacy of people and their relationship to one another.
Selecting partners	Necessary rigorous and fair process to select the best partners who can and want to work together.

Table 2.   Partnering essentials

3B - Integrated Solutions: Three forms of integrated solutions will be explained: Competitive Dialogue, Integrated Project Delivery, and Delivery Consortia/Partner.

3B-1 Competitive Dialogue (CD). Mieke Hoezen undertook a PhD in the history and development of the CD procurement approach (Hoezen, 2012) after having published widely on CDs with her colleagues during her PhD journey (Hoezen, Van Rutten, Voordijk, & Dewulf, 2010; Hoezen, Voordijk, & Dewulf, 2012a; 2012b). She provides one the most authoritative descriptions and comprehensive analysis of the CD process. Referring to the European Commission's Green Paper (Commission of the European Communities, 1996) as a mechanism that had opened up possibilities for more flexible procurement rules in the European Community (EC), she defines the CD thus:

> "The CD procedure is a procurement method that consists of several rounds of discussion between the principal and potential contractors, during which all aspects of the tender are open for discussion" and continues to state that "It regulates the negotiation process during the procurement stage, thus expectedly affecting the commitment and possible renegotiations between principal and contractor. Main expectations with concern to the procurement stage as a result of using the CD procedure were stronger contractor competition than possible with the negotiated procedure, and improved dialogue between procuring agency and potential contractors than possible with traditional procedures. Thus, complexity and renegotiations during the execution stage of the project were expected to decrease" (Hoezen, 2012, p. 15).

An important point to remember is that CD applies to *any* procurement form. It is used primarily in D&C, alliances, and PPP approaches to inject greater collaboration, sensemaking, and understanding of the project context and values. It can be used to enhance collaboration by including the project owner, key design consultants and contractor (and even significant supply chain partners), but seems not to have been applied to that extent. What follows is some discussion on case studies that have been written on how it was applied to better integrate the project owner and contractor.

Hoezen et al. (2010) provide a more detailed explanation of how CD operates in practice in their paper, moving from a prequalification phase where open competition is used to attract potential bidders for a project and where a process is put in place and potential bidders are invited to take part in a dialogue to make sense of the project proposal and to engage with the project owner to define terms and conditions. Through this process, they explore options and prompt innovative solutions that aim to result in a win-win solution for both parties while meeting the need for market testing. It also requires maintaining a collaborative approach between the PO and bidding contractor that is flexible and open to technical and other elements of the project proposal. The process filters numerous project proposals that are screened for viability and expertise of the proponent to ensure that only acceptable proposals are likely to result in a successful project delivery outcome.

Case studies described and presented in Hoezen et al. (2010) involved three screened competitors who were separately engaged in a CD in which an exhaustive process of questions and answers took place in which the full implications of the proposal was explored and explained. Numerous options and varieties of solutions were discussed, and a firm proposal was made by the three tenderers following the CD process. These were tested for viability and judged, resulting in one successful tender being accepted.

Key elements of the CD process demonstrate that an integrated collaborative project delivery solution is achieved. The PO conducts a purposeful and open dialogue about the project's needs, constraints, stakeholder values, potential for innovative solutions to be jointly developed through the dialogue, and full sensemaking from both sides. The allows the PO and bidder to be clear about what risks may be apportioned to various parties, how disputes and clarification during project delivery may be structured and how both parties' interests may be respected and protected. The PO may call upon expert design consultant advice, though this seems to be restricted to in-house expertise rather than engaging design experts to provide independent evaluation on technical issues, so the dialogue does demonstrate limitations in its collaborative capacity. It has advantages over D&C options. The dialogue, for example, engages parties more fully, and so better sense can be made on particularly uncertain or risky conditions. The cases that Hoezen and her colleagues present seem to be mainly rail and infrastructure projects in which there is a PPP or project servicing component involved that opens up greater uncertainty about the condition of the existing facilities and how they will be taken over for operations and maintenance.

3B-2 Integrated Project Delivery (IPD) is an approach that was developed in the U.S. and is an interesting project procurement form, allowing the PO to not only engage and collaborate with the design team on construction projects (which is the traditional approach), but also collaborate from the project initiation stage with the main contractor and also significant subcontractors, whose volume of work and impact upon the project outcome can justify their early involvement in project definition and design (American Institute of Architects - AIA California Council, 2007; Cohen, 2010; Dal Gallo, O'Leary, & Louridas, 2009). This approach developed from a lean construction approach into an integrated contractor and main sub-contractors supply chain management project procurement and delivery form that, together with design consultants and the PO, aimed to drive out waste, rework, and inefficiencies (Mathews & Howell, 2005). Cohen (2010) describes case studies in which hospital and office construction projects used an integrated cohesive team approach that collaboratively decided on a project solution that met the PO's best-for-project behaviors while reducing adversarial behaviors about agreement to design changes, dealing with various uncertainties and risks in a way that eliminated most of the administrative burden and energy of documenting design changes, for example, to make or defend claims for additional payments. This IPD form shares many features associated with partnering and alliancing (discussed shortly), and as Lahdenperä (2012, p. 973) observes, "IPD has mostly been used for social infrastructure, or 'vertical' building construction, where the uncertainty is largely related to complex systems, their compatibility, functionality, and response to the owner's needs. There, the risk can be minimized by intensified, cooperative early planning where model-based collaboration and review can be of great benefit." We have not seen examples of IDP for engineering infrastructure projects that are highly prevalent in Australasia (Mills & Harley, 2010; Walker, Harley, & Mills, 2013a; Walker & Lloyd-Walker, 2011a; Wood and Duffield, 2009). IPD appears to be more collaborative and structured than partnering, but less committed in terms of all parties adopting a sink-or-swim-together stance, as is the case with project alliances. However, IPD seems to offer greater inclusivity of sub-contractors that PAs. IPD is used on building rather that infrastructure engineering projects, in contrast to PAs, although we only find rare examples of PAs used for building projects (Walker and Hampson, 2003c).

Heidemann and Gehbauer (2011, p. 24) compared two different approaches to collaborative project procurement. They describe IPD using the term: integrated form of agreement (IFOA). This is the collaborative approach used by Sutter Health in the U.S. and which is commonly termed IPD. They contrasted IFOA/IPD with the Westgate Freeway Alliance in Australia that was delivered using a similar approach, which is termed project alliancing or a project alliance (PA). The table Heidemann and Gehbauer (2011) produced from the comparison they conducted illustrates the similarities, and differences, between these two collaborative procurement forms. Principally they note that IPD on the Cathedral Hill Hospital case study project in San Francisco had no external control, while the Westgate Freeway PA did through external probity and financial auditors as is normal practice for Australasian PAAs (project alliance agreements). Behavioral strategy aspects were highly correlated and tools and techniques used in the project delivery were similar, except that there was a greater focus on Lean construction techniques on the U.S. project than was evident for the Australian project. At a recent conference (2013 CIB [International Council for Research and Innovation in Building and Construction or Conseil International du Bâtiment] World Congress Brisbane), two keynote speakers discussed IPD as it is used within the U.S. Professor Martin Fischer from Stanford University illustrated how building information modeling (BIM) and greater collaboration between the design team and subcontractors with the head contractor provide a very high level of design integrity through all parties sharing a common BIM platform and ICT groupware systems. A later keynote presentation by Brian Krause from Turner Construction Company stressed the high levels of system and project control tools used in IPD projects, and that the use of advanced level modeling and simulation together with integration of many freeware software tools into an integrated process improvement toolbox, appears to be the norm for such projects, and the approach is also creeping into the normal BAU practice for Turner Construction in the U.S. and elsewhere. Sutter Health appear to be a key driving force for championing IPD in the U.S., and this illustrates the key role that a sophisticated client has in the effective delivery of projects through true collaboration.

3B-3 – Delivery Consortia/Partner (DC/P) Approach, an interesting example of which is a recent mega project that applied a sophisticated form of systems integration and advanced SCM. This was the approach taken by British Airports Authority (BAA) on their Terminal 5 (T5) project (Davies et al., 2009). It has been hailed a successful approach despite the humiliation felt by BAA at that project's opening when the final commissioning stage of the integration process was rushed and improperly pursued (Brady and Davies, 2010). T5, nevertheless, provides an excellent case study of an attempt to change the paradigm of project delivery through SCM principles and principles of partnering and alliancing (discussed later in this chapter). The account of T5 prior to its final stages before opening reveals a highly purposeful attempt to select a limited number of suppliers and subcontractors, to integrate them intimately into the project design, project planning and delivery so that their knowledge of constraints, opportunities, and the impact of overlaps and gaps could be better visualized. T5 also deployed highly sophisticated building information modeling (BIM) and simulation software that allowed better visualization of how the many components could be integrated. There was a conscious knowledge-sharing effort made to facilitate collaboration. Clearly, many lessons were learned from the debacle and many of these were about stakeholder engagement and the need for more rigorous system integration testing for such highly complex projects such as T5 (Bourne, 2011b; Brady & Davies, 2010), as shown by the highly visible problems at the project opening when thousands of passengers were disrupted because the baggage handling system failed to operate as expected (Brady & Davies, 2010). The T5 approach extended far beyond traditional SCM approaches to place greater focus on team alignment and integrated collaboration.

Experience of the T5 form of delivery led to two related forms of procurement in the U.K.: the Delivery Consortia and Delivery Partner (DC/P) approach. HM Treasury and Infrastructure U.K. refers to the Delivery Consortia (2013, p. 29) approach in the following terms "The Delivery Consortia approach is adopted in sectors such as the regulated utilities where clients seek to transfer high value performance based contracts to a 1st tier organization over the course of a regulatory control period. Under the contract the supplier undertakes the design of the projects from solution development stage against an output specification. The supplier also provides program management services alongside a design and build capability." The emphasis is on a program of work undertaken over a contracted time, a five-year or three-year term, for example. Individual projects may vary in size. This can be contrasted with the situation for complex mega projects that are constrained by the overall project which may be managed via a series of projects in a program of work. Examples of this would be the Olympic Delivery Authority (ODA) and Crossrail in the U.K. HM Treasury and Infrastructure U.K. (2013, p. 30) states that "The approach taken on both projects is subtly different. The ODA appointed a delivery partner 'CLM' (CH2M Hill, Laing O'Rourke, and Mace) to provide program management and client integration, project management and construction capability. Crossrail appointed a program delivery partner (Consisting of AECOM, CH2M Hill and Nichols Group) to provide program management capability and client integration, and a separate project delivery partner (a consortium consisting of Bechtel, Halcrow, and Systra) to provide project management. The Crossrail project relies on separate competitions for each work package to procure construction services."

Integrated solutions at the IDP and DC/P approach share a number of common threads with alliancing; however, the focus on these two forms as was the case for the T5 procurement approach was deeper penetration of formalized and contractual collaboration beyond the first-tier delivery participant further down the supply chain.

3. – Alliancing: Three forms of alliancing will now be discussed. Project alliancing is the most commonly and best understood, and so we will discuss this first as a template for other forms. The second form is centered on alliances that occur at the earliest stage such as a design alliances. The third type is program and service alliances, where alliancing occurs across projects, time, and/or space.

3A - Project alliances (PA): The project alliance approach to an RBP system has gained a great deal of attention, in Australasia in particular. Walker and Hampson (2003a) provide a useful history of alliancing from initial oil and gas examples from the literature in the late 1990s (KPMG, 1998; Australian Constructors Association, 1999) to the case study of the National Museum of Australia that they undertook and reported upon in their book (Walker & Hampson, 2003c). Other doctoral studies on project alliancing in Australia have added to our knowledge of alliances, their strengths and weaknesses, at a deep level (Davis, 2006; MacDonald, 2011; Sweeney, 2009). A recent study on project alliancing and the KSAEs required was also recently published and provides a rich stream of knowledge about the ambience of a PA that required a particular mindset of those involved (Walker and Lloyd-Walker, 2011a;2011b;2011c).

The selection process for alliances is quite different to other forms of project procurement. It has also evolved over the last five years from a single Target Outturn Cost (TOC) basis to a dual TOC (sometimes referred to as competitive TOC). Both approaches follow a similar path but with an important distinction. First we explain the single TOC process.

The PO advertises for expressions of interest from a consortium of parties that will form an alliance, usually with the PO/POR. The concept is that the consortium parties first agree to a commercial arrangement of what resources will be committed and how these will be reimbursed by the PO. They also agree to a pain-sharing and gain-sharing arrangement based on the negotiated percentage of each alliance participant's profit margin that is placed at risk, and is subject to performance based on agreed key results areas (KRAs). This then forms the basis of an incentivized risk-reward model. The risk-reward model places the participants' profit and company overhead contribution into an 'at-risk' account. Variance from the final agreed project cost is shared between parties in accordance with the incentivization contract clause based on agreed percentages between PO and NOPs. These either eat into the at-risk account until it is extinguished or, if there are savings, then distribution of "gain-share" is made using the agreed percentages. A worked example developing a risk-reward formula is provided in Ross (2003, Appendix 1). Participants also agree to a relationship agreement to work together in the prescribed alliance format of collegiality in decision making and undertaking the work, and transparency and accountability. Finally, they agree to a no-litigation clause for any reason other than criminal or malicious behavior (Hutchinson & Gallagher, 2003; Jones, 2001). Each alliance consortium puts forward named individuals from the cluster of organizations within the alliance consortium that they commit to the project for the project duration and the quality of the bid is judged on the quality of the team put forward. They either allow probity consultants (often with recognized auditing and compliance expertise) to determine the "reasonable fee" structure, or they set that structure and allow the probity auditors to check their financial records to validate that the fee is not excessive when compared to average profit levels over past years. This reduces the selection criteria process from haggling over a contract price to determining a reasonable return for the input of the expertise of the team to form the AMT and ALT. All direct costs, including the project site staffing and ancillary cost of materials, subcontracts etc. are treated in a similar way to the cost-reimbursable arrangements discussed earlier in this chapter based on a 100% open book approach. The tender process is rigorous and involves extensive interviews of proponent consortia. A detailed account of the selection process can be found in Walker and Hampson (2003d), and a model for demonstrating VfM has recently been developed from a number of sources, including government guides (Department of Treasury and Finance Victoria, 2010; Department of Infrastructure and Transport, 2011) and in the thesis written by MacDonald (2011).

The dual TOC (or competitive TOC) approach varies from the selection process above that selects the best team available. It has a primary focus on selecting the best-priced solution with the most attractive team skills package, TOC price, and proposed project delivery strategic solution. The Dual TOC approach somewhat resembles the CD approach discussed earlier. It selects and screens two consortia of proposed alliance partners (similar to the CD) that work independently, but in collaboration with the POR, to arrive at a project delivery solution and TOC. Usually the lowest TOC wins and the unsuccessful consortium is usually compensated to a degree, but not fully, for the effort expended in the TOC development process. This approach has been seen (particularly by government treasury departments) as providing a more competitive result because it is thoroughly "market tested," but it has drawbacks.

One drawback to a dual TOC approach is that two consortia work with the POR to arrive at the TOC *after* being screened as a contending alliance. Participants we interviewed referred to this process as a "beauty parade" in that the first step is to identify and build a team across the various NOPs that will be dedicated to the project, so there is great competition to source the most attractive and talented team. We see many of these PAs comprising two contractors who, in a BAU setting, would be fiercely competitive. However, they recognize that within a PA setting, it is vital to have a balanced and talented team. Their pool of professionals and operational skilled workers, designers, and other staff need to provide a balance of depth of experience and balance a "competitive" cost while presenting the most attractive and talented team.

A second important drawback is that the dual TOC process places the onus on the preliminary design, planning, and costing effort on the competing consortia at a stage *after* being screened to be contenders but *before* being awarded the project PAA. This has two important implications. First, this approach leads both consortia to place more focus on cost than value because, at the end of the day, cost (the TOC) usually trumps value if value cannot be expressed in monetary terms. This seems from our findings (there is little empirically based literature, if any, on this subject at this stage) to suggest that the dual TOC process drives a lowest-cost solution that the PO may hope represents a VfM rather than a best-value solution. There is a fine line of debate about the nuance between cost and value. We will be undertaking more research into this fascinating quandary during 2014. The second implication of the dual TOC approach is that it places greater pressure on the successful PA team to begin the project immediately after the TOC is accepted by the POR when the PAA is signed. Under the single TOC approach, the POR assumes that selection of the "best team" will lead to a best solution, and more open and divergent thinking about the project situation and options that may be considered. However, a dual TOC approach tends to narrow down options much earlier than a single TOC approach. This reduces potential innovation, particularly radical innovation, from emerging through the TOC development process.

We acknowledge that the above discussion is based on data gathered for the study reported upon in this book and is somewhat preliminary. Other researchers need to undertake studies that triangulate data on how single and dual TOC approaches vary so that we can be better informed about what happens within a single and dual TOC process and how advantages and disadvantages between approaches can be perceived. The main tension that is being grappled with at present is that one view of alliances says something akin to 'get the best team based on rigorous selection criteria and they will deliver a superior VfM outcome' while an opposing camp holds the view that 'without market testing on price we cannot trust that team to deliver the requisite innovation, demonstrated VfM, and commitment to a best-for-project outcome.' This is an emerging debate that has a great deal of debate to be contributed and research undertaken and analyzed before any stable position can be agreed upon. It offers rich research opportunities.

A defining set of attributes emerges from the PA literature and our study findings to show that alliancing is an extension to the partnering concept that appears to surmount weaknesses inherent in the partnering approach. These attributes include:

1. A contractually structured way to at best overcome or at least minimize potential exploitation of one or more alliance participants by others through an "all sink-or-swim-together" mindset;
2. Closer integration of alliances between the PO/POR and NOPs through an alliance organizational structure with a high-level alliance leadership team (ALT) comprising the project sponsor/POR and senior champions (often board-level individuals from NOP organizations), plus an alliance management team (AMT) that has representatives from each NOP. Decision making is contractually obliged to be by consensus. While this can be time consuming and energy sapping at times, it results in no party (NOP) being able to point a finger at, or blame, others for decision failures by the AMT and/or ALT. This results in a no-blame culture that facilitates the "all sink-or-swim-together" mindset because failure cannot be attributed to any single party (Walker & Hampson, 2003a). The role and composition of the ALT is relevant. Respondents to our research study stated that "effective ALTs" tended to be composed of high-level executives from their represented organizations and could make authoritative decisions that they could enforce whereas less effective ALTs were composed of "second tier" management level personnel. These ALT members were obliged to seek authority and that took time and lobbying energy that detracted from delivering authoritative decisions that could take immediate or near-immediate effect.
3. A selection process that is predicated upon all participants accepting the alliance principles and charter that is established for each project with contractual force;
4. An agreed pain-sharing and gain-sharing commercial agreement that all sign. The TOC is agreed by all parties and is referenced to an independently estimated benchmark cost and then developed to factor in innovation. The TOC becomes the baseline that further innovation and efficiencies reduce to release potential gainsharing. The static nature of the TOC acts as an incentive to ensure that costs do not exceed this value because painsharing arrangements on all participants mean that all parties hurt if there is pain. This contractual arrangement strengthens the motivation for collegiality and cooperation;
5. The nature of the project alliance agreement reduces power distance so that all parties in the AMT and ALT have an equal voice and their expertise is respected;
6. The inclusion of a no-litigation clause that all parties agree to results in all disputes or variances in parties' perceptions of fair treatment being tested through the ALT and not through arbitration or legal recourse (Jones, 2001, p. 155). The advantage of this is that time and energy-consuming effort to prepare documentation attributing blame for potential disputes is eliminated—consensus ALT/AMT decision making defuses arguments that attribute blame if things start to go wrong; and,
7. The alliance values are explicit and more specific than a partnering charter.

The alliancing selection processes demand transparency and accountability. Alliance NOPs agree to, and expect to, be audited and subject to probity checks. The ambience of an alliance goes beyond "culture" because the actual outcomes characteristics reflect feelings and sensations invoked by agreed behaviors and principles, mutual trust and respect, aligned motivation, and best-for-project commitment. These are based on realized expectations of transparency, stakeholder focus, joint decision making, no-blame pragmatism in fixing problems, and collaborative risk sharing, as illustrated in Figure 5. For a more detailed explanation of what we mean by the ambience of an alliance we direct readers to Walker and Lloyd-Walker (2014).

The advantage of the PA approach is that it encapsulates collaboration, innovation, transparency, and accountability. The collaborative nature of the arrangements means that there is far more flexibility and better mechanisms developed to cope with uncertainty than with other procurement forms. We use the word *cope* because alliance parties struggle and ingeniously use initiative and knowledge to manage their way through issues. This is because the POR, being locked into the alliance with the NOPs, allows priorities to be agreed to be changed and new ideas and innovations to be trialed. It reduces, if not illuminates, the energy absorbed in participants engaging in a paper-chase to cover themselves for risk and potential litigation. This is a positive product of the no-litigation agreement, which, in turn, is supported by the consensus agreement of AMT and ALT decisions, so that grounds for litigation are undermined by this structure. The role of the PO/POR cannot be understated in alliances. Frequently they provide a driving authority for their (internal) organization to commit to changes in process, operational or strategic direction,

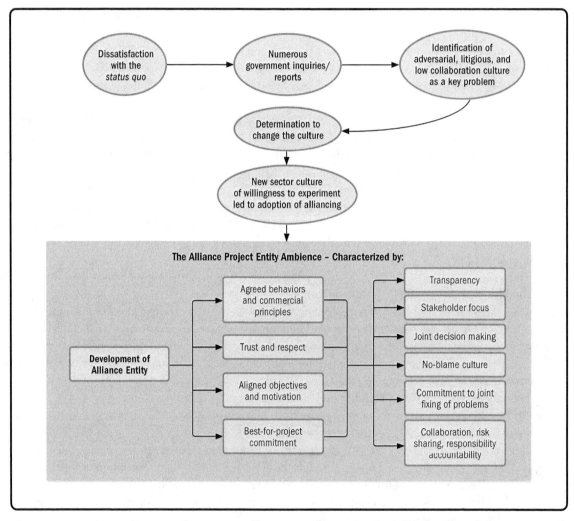

Figure 5.   The ambience of a project alliance (Source: Lloyd-Walker and Walker, 2012, p. 2)

so that a best-for-project outcome can be achieved. The PO/POR is placed in a unique position of influence to enact 'exceptions to the rule' that can present vital opportunities for innovation and pragmatic action.

This procurement approach does require particular and hard to source skills and attributes of participants and team members. This means that there is a structural impediment to its widespread adoption. Even if it became the preferred choice in the near future it would be difficult to roll out globally or even extensively in any one country or region.

Individual project alliances may be part of a larger program alliance arrangement. Program alliances can be designed to collaboratively deliver a series of major projects as part of an overall strategic initiative, some of the projects may be undertaken as project alliances while others mat adopt D&C, DBB or other more conventional delivery forms. We see this typically occurring in road and rail expansion or upgrade projects. Program alliances may also be designed to undertake a series of mini-projects (that may be of hundreds of millions of dollars cost) and they may also be designed to deliver maintenance and operations (see service alliances later in this chapter). Readers that are interested in details on these aspects should refer to the alliancing guide produced by AECOM (Morwood, Pitcher and Scott, 2008).

3B - Design alliances (DA): can be formed as a project front-end process at the design stage where the key problem to be addressed is to understand the complexity, scope and likely ramifications of a project concept. It is used when the skills required to make judgments are rare and external to the PO, the project may need specialized expertise not normally found in PO, POR or design consultancies, or where there is an identified need for freer collaboration to explore options that may take on an experimental character. Additional complexity may arise where some construction work, often temporary safety measures (which could range from several million dollars to several tens of million dollars) need to be put in place while concurrent survey work, design work and prototyping may be necessary. How can a PO procure this type of project? It may present the need for a recursive solution approach on a road upgrade project, for example, where an expert team of disparate professionals need to undertake concurrent preliminary works. This may evolve from testing soil and ground conditions, preparing a model (usually in electronic form) of the road layout and testing its probably physical performance, safety, and impact on surrounding communities, and the physical environment as well understanding how legislative and various government authority requirements can affect a project design. The DA concept is that the PO has the flexibility to call for an alliance proposal that permits a feasible design to be developed and pass through decision stage gates for approval to move through concept to pre-engineering phases of the project definition phase, where a fully informed procurement decision can be made (Alliancing Association of Australasia, 2012). In our study, we interviewed several NOPs and the POR for a water treatment project in which there was a need to test new technologies to respond to a new need to recycle industrial waste water in a safe manner that could be integrated into the general water treatment process. In that case a DA was formed to develop, experiment, and test a design that subsequently was delivered on an engineering, procurement, and construction basis that resembled the MC approach described in this chapter. There are advantages to the DA approach:

1. The PO may have difficulty in sourcing the experts who can collaborate openly to develop a feasible design by calling for an alliance a consortium of organizations that can combine their expertise under a PA with all the advantages that have been discussed for "normal" alliances. Such an alliance is likely to be better coordinated and can collaborate more freely than the PO taking over the role of integrator of the various expert entities. The DA becomes an entity with a coordinated well understood vision and purpose;

2. Necessary temporary works can take place *as part* of the alliance and provide valuable knowledge and input into a holistic perspective of the project. Often there may be urgent temporary work required, especially if the project need has been triggered by a disaster (earthquake, landslides, flood damage, etc.), mitigating long overdue maintenance or upgrade work, or responding to radically changed technology adoption opportunities (such as signaling, IT mobile phone apps for road users, etc.); and

3. The most difficult and complex part of the project may be in its definition stage, after that it may be possible that a traditional D&C or series of DBB packages may be appropriate and a DA allows for this path to be prepared. If the complexity of the project justifies a continued alliance to deliver the project from that point then a PA can be procured or a new alliance novated from the DA or a hybrid form can evolve.

A significant difference between a DA and a PA is that a DA is needed when the project concept is insufficiently clear to procure a PA. We cite a typical example of a DA from the Pacific Highway Upgrade. This is a well-recognized and highly dangerous road running from Sydney in NSW to Brisbane Queensland that for decades was renown as requiring an upgrade to being a dual carriageway with numerous bypass sections around regional towns and for construction of new sections to obviate dangerous curves and traffic black spots. There has been urgency for both short-term measures to improve the safety of the highway as well as a need for urgent complex exploratory works that were subject to difficult geotechnical conditions. Compounding this issue was the need to accommodate preserving indigenous cultural artifacts and sacred sites. In such circumstances, it makes sense for a PO to undertake a combination of approaches. Faced with new challenges requiring novel and innovate solutions, a PO organization has the choice to take time to develop expertise in-house or to put significant effort into sourcing external expertise and collaborating with them to resolve the challenging issues. In essence, this is an outsourcing decision for temporary and rare resources. DAs are appropriate for those projects where the project concept is unclear and cannot be made clear without extensive preliminary work requiring specific expertise that is not readily available to POs/PORs—in such cases it may be near impossible to find a reference case or comparable project to establish what a reasonable benchmark cost/time should be to satisfy best-value comparison. PAs may be appropriate where the concept is clear, but other conditions such as the need for innovation, close collaboration, and perhaps speed of delivery may be high priorities. D&C or DBB may be appropriate for low-complexity, low-uncertainty parts of the project.

A project example illustrating an *alliance design and construct* form of delivery in conjunction with a dependent long term maintenance contract is the Pacific Link Alliance Tugun Bypass Project, which is part of the Pacific Highway upgrade. A case study report provides some insights into how a DA may work (Alliancing Association of Australasia, 2008). The report explains that in August 2002, the initiation of the project when Queensland Main Roads and Parsons Brinkerhoff commenced work on a staged approval process, and the New South Wales (NSW) Road Traffic Authority (RTA) formed a team whose ". . . first challenge was to identify, engage and inform these disparate agency stakeholders in order to produce and obtain concurrence for a single set of project approval documents. These documents had to comply with a range of state and federal legislative requirements – a complex and time consuming process. The team's first challenge was to identify, engage and inform these disparate agency stakeholders in order to produce and obtain concurrence for a single set of project approval documents. These documents had to comply with a range of state and federal legislative requirements – a complex and time consuming process." (Alliancing Association of Australasia, 2008, p. 3–4).

In 2005, Main Roads sought proposals for a delivery alliance ". . . to design, construct and maintain the bypass" (p. 4). The case study report of the project (Alliancing Association of Australasia, 2008, p. 6) states that "A major task for the project team was ensuring the proposal met all of the legislative, environmental and technical standards set by the various government approval agencies. The project team therefore consulted and interacted frequently with representatives from the Gold Coast Airport, other Queensland Government agencies and NSW and Commonwealth officers from a variety of regulatory agencies." This illustrates some of the levels of complexity to be dealt with.

Often, potential ramifications cannot be understood well at the business case development phase and the PO may need considerable help at the project definition stage (see Figure 2) to explore and understand options to present at decision gate DG2. The DA is a useful means to open up project delivery options with a view to narrow them later.

3C – Program Service alliances (SA): Another form of alliancing that shares similarities with outsourcing service provision is a program services alliance. One option an organization has with operating its facilities such as buildings, roads, rail track, water distribution, etc., is to outsource the maintenance and operations of those facilities completely. However, the organization loses ownership and control over such facilities, and it may feel that this is a strategic asset it must keep. Another option for the organization is to commission a service alliance (Morwood et al., 2008).

Program alliances can, in general, take on two forms. The first is for capital expenditure programs of work. Examples of this are found in Australia, such as in the rail sector where a series of railway crossings have been replaced with a rail/road grade separation bridge project under a long-term program of works. Two approaches may take place. The authority (PO) involved may call for a program alliance to cover a series of those facilities on a one-by-one basis as a project alliance within a program of work. Alternatively, the alliance may be organised to span a set period of time, five years for example, and the successful alliance team then undertakes each of the capital expenditure projects within the program alliance and often contributes to the strategic decision making about which project should be undertaken at any given time based on the POR service (rail, road, or water for example) expectations and a range of other considerations that may include resource availability or cash flow budgets. The second form of program alliances is for maintenance and operations. This would be the case for routine, periodic, and emergency situations where the program alliance maintains the asset to enable its service operations to continue smoothly. The first program service alliance situation can be seen as being managed as project alliances and the second type of program alliance, is managed as explained below.

The PO forms an SA alliance with a business (or alliance of firms to form the service alliance) that has the ability to not only operate the facilities and be responsible for maintenance and safety, etc., through the service alliance, but to also provide advice at a strategic level on how to prioritize any upgrade capital expenditure and routine and emergency maintenance. There have been many such alliances formed in Australia and they can be effective in both capital and ongoing maintenance and operations management. In previous research, we interviewed alliance managers of these types of alliance arrangement, and those we interviewed explained the alliance aims and role within their client organization (Klakegg et al., 2010; Walker and Lloyd-Walker, 2011a; Walker et al., 2013a).

An Alliancing Association of Australasia (2010) case study describes the "us" (Utility Service Alliance) in the following terms: "The five year journey so far undertaken by South East Water's 12 year *'us'* - Utility Services Alliance is a story of transformation from a traditional 'outsourced command and control' contract approach, through managing and delivering assets, to a collaborative model that has yielded customer, financial and cultural benefits" (2010, p. 1). The alliance is a $47 million/year operations and maintenance and $100 million/year capital delivery program in Victoria, Australia. KPIs are set for innovation as well as relational KPIs as evidenced in the case study (Alliancing Association of Australasia, 2010).

The value-adding nature of this type of alliance is that the service alliance brings expertise to the client that is unavailable internally, for whatever reason. This expertise provides more than just cost advantages (because if this were the case, then an outsourcing agreement may be more or equally appropriate). It provides strategic advantage in terms of facilitating innovation, growing the business and bringing in expertise on prioritizing capital expenditure (CAPEX) and routine maintenance project plans. There is a danger, of course, in allowing the entity that will carry out CAPEX projects to have any significant influence in decision making. However, this risk is mitigated by the same alliance governance and project ambience characteristics that are illustrated in Figure 5. If a client is uncomfortable with being committed to a single supplier over a period of time it should consider the use of framework agreements, which tend to have a looser commitment between participants that have been screened and selected based on performance and relationship criteria. Framework agreements tend to not include the strategic decision making element. They are discussed and explained later.

We also see similar arrangements evolving in the Rijkswaterstaat (RWS) public transport infrastructure agency in the Netherlands, where they have adopted an approach that they term an integrated performance contract (IPC). Hartmann, Davies and Frederiksen (2010, p1170) state that this evolved "in order to achieve a greater reduction of the administrative work the idea was born to integrate different disciplines of routine maintenance (e.g. asphalt repair, wastage, green spaces) in one contract." This provides an arrangement where not only do several individual trade contractors collaborate and work together under a single entity but that they emphasize shifts from these small subcontractors individually tendering based on specifications and rigid rules, that are micro-managed by RWS instead they are integrated and through an open book and negotiated basis they have developed a procurement form similar to that of a service alliance.

4 – Early contractor involvement (ECI) can eliminate waste of time, cost, and effort that bedevils projects as they move through the project stages described earlier. Much of this waste can be attributed to poor understanding of the impact and knock-on effects of design decisions made prior to project delivery, because those delivering a project have not had the opportunity to highlight potential problems until design decisions are locked in. Love, Edwards, Irani, and Walker (2009, p. 1) conducted 59 in-depth interviews in their study of project pathogens with a range of design and delivery professionals in the fields of oil and gas, mining, and construction projects and found that "Omissions errors, in particular, have been found to account for as much as 38% of the total rework costs experienced."

Findings that are relevant to ECI relate to systemic conditions that can be minimized through ECI. Many of the pathogens that lie dormant in a project design later emerge as being identified specifically with a specific problem, or are a symptom that may have a knock-on effect that manifests a problem yet remains largely hidden. Love et al. note that "Pathogens can arise because of strategic decisions taken by top management or key decision makers. Such decisions may be mistaken but they need not be. Latent conditions can lay dormant within a system for a considerable period of time and thus become an integral part of everyday work practices. However, once they combine with active failures (which are similar to Deming's common causes), omission errors can arise and the consequences of which may be significant. Active failures are essentially unsafe acts committed by people who are in direct contact with a system. Such acts include: slips, lapses, mistakes, and procedural violations. . ." (Love et al., 2009, p. 1). They found that rework and emergent problems that often required expensive rectification work and were disruptive to project delivery progress could be avoided by improved decision making through closer collaboration and information sharing. This can mitigate against the active failures identified above because ECI provides a structural and institutional response to decision making not having sufficient access to the type of information and knowledge that they need to make decisions. ECI is also useful in avoiding rework through developing and more fully exploring planning and optional issues, as well by identifying potential value engineering advantages from achieving functional benefits with the advantage of the perspective of those who translate design into reality though a more buildable or constructable design (McGeorge & Palmer, 2002).

We can trace the concept of ECI back to the pre-Industrial Revolution times when master craftsmen worked with a client's commissioned agent to build large-scale structures. The masons and architects who built the great ecclesiastical infrastructures of churches, monasteries, and the core communal buildings of Europe relied on the skills and expertise of the workforce that built these structures. It was unthinkable to not seek the voice of those who would build the structures. However, the Industrial Revolution began a de-skilling compartmentalization and specialization of work, with its rationalization and logic of segregating the design chief (architect) from the builders. There was still much interaction, though in a highly class-based power distance way until the beginning of the 1900s, and more stridently from the mid 1900s with further fragmentation resulting in contractors devolving work into subcontract packages that was noted as the source of many of the problems that plagued the construction industry from that point on (Murray & Langford, 2003).

There was an attempt to re-unify segmented roles through early attempts at ECI. The term "buildability" or "constructability" was coined to describe the use of ECI advice on the practicality of realizing designs (CIIA, 1995; McGeorge & Palmer, 2002; Sidwell & Mehertns, 1996). During the 1990s, considerable interest was raised in buildability through the Construction Industry Institute in the U.S. and its counterpart in Australia (CIIA, 1995), and this led to government interest through the Construction Industry Development Agency (CIDA) in a way to improve productivity in the construction industry (CIDA, 1993a; 1993b; 1994). In all these cases, the emphasis was on the contractor and design team developing a collaborative approach that improved their working relationship and the final output. The CIIA report (1995) documented a number of high-profile projects where elements of ECI were evident.

According to the Alliancing Association of Australasia (2010, p. 6), "ECI contracting is best described as a process where the designer and constructor work together in a contractual relationship with the client, firstly to scope and price a project (Stage 1) and then to design and construct a project (Stage 2)." These services include providing an independent estimator and probity and financial audits in an open-book manner. Risks are identified, assessed and can be planned to be allocated to those who can best manage those risks. The project development is finished with a risk-adjusted price (RAP) estimate. If the PO decides to proceed, then the price is agreed to (or negotiated, as there may be various service options as well as other aspects needing clarification) and the contractor may proceed to deliver the project. The open-book nature and close collaboration on defining, understanding, and planning how to deal with risk makes this approach attractive to PORs, designers, and contractors because the probity process keeps relevant data out in the open and thus more credible and trustworthy, and it engenders trust among project participants.

We can view ECI as an alliance-oriented arrangement in that similar alliance principles lie at the core of the relationship. However, ECI acknowledges limitations and potential for options to change procurement methods at the project delivery phase, when greater knowledge and better understanding of the project design is achieved.

5 – Framework agreements: share similarities with strategic partnering (see Table 2-1) and alliancing forms for projects or programs of projects (see Figure 2-3). The Manchester Business School report states that framework agreements ". . . are similar to strategic partnering in that a client selects certain suppliers to supply services for a defined period, and there is a mutual intention to improve the quality of relationships and of performance over that time. The actual works will not be defined at the start of the period but once a project is defined there is a secondary selection process to determine which firm(s) will carry it out. Framework arrangements should be distinguished from framework contracts; in the latter, the relationships are purely contractual with no commitment to mutual improvement. The U.K., particularly, has used this form of collaboration" (2009c, p. 9).

In the Aerospace industry, more specifically, companies such as BAE Systems have used a form of supply chain management that is close in concept to a framework agreement (Green et al., 2005). In the BAE procurement form, a set of suppliers establish their credentials to be part of a small group of subcontractors and suppliers that are called upon to engage with the lead contractor and/or PO to deliver a plane, missile system, satellite, or aerospace product.

Khalfan and McDermot (2006) report on the successful use of framework agreements by councils in the U.K. for building and maintenance work. Mosey (2009, p. 145-150) also provides a useful analysis of framework agreements. He points out that these agreements require careful management to ensure that all parties know what they are committing to and how that relationship will unfold. That is, the partnering philosophy needs to be genuine. This is supported by a report on an IT framework agreement for the National Offender Management Information System (NOMIS) published by the U.K.'s National Audit Office (2009, p. 7). The framework agreement was unsuccessfully applied because the client was insufficiently experienced and lacked the necessary skills in managing the agreement with respect to engagement and project management. This provides a cautionary note of how all such arrangements require authentic behaviors by all parties, including the client.

Framework agreements can be advantageous for organizations that have frequent need to contract service delivery such as building and maintenance, IT, etc., and where there is an available pool of suppliers that can agree on a framework that defines what is to be delivered, how, what the behavioral expectations are for all parties and what performance level is required and how it is to be delivered. They can allow small- and medium-sized enterprises (SMEs) to be able to be rapidly deployed on projects, often on a negotiated or cost-reimbursable basis, when there is uncertainty about how the product/service will be delivered to fit the client's constraints. The advantage of the framework agreement over strategic partnering or a service alliance is that work can be distributed to a pool of suppliers, somewhat similar to the *Baufairbund* (BFB) approach discussed earlier. Therefore, it can include more SME supplier organizations, thus raising the sophistication level of an industry segment that otherwise may not have this exposure to learning. This subsection, however, highlights the need for the establishment of the partnering and relationship principles and obligations of all parties to be crystal clear and made explicit so they will be fully understood by all parties.

Beyond the "Iron Triangle" Performance Implications

In this section we discuss wider performance issues in relation to PM and project procurement. Traditional PM stressed what is termed the "iron triangle" performance criteria, in that projects were meant to deliver on a project brief to the established cost/resource budget, to the planned time and to the level of quality and functionality specified in the brief (PMI, 2008). However, as many thought leaders have pointed out, the iron triangle is insufficient to provide the value expectation of a project. It should also deliver on strategy (Morris & Geraldi, 2011; Norrie, 2008), and projects also have a wider social context to be sustainable in financial, environmental, and societal terms: the triple bottom line (3BL) (Elkington, 1997). It should also broadly consider performance in a balanced-scorecard way. We, therefore, discuss the implications for PM from a broader perspective of project value and performance that encompasses a 3BL perspective and, in particular, social responsibility and ethical behavior and a balanced scorecard/excellence model.

Triple Bottom Line Implications

We mentioned 3BL above, but it is worth reinforcing its importance in a project procurement context. 3BL refers to achieving a commercial, environmental, and social "bottom line" (Elkington, 1997). Economic key performance indicators (KPIs) are relatively easy to measure and reduce to a single monetary comparator measure. The other two "bottom lines" components are far harder to measure but can and are, particularly critical outcomes for PAs.

Economic or financial bottom line KPI concerns are generally met within traditional iron triangle KPIs but this 3BL concept is also about financial sustainability and that is about financial return expectations over the long term as well as for short term gains. Shenhar Dvir, Levy and Maltz (2001) show success in terms of efficiency in the short term, customer impact, business success and preparing for the future.

Figure 6 illustrates this concept modified for project value delivery. If the client specifies 3BL type sustainability KPIs then these will define short term success as well as longer term success. Project effectiveness goes beyond efficiency to effectiveness. The project should be strategically aligned to the client's aims to fulfill customer needs in whatever manner it defines those aims to warrant a judgment of medium term success. Clients (whether an external client to the organization delivering the project or an internal client for organizations that manage by projects) would judge a project's long-term success and value if it contributes to its business surviving and flourishing. Many projects that employ partnering and alliancing in particular require evidence of innovation and learning through KPIs and formal recording of an innovation register as established on the Wivenhoe Dam alliance in Queensland Australia (Rowlinson and Walker, 2008, page 411). Another Australian alliance project (the Tullamarine Calder Interchange (TCI) project, an AUD$150 million dollar upgrade of the interchange between the Tullamarine and Calder Freeways in Melbourne, Victoria) provides an example of where occupational health and safety (OHS) KRAs coincides with a KRA for evidence of demonstrated innovation. In the case study (Lingard, Wakefield and Cashin, 2011) a health and safely index was developed to measure the OHS climate that also provided evidence of a significant 3BL related innovation. Both the POR and alliance demonstrated commitment to not only espousing values relating to workplace health and safety culture but also taking action to develop a tool to manage the workplace culture.

In taking a long-term view and looking to the future, some project types may be strategic experiments. Brady and Davies (2004) identified what they describe as "vanguard projects" that some organizations undertake that do

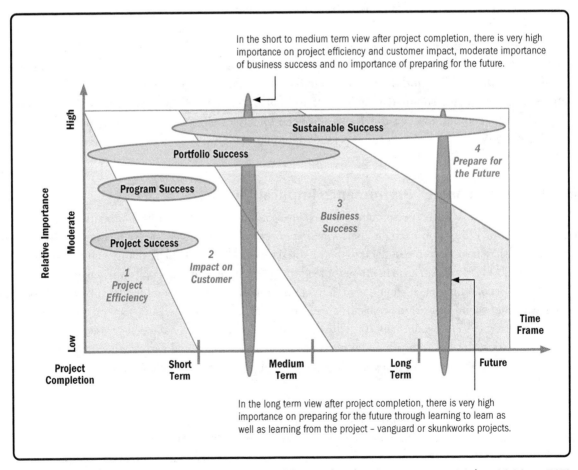

Figure 6.   Value of project success (Adapted from: Shenhar, Dvir, Levy, & Maltz, 2001, p. 717)

not conform to the traditional project KPI because much of their aim is exploratory. The aim is to learn about the environment through the project delivery experience. They may be learning new technologies, new processes, or learning about relationships with collaborators. This project type is sometimes called a *skunkworks* project (Gwynne, 1997; McKenna & Walker, 2008).

We see many instances these days where KPIs are specifically made about environmental measures, both for minimizing waste and pollution but also to be generally positive in an environmentally way. Many alternative energy projects would have these as KPIs as do many construction projects that are aiming to achieve high energy efficiency or reduce the project's delivery carbon footprint. All of the alliance projects that we have studied have had 3BL KRAs and KPIs. The National Museum of Australia project, for example, had specific 3BL alliance team selection criteria as well as KPIs for environmental aspects as well as employment of indigenous workers to enhance their skills and employment capacity (Walker & Hampson, 2003d, p. 92). We have seen similar requirements in all of the alliance projects we investigated in profiling professional excellence in alliance management, as can be seen from quotes from that study. We provide just one indicative example (Walker & Lloyd-Walker, 2011c, p. 9):

> . . . We're trying to work in the forest, you know? And XXX were saying "Well we're not like this. Unless you've got a plan for how that timber you take out, you can give a heap of it to the community, and by the way you can do something else with the timber." And we know that the timber is no use for building timber, and we know - well you know? So then they're there, and the construction answer to that is we'll reduce the timber then, so we'll just go and knock it down. These guys have got another need, like a community need. So it took, I don't know how long, to get the message over that you couldn't start until you had that plan. And that plan changed for instance at every access point, we did different clearing mechanisms. For instance either side and that gave us enough firewood for families and other things. But their idea was "Did you get synergy." You know? So if you could program that into your planning strategy and that's the part - to a construction person the programming is all about doing it tough, and not all of the lead up. And I used to have this problem in YYY, we were producing long term strategies for sewerage and so forth, and you'd say to the guys "The long term strategy, you've got to engage Friends of the Earth, you've got to engage . . . " so how do you program that into our program? So we had to bring different people in."

Clearly, 3BL issues are now moving from being considered as restricted to government projects that wish to appear appealing to the "green vote" and have moved into the mainstream of project performance requirement. With the trend now toward carbon tax or carbon credit trading, we are seeing environmental and sustainability KPIs being demanded by sophisticated repeat clients for construction projects in particular.

Corporate Social Responsibility Implications

The private sector has been taking more interest in 3BL issues through the concept of corporate social responsibility (CSR) of late, and that has certainly been a focus of KPIs for project alliances (PAs). The fall of Enron and other examples of corporate greed and folly as described by, for example, Knights and O'Leary (2005), has led to a greater scrutiny of the responsibility of organizations to their broader stakeholders, that is, society in general.

Much has been written on CSR and frameworks have been developed that help guide clients to specify CSR KPIs (Carroll, 1991; Ehrgott, Reimann, Kaufmann, & Carter, 2011; Faisal, 2010; Matten & Moon, 2008; van Marrewijk, 2003; Wu & Dunn, 1995). KPI safety, health and environment requirements form part of this responsibility (for more detail refer to Walker, Segon, & Rowlinson, 2008b, p. 122–126), but it goes beyond this dimension to respect for community values that are impacted upon by project outcome as well as output. CSR takes responsibility beyond what Morris and Geraldi (2011) refer to as the institutional context, including professional and accrediting bodies that oversee and regulate PM practice. As Dahlsrud (2008) notes, CSR has a multitude of definitions that makes designing KPIs a difficult task. He concludes that "CSR definitions are describing a phenomenon, but fail to present any guidance on how to manage the challenges within this phenomenon. Therefore, the challenge for business is not so much to define CSR, as it is to understand how CSR is socially constructed in a specific context and how to take this into account when business strategies are developed" (Dahlsrud, 2008, p. 6). This leaves us with a key requirement for those who are designing CSR KPIs. They should have strong stakeholder engagement and management skills to identify key stakeholders to be able to help construct feasible and relevant KPI categories and they need to have strong perspective taking skills (Parker et al., 2008) to be able to "stand in their shoes" and understand what CSR might mean to identified stakeholders.

Before leaving this subsection we must mention the role of ethics in CSR. Ethics is a whole topic unto itself (for more detail, refer to Müller et al., 2012; Walker et al., 2008b, p. 122–126). Without guidance on ethical standards, project team members can be caught in ethical dilemmas in which they are placed in no-win situations with poor guidance from the project governance system or, worse still, with team members who mistrust the "system" and that "the system" does not trust its employees. This aspect was explored from a PM perspective through nine case studies in Norway, China, U.K., and Australia, and this research report also provides a useful literature review (Müller at al., 2011). This model that was developed as part of the research that was presented in a report on one of the case studies (Walker & Lloyd-Walker, 2012a, p. 7). The model shows an overarching national/regional culture that influences, and is influenced by, the type and level of trust, governance, and ethical standards expected of the workgroup and organization, and the sense of self-worth of the person experiencing the dilemma. A person is challenged by an ethical issue and seeks guidance from the governance system and if that is thwarted or mishandled in any way, then there will be a loss of trust in either the "system," in that individual or the individual loses trust in the system. The individual also seeks guidance from their own ethical standards and code of life. We will discuss governance further.

One of the key significant implications for CSR and ethical PM value delivery is that this and other elements of the 3BL are being considered when developing KPIs for projects and, as such, they become part of the PM governance arrangements and cannot be ignored or viewed as having no value. Value adding has clearly expanded beyond the traditional iron triangle measures. While they may be seen as a subset of "quality," they do represent a large and expanding focus of project procurement design because 3BL does represent value and hence needs to have well designed KPIs to help plan, guide, and monitor this PM aspect.

Balanced Scorecard and other Performance Implications

Over recent years as complexity in PM has been better recognized, the simple iron triangle performance paradigm has been shifting toward one of a balanced view of value generation. This has entered PM via other disciplines, most notable the accounting and general business performance management sectors of the management discipline. Sveiby (1997) was an early pioneer with most of his work published in Swedish. At the same time, Kaplan and Norton (1992; 1996; 1998a;1998b; 2000; 2004a; 2004b; 2004c) had written widely on mapping value and the balanced scorecard concept and how it can be used to map value, enhance performance measurement and enhance strategy development. One advantage of its application has been helping to identify and map both tangible as well as intangible assets and outputs. The work of Kaplan and Norton appeared in English, resulting in their concept of a balanced approach for appreciating and planning for value generation being better known than Sveiby's.

The balanced scorecard links four dimensions to an organization's vision and strategy (Kaplan & Norton, 1998b, p. 76). The most obvious and traditional dimension is financial and measures various types of returns on investment in tangible terms, usually money. Each dimension poses a question that tests a particular perspective. This dimension provides a perspective that can then be mapped and managed through stated objectives, identifying the most appropriate measures that provide evidence of success, to document targets, and then to summarize initiatives that need to be actioned for the objectives to succeed. For the financial dimension, the question is "To succeed financially, how should we appear to our shareholders?" The second dimension is about internal business process and the question asked is "To satisfy our shareholders and customers, what business processes must we excel at?" The third dimension is about learning and growth with the question "To achieve our vision, how will we sustain our ability to change and improve?" Finally, the customer dimension asks the question "To achieve our vision, how should we appear to our customers?"

This final question has become transformed in recent years to relate to concern for project stakeholders, and this moves this dimension of performance beyond the client or customer concern. Project-related research work undertaken on this aspect has more recently been undertaken (Norrie, 2006; Stewart, 2001; Stewart & Mohamed, 2001) about the perceived need to better engage stakeholders to find out what their value propositions are and how they may fit with a proposed project (Bourne, 2008; Bourne, 2009; Bourne & Walker, 2005) to help project managers manage stakeholder expectations. Similarly, mapping intangible benefits has become important (Nogeste, 2004; 2006), and application of various business excellence models has provided us with a host of potential KPIs to use in designing and managing performance of projects. The analysis by Tan (2002, p. 167) of 16 national quality awards provides a sound set of validated measures and how they may be applied within a PM context. These offer potential KPIs for a balanced scorecard and benefits management approach.

The linking of strategy to designed performance has been a significant change in the "iron triangle" constraints, even though in the international aid development world the use of tools such as the Logical Framework (Logframe) has been used for many decades (AusAID, 2005; The World Bank, 2005). The Logframe links the value, or vision, through the overall objectives to specific objectives or purposes to expected results or output, to, finally, specific activities in a top-down to bottom-up set of questions that pose and answer "What and why is this to be done?" with questions about "How is this to be done?" (Jackson, 1997, p. 10). This potential use of Logframe has been reported in the PM literature more recently (Crawford & Bryce, 2003; Jackson, 1997; Steinfort & Walker, 2011).

Value for Money

One of the greatest paradigm shifts that we have seen over recent decades, called upon by government reports for some time (Murray & Langford, 2003) though most notably Latham (1994) and Egan (1998), has been demands for best value (value for money) over cheapest cost and/or fastest time. Over the first decade of this century, we saw the rise of interest in benefits realization (Bradley, 2010) where the focus for attention is directed on specifying, developing, monitoring, and evaluating tools and attempting to control for value of something that is defined as a benefit rather than a product or even a service.

MacDonald (2011) recently undertook an extensive review of value for money (VfM) systems and arrangements as applied in alliancing projects and offered an extensive enhancement of existing gateway processes that map and help to design and report on the generation of value for money in these projects. The framework was developed from the insights of face to face structured interviews with 27 participants from five specific alliances seeking their views on the definition of VfM and the success of these projects in achieving such an outcome to develop a prototype VfM management framework. This was then extended and refined through a process of Delphi group analysis involving 12 recognized experts in the field of project alliancing who participated in the three rounds of this survey.

A recent review of the post-Egan rethinking construction era by Wolstenholme (2009) identifies a number of blockers in the U.K that have inhibited the outcomes called for by the Egan (1998) report and at the same time, indicated considerable VfM success in demonstration projects that had used partnering arrangements. VfM lies at the heart of many RBP systems, because they tune into stakeholder values. This is an area of potential expansion in our knowledge and expertise in designing effective procurement paths.

Chapter 2 Summary

In this chapter we provided some background theory relating to PM and forms of project procurement. We saw that projects differ considerably in their characteristics and across the project lifecycle and that "iron triangle" project performance measures are inadequate to capture the understanding of the value that a project should deliver and how to recognize achievement of the value generation objectives. Wider measures are needed and 3BL and CSR perspectives provide additional KPIs. A balanced scorecard approach holds much promise.

Business Theory Aspects of RBP

Chapter 3 Introduction

In this chapter, we discuss some of the most relevant business theory and theoretical concepts relating to relationship-based procurement choices.

Figure 7 outlines the subsections for this discussion. We begin with a business justification for outsourcing because the make-or-buy choice is an important strategic decision. This is followed by some fundamentals on governance, because that aspect determines how the RMP approach will operate. We also discuss some relevant issues surrounding globalization and general complexity faced by POs.

The Business Justification for Outsourcing

The rationale for infrastructure projects is to deliver a particular set of facilities that in turn generate the required benefits. The project is a means to an end. The rationale (business case) for these projects should be clear and well enunciated. Risks and uncertainty should be well understood. If the base organization (government or private) is clear about the nature of that need, then a clearly scoped and specified brief can be developed to seek tenders from project deliverers. The rationale for sourcing internally or externally can be made, applying an economical, strategic, or tactical/pragmatic logic.

The Economic Logic

This logic is derived from transaction cost economics (TCE). Coase (1937) is credited with developing the notion of TCE. Williamson (1975; 1985; 1991), who cites Coase, explains TCE as being an economic way to explain the rationale for sourcing products or services internally or externally. TCE theory is about the motivation and rationale behind the decision to either do something yourself or get somebody else to do that thing for you. In essence, TCE theory explains decisions to make or buy an infrastructure item such as a bridge, tunnel, hospital, etc. by a government body. The choice is to source this entirely internally (to make) or to (buy) through a subcontract, or to outsource in other ways to get others to develop the item. Undertaking the work internally may involve hiring specialist skills and resources if these are not available when needed, and that can cost money. Even if an organization has the internal resources, the opportunity cost may be high in terms of money and management effort. This cost may exceed the value gained, because those resources may already be engaged on more valuable projects.

There is a transaction cost for getting others to do the work. This includes obvious costs, over and above the resources that may be common to an internal purchase of required resources, such as a search cost to find and recruit bidder,s as well as the cost of tendering, and, of course, the contract management and communication costs incurred. The rationale explained in purely economic terms is that if the cost to do this externally is less than doing so internally (due to efficiency of external sources and perhaps their innovation and intellectual property being superior to that available internally), then it makes economic sense to source the item externally. However, this is an economic rationalist view. In reality, governments and corporations make these decisions based on a range of both rational and

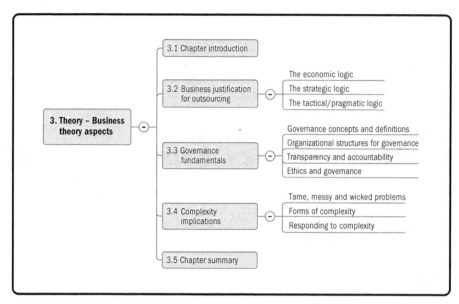

Figure 7.   Business theory chapter structure

emotional criteria—risk assessments, avoiding specialized skill and expertise shortages, social factors (keeping a vibrant and viable private sector), as well as a host of reasons that may be entirely political in nature.

This has an impact upon RBP in terms of the TCE perspective of the cost of trust, because RBP forms are founded upon mutually trusting behaviors between the commissioner of an item and those responsible for delivering it. The cost of trust in project alliances, and ECI for example, becomes apparent in terms of the required probity measures, the cost to the commissioner of the item to supervise the relationship, and costs incurred in developing and maintaining trust. The cost of tendering, selecting, workshopping, relationship building, etc., must be balanced (according to TCE theory) against a comparator of a traditional design, tender, build, or variant of that procurement model. However, a focus on cost has been supplanted by a concern for value (Thiry, 1997; Thiry & Deguire, 2007; Walker & Hampson, 2003b; Walker & Rowlinson, 2008b). The value of developing a mutually trusting relationship as an antidote to wasteful disputation and game-playing tactics to gouge extra money in projects has for a long time been recognized (NBCC, 1989) as a goal worth achieving as a value enhancement and waste-reduction tactic.

Further, the value of knowledge sharing and exchange is now becoming appreciated and ingrained in project procurement decision making (Walker & Maqsood, 2008). This occurs from the perspective of clients better sharing knowledge with a project design team to explain what they need and why they need it, and from the perspective of the design team sharing knowledge with those that will build and maintain the output, for example a hospital, so that not only efficiency is gained but also effective solutions are proposed and considered. While knowledge value in VfM terms has not been very effectively monetized, there is a broad acceptance that even in terms of management energy and attention, the value of effective knowledge sharing is real and should be considered more seriously.

The Strategic Logic

This logic places the organization's strategy as the prime motivator. Thus, if an organization's strategic aim is to divest operations and focus on identified core competencies, and if these do not include "making," then the organization will choose a "buy/outsource" decision. Porter (1985) describes three types of competitive advantage: *cost*, position or *customer focus*, and *differentiation* advantage. As he puts it,

> Competitive advantage grows fundamentally out of value a firm is able to create for its buyers that exceeds the firm's cost of creating it. Value is what buyers are willing to pay, and superior value stems from offering lower prices than competitors for equivalent benefits or providing unique benefits that more than offset a higher price. . . Interrelationships among business units are the principal means by which a diversified firm creates value' (Porter, 1985, p. 3).

All three competitive advantage issues are relevant to both government POs and their NOPs in alliances. *Cost advantage* tracks back to an ability to provide what is quite easily visualized as VfM. The most economical and efficient solutions are developed and delivered. *Customer focus* relates to the ability of alliance team participants to develop a client-oriented, or in the case of PAs, a best-for-project culture so that they are focused on delivering effective as well as efficient project outcomes. This may be also quite easily visualized in empathic behavior of being keen and mindful in understanding the project owner's fundamental need, so that tacit or implicit expectations are met. In this case, NOPs may, for example, challenge explicit assumptions about what is specified and engage in a debate to unearth better value solutions and approaches to project delivery. Differentiation may be evident in a number of ways. Project owners may *differentiate* themselves within their organization by proposing projects that present incremental or radical innovation, for example, a road or rail project that helps a transport system better perform in aggregate. NOPs may differentiate themselves through developing a specialized bundle of skills or having a special history of participating in projects where that potential knowledge and experience may be useful in niche specialized areas or as integrated solutions.

This view of sustainable competitive advantage links in well with TCE in explaining the rationale for RBP and the context of required skills, knowledge, and other attributes. Potential criticism about alliancing centers upon the cost of governance, for example, team establishment costs, VfM reporting, and probity. Many infrastructure projects may be purely focused on VfM, but what does VfM actually mean in this context? How does it compare with more traditional and transactional approaches such as DBB forms or D&C that has its focus purely on cost/time and end product quality performance. This criticism of alliancing needs to be seen in term of differences between cost and value within a context of urgency, long-term sustainability and business viability. A best-value paradigm embraces triple bottom line (3BL) project outcome objectives, which may include general industry upskilling or cultural change to a no-dispute or at least minimal-dispute project environment. For project managers, to understand an environmentally sustainable focus on PM will naturally require additional and different skills, knowledge, and attributes to that of a pure VfM performance paradigm. More traditional transactional procurement approaches involve many hidden costs that are borne by the NOPs through the overall cost of multiple tenderers or high governance costs associated with adopting a high control emphasis on project administration. This can result in high disputation and legal costs. VfM does require attempts to acknowledge the value of intangible outcomes inherent in 3BL outcomes, but the very presence of the word "money" in VfM presents difficult challenges in valuing, for example, knowledge, goodwill, collaborative behavior, and other people-supportive behaviors—all skills and attributes that are essential for alliancing. Adopting a best-value procurement basis rather than a VfM focus can present demanding challenges. Therefore, different skills and attributes are necessary for RBP projects than traditional approaches. This helps explain the need for acquiring these skills in project participants as well as their special competitive advantage skills associated with *customer focus* and service *differentiation*. Often the pool of potential alliance team members with the required skills and attributes is very small, hence the traditional procurement approach for these projects fails on TCE grounds. The search cost and development cost can be very high. Therefore a best for project/client mindset by the PO and NOPs is essential when the competitive advantage of providing a customer focus is a key strategy driver.

The Tactical/Pragmatic Logic

The outsourcing of project design and delivery may be triggered by a purely pragmatic (lack of) choice. The National Museum of Australia procurement choice of project alliancing was made on the basis of it being considered as the only choice that could deliver the project by the required time as a political promise of a gift by the Commonwealth Government of Australia to the nation (Auditor-General of the Australian National Audit Office, 2000; Walker & Hampson, 2003d). While one view of a government project procurement choice of this kind may be seen as expediency or vote-catching, it can also be argued as a pragmatic response to deliver on a "sacred promise" to stakeholders (voters). Certainly, an RBP choice with an aim of selecting, on the basis of local skills, a local workforce as a means to maintain a viable livelihood to an area is both pragmatic and understandable. Much of the Christchurch, New Zealand earthquake recovery project work is being undertaken on an RBP basis to alleviate severe economic and social distress in that area. This makes valid pragmatic sense.

We can envisage instances where an organization has adequate internal resources to design and deliver a project but chooses to outsource to gain a fresh approach that may deliver unanticipated value in terms of learning. The idea of a "skunkworks" (Tulley, 1998; Wolff, 1987) is relevant here where a radical or controversial project is "insourced" to an especially quarantined group to undertake projects that may need to be undertaken under a radically different organizational culture or governance framework. This happens more frequently in very quick-to-market settings such as radical new product development or radical process change projects such as in the communications sector as described by McKenna (2010).

Governance Fundamentals

Much is written and spoken about governance and it has a certain authoritative ring about the term, but what does it actually mean in an RBP context? Klakegg et al (2009, Chapter 2) provides a useful summary of public sector, corporate, and project governance. They point out that the concept can be understood from a number of perspectives and they cite several including bureau-shaping, instrumental-structural, network, cultural-institutional, and environmental perspectives. Projects are instigated by a PO who has certain responsibilities and obligations, and the project is delivered by a team of PM team specialists who also have certain responsibilities and obligations.

Governance Concepts and Definitions

Müller (2009, p. 2) provides a simple and understandable definition of project governance. He states that it is "a framework for ethical decision making and managerial action that is based on transparency, accountability and defined roles. It also provides a clear distinction between *ownership* and *control* of tasks." He later brings in concepts of governance being linked to the values of the organization and further develops a typology of governance frameworks based on an *outcome control* focus or *behavior control* focus on one dimension and a *shareholder orientation* or *stakeholder orientation* on another dimension to create a 4×4 matrix. This provides a useful typology of government paradigms.

Müller refers to a *flexible economist paradigm* for an outcome control focus with a shareholder orientation. This seems to be most aligned with a traditional DBB form of procurement and many D&C variants, where the worldview is very performative in terms of contract wording and conditions while maximizing protection and advancement of the home-base companies involved, so that each team is aware of its obligations to its shareholders as their top priority. There is a high level of concentration on competencies and a tendency to take a knowledge exploitation rather than a knowledge exploration stance.

A behavior control focus with a shareholder orientation is termed a *conformist paradigm*. This worldview, as with the flexible economist, has its shareholders as the prime expected beneficiaries of the transaction while adhering to contract obligations, but there is greater emphasis on following due process and behaving in a manner that relies on setting people's behavior patterns in alignment of objectives rather than relying on output targets and KPIs, etc.

An outcome-control focus based on stakeholder orientation relies upon hard performance measures as well as so-called "soft" qualitative measures that deliver intangible benefits to a broader base. This *versatile artist paradigm* does respect the validity and value in balancing demands of various affected entities, and viewing success in this light rather than by purely economic KPIs.

The final paradigm that Müller (2009, p. 11) identifies is the *agile pragmatist*. This worldview has a behavioral control focus but with a stakeholder orientation. Success is seen to be project efficiency, effectiveness to all parties that have influence, as well as making a contribution to longer-term business success.

Our perspective from Müller focuses on RBP approaches that are clearly more stakeholder than shareholder focused and are more behavioral than control-outcome focused. RBP approaches are designed to be team inclusive and to align best-for-project behaviors, ethical dealings and these generally have a high focus on triple bottom line (3BL) outcomes. We can see how this may affect the way that a procurement approach can influence the requirements for governance arrangements. Figure 8 serves to guide this discussion.

Figure 8 provides us with a framework for discussion for this section. It takes a structural and behavioral perspective that acknowledges an institutional perspective in terms of legal and regulatory requirements. It provides an

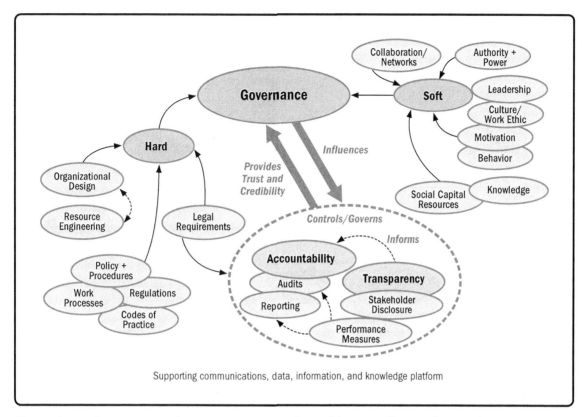

Figure 8. Governance elements (Source: Adapted from Walker et al., 2008b, p. 128)

illustration of the nature of the organizational structures, how these are institutionalized and embodied in the governance arrangements, and how accountability and transparency influence and provide trust and credibility in this system's capacity to deliver the means to enact the designed governance framework. It also helps us to understand how governance can impact upon ethical behavior.

We investigate RBP from an organizational structure perspective of governance to better understand it in a global context and to enable us to suggest and recommend how we can design a procurement system to effectively deliver value and benefit through an organizational form. Clearly, part of this involves designing a protocol that facilitates effective delivery of the benefit and value through the project vehicle, and this means that we need to understand how that protocol might work and what knowledge skills, personal attributes, and experience would be required.

Organizational structures for governance

Figure 8 illustrates the governance system as having "hard" and "soft" features. The "hard" features include elements relating to the organizational structure design and resource engineering to sustain that structure. Finding and applying the required resources to deliver the project will influence and be influenced by the organizational design. The way that resources are distributed and who is accountable and responsible for those, how risks are managed, and how incentives and penalties should apply are all part of the chosen or designed governance framework.

Figure 9 illustrates a generic project organizational design. The top level represents the executive leadership team that makes high-level strategic decisions. In the case of traditional projects, this team would be external to the project and would be positioned in the hierarchy above the Team 1 to Team n organizations. They would lead company boards of suppliers, subcontractors, designers, and the system integrator. In JVs, that executive leadership team may be created for a specific project or the JV may be engaged in several projects accountable to this board. In project alliances, this high-level board would be called the alliance leadership team (ALT) and would be composed of senior executives from participating organizations. A second-tier senior management team would make mid-level strategic and tactical decisions. Each of the teams would have their appropriate hierarchy to undertake the work.

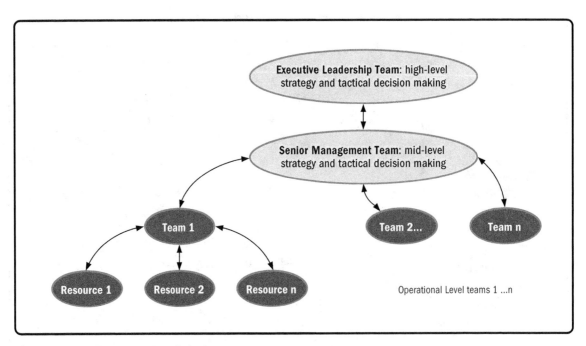

Figure 9. Organizational design

Each level would have its own designated limits and constraints on what it can approve and be authorized to do, and any conflict or questions or required approval would be passed up the chain using a well-understood escalation strategy.

The organizational design may be in the form of a project management office (PMO) or a temporary organization made up of project teams from a range of subcontractors, suppliers, designers, and system integrators. It may be hierarchical or relatively flat in terms of authority levels. It could be co-located or virtual. There are many potential forms: the point we make is that the form should be designed to suit the project design and delivery objective. In more traditional projects, there would be a project integrator organization and each contributing entity would have supporting teams. All teams would have their own reporting arrangements to their organizations, boards, hierarchies, etc. Very large projects would resemble a stand-alone company in many ways as would JVs.

Other "hard" elements illustrated in Figure 8 include the rules, regulations, procedures, work processes, codes of practice, etc. All these are designed, or evolve, to attempt to provide order and guidance to the way that the project is managed and the way that people interact. The external legal and regulatory system that imposes laws, regulations, and processes to obtain and lodge permits etc. provides an addition element of governance to internal and designable governance elements.

Implicit in this, and supporting the governance framework, is a platform that provides communication of data, information, and knowledge as well as decision support through modeling and visualization tools. These may be un-integrated, which may or may not pose interoperability problems, and they may be shared. This platform may be as crucial as the governance system itself in facilitating collaboration and control.

Taking a cultural-institutional perspective of governance led us to include the soft, often forgotten, aspects of governance that include collaborative networks. Even the most transactional and hard-edged procurement approach requires a set of suppliers and subcontractors and unofficial as well as official sources of advice from past projects and associations. These networks have varying value to the project but often they remain unrecognized and/or poorly appreciated. RBP approaches tend to be more active in recognizing their value and, in Australia, the Infrastructure Partnerships Australia (IPA), for example, provides a valuable network of participants in PAs that regularly meet and exchange knowledge. A particularly interesting example of a collaborative network that is used as a governance mechanism to enhance collaboration and business transformation opportunities for change and supply chain integration projects in Latin America is the Atlantic Corridor. Interested readers can refer to Arroyo's doctoral thesis (2009) or several publications that focus on case studies from that work (Arroyo & Walker, 2008; 2009). Collaborative networks can be internal and serve innovation diffusion purposes as illustrated by Peansupap in both Australia (2004; Peansupap & Walker, 2005b) and in Thailand (Peansupap & Walker, 2009). There are many other examples of situated learning networks that can be mentioned—for example, in Sense's various articles (2003; 2005; 2007)—that can be designed as a knowledge creation, sharing, and transfer entity that is designed into how projects are governed.

Other cultural-institutional aspects of our governance perspective are illustrated in Figure 8. These include the designated levels of power and authority that govern approval and decision making, and the leadership style that adjusts and is adjusted by the way that strategy is developed and disseminated, how motivation and behavioral norms evolve, and how the whole cultural ambience of an organization emerges. These "soft" governance aspects transform the designed project intent into action. Frequently unintended consequences arise from poorly thought through "soft" governance elements that can result in rigidity at one extreme and laxness at the other extreme.

From a principal-agency theory perspective, Eisenhardt (1989, p. 58) summarizes agency theory thus:

"Agency theory is concerned with resolving two problems that can occur in agency relationships. The first is the agency problem that arises when (a) the desires or goals of the principal and agent conflict and (b) it is difficult or expensive for the principal to verify what the agent is actually doing. The problem here is that the principal cannot verify that the agent has behaved appropriately. The second is the problem of risk sharing that arises when the principal and agent have different attitudes toward risk. The problem here is that the principal and the agent may prefer different actions because of the different risk preferences."

One way to accommodate this situation is to ensure accountability and transparency. Accountability traces who is responsible for what, how, and when. Transparency provides the rationale (why) and makes the process as clear and unambiguous as possible so that the constructed meanings of the PO and the agent (the POR and all project team members commissioned at that point) can be aligned as closely as is feasible.

Transparency and Accountability

Often a business plan or project brief provides a starting point for transparency but it obliges the PO/POR and those engaged in subsequent steps and phases in Figure 2 to be as transparent and clear about what the project's purpose is, what the expectations and assumptions are, and how the relationship between parties will be conducted.

The PO is usually far removed from the project once the initial stage gate DG0 for business development in Phase 1 in Figure 2 and Phase 2 strategy to feasibility study decision gate DG1 have been approved to allow Step 2 of Phase 2 development of concepts to progress. One of the criticisms made of project alliances in Australia (Wood & Duffield, 2009) has been that many POs or their PORs leapt straight into alliancing as a procurement choice without developing a clear business case and rationale for that choice. Additionally, not only do the outputs (deliverables) and anticipated outcomes (impacts and consequences of delivering the outputs) need to be defined, but appropriate measurement devices are needed to be able to define what precisely is to be delivered and what are the limits and granularity of assessment when measuring performance. As noted earlier in the section on *Balanced Scorecard and other Performance Implications*, the LogFrame approach has been largely ignored by the PM world (Baccarini, 1999), even though it is a useful tool for planning, developing a business plan, and performance measures (Steinfort & Walker, 2011). Once project deliverable output and outcome expectations are clear, it is possible to design a system for reporting on defined KPIs and KRAs and how that may be audited. In defining the KPIs and KRAs, especially if the stakeholder rather than purely shareholder *versatile artist* or *agile pragmatist* paradigm is accepted, the importance of stakeholder engagement is vital for learning about what the anticipated benefits are and how they should be articulated and measured, as well as how they should be communicated so that performance is transparent. Finally, drawing upon agency theory, it becomes clear that auditing is linked to the extent to which an open-book approach to transparency is appropriate and just. We can see that stakeholder engagement is vital in understanding their needs and concerns, as is argued by, for example, Bourne (2009; 2011a) and by Aaltonen for work on international projects (Aaltonen, 2010; Aaltonen and Kujala, 2010; Aaltonen and Sivonen, 2009).

Transparency and accountability feed the governance system in that they provide the designed templates of what is to done and how it is to be assessed. For example, in terms of accountability, a role description should not only define what that person is expected to do and who they report to, and are reported to but it should clarify how that role fits into the governance framework in general, what value that brings to the management of the project, and how performance should be measured and assessed. We discuss this in more detail in the next chapter. In terms of transparency, this provides the means by which stakeholders are engaged with (consulted but and kept informed about relevant and important issues that impacts them). It also helps to monitor and evaluate performance against designated KRAs and KPIs and to allow early warning signs to be visible so that problems can be addressed.

Ethics and Governance

Ethics and governance are linked, along with trust and commitment. We mentioned in the section on *corporate social responsibility and ethics* that an important input into how project managers and team members address ethical dilemmas is through reference to the governance framework. Müller et al. (2012, p. 13) present four types of dilemmas in project managers' decision making:

Dilemma 1: There is a conflict between two equally valid ethical choices;
Dilemma 2: There is a conflict between what is ethically correct and what company policy is;
Dilemma 3: There is a conflict between what is ethically correct and what the law requires; and
Dilemma 4: There is a conflict between what is legally correct and company policy

These can apply to procurement choices and how to respond to external stakeholders and team-member stakeholders during design and delivery of a project in tendering and selecting project participants, choosing which available procurement form should be adopted, and how project design and delivery should be conducted. The research results published by Müller et al. (2012, p. 16–17) present four propositions relating to governance, trust, and ethical stances of people facing ethical dilemmas.

"P1: In order to be able to delegate the taking/facing of challenging situations the governance structure needs to trust staff's ability, benevolence, and integrity to take appropriate decisions

Similarly, the project managers should fulfil the requirements of trustworthiness in order to be trusted by the governance structure. That forms the second proposition:

P2: In order to act appropriately in the face of challenging situations project managers need to recognize the challenging situation, evaluate it, decide on appropriate course of action, and have the ability, integrity and benevolence to take appropriate action

With propositions P1 and P2 representing the ex-ante situation, the following describes the flow of actions when a situation for ethical decision making arises.

The governance structure sets the framework for project managers to act, thus providing limitations and guidance. To that end the governance structure needs to provide help when project managers are caught in an ethical dilemma. For that, the project managers need to perceive the governance structure as being trustworthy by the time ethical decision making is required. That leads to proposition 3:

P3: If staff members feel they cannot act on their own, they need to have trust in the governance structure's benevolence, integrity and ability to refer the challenging situation back to the governance structure

Once the governance structure has been put to the test for resolving the issue at hand there are two possible outcomes. Hopefully the governance structure helps the project manager to address the issue in an appropriate manner which supports the existing trust in the governance structure. Otherwise, the governance structure is of little or no help for the project manager, which leads to a loss of trust in the governance structure. That forms propositions 4A and 4B:

P4A: If the governance structure works to resolve the challenges it reinforces trust of the project manager in the governance structure and he or she will continue to use the governance structure.

P4B: If the governance structure does not work to resolve the challenges, it damages trust of the project manager in the governance structure. If project managers lose trust in the governance structure they will start to circumvent the governance structure and that, in turn, may damage the trust of the governance structure in the project manager."

These propositions were tested through undertaking 28 interviews involving nine case studies in Northern Europe, Western Europe, China, and Australia.

We leave readers to follow up on that work, as further publications will follow during 2013 and beyond, and part of that study involves a survey of PM team members in a range of industry sectors and regions. The important message here is that it demonstrates that project governance has highly significant influence on how questions of ethics in procurement are addressed. The governance system frames expectations of accountability, responsibility, and responsiveness. This need to frame expectations links to a need for stakeholder engagement in defining and refining what performance KRAs and KPIs should be designed into project governance for any given project context or type of project. The way that ethical dilemmas are addressed is influenced by "hard" system elements as well as "soft" elements, as illustrated in Figure 8.

As explained earlier discussion on corporate social responsibility implications the model in Figure 10 illustrates the person being ethically confronted. They have a default position that is influenced by their national/regional/local culture, which forms part of the Figure 8 "soft" elements combined with their own ethical stance on issues. The governance framework plays a critical role as propositions P1, P2, P3, P4A and P4B suggest. The person facing the dilemma must decide whether they trust the governance system to support and guide them or whether it proves meaningless and that they would be better to trust their own ethical instinct that is influenced by their work/regional culture and their experiences of what has proved to be authentic or consistent in the past. People may have quite different individual ethical standards that may be driving their perception of the dilemma. There has been a number of studies on national and regional culture undertaken (Chhokar, Brodbeck, & House, 2008; Hofstede, Hofstede, & Minkov, 2010; House, Hanges, Javidan, Dorfman, & Gupta, 2004; Trompenaars & Hampden-Turner, 2004), and all these show variations in national and regional comfort with levels of power and information access that can affect the extent to which individuals may feel it to be their obligation to do something that they instinctively feel may be unjust or unethical. We will discuss how trust works in Chapter 4. Of course, all the judgments about what to trust, who to trust and follow, and how this all

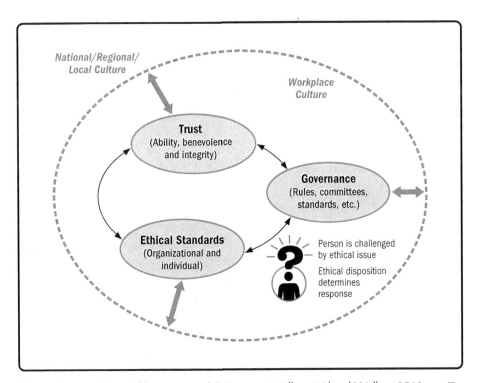

Figure 10.   Ethical dilemma model (Source: Walker & Lloyd-Walker, 2012a, p. 7)

makes sense to the person trying to make sense of it all, their judgment is influenced by their perception of how simple or complex the situation is that they are facing. This proves a natural lead into the next section, the role of complexity in designing and implementing project procurement approaches.

Complexity Implications

We argue in this book that an effective design of an RBP system to deliver a project or program of projects is contextually path-dependent. An approach that is appropriate for a simple situation can be highly inappropriate for a more complex one because simple situations generally present less uncertainty than a complex one, and so we need to gain a better understanding of the situational context to best design an appropriate procurement approach.

Tame, Messy, and Wicked Problems

Situations are seldom straight forward. Hancock (2010) provides an explanation in his book for three situational states: tame, messy, and wicked. *Tame* situations are easily understood and can be dealt with using standard approaches and tools. *Messy* situations are puzzles so that first the mess needs to be understood and ordered systematically so that they can be resolved. *Wicked* situations have no correct answer and indeed the questions may be uncertain, needing the application of divergent thinking and analysis. As Rittel and Webber (1973, p. 161) state, "The formulation of a wicked problem is the problem! The process of formulating the problem and of conceiving a solution (or re-solution) is identical, since every specification of the problem is a specification of the direction in which a treatment is considered."

Making a procurement choice can be a tame, messy, or wicked situation to deal with. If the project objectives are to deliver the project in a quick time and at lowest cost to strictly specified conditions, then this resembles a tame procurement choice problem. However, if the choice involves interpreting European Union directives about contestability and what best value may mean, for example, then the situation looks more messy than tame. Similarly, if we impose upon this situation objectives of maximizing local provider content, delivering excellence in knowledge transfer, and experimentation on a vanguard project, then we may be entering the realm of a wicked problem/situation.

Forms of Complexity

A number of PM writers have attempted to describe and categorize complexity. Baccarini (1996) was an early writer on complexity in PM and mused on complexity in terms of technical and organizational structure and interpersonal network interfaces. Williams (1999, p. 271) built upon the differentiation and interdependency concepts and concluded that project complexity could be decomposed into structural uncertainty (number of elements and interdependence of elements) and uncertainty (in terms of goals and methods). Perminova, Gustafsson, and Wikström (2008) distinguish between risk and uncertainty by claiming that risk is a causal concept while uncertainty is a consequential concept. There exists a risk that an event may happen but the consequence in terms of scope, scale, and impact is unknown or perhaps unknowable. This debate and probing of the concept was later extended by Bosch-Rekveldt, Jongkind, Mooi, Bakker, & Verbraeck (2010) with an extensive literature review of more recent PM complexity work, where they arrived at the technical, organizational and environment (TOE) complexity classification. Clearly from this work, complexity involved something beyond quantitative factors (numbers of people, social links, scope and scale, etc.) to include qualitative factors such as the nature of influence and ability to recognize and cope with it. Remington and Pollack (2007) wrote a book on various types of complexity, including structural, technical, directional (uncertainty in where the project is/should go), temporal (shifting and changing objectives and timing of project elements), and what tools were available to manage complexity. Remington (2011) later wrote a book on leading complex projects in which she provides very useful guidance based on experiences of a wide range of experienced project managers of highly complicated and complex projects with valuable quotations from interviewees to illustrate and explain their insights. She summarizes complexity well when she states that complexity is characterized by uncertainty, ambiguity, and decreasing levels of trust of people in their relationships or behaviors that suggest unexpected emergence of events that regate held assumptions about the situation (Remington, 2011, Chapter 1).

Perhaps earlier PM references to complexity should have referred to complicatedness characterized by messy problems and reserved complexity for emergence of issues that require revisiting and revising assumptions or perhaps to simply probe and respond to complex situations being faced. This leads to a further characterization of messy or wicked situations into chaotic ones where no clear pattern can be discerned, or that they are in ". . .disarray, discord, confusion, upheaval, bedlam, and utter mess arising from the complete absence of order" (van Eijnatten & Putnik, 2004, p. 419). Organizations that can transform chaos into order do so through self-awareness and self-learning and become *chaordic enterprises* (van Eijnatten & Putnik, 2004). Transforming disorder into order can involve numerous strategies that depend upon the knowledge, skills and experience of those making sense of this disorder. Kurtz and Snowden (2003) discuss how leadership groups trained in the use of the *Cynefin* framework understand the nature of exposure to risk and uncertainty posed by their operating environment. The *Cynefin* framework characterizes domains of knowledge in organizations as *known, knowable, complex,* and *chaotic* (2002, p. 106–7). *Known* knowledge is acknowledged best practice in tame situations. *Knowable* knowledge is available from experts who can analyze tame or messy situations and perceive how to respond from understanding patterns and reducing ambiguity, uncertainty, and linkage within and between systems. *Complex* spaces are where patterns are in a state of flux and there is uncertainty about how, why, and when changes occur, but highly expert people can understand the dynamics of these turbulent patterns. *Chaotic* is the space where knowledge and thinking must be entrained then used, when and as needed, where assumptions are totally questioned, and response to experimentation is rapid and intuitively applied.

Snowden (Kurtz & Snowden, 2003; Snowden, 2002; Snowden & Boone, 2007) sees situations as being mainly ordered or unordered with a small zone of disorder—essentially this zone is not yet ordered and so open to individuals to make sense of the situation and make an interpretation of what they see as an appropriate response.

We saw earlier in this chapter that infrastructure and engineering projects were suggested by Turner and Cochrane (1993) to typically have well understood goals and methods of delivery. However, their attempts at project classification on that basis appear to be rather coarse-grained when contrasted with the added dimension of project type offered by Shenhar and Dvir (2004; 2007) who consider novelty, complexity, technology, and pace as important project context considerations. Howell, Windahl, and Seidel (2010) classified PM frameworks and approaches based upon two dimensions of uncertainty (the probability of unexpected events) and consequences (the impact or cost of the unexpected). Projects have also been more recently perceived in terms of complex bundles of projects and associated services where innovation and learning features strongly (Hobday et al., 2000). These examples indicate relevance of project complexity, degree of being inherently complicated or their being delivered in a turbulent or chaotic environment, to RBP choice. Undertaking highly complex projects may have project procurement choice implications.

We can view the complexity of project briefing, design and delivery in terms of what is known and unknown (i.e., risk and uncertainty). The Johari window, originally developed by Luft and Ingham (1955), is a useful tool to map awareness. Its dimensions are "known to self" and "known to others." *Public* knowledge is that which is known to self and others. *Private* knowledge is known to self but unknown by others. *Blind* is known to others but not to self, and *unknown* is knowledge that neither "self" nor "others" are aware of. This idea can be transformed within a PM context into self (project team cumulative knowledge) with known "knowns," and this model can be used to also classify uncertainty and can further be combined with the *Cynefyn* framework described by Snowden and Boone (2007). Figure 11 presents a transformation of these ides within a project procurement context.

Responding to Complexity

Snowden (Kurtz & Snowden, 2003; Snowden, 2002; Snowden & Boone, 2007) recommends strategies to deal with apparent or perceived disorder by shifting perceptions through use of knowledge and perceptions that can be shared and reframed so that the disorder slips back into either an ordered or unordered state. If the project objectives and methods are known and understood, it is relatively simple to take effective action, using well established protocols and, as indicated in Quadrant 1, a traditional procurement approach may well suffice. Quadrant 2 describes complicated projects that may be effectively dealt with using traditional project procurement approaches as long as the client/project owner seeks and uses expert help to formulate scope, scale, and performance expectations. Relationship-based procurement strategies begin to appear more attractive when the PO is blind to potential problems in complex projects. In this situation, a lot of mutual adjustment is required between the PO and project teams in facilitating clear scope, scale, and performance expectations. This is where a panel of experts can undertake experiments and

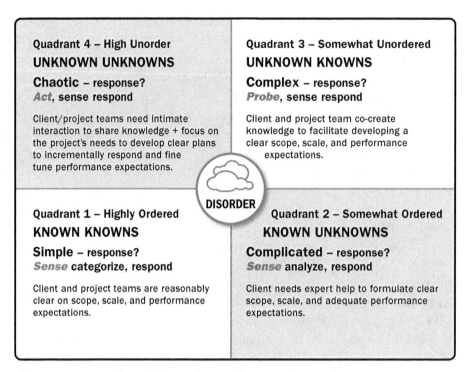

Figure 11. A Johari-Oriented Cynefin Typology of Project Awareness (adapted from Snowden, 2002).

try things out in a measured and professional way. This situation is suggested by Quadrant 3. Quadrant 4 illustrates a chaotic state where the environment is highly turbulent or circumstances and required knowledge are changing more quickly than can be formulated into medium-term plans such that the response can only be reactive, and therefore all team members, including the POR, must be focused on action that moves the project completion forward and be prepared to make sorties or probes into finding a plausible way forward, and be speedy and resilient enough to be able to change plans to adjust to emerging realities. In his YouTube presentation, Snowden explains clearly the role of disorder and explains that most of us are in a state of disorder where we are not quite sure which quadrant we are actually in (see http://www.youtube.com/watch?v=N7oz366X0-8). Our response to moving from disorder (being unclear what is the best way forward) to the apparent order of one of the quadrants is governed by our predisposition. If we convince ourselves that we are probably in an ordered state, then we will use tried and tested 'scientific' approaches, but we may be in a chaotic quadrant, and so our choice of response may have disastrous consequences. In procurement terms, we need to fit the flexibility/rigidity framework to the context, circumstances and capacity of our project team to adapt and adopt the most sensible approach to managing a project.

Figure 11 introduces general issues of complexity and complicatedness in terms of the need for the PO and NOP team to share knowledge, insights on the implications of prescribed (planned) actions, and performance expectations. It hints at the importance of mutual understanding of what is required, what needs to be done and how to resource and mobilize resources to achieve the intended project outcome, as well as the need to define performance expectations. From the PO's perspective, performance may mean benefit realization through the project outcome and this could encompass a number of stakeholders, such as end-users, as well as "the environment." From a NOP's perspective, performance may include financial rewards as well as intangible returns such as kudos, learning, relationship building, and a range of other benefits. Figure 11 is useful because it provides a framework for understanding the need and project circumstance that could govern the degree of relational consideration that the project procurement form must encourage to be effective in facilitating clear enough scope, scale, and performance expectations to enable the PO and the NOP project team to be able to deliver a successful project. Explicit articulation of performance in terms of delivering expected benefits is critical to achieve project success.

Chapter 3 Summary

In this chapter, we provided several business theory aspects of PM. We began with the business justification for outsourcing. This was followed by a section on governance fundamentals in which organizational structures, transparency, and accountability are explained as linking governance and ethics and how that may impact project managers facing potential ethical dilemmas. A section of complexity then followed.

The chapter sets the salient business theory to PM that can help us better understand project procurement rationale in general and RBP in particular. Business justification for outsourcing helps set the context. Governance aspects are critical parts of a procurement system in defining how they will work and understanding any unintended consequences. Procurement system design and delivery needs to take into account varying levels of complexity and its likely impact and implications.

The next chapter deals with the last important aspect of RBP theory that is necessary to understand human behavior aspects.

Human Behavior Theory Aspects of RBP

Chapter 4 Introduction

In this chapter, we discuss some of the most relevant human behavior theoretical concepts relating to relationship-based procurement choices. Figure 12 illustrates this chapter's structure.

We present a section on trust and commitment following this brief chapter introduction, because this is a core and fundamental feature of RBP approaches. Similarly, the section on collaboration frameworks discusses vital aspects of co-learning the ability of people to acknowledge the perspective of others and to the value of empathy. The section on strategic HRM is central to our analysis of the skills and experience part of the KSAE required of RBP forms. This leads into a necessary section on the classification of capabilities and frameworks that may be applicable to the aim of this study. We wrap up the chapter with a chapter summary.

Trust and Commitment

In Chapter 3 in the section on the business justification for outsourcing, we discussed the business logic of outsourcing from a TCE perspective. We pointed out, using a number of cited sources, that trust enabled a cost saving in reducing the investment in the need for vigilance against exploitation of one party by another as well as the cost of preparing countermeasures to ensure that issues such as instructions and their rationale are fully documented. We also highlighted that gaining trust involves an investment in energy and time, and that this includes not only the cost of doing this but also an ability to build trust and commitment.

Further, drawing upon the cost-benefit of trust, Hosmer (1994) directs to our attention to the need for managers to be concerned about fairness and the way that benefits and their costs are distributed so that those they deal with can gain a sense of being treated reasonably and ethically. He further underpins this line of argument with a discussion on the link between ethical behavior and being perceived as trustworthy (Hosmer, 1995), and this reinforces our previously cited quote from Eisenhardt (1989, p. 58) about agency theory, where a prime concern is first how trustworthy parties are, and second how effectively one party can understand another party to be able to interpret what they are negotiating and what the offers and acceptances really mean. Trust and trustworthiness become an asset and a tradable commodity in the sense that it can be used to offset costs that would otherwise have to be expended.

We now draw upon some salient theories of trust and commitment and follow with a discussion of trust and culture.

Elements and Models of Trust

The most frequently quoted theories on trust are based on early work of Mayer, Davis, and Schoorman (1995) and elaborations upon their model. Figure 13 illustrates our adaptation of the original Mayer et al. (1995, p. 715) model. The model makes sense if we assume that people engaged in this set of thought patterns are rational and that they calculate trust in a self-interested way. The key to the model is that trust involves a person willing to take a risk that they are making themselves vulnerable in some way and that the person is making a calculated rather than emotional decision to trust, not trust, or distrust. We acknowledge the criticism made by some authors (Denis, Langley,

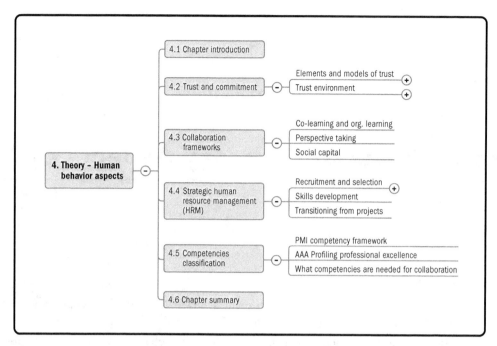

Figure 12. Human Behavior Theory Aspects Chapter Outline

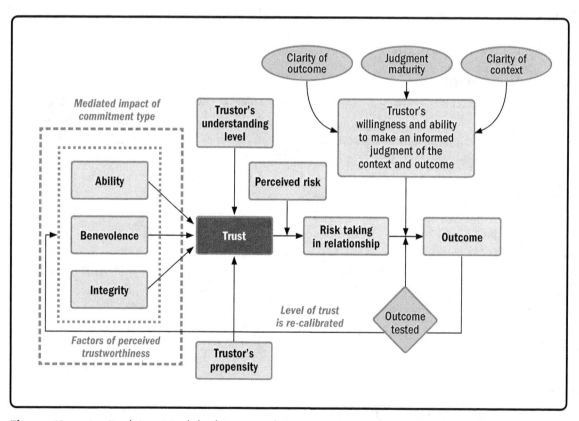

Figure 13. An Evolving Model of Trust and Commitment (adapted from Walker, Bourne, & Rowlinson, 2008, p. 79).

& Rouleau, 2007; Langley, 1995; Langley, Mintzberg, Pitcher, Posada, & Saint-Macary, 1995; Langley, Smallman, Tsoukas, & Van De Ven, 2013) that decisions, and therefore perceptions of trust, are driven by rationality and logic as well as by emotions and haphazard events. This may affect people's cause-and-effect perception and their attitudes toward perceived trustworthiness. However, as much of the literature on trust and commitment has its basis in rational thinking, we will pursue this line of reasoning in this chapter.

The sequence of events that affect trust, illustrated in Figure 13, is as follows: First, there is a residual propensity in a person considering trusting another (or entity such as an organization or governance system). This is driven by three main factors, as illustrated in Figure 13. Ability refers to the capacity and motivation of the other person (or entity), hence it has two elements; the first is about having the ability to do something and the second is about being committed enough to perform to the level of capacity. Benevolence refers to the feelings toward that individual. We would expect and hope for feelings of parties not wishing to inflict harm, but this is mitigated by recognition that harm may occur unintentionally despite a motivation to not do any harm. This element of trust could also be about expectations of benevolence due to reciprocity where favors or some form of obligation is being repaid. The third element referred to is integrity. This is about performance matching rhetoric and that is also mediated by motivation and commitment.

The mediating factor indicated in Figure 13 is commitment. Meyer and Allen (1991) developed a three component model of commitment that Meyer subsequently refined and expanded upon with others through empirical studies (Meyer & Herscovitch, 2001; Meyer, Paunonen, Gellatly, Goffin, & Jackson, 1989; Meyer, Stanley, Herscovitch, & Topolnytsky, 2002). In essence, commitment extends beyond mere compliance, that is, being *required* or coerced to do something. Commitment can be classified in three ways. *Continuance* commitment is a need-to form of commitment in which there is a cost that is implied or expressed in *not* doing something. *Normative* commitment is an ought-to style of commitment, being obliged to or feeling a form of loyalty to do something. The most intrinsic form of commitment is *affective* commitment, which is want-to type of commitment. In this style, there is some form of joint and aligned objective that drives decision and action.

The trustor needs to make sense of the risk and his or her level of vulnerability in the situation that requires trust, as well as the factors described above that affect the trustworthiness of the people/entity involved. The risk-taking situation is then engaged in and the relationships and behaviors of those being trusted are then tested. The value of the feedback that the trustor perceives and absorbs is dependent upon his or her ability at that time to clearly recognize and understand the outcomes. Understanding and judgment is mediated by at least three factors at the time the judgment is being made. First, the clarity of the outcome of the test is determined by perception of not only immediate observable outcomes but also anticipated projected trends. Immediate observable outcomes need to be interpreted, so aspects such as contextual clarity and knowledge as well as the maturity of the situation and trustor in this circumstance also come into play. In this sense the "stickiness" of knowledge, the way that lessons can or cannot be learned, also affects the clarity of context. We will explain knowledge stickiness in the next section. The judgment of the outcome of the testing of trust is then absorbed and the trust level for that person within a similar context is then recalibrated. This could involve a deepening of trust and willingness to accept greater future risk or the reverse situation.

Figure 13 illustrates a highly personal unit of analysis. To extend this, and better understand what may be happening in the trustor's mind at the organizational or societal level, we need to also consider how the model may be more widely applicable. Pinto (2000) discusses how understanding the politics of a situation is an important art, and this aspect is elaborated upon by Bourne (2011b) in her concept of "tapping into the power lines;" knowing how to access credible advice from those who may not necessarily appear influential in a situation but who may offer deep contextual knowledge about the situation. Das (2005) introduces time horizons into the sensemaking process and argues that situations need to be judged on the basis of temporal proximity or distance. For example, if a possible negative outcome is likely to happen a long time into the future, then we can assume that many things can change and there is time for intervention. Others have also argued, based on studies of trust, a range of temporal dimension implications. This dimension ranges from a form of "swift trust" that we see with Internet-connected teams (Bachmann & Inkpen, 2011; Jarvenpaa, Knoll, & Leidner, 1998; Perks & Halliday, 2003) to trust starting at near zero and building with experience (Lewicki, Tomlinson, & Gillespie, 2006). From the institutional perspective, Rousseau, Sitkin, Burt, and Camerer (1998) argue that institutional trust is reasonably stable because an organization's values and reputation are generally stable; however, as we have frequently seen, corporate scandals instantly undermine trust.

Trust can, and often does, cohabit with distrust as Lewicki et al. (2006, p. 1003) remind us with their four-cell model. Parties with high trust and low distrust are characterized as having high value congruence and confidence, hope and faith in their judgment. Low trust and high distrust are characterized by a "trust but verify" approach and features strict boundary distinctions and demarcation and a monitoring system designed to provide accountability and transparency. This latter set of arrangements is most strongly featured in project alliances, many JVs, and frequently in partnering arrangements.

Smyth (2006, p. 102–103) makes the point that the models derived from Mayer's work are predicated on calculative trust. This particular worldview refers overwhelmingly to *self-interested trust* where there is minimal evidence of trust but estimated high levels of mutual self-interest in obtaining a win-win outcome from the relationship. This requires the parties to trust each other and the systems in place to enforce that trust. He contrasts that with *socially-oriented trust* in which the enforcement mechanisms are social and potentially more powerful. He includes such things as social networks, peer values, brand/reputation, and the need for collaboration in these. Trust is realized at "a deeper level, generated through obligations in a social network and comes through reputation, advocacy and especially supportive relationships, where the motive is, 'What can I do for the other party?'" (Smyth & Edkins, 2007, p. 234). Social trust is potentially more effective because while calculating self-interest and motivation is fraught with hazards of under/over estimation and short term perspectives, social trust is much more attuned to long-term assessment and being intrinsic, and so more in line with affective rather than normative or continuance commitment. Smyth (1966) illustrates a model in which conditions of trust (similar to the Figure 13 factors) lead from calculative self-interested trust toward socially oriented trust through mechanisms of faith (unseen capabilities of others parties to perform), hope (that they will perform to that expected), and confidence (based on experience of past performance, reputation, etc., and as an indicator of future performance), building within a socially driven (rather than governance and hierarchy driven) context. The model's building blocks are stated as characteristics of trust, components of trust, and conditions of trust (Smyth, 2006, p. 114–115).

The Trust Environment

The socially oriented trust perspective segues into a discussion on trust and culture. Linked to the above, and highly relevant to trust and culture in an RBP context, is the tension between trust and control. In the earlier discussion on the four-cell Lewicki et al. (2006, p. 1003) model, we saw the coexistence of trust and distrust. Das and Teng (1998) undertook a study of the relationship between trust, control, and confidence in a partner's cooperation and delivery on promises. They investigated JVs and minor and non-equity business alliances (as opposed to project or other alliance types discussed in this book), and their control dimension concerned hierarchal control and ownership control. While this does not have direct relevance to project alliances and other forms of RBP discussed in this book, it does provide an interesting perspective of the purpose of these governance arrangements.

All culture is derived at its taproots from common assumptions that are understood through explicit and implicit shared values. These are manifested through observable artifacts (Schein, 2004). This cultural influence shapes and guides an individual's response to organizational and social pressures.

Figure 14 illustrates the world of cultures that projects inhabit, and each of these has an impact upon people who are the core element of any organization. It illustrates the extent of cultural influence that shapes and guides their behavior and response. Trust, as we saw earlier, involves attributes of benevolence, ability and integrity that are interpreted through a cultural lens. For trust to be possible, and indeed nurtured, the project teams need to have common assumptions and shared values that support these attributes, but people in these project teams are part of and act within a wider world with a range of sub-cultures that have some shared and common attributes but other conflicting ones. Each person will have their own worldview partially, if not largely, influenced by their "home" culture. They also will belong to professions or associations that often have a code of ethics and culture. Organizations and teams or workgroups also will develop a culture. The whole system of interrelated sub-cultures interacts and changes.

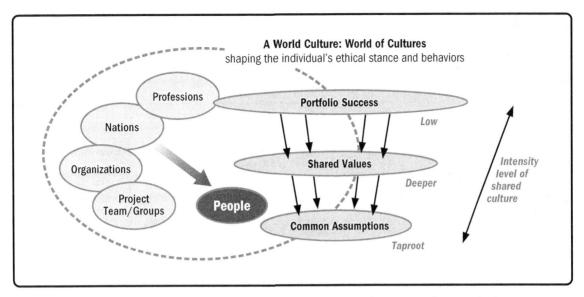

Figure 14. A Systems View of Culture (Adapted from Rowlinson, Walker, and Cheung, 2008, p. 279)

While it takes a lot of time, energy and effort to change the taproot common assumptions and shared values, the observable artifacts can change more rapidly, and we see this as fads come and go (Abrahamson, 1996). Figure 14 helps explain how trust calculus and social trust may function. Observable artifacts can, at the superficial level, suggest a particular culture or subculture. For example, in a partnering culture there may be a partnering charter prominently displayed and even regular partnering workshops being held with all participants badged in some way with a common project symbol or icon. However, this is insufficient for a partnering culture to exist unless participants truly internalize the espoused shared values and absorb those values as core common assumptions about the way that they will behave and interact. When people are testing for trust indicators as illustrated in Figure 13, they are assessing evidence of artifacts and shared values achieving an authentic fit. Similarly, *socially-oriented trust* participants are seeking approval and validation from their valued professional, business, and social network subcultures to recognize their social capital "worth" and trustworthiness as well as their performance on past projects.

In terms of better understanding the values of regional or national cultures, we need to be aware of models and frameworks that help us understand the common assumptions and values. A great deal of research has been undertaken on the study of dimensions of regional/natural culture. The work was pioneered by Hofstede et al. (2010) and others such as Trompenaars (1993; Trompenaars & Prud'homme, 2004), and in a wide scale survey of 62 national and regional cultures (societies as they refer to them) undertaken under the banner of the *Global Leadership and Organizational Behavior Effectiveness* (GLOBE) Research Program. This resulted in two heavy but intensely valuable books (House et al., 2004; Chhokar et al., 2008) with a string of journal publications that may be more accessible to readers than these two books. These articles include House, Javidan, Hanges, and Dorfman (2002) and Javidan, Stahl, Brodbeck, and Wilderom (2005) with many others appearing the *Journal of World Business*. The relevant message from this body of work is that different regional/national cultures have varying shared assumptions about issues that can be categorized across a number of dimensions. Some of the most relevant of these to RBP are the ways that various cultures see legitimacy in power distance, role, and behavior to their fellows. To illustrate these dimensions, we summarize them in Table 3, based on the Hofstede's and GLOBE's dimensions of culture.

It is easier to understand, when the above is considered, how people can misunderstand each other or might take an emotional stance rather than a calculative one if their cultural norms are being challenged by others. This has a direct impact on how trust is established, maintained, and impacted. It also helps explain why different people will experience quite different degrees of discomfort with many ethical dilemmas and respond in a variety of ways.

Cultural Dimension	Implication for RBP
Large or small power distance: Power distance reflects the degree to which a society accepts a hierarchical system and unequal distribution of power.	Large power distance indicates larger inequalities between the members in these societies with power and those without. RBP usually seeks smaller power distance, though roles and escalation level guides are important artifacts.
Masculinity versus femininity: Masculinity reflects the degree to which a society defines achievement in terms of success and the acquisition of money or material possessions.	Some societies with sharp and strict divisions turn masculine; others when the divisions are loose and blurred turn feminine. In masculine societies, people admire success. In feminine societies, people pursue values such as relationship orientation, concern for quality of life, etc. This affects the likely mix of a risk reward design to incentivize parties.
Individualism versus collectivism: Individualism reflects the degree to which a society values independence from group membership.	It is concerned with the form and manner of the relationship between an individual and others in the society. In individualist cultures, people look after themselves and their direct families only, and they are expected to conform; while in collectivist cultures, people belong to larger groups that takes care of their interests in exchange for loyalty—relationships are therefore more tightly structured.
Strong or weak uncertainty avoidance: Uncertainty avoidance reflects the degree to which a society tolerates ambiguous situations and the extent to which it has created institutions and beliefs to minimize or avoid these situations.	In some societies, people do not feel threatened by accepting ambiguity and uncertainty. In others, uncertainty is seen as disruptive and makes people psychologically uncomfortable. Strong uncertainty-avoidance societies reduce uncertainty and limit risk by ordering and structuring things, imposing rules and systems.
High and low Confucian dynamism: Confucian dynamism is associated with the teaching of Confucius.	People in a country emphasize values associated with the future over values that focus on the past or present. In societies with high Confucian dynamism scores, people tend to be pragmatic, future-oriented, and focusing on obligations and tradition; in those with low scores, people tend to be normative and short-term oriented, quick results are expected, and people are more concerned with stability.

Table 3.   Dimensions of Culture (Source: Adapted from Rowlinson et al., 2008, p. 294–295)

To illustrate behavior and reaction by two people with different cultural influences, we need to consider what justice and fairness may mean to them when viewed through their specific cultural lens. Luo (2007, p. 644) identifies three separate types of justice:

1. distributive justice, related to the fair distribution of outcomes within a workplace;
2. procedural justice, the perceived fairness of the process by which outcomes are reached; and
3. interactional justice, the perceived fairness of the nuances of interpersonal treatment.

Somebody with a high power distance stance may be quite comfortable with high-status members of a project team gaining kudos and recognition even though they may have personally contributed little, while those with a low power distance stance may be highly offended and feel that the procedural justice and/or interactional justice aspects of the reward governance arrangements were unfair or even corrupt. In this way, each of the cultural dimensions can be judged by individuals through their own ethical stance and we could observe quite radically different reactions. We can see that this will affect how trust is established and maintained and how one person may perceive actions demanded of them perfectly consistent with their own ethical norms while another may feel pressured and bullied into being unethical.

While we do not argue that any one cultural dimension is superior to another, it is clear that several of the cultural dimensions pose challenges while others enhance changes of collaboration. We do argue that we can be more sophisticated in the design of procurement systems when we understand how culture can impact upon ethical stances, incentives (rewards and penalties), governance, and shared values to build and maintain trust.

Collaboration Frameworks

What does collaboration and collaborative frameworks actually mean? Even if we can understand and agree on what collaboration is, how can a collaboration framework facilitate innovation to result in efficiency and effectiveness? Also, how are benefits fairly shared? Who will gain from any benefits? There are many questions that this section attempts to answer. To do this, we focus on three core concepts that we feel are important to articulate so that these can inform our analysis of data and interpretations from the literature. These are co-learning, the ability of people to take the perspective of others and empathize, and how social capital can be nurtured and mobilized.

Collaboration, according to its root meaning is together (co) working (labor), and this is implied as being directed to the same end. It is linked to cooperation, which similarly means operating (doing things) together, though people may cooperate with few signs of heading for the same goal. This seems to be one difference between cooperation and collaboration. Projects, regardless of procurement form chosen, require teams of people to work together to deliver the project and *de facto* have a relationship, in that they are all parts of the same vehicle that delivers the project. At times they are working sequentially and at other times they are working in tandem. Teams, as we know, take responsibility for various parts of the project enterprise and so it is inevitable that they have a common destination goal, but the path there varies and they have different priorities and different side agendas. One entity generally takes on the role of system integrator to pull together the different threads into a coherent end state of project completion. Sometimes that maybe the POR, other times it is the lead design team's chief, and we also see examples where the lead is the contractor's chief. Thompson and Sanders (1998) provide a typology of four states of collaboration. Competition occurs when there is zero collaboration, as the entities are in direct opposition with only a win-lose outcome possible. Cooperation occurs with low to medium congruence of goals and objectives and the parties working alongside each other toward the project delivery. Collaboration is characterized by medium to high congruence of goals and with teams working together. Coalescing is where the teams join with high to very high objectives alignment. This gives a good picture of where collaboration fits within a continuum, but it only vaguely points to who gains the benefits. Their paper detailed significant savings in cost and improvements in delivery time, and so its focus is directed to the advantages to the lead contractor.

Collaborative networks may be formed for joint problem solving; often they are formed for knowledge creation and sharing. In the context of this book, we focus on them as entities that behave in a collaborative manner to achieve a specific goal. They may include teams of people contracted to jointly deliver a project as well as include wider connected groups and individuals outside the contractual relationship.

A good review of the project collaboration literature is presented by Anvuur and Kumaraswamy (2008) and they go further to describe how relationally integrated networks of project parties can be facilitated (Anvuur, Kumaraswamy, & Mahesh, 2011). A further example of collaborative networks that we mentioned earlier is the Atlantic Corridor, which engaged an entire continent's logistics delivery enterprises in a massive transformation of the way that they did business in response to global competition, deregulation, and the consequences of formation of a massive trading block in Latin America. This organization was established by representatives of government in Brazil to improve the region's network of shipping, trucking, and air freight companies and their clients and supply chain members. It facilitated more effective collaboration to further the aims of the Mercosur, the great South American common market. Arroyo wrote a very interesting doctoral thesis (see URL http://researchbank.rmit.edu.au/view/rmit:7891) on this particular collaborative network from a knowledge sharing and business transformation perspective (Arroyo, 2009). Several case studies from Arroyo's work have also been published (Arroyo & Walker, 2008; 2009), and the Atlantic Corridor concept was explained in Walker (2012). This provides a convenient entry to the next section.

Co-learning and Organizational Learning

Atkinson (1999) alerted us to the weakness associated with the iron triangle of time/cost/quality dominating the discourse on project success and being the sole focus for project performance. The re-thinking PM research group (Winter & Smith, 2006) provided a much-needed boost to reviewing project outcomes, and one strong outcome of papers from that initiative (Winter, Smith, Morris, & Cicmil, 2006) was the findings related to the lack of reflection of PM practitioners and the lack of valuing knowledge and innovation as a viable project outcome.

Several PM thought leaders have stressed the point that projects can, and should, be seen as learning vehicles (Koskinen, 2010; Koskinen & Pihlanto, 2006; Koskinen et al., 2003; Morris & Lock, 2004; Winter & Szczepanek, 2009). The theory of exploration and exploitation (March, 1991) has triggered useful discussion about knowledge management (KM) and organizational learning (OL). Knowledge and routines learned through exploration are then adapted and applied in varying similar contexts as a process of exploitation of knowledge. In essence, exploration occurs as a process of discovery such as when projects are used as experiments or purposeful learning experiences, what Brady and Davies (2004) call vanguard projects and others have termed "skunkworks" initiatives (Gwynne, 1997; McKenna & Walker, 2008; Tulley, 1998;). A critical requirement of those embarking on vanguard or skunkworks projects is that they have the capacity to recognize, reap, and accumulate knowledge—what Cohen and Levinthal (1990) refer to as *absorptive capacity*. However, many clients seem to lack an appreciation of the value of knowledge as a product of the PM process. Indeed, all parties involved are guilty to a varying extent of not absorbing knowledge from lessons learned and project reviews (Eppler & Sukowski, 2000; Gann, 2001; Oaks, 2008; Schindler & Eppler, 2003), indeed, organizational amnesia is a cross-business phenomenon (Othman & Hashim, 2004).

Despite this potentially gloomy picture, we now note a sea-change occurring with repeat clients that expressed value concerns about narrow definitions of project success that did not include innovation and better knowledge retention from project to project. This was highlighted over a decade ago in major reports on the construction industry, such as the frequently cited Latham (1994) and Egan (1998) reports and it appears that this situation has not experienced sustained change in the U.K. during the intervening period (Wolstenholme, 2009), despite the establishment of the Constructing Excellence organization, which promoted and facilitated reform of the construction project industry in the U.K. However, we now see a better appreciation of the role of intellectual capital in enhancing performance in general (Kang & Snell, 2009) and in PM work in particular (Turner, 2011). Learning, innovation, and knowledge transfer between the project team and the client and between team members is now being used as selection criteria (Walker & Hampson, 2003d) and demonstrated proof of innovation in project alliance KPIs (Rowlinson & Walker, 2008). Indeed, where innovation and knowledge transfer have been deemed inadequate, it has been used as grounds for criticism in project alliance performance (Wood & Duffield, 2009). This demonstrates that we have moved, particularly for repeat project clients, from a position of not being aware of the advantages of co-learning, knowledge exchange, and innovation, to requiring evidence through specific KPIs on at least some forms of project procurement. Clearly, an emerging class of clients see the benefit of knowledge and innovation as a project outcome.

How are benefits of knowledge co-creation, exchange, and use shared? Clients and users of project outcomes benefit in theory due to continuous improvement and efficiency gains, and this is the rationale behind the refinement of consideration of value for money that has recently emerged in the European Union (EU) in countries such as the Netherlands (Hoezen et al., 2012a) and Denmark (Gottlieb & Jensen, 2012; Manchester Business School, 2009b). We cited a study on the value of cross-team learning in JVs (Walker & Johannes, 2003) earlier in this book in the discussion of JVs, and we can add to this discussion another on the advantages of learning across supply chain participants in project work (Khalfan & Maqsood, 2012; Khalfan & McDermot, 2006). This suggests that the value of co-learning and innovation is being increasingly recognized and that it can be spread across all participants.

How does co-learning take place in project work? Much of this occurs at the briefing stage when the PO or POR works with the design teams and, in integrated design and delivery procurement forms, with contractors and specialized subcontractors and suppliers. Whenever people are forced to explain concepts or plans to others, they engage in two very important conversations. One conversation is with themselves as they prepare in their mind what to say, how best to frame that, and how best to illustrate their thoughts in a way that others might best understand their meaning. This preparation is vital, as it forms a reality check and self-reflective mechanism to filter poorly formed elements of their thoughts (Emerson, 1983; Luria, 1973; Vygotskii, 1986). The other conversation is with the listener who then reflects on this new information in an act of self-reflection undertaken through the dialog. In this way, the construction of meaning can be a highly creative exercise because as one party to a dialogue explains meaning and nuance, they not only inform the other party but they inform themselves and often take leaps of imagination as a form of creativity (Amabile & Kramer, 2007; Leonard & Sensiper, 1998; Leonard & Straus, 1997).

Co-learning and this form of knowledge exchange continues throughout the project delivery phase as problems arise, which require coordination and self-adjustment to enable solutions to be arrived at. Problems can be resolved more effectively when sufficient knowledge and expertise is exercised together with willingness of all parties to affectively commit to working toward problem resolution through a process of building social capital (Dyer & Singh, 1998). Many projects involve complicated or complex interaction of people, systems, technologies, and exogenous events. This makes it even more important that those engaged in decision making are as aware as is practicable about the context and potential consequences, and understand the motivations and priorities of others. Bakker, Cambré, Korlaar, and Raab (2011, p. 496) refer to three types of collaborative embedding that support the kind of relationship building that helps develop experience in knowledge recognition of the value of co-learning, co-generation of knowledge, and its use and exchange. These are relational, where several project teams from different organizations (or parts of organizations) are embedded in joint problem-solving activities, or where they share concepts, approaches, language, and ways of creating meaning, or being temporally embedded where teams have been working together on previous occasions. However, people can be exposed to and be invited to participate in collaborative processes, but this does not mean that collaboration will happen. The formation of absorptive capacity is one critical element, along with the motivation to collaborate.

We might ask what provides an enabler or barrier to this process. We can find some guidance here to answer that from the innovation diffusion and organizational learning perspective. Szulanski (1996; 2003) provides some useful insights into how knowledge and innovations may be diffused within organizations and communities in the concept he refers to as "sticky knowledge." He uses sticky knowledge to describe difficulties in transferring knowledge about business routine between organizations; this knowledge of how to do something is wrapped up in organizational routines, some of which are well documented, but with tacit or implied aspects of knowledge that is difficult to imitate. Without intimate "inside" knowledge of an organization, knowledge transfer becomes difficult. Knowledge is then seen as sticky or viscous in that it does not flow easily from one source to another. Effective knowledge transfer requires understanding the context of knowledge source; it simply cannot be unquestionably applied in an "off-the-shelf" manner. Many readers will have observed from their own experience how often lessons learned that have been documented are not internalized and therefore lose impact. He provided some good reasons why this appears to be so based on his PhD research. He identified four general influencers of effective knowledge transfer, which are summarized in Table 4.

Knowledge Stickiness Element/Sub-Element	Explanation and Relevance to PM Team Knowledge Transfer
1 Characteristics of the knowledge transferred	It's difficult to transfer practices that have a high proportion of indefinable and tacit knowledge due to the tacit human skills involved, collective nature of the information, or idiosyncratic features of the context in which the knowledge is put to use (when there is ambiguity about why or when a practice works well).
	Most projects are exposed to novel and complex contexts that various project cross-team members would have experience of, but each team tends to use its own jargon and therefore needs a forum to explain and communicate meaning.
2 Characteristics of the source of knowledge	Lack of motivation – project team members may fear losing ownership, privilege, and resent not being rewarded for sharing success. Also, knowledge available may not be seen as reliable, trustworthy, and knowledgeable.
	There needs to be a systemic response to reward and facilitate knowledge exchange and a culture of respect for the expertise of others, including for technical and process knowledge.
3 Characteristics of the recipient of knowledge	Lack of motivation - the "not invented here" syndrome. Lack of ability to value, assimilate and apply new knowledge successfully to commercial ends (i.e., "absorptive capacity").
	Lack of persistence to make it work instead of giving up and reverting to status quo (i.e., "retentive capacity").
	A culture of respect is needed so that potential recipient team members acknowledge the potential value of knowledge offered to be shared and re-interpreted. A command-and-control mindset through use of strict DBB specification and iron-triangle measures of performance inhibits people challenging the status quo.
4 Characteristics of the knowledge context	Creating the climate, culture, or ambience that nurtures knowledge transfer, perception sharing, and the necessary creativity to produce innovation.
	Absorptive capacity relates in part to accrued experience in experimentation, critical analysis of mistakes (rather than attributing blame) engaging in co-learning, and negotiating various perceptions of "truth" and "facts." Collaborative forms of project procurement enhance the richness and reduce the barrenness of a learning and innovative environment.

Table 4.   Project Collaboration and Stickiness of Knowledge Transfer

The characteristics of knowledge to be transferred vary. Some knowledge is highly explicit and not highly contestable, so the receiver of that information and knowledge can accept, believe, and associate with the source's validity. When the strategy for dissemination of "the message" is effective, this enhances motivation to collaborate on co-creation and sharing of knowledge, whereas in other cases where either the message source or recipient is not attuned to receive the message or feedback, then diffusion is retarded.

The first factor relates to the characteristics of the knowledge or message. Much of the most valuable knowledge exchanged in teams is tacit, that is, it is implicitly shared through shared experience so that while it is difficult to state what the whole background context contributes to meaning, the essence can be approximated through this shared experience. Characteristics may suggest inhibition or facilitation of knowledge transfer on this basis. Sometimes the source of knowledge or the message is a "hunch" or other contestable sources. This is problematic in the sense that tacit knowledge is notoriously difficult to transfer without also transferring insights about shared experience (Polanyi, 1997).

The second factor presented in Table 4 indicates the relevance of the source of the knowledge or information. Questions may be raised about that source's credibility and veracity or epistemological validity. We may pragmatically ask, is the source information/knowledge valid in this case? The source must be credible and must be open to being challenged and validated. This is not as simple a problem as clarity of message, though that is important, as it also involves entrainment of knowledge. Söderlund (2010) refers to entrainment as a condition of just-in-time access, when a person receives a message it is timed in a way that all the precursors to understanding the message are in place so the message is internalized. This infers that the context and historical trajectory must be prepared so that when that message arrives it makes sense and connects to the recipient.

The third factor relating to the recipient's view on this will affect the way that the message is interpreted and internalized. This depends upon the recipient's capacity to receive and internalize that message as much as the value of the message. There needs to be an adequate level of absorptive capacity, that is, the ability to receive a message and to be able to apply lessons learned from that message to advantage (Cohen & Levinthal, 1990; Zahra & George, 2002). Absorptive capacity requires certain cultural attributes discussed earlier and to be elaborated upon shortly, but these essentially allow people to experiment and reflect so that they can form mental scripts that allow them to perceive and recognize familiar patterns of actions that they can deploy to advantage. How is this capacity built? Much of it is by trial and error, or experimentation. However, just experimenting is insufficient; there needs to be consistent reflection and redefinition of what is perceived to be "the truth." This is what is referred to as reflective practice (Schön, 1983). Reflection allows the possibility to move beyond cause-and-effect to hypothesize and create possibilities. This is where toleration and welcoming of variety of views is so important, because each party can add their perspective on an issue to "round out" a solution so that it is inclusive. Command and control regimes tend to undermine the collaborative process.

This leads into the fourth knowledge stickiness element, the characteristics of the knowledge context. Szulanski (1996; 2003) refers to this as a barren or fruitful context for knowledge transfer. Many project environments that have a skewed focused on exploitation of knowledge rather than exploration (March, 1991). Knowledge creation can undermine confidence in the knowledge. Others facilitate experimentation and reflection with a no-blame culture for making mistakes in which mistakes that generate learning and transfer of that learning are seen as an asset (von Krogh, Ichijo, & and Takeuchi, 2000; von Krogh, Nonaka, & Rechsteiner, 2012). The importance of creating a learning environment may relieve many of the time-lagged symptoms and causes in innovation and knowledge transfusion that was identified by Peansupap and Walker (2006) at the organizational, work group, and individual level. Many constraints that impose time lags relate to lack of support in the form of time to reflect, and time and resources to probe and experiment. We saw that these are critical to aspects highlighted in Figure 11 as well as being a consistent support of the organization being open, transparent and allowing "dirty linen" in terms of past mistakes to be on view and scrutinized to glean lessons to be not only acknowledged but infused in organizational decision makers.

Co-learning and organizational learning can be seen to be dependent on a form of contract that is supporting of co-learning and collaboration; supporting the intellectual activity of assessing project experience based on theoretical knowledge, experience. and reflection upon experience in an action-learning sense of plan, do, reflect repeat the cycle; and providing an environment that supports teams to learn and reflect in a collaborative multi-team contact context. as illustrated in Figure 15.

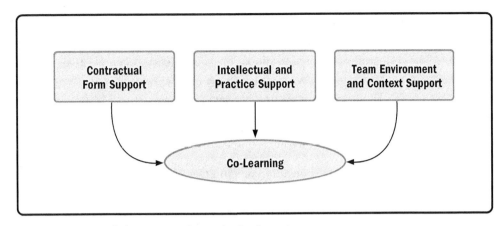

Figure 15. Collaboration Through Co-learning

We argue that knowledge stickiness theory provides a key to understanding co-learning. The governance system can provide support through contractual requirements and performance (KPIs and KRAs) expectations. Support mechanisms need to be in place to provide intellectual stimulation, informed debate and questioning, and access to external expertise to bridge identified gaps as and when they arise. Finally, the team environment and context for support is a vital ingredient.

To illustrate the dynamic process of knowledge creation, sensemaking between people and the nature of gaps, and time lags we present Figure 16 from Peansupap's PhD thesis (Peansupap, 2004; Peansupap & Walker, 2006) in which he studied the diffusion of knowledge about groupware information communication technology (ICT) diffusion

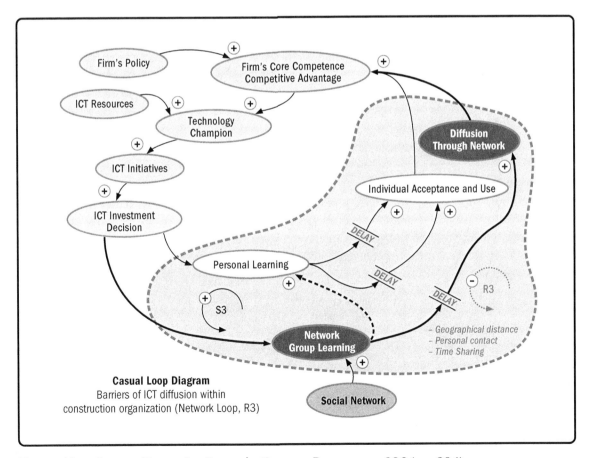

Figure 16. System Dynamics Example (Source: Peansupap, 2004, p. 284)

in four case study construction organizations in Australia that had already been using ICT for simpler applications, and thus had developed a high level of absorptive capacity.

Figure 16 illustrates how co-learning and organizational learning occurred in a case-study example at the group level within a network of project participants for a construction contractor. We see examples of support from the three contexts illustrated in Figure 15. The firm's policies provide some governance and contractual support, in this case through the resourcing of the ICT being diffused. Intellectual and practice support was provided through the technology champion, training and help-desk support as well as a social network. The team environment and network group also provided learning support.

The social network in this case comprised several communities of practice (CoP). Wenger and Snyder (2000, p. 139) describes CoPs as "groups of people informally bound together by shared expertise and passion for a joint enterprise." CoPs are often naturally forming entities though they are also often sponsored by organizations and institutionalized (Jewell & Walker, 2005). In the case study example Peansupap identified a number of intersecting CoPs (2004; Peansupap & Walker, 2005a). These can be seen from Figure 17 as including personal, professional and institutional as well as organizationally enabled CoPs.

CoPs such as the individual's previous workplace colleagues provide a powerful reference source to be able to refer to, even when they are in competing organizations, because they enjoy sharing stories. Teigland (2000) observes that what leaks from one competitor in terms of time and intellectual assets in solving problems is repaid at some future date due to a feeling of mutual obligation that becomes a motivation for social trust as discussed earlier. This form of collaboration among competitors appears to have advantages for all parties involved. It is tantamount to hiring short-term consultants on demand.

Another RBP dimension of collaboration through co-learning arises when people from different organizations voluntarily collaborate in CoPs as an alternative governance arrangement, either formally or, more often, informally.

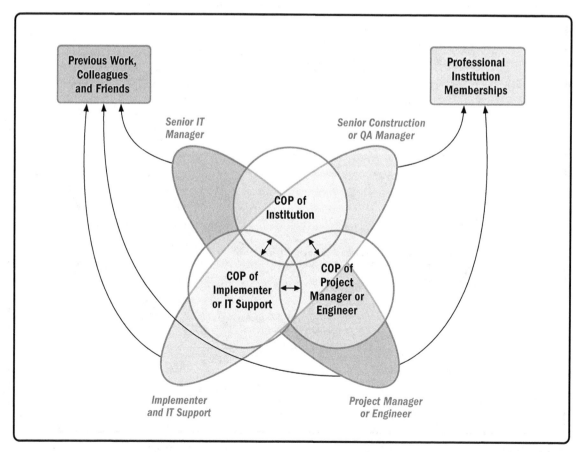

Figure 17. Relationships of CoP Between Organizations (Source: Peansupap, 2004, p. 238)

A project's governance system may be described as *thick* or heavily rule-and-regulation bound so that reliance of collaboration is assumed by prescribed organizational routines and processes defined in rulebooks or operational handbooks (Storck & Hill, 2000). Thick governance may lay much emphasis on aligning to strategy through artifacts by using manuals as boundary objects that proscribe activity. Governance may be described as *thin* when the governance measures are offered for guidance rather than for compliance. A well-functioning CoP can provide a more eclectic thin governance system by members drawing upon what pragmatically works using routines and processes from host organizations and those developed through interaction. This approach was shown to work with Xerox in the 1990s while undertaking a major transformation in the use of computers (Storck & Hill, 2000). We see the building of intellectual capital as effectively occurring through collaboration and co-learning within a company.

The relevance of OL to this section is that it is important that we understand how organizations learn through projects, and that they can optimise their learning through collaboration and reduce knowledge stickiness. Initial work by Nonaka and Takeuchi (1995) introduced the concept of knowledge creation and sharing through their SECI model in which tacit knowledge (implicit knowledge known to an individual through practice that is difficult to explain) is made available for sharing and being made explicit through a four step process. The first step of knowledge *socialization* allows tacit knowledge sharing among individuals. Articulated tacit knowledge is made explicit though a process of *externalization* of this knowledge followed by a process of *combination* of the different entities' explicit knowledge with the recently explicit tacit knowledge. This is then *internalized* by embodying explicit knowledge into tacit knowledge. They also argued that this needs to take place in a specially constructed knowledge-friendly environment referred to by the Japanese word *ba* (Nonaka, Toyama, & Konno, 2001). This approach had a focus on turning tacit knowledge into accessible explicit knowledge, and much interest was then applied to technologies and ways in which knowledge could be created, stored, transferred, and accessed for use. Much debate arose around optimum models for use of a technology-centric or people-sharing-centric approach to that process.

Hansen, Nohria, and Tierney (1999) argued for an either/or strategy and claimed that a simultaneous focus on both strategies was divisive. However, Scheepers, Venkitachalam, and Gibbs (2004) later provided evidence from case studies where a simultaneous combination strategy was effective, and so the mix of focus on people and technology was contingent on environmental factors. Evidence on the way that a people focus for knowledge sharing on projects that were very strong on partnering and supply chain integration (for example, the Heathrow T5 project (Davies et al., 2009), or project alliancing (Walker, Hampson, & Ashton, 2003) and other similar collaborative RBP projects (Radosavljevic & Bennett, 2012)) indicate the need for strongly integrated and functioning common communication platforms for groupware applications and for sophisticated building information modeling (BIM) seen in many complex construction projects these days (Aranda-Mena, Crawford, Chevez, & Froese, 2009). Much of the debate about how best to establish mechanisms for effective OL revolved around codifying lessons learned so that knowledge gained through exploration could be exploited (Eppler & Sukowski, 2000; Maqsood, Finegan, & Walker, 2006; Schindler & Eppler, 2003;).

The mechanism for integrating individual's intuition knowledge to be developed at varying organizational levels into institutional knowledge is as important as individual and small group learning. Crossan, Lane, and White (1999) illustrated a framework for knowledge creation that is congruent with ideas of knowledge, being a series of stocks and flows of knowledge as proposed by Bontis, Crossan, and Hulland (2002). The mechanism by which these are facilitated by group processes of influence, social acceptance pressure, and the power of authority within an organization sanctioning the flow-forward and feedback loops, and also knowledge being reconceptualized and validated by people and groups, was demonstrated by Lawrence, Mauws, Dyck, and Kleysen (2005). Other contributions to OL have helped us better understand the mechanisms of KM. Järvinen and Poikela (2001; 2006) combined ideas from Kolb's (1984) experiential learning model of concrete experience being reflected upon, leading to abstract conceptualization into an hypothesis or proposition that is then tested along with the flow of knowledge through organizations from the individual perspective through a shared learning context to the organizational context. All these theories rely on reflective practice where participants in co-learning first need time and space (*ba*) to make sense of their experiences and are in a safe environment to do so. The call for reflective practice is not new (Schön, 1983), and more recent contributions highlight the value of reflection in both internalizing knowledge and in conducting essential internal conversations which allow that knowledge to be framed for external explication to enable tacit understanding (Raelin, 2007; Selvin, Buckingham Shum, & Aakhus, 2010; Shelley, 2012; Smith, 2007).

The whole field of OL and KM can be seen as evolving from at least three paradigms (Firestone & McElroy, 2004; Vorakulpipat & Rezgui, 2008). The first is about applying knowledge sharing through ICT platforms using a supply-side perspective. The second has a focus on best-practice and normative frameworks for converting tacit knowledge into explicit knowledge that can be shared by groups and organizations taking a demand-side perspective. The third scrutinizes OL and KM more holistically and probes into how individuals and groups interact and make sense of actions and environments and how they share these perceptions and perspectives (Firestone & McElroy, 2005). This critically questions KM because knowledge is not information; it is a perceived reality based on information and other stimuli. We are all individually constructing, therefore we can never "really" share knowledge but only close approximations of that knowledge, because our realities are shaped by and all stimuli being received (or rather perceived) in slightly different ways. This changes the dynamics of understanding co-learning so that KM tools such as portals, data/information mining, CoPs, knowledge cafes, storytelling, social network analysis, etc., are vehicles for managing information as a feedstock that an individual's brain processes and adapts to their own ontology or paradigm to create knowledge. As Firestone and McElroy (2005, p. 202) argue:

> "Portals, like best practices systems, do not provide a way of distinguishing information from knowledge. As a consequence, any support they provide for integration functions such as broadcasting, sharing, teaching (through e-learning applications), and search and retrieval, is restricted to information, rather than knowledge, integration. Nor do portals generally provide targeted support for problem recognition, or for individual and group learning, or for knowledge claim evaluation."

This leads to a fundamental issue in how OL and KM literature is useful in studying and understanding RBP. The fundamental building block we suggest is not OL or KM *per se*, but rather the act of collaboration of people challenging assumptions and making sense of problems they solve through practice and through jointly working to make sense of action and potential consequence. Cavaleri (2008) poses the question: Are learning organizations pragmatic? He states that the pragmatist framework is built on foundations of facilitation of people to learn over time, more specifically (Cavaleri, 2008, p. 478) by:

1. Thoughtful interpretation and enactment of one's environment;
2. Learning from the feedback of experiences;
3. Reflecting on past experiences;
4. Imagining how discovered patterns of cause-effect will potentially impacts future states;
5. Engaging in inquiry to assuage the irritation of doubt;
6. Taking targeted action to achieve a desired result or state of affairs;
7. Carefully reasoning to apply rules for action or create new rules;
8. Building knowledge through experimenting with one's actions;
9. Improving the quality of one's knowledge by incorporating discoveries from action and
10. Clarifying beliefs by paying heed to doubt, and using inquiry to improve performance.

This is clearly a more intellectual and collaborative process that the first order KM/OL paradigm of information sharing and interacting with an assumed or accredited concept of knowledge as some form of truth. The third-order paradigm of KM/OL is one of seeing a flow of knowledge that is created, challenged, and validated to be incorporated and embedded into the organization as the foundation of its cultural assumptions. As illustrated in Figure 14, however, when the culture is open, rich, and strong enough to embrace contest, as illustrated by the above 10 points, assumptions and knowledge are constantly adapting.

This model of a knowledge life cycle sees a distributed organizational knowledge base (DOKB), which we argue is an agreed and socially mandated approximation of knowledge-as-truth. It comprises both subjective and objective knowledge that forms a bundle of beliefs and claims. These are applied within a business processing environment, and that knowledge-processing environment mediates the DOKB. This helps to validate and assess the extent of truth of a knowledge claim. A knowledge claim thus passes through a knowledge production process in which individuals within groups shape a knowledge claim using subjective and objective information and existing knowledge, evaluate that claim and, through that processes of challenge, carry out re-conceptualization and validation work and decide how to integrate that knowledge into the organization for broadcasting, searching, teaching, and sharing perspectives (Firestone and McElroy, 2005, p. 196).

Zahra and George (2002, p. 195) identify three competency traps that can occur when organizations are collaborating and gaining absorptive capacity through a KM mechanism. They can become overly familiar with exploitation of knowledge and lose capacity or willingness for exploration. They may suffer a maturity trap resulting from being unable to conceptualize reliable and predictable outputs from knowledge exploration (such as a definition of value for money encompassing knowledge and competence), or they may suffer from what they call propinquity (nearness) traps, which is their disposition to explore knowledge in areas closest to their existing expertise so that they do not take advantage of radical changes. This latter trap is often one of being successful and not noticing when disruptive change is looming (Christensen & Overdorf, 2000; Gilbert & Bower, 2002). This can be dangerous and is one reason why exposure to alternative perspectives through collaboration and co-learning across firms or within organizational boundaries is an often unacknowledged advantage and value to collaboration within projects.

The final key point we make to conclude this section is that we argue, based on sound literature as well as our own research into how project alliances operate, that reflection, challenge/contest, and absorptive capacity to embed and integrate knowledge is based on the capacity of individuals and of their organizations to allow their employees to take the perspective of others.

Perspective Taking

The ten points of the pragmatist framework illustrated above stress several qualities of individuals and, by extension, organizations. One quality that stands out is humility. By humility we mean the capacity to acknowledge and accept that one is probably continually misinterpreting signals. This is an ontological and epistemological issue. The worldview that this represents is one where truth is considered contestable and highly subjectively constructed. If this is reasonable, then we must take the point of view of others into account and respect their opinion. This does not mean that the "other" is always right, rather their perspective may be useful in filling gaps or for challenging our own held assumptions. If we accept the likelihood that we are often misinterpreting signals, then it makes sense for us to avail ourselves of any tool that challenges our interpretation as being valid, invalid, or incomplete. In epistemological terms, others' values and validity measures are also useful. If we believe that truth is constructed and not an objective reality, then we must accept that we are constantly working in clouds of approximations. Availability of guidance by others is, therefore, highly important.

Collaboration is, from the root formation of the word, "working together" and not engaging in a battle for a dominant truth. It requires consensus. Beliefs are based on current conceptualization of knowledge and reasoning about the validity of governing rules, assumptions and ways of assessing what is observed and experienced. When people take the perspective of others, they attempt to understand how others came to believe what they profess. By applying a temporarily adopted set of rules, assumptions and values when reasoning about a problem we can interrogate a problem, from a richer position; by doing so, we often modify our beliefs. We may totally reconceptualize a problem and this is what is often meant by "out-of-the-box" or, as Leonard terms this, thinking empathic design (Leonard-Barton, 1995; Leonard & Rayport, 1997; Leonard & Straus, 1997).

Parker et al. (2008, p. 4) provide a useful definition of constructive perspective taking as:

"Active perspective taking occurs when an observer tries to understand, in a non-judgmental way, the thoughts, motives, and/or feelings of a target, as well as why they think and/or feel the way they do."

They go on to describe perspective effectiveness as:

"The degree to which the observer has a relatively accurate, comprehensive, and objective understanding and appreciation of the target's thoughts and/or feelings and the reasons they are thinking and/or feeling that way." (2008, p. 6)

This provides a very useful framework for understanding what perspective taking means and its value in an RBP context. In their paper, Parker et al. (2008) present a figure that describes a model of outcomes of perspective taking. In that model they outline positive outcomes that include a more empathic approach to conducting a dialogue. The literature on innovation (Leonard & Rayport, 1997; Rogers, 2003; Sundbo, 1997; Thomke, 2001; van de Ven, 1986; von Hippel, 1990) suggests that empathic listening in a truly engaging manner provides a powerful driver for reconceptualizing both problems and solutions. People who are expert at perspective taking improve their cognitive responses, reasoning power, and effectiveness in understanding complex situations as a positive outcome. This ability expands their repertoire of perceived cause-and-effect loops that may operate and the awareness of their and others' potential preconception bias of situations. The final positive outcome of perspective taking is greater clarification of meaning and identity between people engaging in any kind negotiation. Unanticipated ways of working can be developed that are more intrinsically rewarding by project team members consciously considering the client's and other team members' perspective and their value proposition (Anderson, Narus, & van Rossum, 2006) through reconceptualizing the value and nature of tasks. Other personal dyadic outcomes that are presented in the Parker et al. (2008) paper includes: improved interpersonal relating; self-regulation; citizenship behaviors; improved dispute resolution and negotiation; and reduced prejudice, stereotyping and discrimination. All these qualities are associated with high levels emotional intelligence that has been shown to be valuable attributes of project manager team members (Goleman, Boyatzis, McKee, & Buntine, 2002; Turner, 2007; Turner & Lloyd-Walker, 2008; Turner, Müller, & Dulewicz, 2009).

The Parker et al. (2008) paper also identifies some negative outcomes. These include exploitation as well as conflict and self-interest and positive bias that need to be guarded against. Undue sympathy can result in manipulation and positive bias that transgresses the ethical process when making choices for example.

The broader outcomes are listed by Parker et al. (2008) as improved team and organizational performance. It is worth noting, particularly in response to the earlier section on the impact of culture, that perspective taking should be considered within context. Parker et al. (2008) do acknowledge mediating factors such as degree of independence. but their model ignores the type of dimensions earlier discussed in the GLOBE study. For example, perception taking may be inhibited by respect for authority levels, and feelings of discomfort with open communication in cultures where some forms of information disclosure may be considered disrespectful or even insulting. Those involved in perspective taking should also understand organizational culture constraints such as the importance of following organizational strategy and an insistence that all 'singing from the same song sheet'. Without considering these dimensions a person engaged in perception taking may in fact be engaging in self-delusion.

Perception taking is vitally important in effective decision making, particularly when there are many ways to frame and explore a problem/situation, because it expands possibilities and ways of looking at a problem. This aids perspective divergence for pursuing innovation. However, it does have some disadvantages including vulnerability to potential manipulation either through conscious or unconscious influence. It also is more time consuming, and in circumstances where a rapid decision to act (in an emergency or crisis, for example), it can be too time consuming to be of value. This latter point is cautionary.

Social Capital

Social capital is the glue that binds people and organizations together. It refers to features of social organization such as networks, norms, and social trust that facilitate coordination and cooperation for mutual benefit (Putnam, 1995; Tsai & Ghoshal, 1998). Figure 18 illustrates the linkage of social capital and knowledge transfer activity that supports collaboration.

Nahapiet and Ghoshal (1998) discuss and illustrate how people in groups create links across project and home organizational boundaries through having shared codes and language to be able to share perceptions, perspectives, and have common language to communicate these. Having the required trust, commitment and cultural norms and values enable people to work together in co-creating knowledge and learning from the tasks and routines they undertake. This drives the development of project capital (Brookes, Morton, Dainty, & Burns, 2006; Turner, 2011). Brookes et al. (2006, p. 477) define project capital as:

> the sum of resources that can be used to achieve a project's goals that are available through the network of relationships associated with that project. It is therefore a function of not only the level of resources possessed

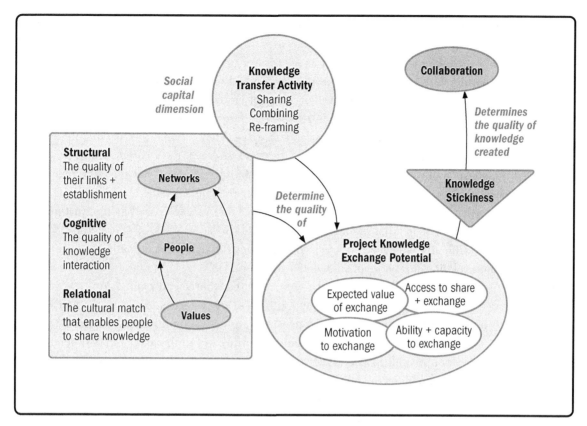

Figure 18. Social Capital in Context

by individual project actors but of the interconnectivity of actors in terms of the number of relationships between them and the resource conductivity of those relationships." This way of looking at how organizations learn through collaboration is vital in understanding the importance of transparency in communications between team members about motives, aims and expectations.

Figure 18 illustrates how social capital dimensions determine the quality of potential knowledge capital for a project. Various actors within the organization have the potential to marshal their structural, cognitive and relational resources and the quality of their contribution can result in determining the expectations of various actors concerning what they will gain from the process, their motivation to exchange knowledge and information, and their access to sources of knowledge, as well as their ability to exchange knowledge. As we discussed earlier, the factors that determine knowledge stickiness mediate the knowledge creation, transfer and use activities and this in turn impacts upon the collaboration quality. Aspects discussed in this chapter and Chapter 3 will influence the nature or model of collaboration that is likely to occur. To an extent, this model can be designed and an optimum solution developed to configure governance and how best to facilitate the interaction of people to share knowledge that improves risk management and overcomes problems associated with dealing with uncertainty.

There is no shortage of subject matter experts in academia who have written widely on the value of social capital. These thought leaders, based on their research studies, write about the need to make the most of the link between the creation of human capital and a supportive workplace environment, personal motivation, personal competence and engaging and rewarding interpersonal contact (Brockbank, 1999; Dessler, Griffiths, & Lloyd-Walker, 2007; Gratton & Ghoshal, 2003; Lawler III, 2001; Ulrich, 1998). The workplace environment and the quality of interaction between parties are seen to be critical factors.

The interaction dynamics of collaborating individuals and teams when problem-solving in projects can be highly relevant to the procurement design. If we look through the analytical lens of exploration and exploitation, we can see that traditional transactional project procurement choices have a dominant focus on exploitation. Traditional forms of project procurement tend to reward exploitation of contract conditions, use of uncertainty as a lever to extract additional money or time, and a view of people in other teams as being "objects" with exploitable sources of knowledge and potentially lucrative mistake-makers to be used as sources of blame that can be sued. With RBP, by contrast, particularly for strong partnerships and alliances, people are brought together and rewarded for being collaborative. This is suggested by Groysberg and Lee (2009) in their study of employee "stars" in the financial services sector. They found that stars that based their career mark on exploration failed to live up to expectations when placed in a work situation that demanded predominantly exploitation strategies. They seemed to miss the hidden and often assumed culture of knowledge and perspective sharing that they had grown in their career within work environments that placed a high emphasis and reward on people sharing and building ideas. That is a workplace setting where there were high levels of social capital support. As we see from Nahapiet and Ghoshal (1998), the quality and number of network links is important—the openness and common language and values as well as the trust and relationship-building qualities. This is similar to what Szulanski (1996) refers to as aspects of sticky knowledge that inhibit effective learning, where difficulty is caused in knowledge transfer through what he calls "a barren organizational context" and an "arduous relationship between source and recipient."

We could argue, based upon our observations and past research, that social capital also provides a safety net where mistakes are able to be converted into learning opportunities, and where openness to recognize and broadcast enables colleagues to help overcome adverse consequences and to thereby build social capital and trust. Projects procured under alliances, for example, have KPIs that include learning within the team and between teams on a project. This encourages exploration as well as exploitation when attempting to be innovative and within the continual stream of small but significant problem-solving activities that these project teams engage in. Our studies on the National Museum of Australia (Hampson et al., 2001) and quotes published in Volume 2 of the AAA study (Walker and Lloyd-Walker, 2011c) suggest that encouraging innovation through specific KPIs and KRAs that demand both knowledge exploration and exploitation encourages social capital building within the project delivery organization.

Strategic Human Behavior Aspects

In this section we discuss a number of issues related to HRM that while they specifically relate to alliances they may also be highly relevant for other similar RBP forms.

Managing People Across RBP Forms

To a large extent, this research has been conducted and this book written because projects have become the common way of organizing work in all sectors of the economy (Lindgren & Packendorff, 2006). The way work is carried out has been changing, with project-based organizations completing their core business through project teams, and project-oriented organizations forming teams to deliver products and services within their traditional organizational structures (Huemann, 2010; Huemann, Keegan, & Turner, 2007), thus much of the activity in these organizations is now carried out within temporary organizations, or small project teams (Ekstedt, Lundin, Söderholm, & Wirdenius, 1999; Pettigrew et al., 2003; Söderlund, 2012). Huemann (2010, p. 362) stated that "there is a paradigm shift in the nature of 21st-century organizations with projects as a specific and significant characteristic." People from a growing range of professions and backgrounds are involved because project teams are now used in health, education, the voluntary sector, and the public sector (Clark & Colling, 2005) as well as construction, mining, manufacturing, and research and development (Bredin & Söderlund, 2006). Indeed, the growth of project management as a profession confirms that the structure within which people work across a broadening range of industries, organizations, and roles has changed. The PMI-predicted growth between 2010 and 2020 in the demand for project managers would be strongest across seven project-intensive industries, leading to15.7 million new project management roles being created by 2020 (www.PMI.org/Pulse). Employment that involves project work is, thus, both already common and growing.

Fixed roles, reporting only to a divisional or business unit head, are no longer the norm for a large percentage of today's workforce. Permanent employees are now commonly deployed into roles within project teams where they may have a reporting relationship and deliverables to their project team leader while retaining responsibilities within their appointed role. For others, their project team duties may constitute their total work role for varying periods of time. In addition, contracting has become a career (Peel & Inkson, 2004) and these project managers join teams to work for a set period of time to deliver an agreed outcome, leave the organization on completion of their contract, and then seek new contracts with the same or other organizations to complete future projects. Project teams are now the common structure through which work is completed in organizations, and, at the same time, we have seen changes in the way in which project teams form and operate as new relationship forms evolve over time.

This confirms that in a broad range of workplaces work is now carried out differently to the way it was just 40 years ago. Human resource management (HRM) systems in use in today's organizations were designed to address the needs of organizations according to the way they operated in the past; they were designed to suit traditional organizational structures and ways of working. Bredin (2008) argued for the need to extend existing HR frameworks for use in project-based organizations to include people capability. This would involve developing people management systems which integrate "people capability with strategic, functional and project capabilities" (Bredin, 2008, p. 566), for instance building on the principles of capability framework models developed by Davies and Brady (2000).

It is necessary, therefore, to consider changes required within HRM systems to adapt to the use of temporary organizational forms, but additionally, we would argue, these systems need to be further adapted to suit the various different RBP forms. This needs to be addressed because HRM is "is of strategic importance in all organizations" contributing to their success and creating competitive advantage (Huemann et al., 2007, p315). Huemann et al. (2007) argued that project-oriented organizations create HRM challenges and Bredin (2008) referred to a range of studies that indicated that the people management systems developed for traditional ways of organizing work may not meet the needs of temporary organization forms. We would argue that this applies to all organizations that use projects to organize work and that additional challenges are presented by recent RBP forms.

We now discuss a range of areas where human resource (HR) expertise and input is required, and then discuss the role of the project manager and the alliance project manager. Next we consider a range of HR activities, many of which may now be devolved to line managers within traditional organizational structures and to project managers as a result of project intensification in organizations.

The need for HR to be closely linked to the business of the organization, to understand its core business and develop ways of supporting achievement of organizational strategy through people management policies and practices that enable goals to be achieved is not new. Ulrich (1997) and Brockbank (1999) were among several who identified this need for organizations in general, and Huemann (2010) outlined the specific need for HR to be aligned to strategy in project-intensified work environments. HR policies and practices have largely been designed for permanent, not temporary organizational forms, and don't generally acknowledge the ways in which projects are embedded within the organization or the temporary systems which are established, for instance to monitor task performance during projects (Sydow, Lindkvist, & DeFillippi, 2004) that need to feed in to permanent systems, such as the organization's overall employee performance management system.

It has been observed that within all organizations, in an effort to better support HR to become a strategic partner, a range of HR activities formerly believed to the domain of the HR or people and culture department have been devolved to line managers (Kulik & Bainbridge, 2006; Kulik & Perry, 2008). With people spending increasing amounts of time in project teams, or spending their career working on sequential projects, it is the project manager who now implements HR policy and practices across their project team. Project team members experience the employment relationship through their project leader and the way they manage their project team. As a result, there has been a call for new ways of managing the employment relationship that acknowledge the new way of working within projects (for example, Bredin, 2008; Bredin & Söderlund, 2011a; Clark & Colling, 2005; Huemann et al., 2007). Söderlund (2012, p. 1) has suggested it is time to analyze "different modes of organization of human resources" in project-based organizations. Bredin and Söderlund (2011a; 2011b) have provided the HR quadriad as a framework to analyze HR roles in project-based organizations.

Importantly, HR professionals in organizations that use projects will need to work with project leaders to agree how they might best support project team selection, development, performance management, and redeployment on project completion. This has been linked to their new strategic partnership role. The development of project leaders suitable for all relationship forms will require HR involvement to ensure that the knowledge, skills, attitudes, and expertise required to succeed across the full range of RBP forms is available to the organization, using permanent or temporary contract employees. HR practitioners will need to develop relationships with both line and project managers to support them in the conduct of an increasing range of HR activities that have now become part of their domain.

Project Manager and Alliance Manager Capabilities

In Chapter 4 (Table 5), we detail the expertise, competence, and knowledge required of project managers from entry level through to expert performer. This model of professional expertise and development is expanded in Chapter 4 (Table 6) to highlight the specific capabilities required of alliance managers.

Project managers and leaders of major projects, especially those leading major infrastructure alliance projects with budgets in excess of one billion dollars, now manage budgets greater than that which some CEOs are responsible for. For successful technology projects, Beheshti (2006) maintained the project manager must both understand the change and have a good understanding of the business in addition to their understanding of the technology. Extensive research into the professional skills required of alliance managers revealed a "defining characteristic of the highest level AM" which set them apart from other project managers was "being able to interact and influence at the business board" and that this understanding of the business may "have been grounded in experience in general management" (Walker and Lloyd-Walker, 2011b, p. 11). This would indicate a need to move employees between line and project roles or for project management education to include business management skills development including the management of budgets, systems and people.

Traditional project management skills, concentrating largely on planning and control, are still required, but people with strong technical skills now also require business management and relationship management skills to manage projects, and the people who will bring them to a successful conclusion. Project managers now commonly perform activities formerly viewed as the responsibility of HR (Legault & Chasserio, 2012). Project managers now require an understanding of why a range of HR policies and practices need to be implemented within project teams. These additional capabilities will be especially needed as project procurement form moves from traditional delivery forms toward alliancing (as discussed in Chapter 2). These changing needs involve HR and project leaders working together on activities such as workforce planning, employee performance and development, rewards, and employee health and safety.

Traditional project management education and training has not prepared project managers for this more "people management"-oriented role that devolution has created. Indeed, it was found that within engineering organizations, the way that project management was practiced had worked against achieving the desired impact of HR strategies (Clark & Colling, 2005). Devolution of decision making to line, or project, management has brought with it the possibility of increased "disparity and inconsistencies between policy formulation at senior HR level and the decisions that are taken by these managers" (McCarthy, Darcy, & Grady, 2010, p. 157). Current project management training and development is inadequate for alliance management preparation, but what is also missing is a people management system flexible enough to continue to support the rights of all employees and which ensures equality of work conditions while supporting coordination of the development of employees so all may pursue their desired career path.

As stated earlier, organizations expect much more of those now delivering alliance and other RBP forms than they expected of them when delivering traditional projects (Ezulike et al., 1997; Grimsey & Graham, 1997). It has also been established that just as HR activities are being devolved to line managers so are project managers now taking on an increasing range of activities formerly considered the domain of HR. The temporary work processes and relationships that project team formation demands of employees leads to fluctuating workloads (Turner et al., 2008) and to changes in reporting relationships. It raises questions such as with whom will the project team member or project manager have their performance review conducted, and who will ensure the project team member is made aware of career development opportunities? Who will recommend the project worker for positions that would support their career advancement? Is this the role of the project leader or the supervisor of their substantive position?

If decision-making responsibilities in relation to these issues are to be devolved to line and project managers, HR professionals will need to ensure that these managers have been provided with the necessary understanding of the issues influencing policy development and provided with the knowledge and skills required to implement the policy as intended.

As we work through the full range of forms of project procurement discussed in Chapter 2, we begin to understand that the demands on project team members, project managers and project leaders change as the choice of procurement form changes. As the need for greater collaboration and coordination increases, in particular, so are greater demands made of all project team members to develop new and different ways of working. A new set of capabilities now needs to be added to the technical knowledge and skills developed for success in traditional projects.

Selecting, Inducting and Redeploying Team Members

On traditional projects, or when forming small project internal project teams, organizations may first consider two issues: availability of staff and the fit between the individual's KSAEs and those required across the project team to achieve successful completion. On occasions, perhaps where a new IT system is being implemented and there is no employee with a high level of knowledge of the new system, expertise may be "imported" through contracting specialists to work on the team.

When selecting teams for an alliance, it is not just a matter of looking at the organization's staff profile and selecting suitable staff from within it. Alliancing requires HR and project leaders to work with otherwise competitor organizations to develop a balanced and talented staff profile for the alliance entity. This is the joint responsibility of the two or more organizations forming the alliance entity, for they stand the potential of sinking or swimming together. Strategically, learning to work with competitor organizations, therefore, is an important relationship management skill for HR staff and project managers. It acknowledges the multi-systemic situation that is created when an alliance is formed. That is, two or more sets of employee data, including performance achievements need to be considered. Another step is required, compared with staffing an internal project. Here, locating a person with related knowledge and skills who currently is not working on a project will not be sufficient.

Alliance partners come together to discuss the full range of shared responsibilities and resources, including people. Staffing an alliance involves selecting the best people from across the member organizations. This requires HR staff to communicate with one another and work together to ensure that the best possible team is assembled. On one alliance, two major construction companies were attempting to balance experience, knowledge, expertise and relationship skills through the contribution of staff from each company to match needs and ensure that gaps were not present within the alliance entity. The advantage here is that two pools of experience, knowledge, expertise and relationship skills can be drawn from despite coming from competing companies to ensure an appropriate and effective workforce within the alliance. Participant 47, (P47) an HR practitioner who worked on this alliance, said:

> . . . you judge your capacity to be able to provide enough personnel with the right skills and at the right levels to manage the project properly and if you think you're not going to be able to do that that actually makes sense to joint venture with another group because that just increases the pool of available engineers, supervisors and other skilled people to make sure you've got coverage in all of those areas and we found at different levels that [Organization X] and [Organization Y] for instance complemented each other quite well. [Organization Y] had many more engineers at a certain level, probably at the five year level or less, but [Organization X] were able to provide some other key people in other areas that [Organization Y] would have struggled to provide. The other complicating factor is what other jobs you've got going at the moment and where you've got your other people occupied. Because . . . people can't work on more than one job at a time so they can't do it justice. You might have your environmental person going between projects and playing surveillance and that sort of stuff but in the set up and the initial phases of a project you need all your key people especially your leadership people 100% committed and just totally focused on getting that project off the ground and running in the right direction, otherwise, you've got problems and you spend the entire rest of the project trying to claw back that lost ground. . . . At [PA 1] you had [Organization X] as a civil contractor and [Organization Z] as a mechanical systems and electrical contractor and so they were complementary. [Organization X] deals with the civil parts and [Organization Z] come in and install the mechanical gear, put in the electrics, control systems and that sort of thing in, so you really did have some civil engineering teams and some process engineering teams and they'd come in and you had all these different phases of the project to build the thing first then you had to come in and install all of this gear, but you still had quite a bit of overlap, for instance, there was a [Organization X] senior electrical or process engineering manager. He was a civil engineer by trade but he had the ability to manage these teams of electrical

and process engineers as well and at the end of the day it became more about his project management skills and his co-ordination ability to get things done rather than his actual expertise in the [engineering] area which should have been provided by the team members he's controlling.

Badging an alliance, ensuring that people feel part of the alliance regardless of which organization they came, from is important if the alliance is to succeed. Interviewee P47 commented: "We did some very strong branding basically to try to get people away from the mentality of . . . I work for A or I work for B.' He advised that they aimed to have people feeling part of the alliance entity and going about their work abiding with the agreed code of behavior, whether that was the way they behave in their parent organization or not. P47 went on to state that they "tried as much as possible to get these teams to be multidisciplinary and multi organization . . ." They worked on developing an understanding that:

> . . . you work for the X Alliance; you work for the alliance regardless of who pays you you're working under the same rules, the same behaviors, the same way you speak to your people out in the field, the same position description that you hold as a foreman or as a whatever you're employed as . . . And I think we were relatively successful in that.

However, it was acknowledge that some team members more quickly adapted to this environment, working cooperatively with those who, under other project forms, would have been competitors.

P47 said that the work done on developing a culture to support the stated aims and code of conduct agreed for the alliance had succeeded in creating a unique ambience within the alliance.

> . . . it is good team building as much as you can to try to create a culture and I guess use the word ambience, it's a good word, it's the general feel of the place when you walk in in the morning are people happy, are they talking to each other . . . So team building workshops were good . . .

HR commonly supports line management to build the team skills of project team members within a single organization to support improved team performance. The development of emotional intelligence skills to complement strong technical skills has been demonstrated to improve project team performance (Rezania & Lingham, 2009; Turner & Lloyd-Walker, 2008). When creating teams within alliances, HR practitioners may need to liaise with HR and alliance leadership staff from the other alliance member organizations. P47 provided an example of how alliance organizations had employed a facilitator to work with staff from alliance member organizations to establish the culture of the temporary alliance entity:

> . . . you do try to team build. We actually ran some cross functional team workshops to start . . . got a professional facilitator in to come in, . . . and said okay, well, you're the team that's responsible for all these areas . . . for each team [he asked] who are your key interface points, well, first of all who are we as a team, what do we want to achieve, what are we going to stand for as a team and talk about behaviors and attitudes and that sort of thing, what are we not going to stand for within our team, what are we not going to stand for from other teams. This is people coming together right at the start of a job, so they're really challenging questions to ask.

DeFillippi and Arthur (1998) identified the single-project organization that is dissolved when the project is completed. Alliance entities are created to deliver an agreed outcome and disbanded on completion. They may operate for a short period of time or as long as 3–5 years. Redeployment is an issue for consideration on completion of the project, as employees will return to their employing partner organization and contractors will need to negotiate a new contract with another organization, for the alliance entity no longer exists. Maintaining communication with employees throughout the life of the alliance will be important both for the individual and the organization in redeploying the employee to a suitable position, based on continued tracking of their performance and career preferences during the life of the alliance.

Employee Rewards

People management policies and procedures to ensure compliance with employment law, including health and safety, equity, and conditions such as pay must be maintained within the alliance, but how these policies and procedures are implemented in each of the partner organizations may vary. Employee rewards may encompass salaries and wages, benefits, and incentives but can often also be viewed as incorporating the provision of a safe and healthy workplace, ensuring equity and fairness.

P47 was asked: How does the HR person reconcile possible quite large differences between the HR systems within the merged companies? In his experience with a recent alliance, payroll was not changed. P47 advised "we weren't responsible for that on the project, they were paid from their parent organization." In other instances on alliances, efforts have been made to ensure equity across similar roles with similar responsibilities. However, as pay rates are not commonly discussed, and years of experience and length of employment may impact on the current rate of pay, annual salaries may remain the responsibility of the employing partner organizations.

Employee benefits and incentives that may be visible to others on the job will need to be discussed to ensure that lack of equity of treatment does not lead to resentments and possibly interfere with cooperation, trust, and sharing. Issues such as hours of work, or work-life balance (WLB) policies may be best discussed and agreed across the alliance entity. We use a WLB example here to demonstrate how a proactive approach to health and safety, one which goes beyond compliance, can support improved employee morale and job satisfaction, and lead to project success. It can be viewed as a "benefit" provided by the organization, and act as an incentive motivating employee performance.

One of the issues we identified in our earlier research (Walker & Lloyd-Walker, 2011b; 2011c) was the high level of commitment to success that develops within an alliance. The high level of cooperation, commitment and trust that develops across team members in this project relationship form provides many positives, but it can also lead to people overcommitting their time and efforts to the detriment of other parts of their life and their health. There is the potential for issues of overwork or lack of attention to employee well-being or for those not currently falling within the traditional structures that current HR practices are designed to work within being treated less well across a range of areas than those with one reporting relationship only in a continuing role. For those choosing contracting as a career (Peel & Inkson, 2004), moving from organization to organization to take on a variety of roles within project teams, the issue of "employee wellbeing and ethical treatment" (Turner et al., 2008, p. 577) may present even greater challenges.

Project managers are provided considerable latitude in relation to decision-making power in alliancing. Legault (2005) points out that this situation could have the potential to lead to organizational policies not being fully implemented or applied as intended, and perhaps project team members being denied their workplace rights. On some projects, working extremely long hours may occur as a result of the enthusiasm team members have for bringing the project to a successful completion. This has been observed within the performing arts (Lindgren & Packendorff, 2006). Or team members may be expected to work through weekends. Indeed Clark and Colling (2005) cite Scase's (2001) investigation into the possible link between project management and the U.K.'s long-hours culture.

Regard for worker entitlements may then be "lost" when the leader driving the project to successful completion is responsible for activities formerly the purview of HR (Legault & Chasserio, 2012). In striving to meet deadlines, the needs of employees and their rightful entitlements may be overlooked. The reward, or incentive, may be perceived to be satisfaction in having met the challenge and delivered the project, or it may incorporate some financial reward according to the extent to which time lines or quality issues are met. Establishing fair and equitable rewards that do not deny employees their entitlements can require considerable effort and expertise at the planning stage.

Careful consideration of project team members' WLB can contribute to a proactive approach to workplace health and safety and contribute to improved project performance. Lingard, Brown, Bradley, Bailey, and Townsend (2007) provided interesting insights in this regard in their research into work/life balance on the Wivenhoe dam alliance project in Queensland, Australia. The alliance team members agreed to work longer but fewer days. The location of the dam works meant that the team members lived away from home during the week and had been returning home too late on a Saturday to, for instance, see their children play sports. Changes to work hours enabled employees spend weekends with their families. The result of the new working conditions was a higher level of employee satisfaction, completion six months ahead of schedule and below the original estimated cost, despite working fewer days. This led Lingard et al. (2007, p. 813) to claim that using "traditional metrics of cost and time, the Wivenhoe Dam project was therefore a remarkable success." This research demonstrated that alliancing, as a project procurement method, provides an environment in which HR issues, in this instance work-life balance, can be discussed, agreed, and implemented, contributing to the creation of high performance work teams in a team environment that enables open discussion, such as alliancing (Lingard et al., 2007).

Performance Management and Review Processes

Performance reviews can present some challenges even when people are working only part time on a project within their own organization. Gaining input from the project team leader may assist the supervisor to gain a better understanding of the overall performance of their direct report for the review period, however when the employee is located within a separate entity, as is the case with an alliance, maintaining contact and tracking the performance of an employee, who will in due course return to that supervisor's area, can present greater coordination demands. One example provided by an interviewee when researching on project careers was that they had an annual meeting with the supervisor of their substantive position to update them on any structural changes or future projects that may provide career opportunities and the alliance project manager provided some information on the team's and individual's overall performance to the supervisor. P47 stated that on an alliance project involving two main member organizations only (some subcontractors were also involved) performance reviews could present some issues:

> When it comes to performance reviews we had the issue, the big issue that we felt, okay, I'm a B Company team member I report to an A Company person, that A person reports here to a PO person or something or other or a combination. A person doesn't know B's reporting process or performance arrangement process so how are they going to affectively give me a performance review every six months and it might be reversed too of course, or, ... they might favour the other three A people . . . on the team versus the one or two B people or vice versa. . . . for the most part yes, there's an organization requirement from each of their partners to use their own process because they still need to manage the on-going performance and development of their team members because otherwise there's a risk of putting their team members out on the project that they're going to lose them because they're not managed effectively or they can't guarantee they are, or, this person perceives that they've been cut off from the performance or the development opportunities that come within the organization they work for.

Concluding Comments

HR has a role to play in alliancing. This involvement may take different shapes and forms, according to the needs of a specific alliance team. As part of our research we spoke with groups, including a group of HR managers from project-based and project-oriented organizations, separate from the 50 participants interviewed for the main study reported upon in this book. Of the 23 practitioners present at one presentation, only one HR manager commented that it was necessary to speak with the alliance leadership team to determine what they required of HR to support successful involvement in the alliance. Another HR manager commented that their organization had recently been involved in an alliance where the member organizations decided that in order to support creating the desired alliance culture and to ensure equity and fairness across all participants, an HR consultant would be employed to work on policies and procedures to guide people management within the alliance entity and maintain contact with partner organization HR departments.

How HR should be configured to support operations in project-intensified industries and organizations and how this alters the KSAEs required of HR personnel in these organizations is a matter for further research. Preparation of project managers to perform the increased range of activities for which they are now held responsible is also another area requiring more research. The development of project leaders suitable for all relationship forms will require HR involvement to ensure that the knowledge, skills, attitudes, and expertise required to succeed across the full range of RBP forms is available within or to the organization, using permanent or temporary, contract, employees.

Because HR departments tend not to intervene in the project manager/employee relationship (Bredin and Söderlund, 2011b) on a range of issues, including hours of work and applying the organization-wide WLB policies, project managers will require guidance to ensure equity and fairness. Clark and Colling (2005) found that in engineering organizations there was the potential for "highly specific project management practices" to constrain the impact of HR strategies. The suggestions by several researchers [including Bredin, Huemann, Keegan, Legault, Söderlund, and others] in the area shows that new ways of analyzing these issues and new frameworks for managing within project intensified industries is, thus, well justified and needed.

Competency Classification

Within the context of this book, what do we mean by competencies and capabilities? This section will provide discussion and framing of three sets of competencies that are important to gaining a better understanding of what is required of teams undertaking projects that expect a relationship based project delivery approach.

Hoffmann (1999, p. 276) undertook a literature review of the terms relating to personal competencies and found no single accepted consensus on what the term meant. He found three dominating themes: observable performance; the standard or quality of the outcome of the person's performance; and the underlying attributes of a person. He concluded that to enable performance standards to be defined and proscribe competencies, two questions need to be asked—what needs to be done, and how well does it need to be done? Much of the competence frameworks we will discuss do this.

We do, however, express reservations and qualifications concerning the concept of competency standards. The term competency is somewhat minimalist. It expresses the bare minimum needed to do something and that is not a strong basis for achieving sustainable human capital or sound relationship building. Competence is similar to compliance in the earlier discussion in this chapter on commitment (Meyer & Allen, 1991). Most alliances agreements and literature, for example, term business-as-usual (BAU) behaviors and abilities as unacceptably low and expect best-for-project attitudes. Therefore, we view competencies as minimum standards to describe various levels of attainment. Perhaps capabilities would be a better term to use, as it implies a range of abilities that assumes competence as being the base level platform of ability. It is interesting to note that guides such as the PMI Competency Development Framework (PMI, 2007) refers to competencies rather than capabilities. We aim in this book to identify gaps in that framework, and so we primarily refer to competencies but also discuss how that base level can be extended to a level of excellence.

Organizational competencies refer to organization's set of abilities (Prahalad & Hamel, 1990) and for many firms, their successful competencies and routines actually inhibit them exploring new boundaries (Leonard-Barton, 1992) because it makes them myopic (Levinthal & March, 1993). Firms and individuals who focus on what they are good at can miss understanding what they need to be good at to meet the expectation of a client/customer/collaborator's value proposition, what the really want (Anderson et al., 2006). We stress the need for understanding what is *really* needed and expected, not what is the minimum that can be offered to comply.

This leads us to focus on knowledge and skills that build the intellectual foundation of reflection. Thus, we consider the Dreyfus (2004) model that offers a five-stage model of professional expertise development, and combined this with the Cicmil (2003; 2006, p. 35) model that further developed this application of the model to PM skills development. This model is useful for this chapter because it illustrates a defined level of PM background technical and PM-related knowledge and sophistication. For example, Table 5 suggests that the novice and advanced beginner-level project managers might be well qualified, having gained much theoretical knowledge but have limited experiential knowledge to reflect upon which we have shown to be critical in RBP situations. Further, their ability to advance from this level to higher levels of knowledge and expertise (proficient performer or expert) is limited by their capacity, ability, and environmental conditions to reflect upon experience based on their ability to theorize and through reflection, and consolidate their knowledge and this is enhanced by exposure to RBP forms of project delivery. These last two levels push project managers' expertise beyond technical skills toward political and human relationship skills, where their ability to use reflection transforms their deep understanding of cause and effect links to inform their actions.

Proficient performer/expert level requires a broader understanding of relevant theoretical concepts and an ability to apply them to relevant experiences to build reflexive mental models that can be instantly called upon when needed. This level of proficiency is built through participating in organizational learning opportunities such as CoPs and other forms of social capital building, which is perhaps more important to RBP projects that traditional BAU projects. A lack of knowledge and ability to reflect could be caused by an absence of the necessary theoretical and methodological knowledge of how to reflect and undertake reflective research. Limits could be institutional or systemic so that the PM organization does not facilitate and perhaps even hinders reflection. This illustrates how RBP approaches can enhance OL and competency development.

Level	Experience	Real-Time Action in Context is Driven by
Novice	Faces a given problem and a given situation for the first time	• Instructions (training courses, *PMBOK® Guide*) • Learning to recognize objective facts about and characteristics of the situation (models and definitions of project) • Learned generalized rules for all similar situations on the basis of identified facts, thus context-independent (project management methodology, procedures) • Evaluation of the performance of the skills on the basis of how well the learned rules are followed
Advanced beginner	Has gained some real-life experience	• Learning to recognize relevant elements in relevant situations on the basis of their similarities with previous examples (e.g., awareness of a typology of projects) • The awareness of the importance of the context of experience; thus making a choice about what are the key elements of the given situation, in addition to context-independent rules (learning from experience, limited reflection, *PMBOK® Guide* recommendations) • Trial-and-error
Competent performer	Amount of experience increases and the number of recognizable learned elements and facts becomes overwhelming	• Learning from own experience and from others to prioritize elements of the situation • Organizing information by choosing a goal and a plan • Dealing only with a set of key factors relevant to the goal and plan, thus simplifying the task and obtaining improved results • Deliberation about the consequences of using own judgment in relation to the given goal and plan (simultaneous subjectivity and objectivity), the relationship of involvement between performer and environment • The model of analytical, proficient performer: Elements-rules-goals-plans-decision • Ability to think on one's feet (confidence, reflection, choice of action, and risk taking)
Proficient performer	Away from cognitivist, analytical rationality (rules, principles, and universal solutions) toward perceiving situations rapidly, intuitively, holistically, visually, bodily, relationally	• The awareness of interpretation and judgment involved in such decision making, rather than logical information processing and analytical problem solving only • Understanding of the situation on the basis of prior actions and experience, acts as deeply "involved-in-the-world" manager/performer who already knows • Reflective understanding and participation in power relations
Expert or virtuoso		• Reflective learning; simultaneous thinking and doing • Intuitive, synchronous understanding of the situation, with an overarching participative critical reflection of the self and the group • The thought, body, knowledge, and action are inseparable, are simultaneously forming and are being formed by one another; • Understanding that power relating is an intrinsic part of intersubjective relating, always there • Considerations for the present and deliberations about the future

Table 5.   PM Expertise, Competence and Knowledge (Source Walker, Cicmil, Thomas, Anbari, & Bredillet, 2008a, p. 23)

Developing PM professionals at the novice level can be effectively accomplished at the workplace through on-the-job training, short courses, and training programs, which are part of the KPIs and KRAs seen in project allianc-ing. As the skill level moves from novice toward advanced beginner and beyond, emphasis is placed (consciously or instinctively) on combining theoretical knowledge with practical experience and reconciling how gaps affect performance. RBP forms achieve this through mentoring and coaching. Novices and advanced beginners widen their repertoire of potential responses to situations through broadening their frames of reference beyond their current experience, which requires a supportive PM delivery form environment. At this stage, they may then best benefit from extensive networking and communication with others at their skill level or higher. Opportunities for this are prevalent in alliance projects. This may enable novices to use learned explicit knowledge and reframe it based on the experience gained that generated tacit knowledge. This can then be internalized and reformulated in more flexible and reflexive routines and approaches to cope with ambiguity and complexity. This is where a no-blame environment that is characteristic of alliancing is essential (Walker, Lloyd-Walker, & Mills, 2013b) because it allows people to make mistakes, acknowledge them, learn from them, and turn the experience into a valuable learning episode rather than merely an error to be buried and forgotten about. Project alliance learning KPIs play a useful role in providing the environment, means, intellectual support and "safe playground" for people to experiment, fail (if necessary), learn from feedback, self-critique, and reflect to fast-track building experience and moving toward being competent and perhaps proficient performers.

Reflective learning is of value at all levels of expertise. At the "novice" level, we can see that potential to gain from reflecting upon experience is likely to produce a shallow result simply because many situations are encountered for the first time, therefore, these do not offer the opportunity for any action learning feedback. We can see from this model that RBP can produce valuable collaborative synergy. How does this relate to accepted professional PM institutional frameworks? The next sections provide some insights.

PMI Competency Framework

The PMI's Project Management Competency Development (PMCD) Framework 2nd Edition (2007) is an extensive set of guidelines and requirements that describe the role and competency needs of project management teams undertaking project work. It is aligned with the PMI standards and guides based on a particular view of "relevant knowledge" such as *A Guide to the Project Management Body of Knowledge (PMBOK® Guide)* (PMI, 2008) and also describes some of the PM-related competencies required of program and portfolio management positions, as envisaged by the PMI standards for those roles (PMI, 2006a; 2006b). It is by nature limited by what the PM professional associations perceive is "relevant knowledge." The *PMBOK® Guide* and the competency framework are useful for certification purposes, reflecting PM knowledge as proscribed by the *PMBOK® Guide*. However, as Morris, Jamieson, and Shepherd (2006) highlight the PMI's sister organization, the U.K.-based Association for Project Management (APM), Body of Knowledge 5th Edition (2006) shares similar limitations to that of the PMI's *PMBOK® Guide*.

Professional associations such as PMI and APM have a strong practitioner tradition, and their volunteers who help develop and vet any competency framework are doing so from a normative and shared ontology that these standards and expectations are "facts," whereas they are socially constructed. Some of the standards are based on academic research and some are based on tradition. This leaves these competency standards potentially backward-looking, or at best "in-the-moment" looking, being framed by the worldview of a volunteer group that has more of a great focus on current and past practice than speculating on the future. The purpose of these standards are to reflect current practice expectations, as they are generally linked to accreditation and examination processes and it would be unfair to expect practitioners to prepare themselves with capabilities that may or may not be in immediate demand.

There is also danger that fads may creep into competency frameworks that are difficult to exclude later, particularly if a constituency evolves that has a vested interest in these fads. Abrahamson (1996) wrote an influential paper on the emergence and dangers of management fads. Whitty (2005; 2009; 2011; Whitty & Maylor, 2007) has also written about the development of PM trends and fads around perceptions of complexity and how current practice can blind us to the competencies that are really needed to prepare professionals for current and future challenges, including inclusion of the many industry sectors that currently do not currently recognize PM practice. This problem is not restricted to professional qualifications, as the education literature also draws our attention to problems associated with curriculum development to prepare present and future project managers when dominated by paradigms of the past (Bennis & O'Toole, 2005; Crawford, Morris, Thomas, & Winter, 2006). There is also a dilemma of how to best integrate theory and practice in competency development (Berggren & Söderlund, 2008; Raelin, 2007) and to value reflective practice as a key competency.

The PMI (2007) Competency Framework has a focus and is structured around the PMI-defined project life cycle processes of initiating, planning, executing, monitoring and controlling, and finally closing. It has a well-structured approach that splits the processes into elements, and then performance criteria and evidence that needs to support evaluation of that competence. However, despite its logic and usefulness in general terms, it does not specify how these elements and performance criteria should be met or how these outputs should be measured. Figure 19 illustrates the procurement performance criteria as an example.

Thirty separate competencies are identified. The "2.0 planning a project" performance competency, for example, defines 10 separate units of that element. The unit "2.9 Procurement plan agreed" is one of those 10 in that life cycle elements. This performance criterion has five components of analysis material requirement evidenced by the project procurement plan and bill of materials, and as illustrated in Figure 19. However, as is evident from the framework, there is little to guide a PM team member on how to discern between an excellent or poor project procurement plan other than by reference back to the *PMBOK® Guide* (PMI, 2008), and that is not sufficiently expansive in its explication of how to produce a procurement plan to be definitive. Other definitional gaps are evident. For example, how should a plan accommodate concepts such as best value or value for money and how does this fit together with, for example, a form of gateway system suggested by MacDonald (2011). This lack of detail hinders assessment, which must, as a consequence, be subjective and neither uniform nor consistent.

The framework also includes six personal competences (PMI, 2007, p. 24) to provide background their technical and PM knowledge as follows:

1. Effective *communication*, defined as using suitable methods for accurate, appropriate, and relevant communication with stakeholders;
2. *Leading*, defined as guiding, inspiring and motivating stakeholders to manage and overcome issues to achieve project objectives;
3. *Managing*, which is defined as administering and deploying resources;

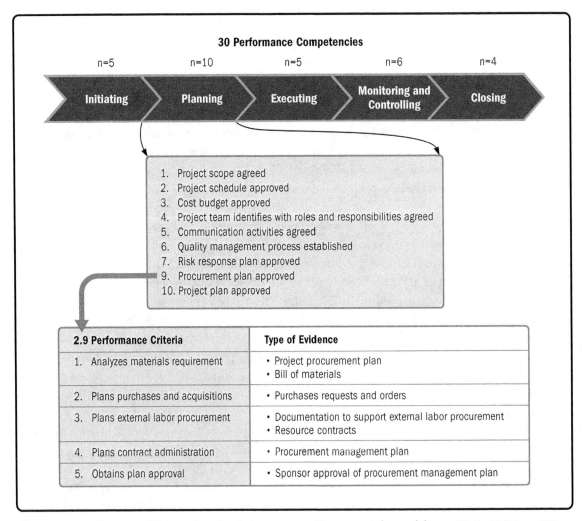

Figure 19. Illustrated Example of a Competence (Source: Adapted from: PMI, 2007, p. 17)

4. *Cognitive ability*, defined as having depth of perception, discernment, and judgment to direct a project within a dynamic and evolving environment;

5. *Effectiveness*, producing desired results using appropriate deployment of resources, tools and techniques; and

6. *Professionalism*, defined as conforming to ethical behavior governed by responsibility, respect, honestly, and fairness in practicing PM.

These are explained more fully, and Figure 20 illustrates an example for the communication personal competency.

Each of the 25 personal competencies has associated performance criteria and types of evidence. Figure 20 illustrates the four communication competencies and their performance criteria and types of evidence.

What becomes clear is that the paradigm, worldview, driving these competence standards is highly positivist and instrumental. PM, as the professions have seen it for decades, is more of a science than an art, but that view is changing to PM being seen as a craft and art (Smith, 2007; Smith & Winter, 2010). Morris (2011) points out PM has evolved from an operations research (planning and scheduling, optimising resources etc.) basis to a strategic implementation activity that is intensely people-oriented. Traditional PM-espoused values concern containing uncertainty, planning and control, and belief in an ability to optimise. Most of the PM discipline's short history has been centered on designing a problem solution, using design drawings for visualization and representing the project to enable components and constituent parts to be numerically measured and their integration and assembly to be predicted in plans. This has led to PM training and education to be highly technically and process oriented, based on its internal research and practice development in a way that has been referred to as trained technicians (Crawford et al., 2006). As PM embraced not only the IT sector but also "soft" sectors such as professional services, events management, public administration delivery, and scientific exploitation such as pharmaceuticals, it became evident that many

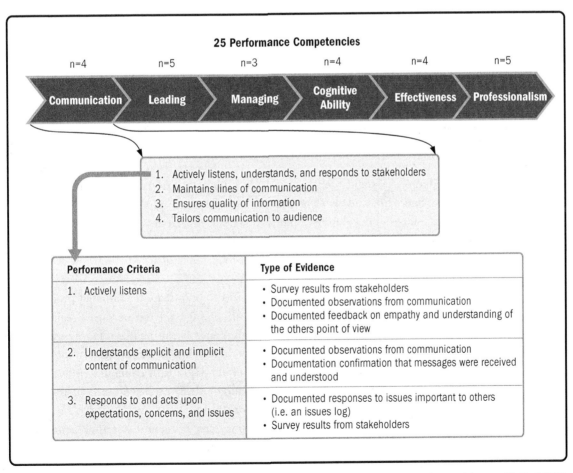

Figure 20. Illustrated Example of a Personal Competence (Source Adapted from: PMI, 2007, p. 25–26)

projects were combinations of technology, systems integration, and service delivery, with a great focus on how people deliver project outputs and outcomes. It also became clear that PM has a strategic dimension and that its aim is to deliver on strategy, thus having a strong institutional purpose (Morris & Geraldi, 2011, Morris & Jamieson, 2004).

The rethinking PM research network deliberations (Winter & Smith, 2006) led to a different way of conceptualizing what PM is really about. This work, together with that of Hodgson and Cicmil and their colleagues who contributed to a landmark book (Hodgson & Cicmil, 2006), highlighted the need for project management reflective practitioners (Winter et al., 2006) and for PM knowledge and competencies to be broadened. Others in Scandinavia were reconceptualizing PM as ways of organizing work in temporary organizations and so had a focus on organizational and business delivery terms (Artto & Kujala, 2008; Artto et al., 2008; Lundin & Söderholm, 1995; Packendorff, 1995). PM was also perceived in terms of projects not only being undertaken by project-based organizations but by managing business through projects (Gareis, 1989; Turner, 2000; Turner, 2006). These contextual observations introduced the need for business knowledge, skills, and attributes of people as working in project competencies. Taking a view of PM as systems integration of complex products and services (Davies & Brady, 2000; Davies et al., 2005) led to additional competence requirement insights. Additionally, as has been highlighted earlier, projects when seen as learning vehicles (Brady & Davies, 2004) in project-based organizations (Koskinen, 2009; 2010; 2012) add competencies required related to KM and OL. Books such as Smith (2007) and Winter and Szczepanek (2009), with their use of metaphor, broadening the scope and scale of project work, highlight the need for PM team skills to be far more extensive for the more complex projects seen frequently today than the instrumental and more rigid view of PM requirements for skills, knowledge, attributes and experience.

Taking this broader perspective of PM and how it is evolving from the literature cited above, we can see that competencies, knowledge bases, and perceptions of PM and what PM practitioners need as personal competences have moved far beyond the PMI Competency Development Framework (PMI, 2007).

Alliancing Association of Australasia (AAA) Profiling Professional Excellence

This section draws upon an independent study for the AAA that relied upon extensive PA literature, several recent Australasian studies on PAs (predominately undertaken in Australia), and others elsewhere, as well as results from a recent research project undertaken with the Australasian Alliancing Association in which 17 Alliance professionals, including 11 project alliance managers (AMs) and 3 unit managers to whom the AMs report, were interviewed. The study generated 13+ hours of taped interviews and over 250 pages of transcription that were analyzed using NVivo with a grounded theory approach to make sense of the results. Results were used to develop a profile of the skills, attributes, and experience needed of AMs and the framework developed to differentiate between new and inexperienced AMs, emerging proficient and expert levels of preparedness for the AM role. A capability maturity model was developed to not only profile AM stages of development but to also be used as a developmental tool by those pursuing careers in alliancing. While results may be specific to Australasia and for AMs, the profile and results presented may form the basis for wider application, because it incorporates the broad range of KSAE required of project managers in new and evolving RBP forms discussed in this book.

Earlier in our discussion on partnering and alliancing forms in Chapter 2, under forms of project procurement, we highlighted an institutional differentiation between project alliancing and partnering. Bresnan and Marshall (2011) argue that there is a prevailing industry experience-logic that has institutionalized highly competitive behaviors in the construction industry. This has caused many of the ills highlighted by Egan (1998) and Latham (1994). On the positive side, partnering has been institutionalized as a service-logic with commitment to a customer focus. An analysis by Murray and Langford (2003) of a series of reports into the U.K. construction industry conducted since 1944 indicates a cultural shift under which the industry is demonstrating a genuine desire to turn its back on the past and at least to seriously consider the value of closer relationship-based procurement approaches. In Australia, a similar trend, starting with the "No Dispute" report (NBCC, 1989), led to a more recent move toward the current situation where, according to a recent report (Wood and Duffield, 2009, p. 7), "The total value of alliance projects in the road, rail and water sectors in New South Wales, Victoria, Queensland and Western Australia, over the period 2004 to 2009 was $32 billion." This represents a significant institutional shift in attitudes and practice that is a necessary precursor to acceptance of partnering and alliancing. Therefore, POs as institutionally being represented by major corporations and government clients, together with the consultants and contracting firms representing NOPs to an alliance, all have now oriented their focus on the need for a best-for-project culture being both desirable and necessary for project alliances.

The AAA study (Walker & Lloyd-Walker, 2011a; 2011b; 2011c) resulted in the AM's knowledge, skills, attributes and experience (KSAE) model illustrated in Figure 21. It categorizes KSAE into "hard" core competency baseline knowledge and skills, which are necessary for project team members and leaders. These relate to the technical business such as IT, construction/engineering, aerospace, or professional services, change management, and other emerging fields of operational/organizational endeavor that are managing their business by and through projects. This also categorizes baseline experience: in the technical context; managing projects; the organizational context; systems integration within cross-disciplinary teams; working in cross-cultural (business as well as nation) teams; experience in recovery from crises or distressed projects; and being exposed to the need to engage in system and holistic thinking.

This prompts the need to understand what a PA requires of an AM to fulfil its goals. Alliancing implies that there are additional or different KSAEs required for managing project alliances compared to more traditionally procured construction infrastructure projects. Knowledge is embodied in processes, texts, and papers, and tacitly through

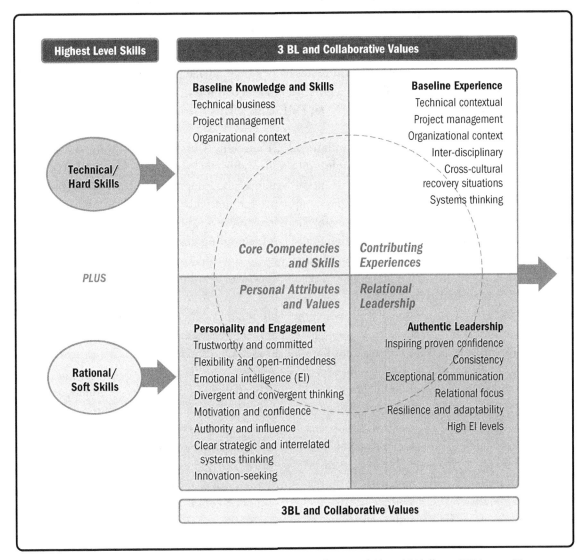

Figure 21. Alliances Managers KSAE (Source: Walker and Lloyd-Walker, 2011a, p. 8)

lived practice. Skills gained from formal and informal knowledge acquisition and training are acquired though study and apprenticeship. Attributes are personality traits that are innate, developed, or adopted from role models. Experience represents practice and learning from reflection on practice. Arguably, this experience requires "soft skills" categorized as personal attributes and values that lead to building and maintaining relationships. These include having the personal attributes and having values that support being trustworthy and committed, being flexible and open minded, developing emotional intelligence, developing a repertoire of divergent and convergent thinking, being motivated and building self-confidence as well as developing the confidence in others, developing authority and being able to influence, developing clear strategic thinking and systems thinking, and being innovation-seeking. Authentic leadership has been identified as an important "soft skill" as detailed in some depth by Lloyd-Walker and Walker (2011). Briefly, this is about being able to inspire confidence; being consistent in espoused and practiced behaviors and actions; have exceptional communication abilities to be able to clearly state positions, intensions, plans, and expected performance; having a relational focus in which there is genuine connection and engagement with people within teams and external stakeholders; having resilience and being adaptable; and demonstrating emotional intelligence.

We also showed underpinning values for a collaborative RBP form of triple bottom line (3BL) discussed through this book thus far, together with valuing collaboration as a business operational paradigm. We also observed in our AAA research the existence of advanced business-level skills that one normally finds in high-level executives who can comprehend and discern the project purpose.

Because we are also interested in *how* AMs develop KSAE, we used a capability maturity model (CMM) approach adapted from existing CMM models (Judgev & Thomas, 2002; Paulk, Curtis, Chrisses, & Weber, 1993; PMI, 2003) and the concept of maturity development in professionals from novice to expert virtuoso (Cicmil, 2003; Dreyfus & Dreyfus, 2005) and illustrated in Table 5, as well as reference to work on PM competencies (Dainty, Cheng, & Moore, 2005; Lopez-Cabrales, Valle, & Herrero, 2006; PMI, 2007). This literature framework led to the development of a four level maturity profile of AMs.

The four-level AM profile comprises 1) foundational, 2) nascent, 3) developing intermediate, and 4) mature experienced levels. *Foundational AMs* are comfortable and highly competent in structured traditional "tame" situations (Hancock, 2010) and may be proficient in briefing and scoping to help narrow down operational options. They need to have divergent thinking and an appetite for ambiguity to be able to influence team thinking to consider wider approaches, more innovation, etc. They may, however, lack confidence in prompting divergent thinking and have some limitations in recognizing and understanding some of the systems that problems and situations are located in. They may be recent graduates, new to the role and under close tutelage, perhaps in an acting role or assistant AM role. They have as a "given" high-level knowledge of the technology dominating the PA scope.

Nascent AMs recognize how technical systems interact with other systems in messy situations (Hancock, 2010). They have good convergent thinking and are capable of encouraging divergent thinking. They have as a "given" high levels of baseline traditional project management knowledge, skills, and experience. *Developing Intermediate AMs* can effectively use divergent thinking to see innovative solutions and to be able to switch to convergent thinking. They may still be uncomfortable with or unable to be effortlessly effective in highly messy situations. They are good systems thinkers and have wide enough experience to be aware of systems and subsystems that nascent AMs would miss. They have as a "given" high levels of advanced project management knowledge, skills, and experience, with well-tuned "people-related" skills such as stakeholder engagement. *Mature Experienced AMs* have true helicopter vision of situations and so are confident to act-sense-respond in highly messy situations. The defining difference is their ability to effortlessly move from systems to real worldviews, trigger divergent thinking in others, be able to achieve rapid and effective reflection, sensemaking, and consequence-coping strategies so that they can successfully turn highly messy situations into complex situations (Hancock, 2010), and then simplify them into tame and routine situations. They often have advanced chief executive officer or board-level general management experience. It is this higher level of working confidently that we believe separates top-level from mid-level AMs. This also fits with complexity aspects discussed in Chapter 3.

The AAA study revealed three main "hard" knowledge and experience-based skills and seven 'softer' knowledge and attributes that are explained in more detail in Table 6 that further detail and explain the content of Figure 21. The application and development of these is enhanced through reflection on practice.

The CMM framework illustrated in Table 6 was subject to further reflection by the authors over mid- 2011 to 2012 and based on testing and advice from two senior academic experts in this area and four senior project director-level PM professionals. The aim of this reflection was to explore the usefulness of a fundamental framework of dimensions describing expected project team behaviors that could be developed to improve our understanding of what is expected of teams to justify why one procurement form may be suitably deployed over another. Such a framework could help us better understand similarities and differences with procurement choice labels used around the globe.

The aim of the framework is to guide PORs to more effectively choose a project delivery procurement option that facilitates the required team behaviors to deliver their project. The behavioral framework is based upon a set of assumptions.

1. That the PO and POR have an intimate knowledge of the PO organization's business strategy and context but may need to collaborate with and access knowledge from an experienced contractor at the business development idea DG0 point in Phase 1 of Figure 2. The POR is most likely the best person to also lead Phase 2 with close knowledge of, and support from, the PO organization to guide the development of concepts in Phase 2. However, the POR may have insufficient depth of knowledge of the uncertainty and risks associated with project realization solutions. The POR will rely on both organizational internal expert advice and external consultant knowledge to bridge the POR's knowledge gaps. As Williams et al. (2009) point out, the concept stage is one where there is scant information available, and this presents both uncertainty and complexity in foreseeing likely consequences of assumptions being made. In many cases, various forms of ECI would bridge the PORs and Figure 2 Phase 2 team's knowledge gaps, but for this to happen requires collaborative behaviors between the POR and non-owner project team participants (NOPs).

Three Skills and Experience Required of AMs—Hard Skills	Foundational Aspiring	Nascent Recent	Developing Intermediate	Mature Experienced
1. Technical skills and experience	Recognized qualifications, training, and experience in the project-base technology.	Recognized qualifications, training, and experience in the project-base technology. Awareness of knowledge gaps and where to obtain expert advice to respond to these.	Recognized qualifications, training, and experience in the project-base technology. Awareness of complexities and knowledge gaps and analytical capacity to frame questions to obtain expert advice to respond to these.	Recognized qualifications, training, and experience in the project-base technology. Comfort with the sure existence of knowledge gaps and unclear, ambiguous, or unknown technical issues; the ability to frame questions and knowledge of where and how to obtain expert advice to respond to these.
2. PM skills and experience	Knowledge of traditional PM approaches and methods for planning, control, and team management to deliver projects.	Knowledge of traditional PM approaches and methods for planning, control, and "soft-skill" team leadership skills to deliver projects. Understands what causes projects to be successful or otherwise.	Advanced level PM skills to include engaging stakeholders and facilitating commitment through effective leadership by example. Has experience in project turnaround from distressed to "back on track."	Demonstrated embedded and natural authentic leadership that drives project performance through complimenting and combining judgment about the extent and use of hard and soft skills. Has been tested by difficult choices and decisions and learned from the experience as well as knows to have sound judgment.
3. Business skills and experience	Awareness of business imperatives and the need for a coherent business case to frame project mission and objectives.	Understanding the fundamental values and business case for the project to-be-delivered benefits.	Participating in translating the business case into a project brief and supporting the project evaluation process at ALT level.	ALT and board-level experience of active engagement in translating and framing the business case into a project brief and evaluating project benefit realization. Has direct experience of learning from mistakes (self or others) in business strategy and delivery.

Table 6. Three Experiences and Seven Characteristics/Attributes Required of AMs (Source: Walker and Lloyd-Walker, 2011a, p. 12–15) *(continued)*

Seven Authentic Leadership Characteristics/ Attributes of AMs—Soft Skills	Foundational Aspiring	Nascent Recent	Developing Intermediate	Mature Experienced
4. Reflectiveness being a systems thinker, strategic, think-aim-act vs. act-think-aim Reflectiveness level is high and knowing the context as crucial.	Highly reactive to challenges and dependent upon formal learning, textbook advice, manuals, and established procedures. Demonstrates a sense of uncertainty and is restricted to highly traditional responses. Probably unaware of wider or deeper situational context. Sees challenges more simplistically.	Reactive to challenges, while somewhat dependent upon formal learning, textbook advice, manuals, and established procedures; balances this with learning from recent experience. Demonstrates a sense of certainty based on traditional responses. Aware of potential complexity of the situational context. Unclear on how systems overlap or interface.	Contemplates and reflects before taking action to challenges based upon past experience and advice from others. May at times be overwhelmed and struck with "paralysis through analysis." Values facts over hunches or intuition. May overcomplicate the context. Seeks explanatory patterns to justify action based on discussions and advice from experienced and trusted mentors.	Contemplates and reflects while taking action to challenges based upon embedded past experience and critiqued advice from others. Able to take decisive action-based heuristics and comprehensive repertoire of past experience. Values intuition over lengthy analysis of situations. Can simplify complexity in context through rapid pattern matching and holistic solutions. Influences framing of situations and solutions.
5. Pragmatism gets on with the job, is politically astute, works within constraints. Interpreting and re-framing rules to context and way in which action is justified as crucial.	Decision-making governed by ability to narrow options based on available knowledge and approaches. Frames problems and solutions to immediate resolution of issues.	Decision-making dominated by narrowing options based on available knowledge and approaches. Frames problems and solutions to short term resolution of issues.	Decision-making dominated by widening consideration of options based on available and potentially available knowledge and approaches. Frames problems and solutions to medium term resolution of issues.	Decision-making governed by screening many options based on a few narrow but salient criteria. Frames problems and solutions to medium/long-term resolution of issues while addressing immediate demands. Shapes and influences interpretation of the "rules."
6. Appreciativeness understanding the motivations and value proposition of all involved (EI) Being able to judge the most effective response to teams and individuals about their value is the key in influencing others and being influenced by them.	Tends to be unaware of how contextual pressures influence the motives and actions of others. Has a passive approach to attempting to influence others with strong opinions. Lacks awareness of the need to probe to find out what others need or want. Lacks confidence to impose closure on decision making.	Grapples with how contextual pressures influence the motives and actions of others. Lacks confidence to negotiate an agenda when attempting to influence others with strong opinions. Tends to allow discussion to drift when decision making or closes off discussion too soon. Lacks self-justification to know when to enact closure on decision making.	Has a strong sense of personal identity and influence in leading the opening up or narrowing of discussions. Understands the agendas and value proposition of others and appreciates demands placed upon them. Yet to develop total confidence in defending their own agendas and preferred position as short cuts to action when facing strong opposition from others.	Has a strong sense of personal identity and expertly shapes the agenda in effectively opening up or narrowing discussions. Responds to the agendas, value proposition and demands upon others by crafting priorities. Transforms strong opposition from others into innovative proposals through resolving paradoxes via an uncompromising "third way."
7. Resilience adaptability, versatility, flexibility and being persistent. Able to effectively learn from experience. The repertoire of skills and attributes that can be drawn upon is crucial. This is related to absorptive capacity to learn and adapt. Attitude to how to deal with a crisis "next time" is critical.	Shows great promise in rapidly absorbing new ideas and approaches and demonstrates examples of initiative and hard work. Is able to cope with disappointment and setbacks as part of a learning experience. Actively seeks advice from others to make sense of experience, especially unexpected outcomes from action.	Readily absorbs new ideas and approaches and seeks out opportunities to apply them. Uses disappointment and setbacks as part of a learning experience. Contributes to and shares with others making sense of experience, especially in developing explanations for unexpected outcomes from action.	Seeks new ideas and approaches and how to apply them. Assumes that the purpose of dealing with disappointment and setbacks is to learn from experience. Leads a process with others to make sense of experience, especially unexpected outcomes from action, and embeds lessons learned as a personal continuous improvement initiative.	Proactively leads the implementation of new ideas and approaches and how to apply them. Champions the outcome of setbacks and disappointment as learning experiences. Supports creation of learning repositories for those developing leadership skills. Leads a culture of transforming setbacks into positive results and leads others to find problem work-around solutions that lead to sustainable contextual learning.
8. Wisdom being the person with opinions and advice that is valued, consistent, and reliable that others instinctively refer to. To be effective, the key is to be influential based on providing sound advice and being respected for that advice or being an effective broker of wise advice. Judgment of the person brokering advice is crucial.	Generally, advice and information is not sought of this person about technical or PM aspects unless in a narrow specialization field. Seeks to become a "go-to" person by actively learning as much as possible about the "system" project details etc. and offering to assist others in research or finding out about relevant issues.	Proactively and enthusiastically shares knowledge and insights to clarify context and gain confidence from others in their judgment and job-specific knowledge. Could be a subcultural representative that others seek their views from, for example as a "younger" AM or as somebody with valuable outside-group perspectives.	Has highly respected technical and either business or PM knowledge/skills that others actively tap into. Knowledge and advice offered is consistently seen as valuable, reliable, and influential.	Has highly respected technical, business and PM knowledge and skills from others actively tap into as being pivotal to sound outcomes. Often strong business knowledge is the crucial differentiator as well as strong understanding of the strength of other team members to action plans and decisions.

Table 6. Three Experiences and Seven Characteristics/Attributes Required of AMs (Source: Walker and Lloyd-Walker, 2011a, p. 12–15) *(continued)*

Seven Authentic Leadership Characteristics/ Attributes of AMs—Soft Skills	Foundational Aspiring	Nascent Recent	Developing Intermediate	Mature Experienced
9. Spirit having the courage to effectively challenge assumptions Being confident in the value of refining knowledge of context through questioning the status quo or assumed realities is vital to better understand contexts.	Lacks confidence in getting others to openly discuss contentious issues or to "rock" the boat. Assumes that prevailing assumptions must be correct for the context experienced.	Confident in getting others to openly discuss contentious issues or to be skeptical and question the status quo. Tests whether prevailing assumptions may be correct for the context experienced.	Adept in facilitating team members to be courageously skeptical when doubting the majority opinion. Challenges assumptions to inspire and facilitate innovation. Having the courage to make unpopular decisions when circumstances warrant it.	Provides stretch targets for interpreting the business case to arrive at an optimal solution. Encourages and demands "devils advocate" positions and evidence-based challenges so that groupthink does not automatically prevail.
10. Authenticity approachable and trustworthy and being seen as open to ideas, collaboration, discussion, and new ways of thinking. To be an effective broker and "go-to" person, it is vital that this person must be open-minded and be available when needed. They must be collaborative, have integrity, and being therefore perceived as trustworthy.	Having a reputation for being open to something new, adventurous and easy to collaborate with and to discuss ideas with. Being assumed to be trustworthy but not yet had the opportunity to demonstrate this in difficult situations.	Is good at collaborating with others, engenders trust and commitment. Has an "open-door" policy, acknowledging the need for diversity in views when trying to understand issues. Being seen as somebody who will listen to "bad news" without blame or cover up.	Being respected as somebody who has an open mind and is swayed by solid evidence or sound reasoning argument. Collaborates as a natural style and is trusted for the quality of judgment and integrity of approach. Holding several concurrent conflicting views of a situation and inviting challenges to any of these to obtain a clearer understanding.	Have high standards of integrity and a natural collaborator with others. People trust them and they are known for constancy of their action with their rhetoric. Having wide business and life experience to have learned how to resolve paradoxes through seeing complementarities (combines opposites through reframing dimensions to accommodate pragmatic "third-way" perspectives).

Table 6. Three Experiences and Seven Characteristics/Attributes Required of AMs (Source: Walker and Lloyd-Walker, 2011a, p. 12–15)

2. The project risk literature (Ward, 1997; 1999; Ward & Chapman, 2003) clearly indicates that teams with advanced knowledge and understanding of likely risks and uncertainty should be sourced for complex and complicated projects to identify both a justifiable and realistic contingency for risk and uncertainty. These teams should also plan how to manage that contingency to avoid it being wasted or misused.

3. Much of the project complexity issues to be addressed primarily relate to people's behaviors and ability to collaborate rather than to resolve purely technical issues. There is a great need for stakeholder engagement on projects these days (Das, 2005; Holzer, 2008; Mitchell, Agle, & Wood, 1997). A focus on team interaction is vital. Team members need to understand behavioral expectations.

4. It is well known that the PO and POR sophistication is a vital factor in project success (Cherns & Bryant, 1984; Latham, 1994; Walker, 1996; 1998). Their ability to collaborate with NOPs, to be able to question and reflect on assumptions and be open to (and able to engage with) NOPs on solution building is a critical skill.

5. Sophisticated POs and PORs and (NOPs) know how to collaborate, communicate and productively and collegially exercise authority to ensure that responsibility and accountability are appropriately allocated.

Based on the above five assumptions, we reflected on our past research and the literature and we proposed 10 dimensions of POR and NOP behavioral characteristics measured using a 7-point scale, with 1 = very low and 7 = very high (Walker and Lloyd-Walker, 2012b, p. 882–883).

1. Coping with Project Design Instability—extent to which the POR and NOPs cope with design solutions that are ambiguous, incomplete, or have conflicting objectives that hinder realistic project delivery bids to be developed and tendered upon that reflect the PO's prioritized objectives.

2. Coping with Context Complexity—extent to which the project context presents structural, technical, directional, temporal, or relational complexity in developing design solutions to deliver the project. Need for taking a range of perspectives and applying sensemaking to understand the internal/external and political environment.

3. Embracing Risk and Uncertainty - extent to which the POR and NOPs have the willingness, ability in terms of knowledge, skills, attributes and experience (KSAE), and capacity (institutional support delivered through the procurement approach and governance system adopted) to embrace uncertainty and potential risk/opportunity in developing project design and delivery strategies.

4. Challenging the Status Quo - extent to which the POR and NOPs have the willingness, ability (in terms of KSAE), and capacity (institutional support delivered through the procurement approach and governance system adopted) to embrace an open mind in interpreting and re-interpreting the project brief.

5. Balanced Performance Value Position - extent to which the POR is willing and able to clarify which benefits the project vision and aims are required to deliver in both tangible and intangible value performance terms.

6. Ensuring Mutual Trust - extent to which the POR and NOPs are willing and able to develop and maintain trust in each other to deliver agreed project performance outcomes as being the prime and overarching priority.

7. Commitment to Best-for-Project Orientation - extent to which the POR and NOPs structure contractual arrangements toward a best-for-project outcome and avoid opportunistic advantage seeking behavior.

8. Commitment to Consensus-Based Decision Making - extent to which the POR and NOPs have the willingness, ability and capacity to work collaboratively and make strategic and major project delivery decisions that all parties take equal responsibility for in committing to engender a no-blame project culture.

9. Commitment to Knowledge and Ideas Sharing - extent to which the POR and NOPs have the willingness, ability and capacity to raise and discuss ideas within a safe environment to share knowledge about project design and delivery issues to deliver best-for-project process/product innovation.

10. Commitment to an Integrated Organizational Structure - extent to which the POR and NOPs develop organizational structure/procedures to lead and manage the project through an integrated POR/NOP mechanism binding POR and NOPs into a coherent collaborative structure (both physical and virtual).

Before concluding this section we would like to comment further on the need for mature experienced alliance managers. We do this in terms of the PM expertise framework based on the Dreyfus (2004) model that offers a five stage model of professional expertise development refined by Cicmil (2003; 2006, p. 35) into the model of PM skills development presented in Table 5 and links to AM KSAE illustrated in Figure 21. Specifically, analysis from the AAA study and a number of quotes from senior AMs cited in Walker and Lloyd-Walker (2011c, p. 56–62) indicate the need for those considered to be expert or high level AMs possessing what we refer to as "board-level business communication and influencing skills." At the same time that our study was published, another, by a French-based team of researchers funded by PMI was also published in which project managers as senior executives were studied (Debourse & Archibald, 2011a; 2011b). The study involved 22 face-to-face interviews with senior executives from the USA, Canada, Brazil, France, the U.K., and Ukraine, and a web-based survey undertaken in both English and French that captured 445 responses. Their report makes for fascinating reading and like ours, draws similar conclusions. Based on these two studies, we argue that our AM characteristics/attributes CMM model illustrated in Table 6 may be applied to a broader range of RBP approaches.

Innovation Competencies

Organizational learning, organizational behavior, motivation theory and innovation theory help us make sense of how collaboration can lead to innovation that adds value when compared to BAU conditions. We have already discussed in this chapter all the separate elements of innovation except innovation itself. Slaughter (1998) categorizes innovation as incremental or radical, incremental innovation including continuous improvement through exploiting existing knowledge skills and experience. According to Walker and Hampson (2003c, p. 238), innovation is "an idea, practice, or object that is perceived as new by an individual or other unit of adoption" or "a decision-making process to enact change in technology, process, services rendered or other management approaches." It can involve reconfiguring a component or redesigning it, redesigning a configuration of components within a system or redesigning and reconfiguring links between systems. All innovation can lead to unintended consequences and uncertain outcomes. Radical innovation involves changing nimbly and rapidly to cope with, and perhaps benefit from, turbulence, disruptive change, and present danger to the *status quo*.

Parent, Roy, and St-Jacques (2007) describe a dynamic knowledge transfer capacity (DKTC) model that is useful for adaptation to help us better understand the integration of collaboration with innovation for beneficial change. Their model has a generative capacity element based on knowledge discovery linked to a disseminative capacity based on diffusion linked to adsorptive capacity based on ability to apply and use new knowledge to advantage leading to an adaptive and responsive capacity. All this occurs within an environment of knowledge availability and need. In a study on innovation in construction firms adopting RBP practices, Chen, Manley, and Lewis (2012) hypothesize learning capability as being shaped by three forces: exploratory learning, exploitative learning, and transformative learning. Explorative learning is about knowledge identification, articulation, and acquisition. Exploitative learning is shaped by knowledge internalization, transformation, and application. These two themes—exploration and exploitation—are well grounded (March, 1991) and have formed the basis for recent scholarly work on innovation and knowledge transfer (Brady & Davies, 2004). However, being able to identify, disseminate, and harvest knowledge is necessary but insufficient for innovation diffusion as has been discussed earlier in this chapter. Organizations need to overcome barriers to sticky knowledge, to enhance fluidity and flow of knowledge through having a sufficient appetite and requisite resources for enacting innovation. The use of collaboration that includes action learning in which reflection, translation of shared knowledge into plans of action, and transformation of plans into action is a necessary platform, along with the ability to absorb innovative ideas to enable innovation to be embedded in routines, values, and culture in general.

Figure 22 illustrates an adaption of the DKTC model to illustrate innovation by and through collaboration.

Figure 22 illustrates an action-based model to not only develop innovative processes, products, service routines, and strategies, but to embed them within the organizations participating in the collaboration. The capability and capacity to undertake innovation and effectively transfer knowledge about the actual innovation and its diffusion can be linked into the capability maturity model (CMM) form used widely these days in information systems and ICT, for example as developed by Paulk et al. (1993) and PMI (2003) with their Organizational Project Management Maturity Model (OPM3), and developed as a conceptual model in gaining a knowledge advantage (Walker, 2004).

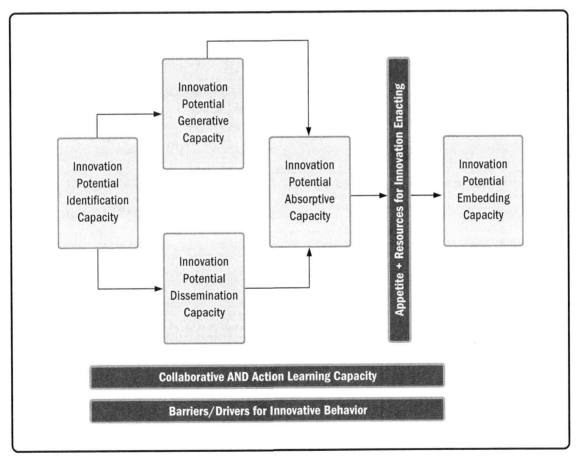

Figure 22. Innovation and Collaboration Linkages

Part of this model illustrating a CMM for sensemaking and its contribution to the knowledge advantage is illustrated and explained in Walker and Nogeste (2008, p. 203–204).

CMM models tend to segregate maturity as moving along five levels of maturity, for example Paulk et al. (1993) use: (1) initial, (2) repeatable, (3) defined, (4) managed, and (5) optimized. Walker (2004; 2008, p. 203–204) use (1) inactive awareness, (2) pre-active initiation, (3) active adoption, (4) pro-active acceptance and adaptation, and (5) embedded routinization. We offer a suggested CMM based on the CMM approach described above in RLP projects for innovation and collaboration, in Table 7 below.

Table 7 represents a suggested approach to assessing a CMM for the way that collaboration within RBP projects create and develop innovative products, processes, and approaches, and how they share knowledge about these innovations. The first level suggests highly *ad hoc* and isolated examples of project team groups that are locked in "silo thinking" within, so that when innovation emerges it happens by chance or by the efforts of a few pioneers, but knowledge about how innovation emerged is quickly lost. Level 2 represents attempts to pilot and test how innovation emerges and represents wider group knowledge, but any innovation diffusion is likely to be limited and poorly systemized and so never enters any wider culture due to the stickiness of the innovation knowledge. Level 3 indicates that innovation is systemically encouraged, knowledge about it is transferred within the firm (and/or within cross-team project participants) and the knowledge has some "half-life" to be passed onto other situations and projects. Level 4 illustrates a more systematic way to ensure that participating project teams and parent companies gain value from knowledge about the innovation, its context and impact. The final Level 5 represents a somewhat ideal state where the whole industry sector has the ability and means to nurture innovation and its diffusion throughout the sector. Here, not only individual firms benefit, but clients/project owners and society in general gain benefit from a more effective and productive industry sector.

This CMM section is closely tied to earlier sections in this chapter where the mechanism of human behavioral impact is explained. We should add that technical advances also have a part to play in our understanding of innovation created and sustained through teams collaborating on problem solving and on developing more effective ways

Maturity	Identification Capacity	Generative Capacity	Dissemination Capacity	Absorptive Capacity	Cultural Embeddedness Capacity
1. **Initial** baseline *ad hoc*	*Ad hoc* experimenting and developing common terms for innovation characteristics	Emergency of innovation is *ad hoc* and isolated and restricted	Protocols for exchanging innovation experience is absent or nascent	Isolated and *ad hoc* individual capacity to internalize use and experience of innovation	*Ad hoc* and isolated retention of the what, when, how, and why of past innovation
2. **Repeatable** developing systems	Within team piloting of common terms for innovation characteristics	Piloting and testing—review of products, process, and routines for improvements	Piloting within team protocols for exchanging innovation experience	Within team capacity to internalize use and experience of innovation	Within team piloting of sense-making of the what, when, how, and why of past innovation
3. **Defined** stabilized systems being adopted	Agreed within firm standard registers and protocols developed	Agreed within firm protocols for challenging assumptions	Agreed within firm protocols for exchanging innovation experience	Agreed within firm capacity to internalize use and experience of innovation	Agreed within firm standardized sense-making of the what, when, how, and why of past innovation
4. **Managed** accepted and managed systems	Cross-team and organization standards translatable	Cross-team and organization focus on continuous improvement	Cross-team and organization protocols for exchanging innovation experience	Cross-team and organization systems for internalizing use and experience of innovation	Cross team and organizational standardized sense-making of the what, when, how, and why of past innovation
5. **Optimized** culturally embedded systems	Industry sector level protocols embedded for recognizing and classifying	Industry sector level protocols for continuous improvement	Industry sector level protocols for exchanging innovation experience	Industry sector level systems for internalizing use and experience of innovation	Industry sector standardized sense-making of the what, when, how, and why of past innovation

Table 7.   CMM of Collaborative Innovation

to deliver projects. Levels 3, 4, and 5 would benefit, for example, from compatible information processing systems such as building information modally (BIM) that has much to offer in allowing compatible information and knowledge about that information to be easily transferred (Aranda-Mena et al., 2009; Cohen, 2010; Radosavljevic & Bennett, 2012). Social capital and shared language, co-location and close team interactions all can help to improve innovation and knowledge diffusion.

Chapter 4 Summary

In this chapter we have focused upon the human behavior of individuals working within teams and across multi-teams in a collaborative context. We discussed trust and commitment and the nature of co-learning through collaboration as linked elements that are core to RBP expectations and indeed, this discussion helped to frame KSAEs required of effective participants in RBP project teams. We also provided a short section on strategic HRM issues, because it is critical to contextualize the recruitment, selection, and, importantly, development, of project team participants. We also added a short discussion on the transitioning of people within RBP project teams because there is often a flow of people between BAU and RMP projects and within RBP project forms, and the way that people transition between projects is important for them as developing human beings as well as for the project sectors they contribute to so that valuable talent, knowledge, and capabilities are not lost.

The previous section dealt with important aspects of competency frameworks and classifications. We drew upon the PMI competency development framework (PMI, 2007), which provides valuable models of how to describe capabilities and levels of attainment required of project managers. The AAA profiles of project alliance manager KSAE illustrated in Table 6 (Walker & Lloyd-Walker, 2011a; 2011b; 2011c) provide a more detailed CMM model that can be used to better manage people's careers in RBP projects. More specifically, the AAA CMM is designed for project alliancing. The CMM of collaborative innovation presented in Table 7 illustrates in a course-grained manner, including suggested levels of KSAE required at the five levels of maturity of people working within a collaborative forums such a project alliance, projects that have partnering arrangements, or more closely integrated supply chains such as that that was evident on London Heathrow Terminal 5 (Doherty, 2008).

This chapter concludes discussion of the salient literature and leads into Chapter 5, which explains our research approach and methodology for the study as well as the research findings.

CHAPTER **5**

The Research Study Approach

Chapter 5 Introduction

In this chapter, we discuss some of the most relevant human behavior theoretical concepts relating to relationship based procurement choices. Figure 23 illustrates this chapter's structure.

This chapter is presented in four sections. This section introduces the study in general and is followed by a section that outlines the study approach, the worldview perspective of the researchers, the data gathering approach, and the validation approach. We then explain how we obtained data and information resources from reports, reflections on the literature, data gathered from interviews with SMEs and our own reflection on insights gained from previous and in-parallel research work. The chapter concludes with a chapter summary.

The Study Approach

We develop this section with a discussion of the perspective that we took in undertaking the research. We then explain our research methods, how we chose the literature and sources of information, and data for our study that we considered when determining which subject matter experts (SMEs) we should contact and discuss their view on this whole topic of RBP. We also justify our research approach with respect to which academic and practitioner SMEs we should interview and how we designed and undertook a validation workshop to seek feedback on our results.

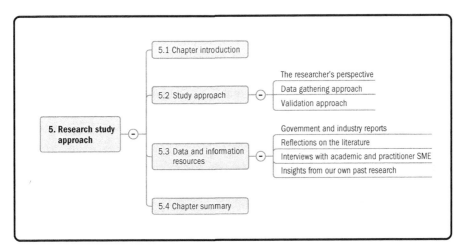

Figure 23. The research study approach chapter 5 mindmap

The Researchers' Perspective and Worldview

When undertaking research, it is necessary to be clear about the researchers' perspective and worldview about the research being undertaken. We all see the world slightly differently and this is shaped by our experience and our interpretation of what we see. Differences in perception explain how we make sense of what we observe and what we believe to be the "truth" about what we see. They also explain how perceptions of truth between people can vary. Readers of this book can best understand the basis of our claims to the veracity of our findings and conclusions and the credibility of that work by understanding our worldview and how we value and attribute truth to evidence. Readers can make their own minds up, based on their worldview, on how convincing our conclusions and analysis are.

One aspect of our worldview is the prevailing paradigm that governs our thinking. According to Smyth and Morris (2007), a *paradigm* is an intellectual purposeful framework embodying systems of ideas and beliefs, sets of common assumptions, and accepted versions of the "truth." Morgan (2007) states that many researchers use the term loosely. He describes the concept of a paradigm in the following way:

- paradigms being all-encompassing ways of experiencing and thinking about the world, including beliefs about morals, values, and aesthetics (p. 50);
- epistemological stances such as realism and constructivism as being distinctive belief systems that influence how research questions are asked and answered and taking a narrower approach by concentrating on one's worldview about issues within the philosophy of knowledge (p. 52);
- shared beliefs in a research field within a community of researchers sharing a consensus about which questions are most meaningful and which procedures are most appropriate for answering those questions (p. 53); and
- model examples that serve as "exemplars" for how research is done in a given field (p. 54).

Cicmil (2006, p. 30) provides a useful table to interpret PM knowledge. She refers to three types of paradigm in terms of knowledge. A functionalism/positivist paradigm is relevant to PM technical knowledge of how to control project activity. An interpretative paradigm relates to understanding practical knowledge, and a radical/critical paradigm is appropriate to knowledge about emancipatory or freedom issues. Creswell (2009, Chapter 1) describes four worldviews that add to our understanding of the paradigm concept that describe various philosophical stances as follows:

1. The *positivism* philosophical stance is about determination, reductionism, empirical observation and measurement and theory verification. It has a belief system that assumes that there is a rational and objective 'truth' that can be observed (independently) and exists because if we died this truth would still be "out there."
2. The *constructivism* philosophical stance is about creating reality through interpretation. It is based on understanding some phenomena, with multiple participants' meaning being seen as being valid and useful; it is a social contextual and historical construction of "truth" as something that is generated; and emergent as relevant data, information, knowledge, perceptions and interpretations are drawn together to make sense of a situation.
3. The *advocacy/participatory* philosophical stance is about understanding the politics of a phenomenon, the issue of which parties have various kinds and extents of power, how participants do or do not collaborate and how change occurs between relationship that affect the phenomenon.
4. The *pragmatism* philosophy stance is eclectic in that it seeks understanding from whatever means are at hand. It is concerned with the consequences of actions, is problem and solution centred and sees 'real-world' practices as being of critical importance. This worldview takes whatever insights and perspectives that are perceived as useful, workable and valuable in a practical sense.

It is useful to see the paradigm concept in terms of being a worldview. The worldview as a paradigm is useful because it helps us to work out what is necessary to satisfy the doubts and gather important evidence to justify an interpretation of "truth." Worldview one above, having a *positivism* philosophical stance, has a need for "facts and figures," "hard science," and objectivity. Worldview two, having a *constructivism* philosophical stance, is all about relationships and interpretations about what can be supported as 'truth' by strength of arguments. It has entirely different criteria for determining or accepting what is "truth" to the first view. Worldview three, having an *advocacy/participatory* philosophical stance, has a highly social and relational perspective of what is valid and what is truth. This takes in a stance that strongly refutes the validity of independence, in fact it stresses that politics, power, motivation are all crucial to determining "truth."

Worldview four, having a *pragmatism* philosophical stance, is highly eclectic and makes use of whatever evidence and support is useful, be that positivist evidence, advocacy or constructivism. From this we can see what constitutes "real" evidence and how to design a way to best support understanding of "finding the truth" rooted in an appropriate paradigm.

Before we explain our research findings from the literature and from interviews with SMEs, we need to clarify three other aspects of how we see the world. We will now explain our *ontological* position, our *epistemological* stance. and our *axiological* values. This will provide readers with a better understanding of what we include and exclude in our discussions and what we offer as exemplar models, as well as how we judge the validity and usefulness of what we present.

The term *ontology* is usually understood as a worldview about what constitutes "truth," what is "out there" to know (Grix, 2002, p. 175). Grix (2002, p. 177) further explains that "ontological positions are those contained within the perspectives 'objectivism' and 'constructivism'." Broadly speaking, the objectivism perspective holds "an ontological position that asserts that social phenomena and their meanings have an existence that is independent of social actors." In other words, we can be positive that the objective truth exists. The constructivism perspective, on the other hand, asserts that social phenomena and their meanings are continually being accomplished by social actors. In other words, truth is subjective and is socially agreed to be true. An objectivist perspective leads toward a positivist ontological stance in which truth is objectively out there whether we are alive or not.

People with *constructivist* ontology will believe that knowledge about what is true or valid is constructed in the mind and is influenced by perceptions gained though a particular viewing lens. That lens could be from being an individual within a group of people, from a shared group view within a larger organization, or from a shared view of one organization within a project team composed of and represented by numerous organizations. A *constructivist* ontological stance holds that truth is not objectively real and is, therefore, subjectively real. Truth is a complex concept about belief in something because we tend to interpret what we see in way that is influenced in many ways. For example, if we are studying how people in an organization view a particular phenomenon, there may be quite different perspectives held from people who are engaged in working directly for the organization. They may be employed full-time or part-time, employed as volunteers, as interns, or as contingent employees working on projects as an independent contractor. There can be a range of ways to interpret the organization as perceived by those employed in it.

We are faced now with having to be clear about what *we* mean by reality, which of many possible perspectives is being taken. We, therefore, take an ontological position when studying anything and by recognizing that position, we have a responsibility to state our position. Researchers may use data from records of how many people are employed in various categories of employment and thus state they are taking an objective *ontological stance*, state from the overall organizational ontological perspective. However, if they are studying how people "feel" about the organization based on interviews, then they are taking an interpretivist or *constructivist ontological stance* of a firm from individual, project team, and home-organization ontological perspectives, because the questions they ask and the answers they get have to be interpreted in both the participant's and researcher's mind. The certainty of "truth" is contestable, and we need to be clear of both the perspective taken and the means by which data is obtained and analyzed.

Grix (2002, p. 177) states that "*epistemology* focuses on the knowledge-gathering process and is concerned with developing new models or theories that are better than competing models and theories." *Epistemology* is about taking a view of how evidence is accepted as "truth" and the "validly" of that view. A positivist ontological stance relies on the authority and *epistemology* of the scientific method to maintain what are accepted ways of identifying, measuring, and analyzing data. These ways evolve and are improved upon continuously; they are by no means static. An interpretivist ontological stance relies on the evolving *epistemology* of social science theories when identifying, measuring, and analyzing data. Considerable debate continuously rages about techniques and methods to undertake research. In essence, there is acceptance that there "is no absolute truth," therefore, a body or chain of evidence is used to demonstrate the credibility of evidence and analysis to support a position on what is as close as is practicably possible to the "absolute truth" within a specified *epistemological* tradition or school of thought.

The term *axiology*, according to Mingers (2003, p. 561), is about the values held that are important to the research, "that is, what is valued or considered good. This is manifest in what the purposes or uses of the model are, and who (analyst, facilitator, participant) develops and uses the model." Axiology considers the aesthetic qualities

Our Position	Taken from	Notes and Comments
Perspective	SMEs as academics and practitioners	The literature provides secondary data that has been filtered by the writer's perspective and worldview, and comprises the full range indicated above. We have chosen to cite papers based on authors that we consider best and offer peer-reviewed and validated insights that authoritatively helped us understand collaborative project procurement arrangements.
Paradigm	Positivism	We adopted this only where we believed that "things could be measured" reasonably objectively and that what was researched was "out there" and existed independently of people's opinion of its existence.
	Constructivism	We adopted this stance where we acknowledged that data on phenomena were an interpretation, for example in how people perceived a "system," whether it existed and how it seemed to function.
	Advocacy/ participatory	This paradigm helped us to understand tensions and paradoxes created by political factors.
	Pragmatism	PM research is mainly about how project managers and project teams interact; it is a highly practical context, and as practicing academics we tend to take a pragmatic view to sense-making in interpreting data.
Ontology	What is truth?	The ontological position is taken from the point of view of SMEs on how they saw "truth" and reality. These were academics and practitioners observing and researching project phenomena.
Epistemology	What rules apply to what constitutes "truth"	We relied upon peer review for the literature, and we adopted triangulation from our own research and verified results through conducting workshops with participants or others taken from the same sample set. Our interview pool of 50 SMEs, and our other sources of information and reflections on our previous and parallel research in this area, allowed us to reach a saturation point of insights where additional interview data, insights from the literature, and reflection on our research into this area revealed little that improved the extent of our understanding of the topic.
Axiology	What are our values?	Our values and our opinion of what is "good research" is that research data and literature we use is accepted by our peers and by reflective practitioners as a reasonably credible and accurate depiction of the lived reality of working in project teams on RBP projects.

Table 8.   Our research perspective and worldview

of perspective. For example, a positivist stance may see beauty in the elegance of parsimonious formulae describing a phenomenon, whereas an interpretivist stance would find beauty in understanding context, and an advocacy/participatory stance would judge use of power or distribution of pain/gain as being the main criteria for an axiological stance.

While the term paradigm as a "worldview" and embodying systems of ideas and beliefs is a short and neat way to describe the term, it leaves gaps in precision. Slicing and dicing the term into its components of ontology, epistemology, and axiology can add some precision, but can also add confusion. Precision is something that we needed to address in stating our worldview in the research reported in this book. Table 8 summaries our perspective and worldview.

The Data and Information-Gathering Approach

Our data resources are global in nature and comprise government and industry reports; reflections on the literature; interviews with SMEs, both academic and reflective practitioners; and our own insights from our previous and current related research projects. In all, we interviewed 50 SMEs and this generated over 500 pages of transcripts that we analyzed. Details of the interviewees are presented in Section 2 Table A2.

Based on our research perspective and worldview we sought data and information from SMEs who were either academic-researchers or reflective practitioners. For this research, we are taking the perspective of SMEs and their reflections on their experience as our data source, rather than gathering data from specific case studies, surveys, or other empirical evidence. We draw upon the literature discussed earlier, reflect on our own research in this area from over the past decade, including transcripts and notes taken from SMEs who we had previously interviewed as part of earlier research. These were either academic or practitioner SMEs; however, many of those interviewed were both academic and active practitioners. We detail these sources of data and information in more detail shortly.

We purposefully favored practitioner SMEs who had experience of project alliance forms of RBP. This is because we agree with Paulk et al. (1993) that maturity development in experience is hierarchal. People, when operating at one level are unable to clearly understand the next level, rather like reaching halfway up a hill but there is a valley and beyond that another hill that is barely visible. They can clearly see and understand in a backward direction and are aware of gaps between where they currently are and where "lower" levels are situated, but they are unclear about what the "next level" really looks like. Using this logic, we felt that from the literature and our prior research findings that alliancing approximates the highest RBP maturity that we can envisage (though we concede that T5, for example, has SCM elements that may be more advanced in thinking about RBP than is present in many alliance agreements). Therefore, SMEs with experience of alliancing are better placed to situate other forms of project procurement and delivery in a viable context that those who have no experience of alliancing approaches.

We sought and were given ethics clearance from RMIT University, and the plain-language statement and questions asked are included in Section 2, Appendix 1 immediately after Table A3. This provides a list of the semi-structured open ended questions asked of academic SMEs as well as general practitioner SMEs and practitioners who had been engaged in project and/or program alliances.

Validation Approach

It is also important for the reader to understand how we justify the validity of our findings and our interpretation of their meaning and significance. We clarify our approach to validating the interpretation of our findings. We presented preliminary conclusions at several conference forums and by distributing draft versions of this book to academic and practitioner SMEs for feedback. And we responded to their comments and improved the manuscript accordingly. Conference presentations generated debate and provided opportunities for our findings to be challenged through additional informal discussion with SMEs to clarify, elaborate, and calibrate results.

While it is fair to say that challenge and debate is limited during "question time" at most conferences, it would be true to state that far more useful insightful and thought-provoking confronting feedback is generally gained from subsequent conversations with conference attendees after question time. In our case, several PhD candidates and their supervisors who were undertaking research into related topics questioned us, and often their questions were both penetrating and sophisticated. This is because they are deeply engaged in this research area and they fervently needed to know precise details of our research approach, data source reliability, and level of validation.

We also undertook one validation workshop at Oxford on 2 October 2013 with 14 PA SMEs. We presented another validation workshop on 4 October with 24 SME practitioners from the Cabinet Office Major Projects Authority and Office of National Audit Office (U.K.) in Whitehall, London, U.K., to present our analysis and to seek their comment and reflection. These workshops were undertaken purposefully to expose our findings and to allow them to be challenged. This allowed us the opportunity to explain ourselves and in doing to improve our internalization of "knowing" and to re-calibrate where appropriate our understanding of this whole topic. Feedback from both workshops particularly provided added insightful comments and challenging questions surrounding Figure 25. Categorizing Collaboration Forms of PM Delivery and Figure 27. An RBP Wittgenstein's Idea of Family and the KSAE framework presented in Table 6. Three Experiences and Seven Characteristics/Attributes Required of AMs (Source: Walker and Lloyd-Walker, 2011a, p. 12–15). The main reaction by these SMEs was that these models and the framework provided useful and acceptably credible reflections on how forms of RBP could be visualized, and that the KSAE required of project managers engaged in these types of project provided a very useful framework for participant and leadership staff selection as well as appraisal and skills development. Many of the SMEs felt that the models were more generally useful than RBP forms and that they could be applied across a broad range of project procurement types with well identified specific KSAE for each of the identified project procurement classifications, such as for PAs business-as-usual D&C, for example.

In addition, we have written several journal papers and a book chapter from this extended research, and these sources all provided feedback, peer review, and SME review. Details of these validation opportunities are summarized briefly outlined in Appendix 1 Table 1.

Data and Information resources

The following outlines the sources of data and information that we drew upon:

Government and Industry Reports

We accessed a number of government reports that justified the need for changes to project procurement. Two of the most widely cited reports from the U.K. experience that we reviewed were the Latham (1994) and Egan (1998) reports, and we also studied follow-up reports (Egan, 2002; Wolstenholme, 2009) from think-tanks and quasi-government department entities that provided high level research, usually undertaken by well-regarded researchers in the PM and construction/engineering field and/or reflective practitioners of influence.

The U.K. has also been able to provide us with valuable sources of data and information on relevant specific topics, such as the stage gate system of project assessment and approval at the project front-end (Office of Government Commerce, 2007b; 2007c). Several Australian government departments have been an important promoter of project alliances and how to ensure and pursue VfM (Department of Treasury and Finance Victoria, 2010; Department of Infrastructure and Transport, 2011). We also closely scrutinized a doctoral thesis (MacDonald, 2011) that was supervised by one of this book's authors that had a very detailed summary and analysis of VfM normative processes. Additionally, we drew upon a meta-analysis of reports from the U.K. between 1948-1998 that had been published that paints a very vivid contextual picture of attempts to escape from the traditional procurement choices that led to poor collaboration by construction project teams (Murray & Langford, 2003).

Australian government departments, think-tanks and various association has also provided deep insights into the context of RBP and evolving best practice in collaboration forms (CIDA, 1993a; 1994; CIIA, 1995). Auditor General reports in Australia also provided highly credible data, for example in gathering background information for an alliance project in Australia (Auditor-General of the Australian National Audit Office, 2000) that one of this book's authors was deeply involved with as a research study that had significant sets of findings being published in a book (Walker & Hampson, 2003c) and we also used a useful report (Australian Constructors Association, 1999) to inform us about the history of project alliancing and how it developed in Australia.

We were able to access reports and guidelines on the integrated project delivery in the USA from two important sources (American Institute of Architects - AIA California Council, 2007; Cohen, 2010). We were also able to source a very informative report that provided us with detailed context and information about procurement in the EU through a major collaborative research project led by the Manchester Business School (2009a; 2009b; 2009c) and through the report on large-scale infrastructure projects in Europe (Hertogh, Baker, Staal-Ong, & Westerveld, 2008).

Reflections on the Literature

Our literature review in chapters 2, 3, and 4 was based mainly on peer reviewed journal articles sources and books. We occasionally cited conference papers where these had not been (to our knowledge) updated and upgraded to journal papers. We were purposeful and cautious in our choice of literature to review and cite to enable confidence that these were indeed authoritative sources. There were instances of books that were published that provide seminal details that provided valuable historical and contextual information, for example the book on the London Heathrow T5 project (Doherty, 2008).

We also ensured that we considered relevant doctoral thesis work, as this provides highly valuable and insightful leading-edge content. Some of these were supervised by one of the authors (Derek Walker), and so the insights are deeper than would be the case for reading a thesis. Theses were directly about topics on RBP forms (Davis, 2006; Johannes, 2004; MacDonald, 2011) as well as wider issues concerning PM in a wider but relevant context to RBP (Nogeste, 2006; Norrie, 2006; Christenson, 2007). We also accessed and read other relevant theses that informed, and was very important, for our reflections on RBP (Ahola, 2009; Hoezen, 2012; Klakegg, 2010; Nyström, 2005b; 2007).

These academic sources provided a wealth of previous work that had been thoroughly researched, was rigorously validated through peer review, doctoral examination or by other similarly rigorous means. We have been both intensely engaged in research and writing for several decades and have had many papers, book chapters, and research reports published, and so we have spent many years thinking about, writing on, searching for literature on, and reflecting on RBP and its impact on strategic HRM and skills development implications. This depth of thought, applied with a renewed focus for this book, has allowed us to apply fundamental and summative reflection on this field of study.

Interviews with Academics and Practitioner SMEs

It has been our experience over several decades that research colleagues have consistently told us that when researchers undertake any significant volume of research, they often sense that the process of dissemination is often incomplete with papers being perhaps rejected and other papers started but not completed to the publication stage. Interesting avenues of further exploration and sensemaking are also abandoned due to time and resource constraints. Additionally, an author will often reflect upon a paper after some time and draw alternative conclusions to that originally published by them. This reflection is based upon their reflection and the influence of subsequent research and literature reviews upon their views. This represents untapped reserves of data and knowledge that we sought.

Part of the rationale for undertaking this research was to take advantage of the above hidden sources of insights. We proposed in our research grant application to the PMI, that underpins this book, to speak to a range of SMEs, both academic and practitioner, and to question them about their work, what was missing from the published versions of their work that they wished to explore through dialogue with us and to express their (expert) opinion of trends and directions in which RBP is heading. In this way, for our academic interviewees, we were taking a retrospective reflection upon past research, connecting it to the present and projecting it into the future. This delivered to us deeper access to past knowledge, re-framed current knowledge and hypothesised or speculated knowledge of the future.

We also pursued a similar strategy with practitioner SMEs, except that many of them had not directly published their opinions, views, and experiences of their lived reality of being a PM practitioner engaged in RBP forms. The interviews were recorded and transcribed and copies were sent to them to make any clarifying comments or observations and to add any further data. An outline of the interviewee perspective and rationale for choosing them is presented in Appendix 1, Table A2 of Section 2. In addition to those specifically interviewed for the research project funded by PMI, we also interviewed practitioners in a series of case studies that formed part of the work undertaken on a parallel research project into project alliancing in Australia. This gave us an opportunity to gather additional insights into the working ambience of the PAs studied as well as to ask information about the necessary skills, knowledge, attributes, and experience required of PA team members.

The data gathered from notes and transcribed interviews (500+ pages) were used with the software package NVivo10 to develop and code themes and subthemes using a grounded theory approach (Corbin, Strauss, & Strauss, 2008; Glaser & Strauss, 1967; Locke, 2001) to help us make sense of content related to the four research questions. We were able to interview and gather data from 14 leading academic SMEs and 36 senior SME practitioners.

SME Insights from our own Past and Current Research

We also had the advantage of having already researched and published on several related research projects in the past and were able to combine reflection upon these along with current case study work on project alliances undertaken as part of a related and complementary study. These are briefly outlined in Appendix 1 Table 1.

In addition, we were able to inform this book's content and our research with other self-funded and *ad hoc* research with other colleagues as part of our normal scholarly duties. For example, Beverley Lloyd-Walker undertook research with others on career development of AMs and their transitioning in and out of projects. All the above intellectual property was able to be marshaled to inform this research project and writing this book.

Chapter 5 Summary

While for some readers, this chapter may not be as interesting as others, it was essential that we explain our research study approach and our worldview in undertaking the study. We explicitly state our perspective, operating paradigm and our ontological, epistemological, and axiological stances so that readers may fully understand our rationale and approach to undertaking this study. We presented our validation and feedback approach that are detailed in Appendix 1 Table 1 in Section 2, as well as coded summary information to indicate the sources of subject matter experts that we interviewed in Appendix 1, Table A2, Section 2, and in Appendix 1, Table A3, Section 2 we presented a summary of previous and concurrent studies that we drew upon to inform our research and this publication.

Our aim has been to clearly and transparently present in this chapter how we undertook the research and what influences shaped our conclusions.

CHAPTER 6

Findings and Models

Chapter 6 Introduction

In this chapter we present our findings and models of relationship-based procurement forms. This book forms a research report as well as a research book publication. Some readers will be mainly interested in summary findings and models while we anticipate that many others will be interested in the detailed findings that support and underpin our summary findings. Detailed findings are contained in Appendix 2 on Section 2.

Figure 24 illustrates this chapter's structure and content. Through this structure, we present several perspectives on the way that RBP forms and concepts evolve to help make sense of this unfolding evolution in improving value generation through projects.

We first discuss RBP through an emerging geographical influence and adoption of forms of collaboration lens. This leads us to take the perspective of depth of collaboration, and we present that as four orders of collaboration. This leads us to the perspective of relational focus intensity between the project owner and the delivery team and within the project delivery team. While this is useful, it leaves us unsure how to categorize RBP forms, especially as the terms used are not registered trade names and there is no globally agreed nomenclature or standards for them. This leads us to draw upon a useful device from the literature (Nyström, 2005a) that helps us create a model that presents core salient features of the RBP forms we identified in Chapter 2. This model helps us synthesize, albeit in somewhat coarsely grained measures of identified characteristics. This model provides us with the means to map identified features and characteristics against the identified RBP forms. Typologies, taxonomies, and frameworks are useful devices that are used to facilitate closer group and universal understanding of complex concepts. Figure 27 illustrates our model. An RBP Wittgenstein's Idea of Family together with its accompanying explanatory tables with suggested measures of the identified elements for Figure 27 in Table 11, Table 12, and Table 13, enables us to map RBF forms to the family of elements. This device enables us to map the KSAE, elements that we had previously developed to provide a profile of PA excellence (illustrated in Table 6 presented in Chapter 4). This framework illustrates the KSAE requirements of leaders of the delivery team and major constituent supply chain teams such as the design team leaders and first-tier supply chain delivery team leaders.

Emerging Forms of Collaboration Terms

RQ1 sought an answer to the question—what are the fundamental characteristics of emerging RBP forms? RQ2 sought an answer to the question—do these RBP forms vary in different parts of the globe and, if so in what way?

In Chapter 2 we outlined a range of project procurement arrangements. These were illustrated in Figure 3 and summarized into three main groups: *traditional* (design-bid-build and cost-reimbursable); *forms with a focus on integrated design and delivery processes that emphasize planning and control* (D&C, integrated SCM and MC; joint venture consortia; and the BOOT family/PFI/PPP arrangements); and *forms with a focus on integrated design and delivery processes that emphasises collaboration and coordination* (project/strategic partnering, integrated solutions that includes the competitive dialog and integrated project delivery approach, alliancing, ECI, and framework agreements).

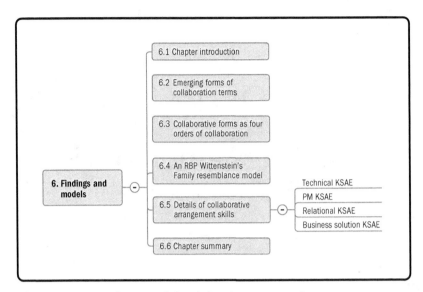

Figure 24. Findings and Models Chapter Mindmap

Lahdenperä's (2012, p. 62) map of the emergence, dissemination and interaction of different relationship based delivery arrangements across the globe is instructive. He traces the whole system from partnering in the U.S. from 1988, but this was informed and molded from practices developed in Japan relating to quality management and lean production that he describes as "gentlemanly principles" that resonated with Japan's traditional cultural norms of respect for quality delivery and continuous improvement *kaizen* (Imai, 1986), often undertaken almost as an art form. Lean production and kaizen and other gentlemanly principles emerged in the U.S. and U.K. as partnering from around 1995. Close cultural and economic links between the U.S. and U.K. have long fed a cultural category recognized as the Anglo-world (Ashkanasy, Trevor-Roberts, & Earnshaw, 2002) and so partnering quickly became popular across the Anglo sphere of influence, including countries such as Australia (Lenard et al., 1996; Testi, Sidwell, & Lenard, 1995; Uher, 1999) and Hong Kong (Chan, Chan, & Ho, 2003). Project partnering then developed into project and strategic alliancing from around 1994 in the U.K. and Australia, mainly through the oil exploration and extraction industry, though this was extended to engineering infrastructure projects and further into building construction projects such as the National Museum of Australia cited earlier in this book, and more recently with the completion of extensive renovation and remodeling of the Hamer Hall concert hall in Melbourne completed in late 2012. Partnering together with a revisiting of *kaizen* and lean production led to the emergence of integrated project delivery in the U.S. around 2005.

Lahdenperä's (2012, p. 62) map does not explain in detail sources of the flows of influence of RBP forms, for example from research that he has been undertaking on recent PAs in Finland (during 2013), which was cited as under development in the Manchester Business School (2009b) report. PAs have also been used in the Netherlands (Laan et al., 2011). These have been modelled on early Australian adaptation of PAs. A range of framework agreements seen in the U.K. (Khalfan & McDermot, 2006) have being extended to adaptation in supply chain integration through absorbing partnering principles, kaizen, and lean production concepts. These have been undertaken in Nordic countries as well as the U.K. (Brady, Davies, Gann, & Rush, 2007; Eriksson, 2010a; Manchester Business School, 2009b).

Table 9 summarizes the family of terms used for RBP in several regions of the world. D&C is extensively used globally, and BOOT/PPP/PFI forms are prevalent for many infrastructure projects. This provides a sound basis for answering RQ1 and RQ2.

This provides a lens through which to trace the development of RBP in the extent to which collaboration reflect contractually binding sink-or-swim-together arrangements, a coalescence of project outcome vision, aims, and objectives expressed through common and joint motivation in a best-for-project mindset illustrated in Figure 25. In essence, it is an "excellence in value delivery" mindset such as that proposed as an evolutionary path of project management by Lechler and Byrne (2011). We can now see four orders of collaboration emerging in project delivery.

Region	Dominant Term and RBP Approach	Characteristics and Comments
U.K.	Partnering, integrated SCM, framework agreements, project alliances (PAs)	Partnering is mainly well known and adopted with a long history, Framework agreements are also used quite extensively, particularly by local authorities and in programs of work. PAs are used rarely but are present in the rail construction, development and maintenance sector. Integrated SCM was pioneered by British Airports and is particularly well known for the T5 Agreement. More recently this has been evolving into a delivery consortia and delivery partner (DC/P) approach (HM Treasury and Infrastructure UK, 2013).
U.S.	Partnering, lean construction, integrated project delivery (IPD)	Partnering has been in use for decades. More recently, IPD is being seen more frequently as a mode of effective collaboration in the health care delivery sector.
Europe	Partnering, PAs	Partnering is often a natural way of doing business in Nordic countries. Finland and The Netherlands are using PAs on a few projects, but not extensively. In Germany, the procurement rules and regulations Vergabe- und Vertragsordnung für Bauleistungen (VOB) strictly prohibit integration of design and delivery and demands competition between bidders at tendering time, which acts as a barrier for integrated project delivery forms (Heidemann & Gehbauer, 2011). However, as Lönngren et al. (2010) report, the Baufairbund (BFB) approach used in North Germany uses a form of partnering. In Norway, the St Olaf Hospital project used some forms of partnering and integrated design with ECI, according to a recent paper (Bygballe, Dewulf, & Levitt, 2013)
Japan and Korea	Integrated SCM as *keiretsu* (Dyer et al., 1998), an interlocking set of companies with business relationships and cross shareholdings. This is similar to Korea, with its *chaebol* form of integrated businesses.	The Japanese pioneered use of lean techniques including extensive and deep integrated SCM as *keiretsu* and in Korea as *chaebol*. Many of the major contractors are owned by banks, and so the project chain includes development and project owners with the contractor. Subcontractors are closely linked into the main contractor through SCM approaches.
China and Hong Kong	Partnering, joint-venture forms and strategic alliances (Anvuur et al., 2011; Xu, Bower, & Smith, 2005). A single TOC and ECI form for some MTR projects.	In Hong Kong (HK) an initiative, relationally integrated value networks (RIVANS) indicated strong interest and practice in partnering and SCM forms of collaboration. In mainland China in particular, but also in HK (Johannes, 2004), there are many examples of joint ventures being formed to combine Chinese local knowledge and highly cultivated family-business connections (*guanxi*) with technology, finance. and other assets of foreign entities (Xu et al., 2005). After a recent site visit to an MTR (mass transit railways) project, the construction manager explained that there was much ECI and a negotiated and verified TOC form of agreement used, due to extreme complexity of the project.
India	One pilot case of a PA	A colleague of ours in India (Dr. Ashwin Mahalingam) is currently undertaking a study on a PA for an IT company in India using the Australian contractor Leighton Contractors and a U.K.-based PA facilitator, together with the client, Indian design NOPS, and several subcontractors.

Table 9.   RBP Terms used globally

Collaboration as Four Orders of Project Team Collaboration

Figure 25 illustrates a notional increase in early contractor involvement (ECI) from one order of collaboration to another. The extent to which an incentive contract allows for pain-sharing and gain-sharing varies across the RBP types. For example, in the first order of collaboration there are no formalized incentives and this is limited if at all present in the second order of collaboration. It is more likely in third order collaboration and a strong and defining feature of fourth-order collaboration. The third and fourth orders of collaboration have levels of blurring and overlap.

Figure 25 illustrates four orders of collaboration and each builds upon its antecedents. It also illustrates how the extent of ECI builds across the four orders of collaboration and how the extent of collaboration, sink-or-swim together mindset and coalescing of common and joint motivation intensifies with a deepening level of a POR's "hands-on" involvement with the project delivery team.

The first order was concerned with product, mainly with a dominant efficiency focus but also some consideration of effectiveness, however, cost and just-in-time collaboration to achieve efficiency is predominant in this mindset. In the

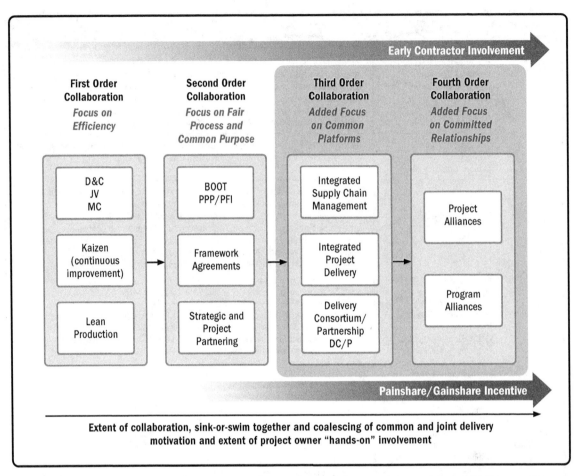

Figure 25. Categorizing Collaboration Forms of PM Delivery (Adapted from Walker and Lloyd-Walker, 2013, p. 9)

design and construction (D&C) form, for example, the PO/POR will typically have already developed fixed ideas about the general project design characteristics, so ECI opportunities for being effective are limited and are confined to efficiency advice. Lean production was developed out of ideas of just-in-time delivery that required a close liaison and coordination logistics role. This led to closer form of integrated businesses supply chain and cross-ownership interests in the supply chain, as seen in the *keiretsu* arrangements within the Japanese context and *chaebol* in Korea (Dyer et al., 1998). However, the focus is on driving out waste, efficient logistics, and continuous incremental improvement, rather than more radical innovation or invention. Relationships are quite hierarchical and subsidiary supply chain interests or first tier sub-contractors and suppliers tend to work in a more paternalistic and even servile relationship. It can be argued that *lean* by definition drives out the requisite variety and surplus resources needed for reflection, challenging the norm and out-of-the-box thinking such as that famously cited as been a feature of 3M in the 1970s and 1980s through time to write reflective stories and time to experiment and "tinker" (Nonaka & Takeuchi, 1995; von Hippel, Thomke, & Sonnack, 1999).

The second order of collaboration takes a greater focus on processes that deal with team interaction and fairness in dealing with each other while pursuing a clearly stated common purpose. Greater emphasis on effectiveness than efficiency is more clearly evident in this order of collaboration. The various evolutions of the build-own-operate-transfer (BOOT) family of procurement forms, including PFIs and PPPs, require high levels of effective collaboration between the design, construction, and financing project teams so that they can translate a PO's brief, respond to the bid proposal, and negotiate with the POR periodically across the life span of the facility to refine KRAs and KPIs as well as the transfer phase of the PPP/PFI/BOOT scheme back to the PO (Akintoye, Beck, & Hardcastle, 2003). Framework agreements open the scope of collaboration so that a range of small business entrepreneurs and firms can prequalify and agree on how to normalize delivery quality standards and remuneration forms so that a larger cluster of actors can combine or work independently within programs to obviate potential problems of domination by a few actors and enhancing diversity in supply of professional and project execution expertise. Partnering forms are another second-order development that emerged from the first-order approaches. Partnering, as discussed in Chapter 2 and with characteristics illustrated in Table 2, critically examines partnering and helps us understand what partnering may look like. Green (1999a; 1999b) cautions us about the rhetoric-reality gap in partnering and points to the many ways that it can be used coercively and in ways that provide advantages for "strong" players within a partnered group, and how it may exploit the weak or naive. Bresnen (2003) discussed seven deadly sins of partnering in a similar vein. These criticisms expose the potential for abuse that a partnering agreement can impose upon unwary participants.

Table 2 can be project-specific or involve strategic partnerships. The essence of partnering is that it moves toward having a charter of behaviors and attitudes that promote collaboration, dispute resolution, and trust building, with an emphasis of performance to enhance project delivery of benefit. However, even long-term strategic partnerships do not guarantee that exploitation between partners may not occur and that charters, while sworn to, are not legally binding. It must be acknowledged, though, that this second order purely advances efficiency-seeking for individual actors' benefit while attempting to fit into a holistic project-successful outcome, but the weightings on which actor within a network of collaborators wins and which one loses and how much each would relatively gain are not defined through legally binding forms or even by wholehearted mutual agreement.

The third order of collaboration takes a greater focus on effectiveness through the use of common platforms such as those for communication and design development and many using a common BIM technology. Three forms of this order have been identified and illustrated in Figure 25. Integrated supply chain management builds upon the foundations of FAs but moves well beyond that approach. The SCM concept originated in the automotive and aerospace sector, but has more closely developed in recent times (at the time of writing) to approaches taken by Network Rail in the U.K. This is particularly evidenced by the London Cross Rail project (or program of projects) that illustrates examples of enhanced information and communication modeling through a common platform. The Heathrow T5 co-location of contractors project experience (Doherty, 2008), particularly as Gil (2009, p. 151) states, "Inter-firm cooperation and sharing of technical knowledge and confidential information were prerequisites for institutionalizing a production strategy on the T5 project," illustrates a more highly cohesive relationship that is expected of partnering arrangements as they evolved from the 1980s through the 1990s. While there is no contractual arrangement to ensure a sink-or-swim-together outcome for project actors, the scale and depth of collaboration is intense and appears to be culture-changing. A second type of arrangement, IPD, also can be placed within this grouping of arrangements. The main characteristic of IPD is that fewer actors may participate in collaborating as a single team. IPD has been described as being adopted in three levels of collaboration. Collaboration Level One is described as being "Typical," collaboration is not contractually required. Collaboration Level Two is described as being "Enhanced," with some contractual collaboration requirements being evident. Collaboration Level Three is described as being "Required," collaboration is required by a multi-party contract. Levels 1 and 2 are analyzed as having a collaboration philosophy, whereas Level 3 is described as having collaboration as a contractual basis (NASF, 2010). Not all subcontractors may, however, form an integrated supply chain in an IPD entity, but the major actors, including the client, do collaborate on an arrangement that moves beyond partnering and often includes common information modeling platforms and greater co-location of teams. In this order of collaboration, we also observe moderate evidence of increasing ECI because the PO, major consultants, and contractors and sub-contractors become more intensely engaged in exploring options, gaining more holistic and shared understanding of opportunities and constraints, and more collaborative planning and decision making. The IPD approach has perhaps greater attention to ECI, but examples of integrated SCM as exemplified in the Heathrow T5 project experience (Doherty, 2008) show that considerable ECI was evident. For example, Gil (2009, p. 151) states that "The consultants were tasked to visit the suppliers' facilities and assist them in improving productivity and quality. BAA did not charge the T5 suppliers for the consultants' time, but expected suppliers to share confidential data on their production processes and costs. The consultants would then apply value stream mapping to examine the processes and find ways to help the T5 suppliers achieve the following objectives: reduce variability in production and installation rates; identify critical information flows and feedback loops; eliminate non-value-added activities; reduce lead times and batch sizes of manufacturing releases; coordinate work flow between feeder and primary workstations; and maximize the number of deliveries of materials and components just-in-time for assembly on the construction site." This indicates a step change from the second order of collaboration demonstrated by not only a focus on effectiveness but also on the quality of between-team relationships. Recently, the U.K. Treasury has added another project procurement delivery approach through a delivery partnership and delivery consortium (DP/C). On closer reading, this appears very much like a version of T5 and IDP and alliancing, but as yet there are no published case studies of this approach as the term has only recently been coined (HM Treasury and Infrastructure UK, 2013).

The fourth order of collaboration takes a greater focus on committed relationships and reducing power and information asymmetry. We include alliances in this category, both project and program. The main differences we see between the highly sophisticated third order of collaboration and this collaboration order is the legal framework and form of temporary integrated organization. Some features do overlap. For example, Doherty's (2008) account states that one feature of the T5 Agreement was that there was a common accounting payment and that materials, equipment, and labor used a common set of accounts that can be inspected and probity checked by all parties, and that this was established by the project owner. Also, common project insurance was arranged. Both arrangements are also common on project alliances. The T5 Agreement was legally binding and enhanced governance arrangements to allow assurance that transparency and accountability was established and maintained. This makes this arrangement very similar to alliances and places it at the cusp of the fourth-order collaboration group. Also, Level 3 IPD shares many characteristics with project alliances. Project alliances have specific clear legal agreements for no litigation unless gross negligence or criminality occurs, and this has special implications for reinforcing a no-blame culture when combined with the requirement for unanimous decision making in clarifying relationships and settling disputes. This provides the sink-or-swim clincher of the deal that characterizes this form as truly fourth-order collaboration (Walker et al., 2013b). Program alliances are similar in many ways to project alliances except that they are undertaken as term relationships. Many program alliances last over five years and may be renewed. The relationships on program alliances enable greater embedding of lessons learned so that KPIs and KRAs can be continually refined over the program period. The relationship between the POR and NOPs can be refined and enhanced to mutual benefit.

The above sense of the trajectory and emergence of current trends in RBP approaches helps us gain a sense of evolution of ideas and a sense of reality of the current (as at 2014) snapshot of the dynamic state of play in how project owners engage and recruit other parties to participate in a relational and collaborative process of delivering projects. Figure 25 provides a sense of emergence, but what of the elements that make up those four orders of collaboration? Figure 25 also helps to fill that gap though, as with many such models, a visualization such as this figure can only illustrate a fleeting glimpse of the dynamic way that industry perceives various RMP categories. We particularly see this with the way that the IPD Collaboration Level 3. The T5 Agreement third order of collaboration may be similarly described as a form of integrated SCM but has many characteristics that could been seen as morphing into the fourth order or perhaps forcing a reclassification of it as a third-order collaboration form. Such categorizations and classifications are, after all, only our social constructs to attempt to make sense of a complex and evolving reality of how business is done. We should not pretend that our classifications or categories change anything in the "real world." Project owners face complex and messy problems and situations about how they should configure the delivery of projects that deliver an identified benefit and they pragmatically go about marshaling practitioners to realize their desired results. Academics come along later, as we do in this book, and merely help practitioners and our scholarly colleagues to make sense of "the reality" so that good ideas are not lost in a miasma of confused history. In this analysis of these RBP forms, we offer some clarity about the development and trend trajectory of each evolving experimental collaborative practice that is illustrated through our models, analysis, and explanations.

One fundamental principle that we can grasp as a starting point to understand the multiple and complex forms of designing or even understanding project procurement collaborative categories, is the extent of integration or segregation of the teams who develop a project brief, design a project delivery system, and then deliver the project. Before we can understand what KSAE are required of project team participants, we need to understand the overall and basic structural possibilities for project delivery.

Figure 3 in Chapter 2 categorized project delivery forms as traditional and integrated forms of project procurement. Each part of the project supply chain may be seen as comprising a host of teams. The PO or POR, for example, will have an internal organizational structure to collaborate with, coordinate, and communicate with internal stakeholders. The design team leader will have various specialist design teams and organizations to collaborate, coordinate, and communicate with, including external stakeholders. Similarly, the project delivery team will be led by a person who collaborates, coordinates, and communicates with specialist suppliers and subcontratcors and also work with external stakeholders.

Traditional segregated forms such as DBB and cost-plus comprise three distinct and separate entities. The segments highlighted in dark grey in Figure 26 indicate that the design team and project delivery team are integrated for the procurement forms under the Figure 3 elements labeled "Focus on integrating design & delivery processes with an emphasis on planning and control" and "Focus on integrated project teams design & delivery teams with an emphasis on collaboration and communication." Each project team includes the POR, the design team (Des-T) leader, and delivery team (Del-T) leader, and interacts with various specialized project teams as well as with their relevant external stakeholders as illustrated in Figure 26.

The POR has internal stakeholder constituents to deal with, as well as a range of external stakeholders. For example, in healthcare projects there will be clinicians, administrators, facilities managers, faculty members and a host of others concerned with the project outcome and similarly, in a university setting, academics, facility managers, and university administrators. The POR will filter the wants and needs of various project user groups and has to manage these requests and demands in developing the project brief (Barrett & Stanley, 1999). The project design team leader will have teams of specialists to collaborate with, both in-house and outsourced. The project delivery team leader will have teams of suppliers and subcontractors and may be engaged in a JV with other main contractors, and so the range of teams to work with can be highly complex. There may also be an overall project director for integrated design and delivery projects coordinating and managing the leaders of the design and delivery teams. Figure 26 illustrates the complex lines of possible collaboration, coordination, and communication.

When we consider Figure 25 and Figure 26, we see a broad typology of RBP emerging from the literature, and when combined with consideration of Figure 3 under the subheading given as "forms of project procurement," we start to see a way of better understanding a taxonomy of the relational intensity and characteristics of various identified RBP Forms. Table 10 summarizes their broad characteristics to further refine and provide finer granularity of

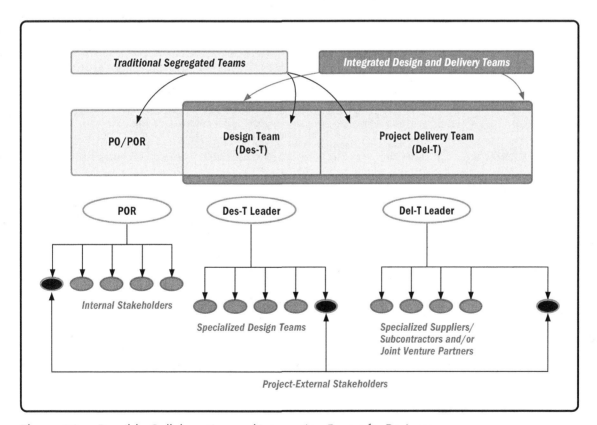

Figure 26. Possible Collaboration and Integration Forms for Projects

RBP Form Name Tag and Relationship focus intensity	Relationship Characteristics
Design and construct (D&C) *PO/POR with delivery team = Low* *Within the delivery team = varies (depends on the head contractor's workplace culture)*	D&C is integrated in a single contract between the project owner (PO) or its representative (POR) and the project delivery entity, which may have an in-house or outsourced design team and a project delivery production team. The relationship between the PO/POR and project delivery entity is purely a "hands-off" business one. The project delivery entity may have its own internal ways of collaborating and coordination, but the PO/POR would not take any intense interest or involvement in that process being concerned more with a solution based on the PO's brief or conceptual design specifications. Collaboration between design and delivery team members at an early stage would occur in developing the D&C bid, but the intensity and quality varies.
Integrated supply chain management (SCM) *PO/POR with delivery team = Low (unless leading the approach such as in T5)* *Within the delivery team = High*	This may range from a contractor, acting independently of the PO/POR, managing its supply chain through purposeful and tiered arrangements to minimize the numbers of parties in the supply chain, to an integrated PO/POR and contractor SCM approach similar to that discussed earlier in the way that BAA developed the T5 Agreement. In SCM, the approach, relationships, accountability, and transparency are well defined and expressly stipulated. The recently developed delivery consortia and delivery partner (DC/P) approach shows many shared aspects of T5 combined with that of IDP and PAs.
Management Contracting (MC) *PO/POR with delivery team = High* *Within the delivery team = High*	The MC entity may have an agency (fee-based) contract or a direct (profit) contract with the PO. In either case, the work packages are undertaken directly under the POR (for-agency MC) or the head contractor (for-profit MC). The main feature of MC is ECI advice about logistics, project methods and other technical issues that helps to develop a more "buildable" solution. The relationship between POR and the MC is usually close and collaborative and work packages may be undertaken in a similar vein between the sub-contractors and head contractor.
Join venture (JV) consortia *PO/POR with delivery team = Low* *Within the delivery team = Varies*	This is very similar to a traditional design-bid-build project, except that the head contractor of the project delivery team will form a contractual arrangement with other contractor(s) to be able to cover all technical, cultural or other needs of the project. The JV may operate in a variety of ways, depending on how well disposed each party is toward building and maintaining relationships.
BOOT family, PPP/PFI *PO/POR with delivery team = Medium to Low* *Within the special purpose vehicle project delivery team = Very High*	There is an intense involvement of various parties to the project delivery team but with little involvement of the POR at the early stages beyond acting to clarify any questions and issues and ambiguities presented by the project brief. The project is also in this case a very long term one in that the entity that "owns" the project has possession of it until it is transferred to the commissioning client. Thus the BOOT/PPP/PFI entity can be considered the PO in one sense. A key element in this procurement form is that there is a more distant initial relationship between the PO and special-purpose vehicle entity but there is a far greater immediate and continuing relationship between the design and delivery teams within the special-purpose vehicle as the project proposal develops. In this form, there is also greater engagement between the leading organization within the special purpose vehicle with financial and legal participants.
Project partnering (Proj. Pntrg.) *PO/POR with delivery team = Varies* *Within the delivery team = High*	A partnering agreement is established as a form of relational compact rather than contract, in that is somewhat volunteered. This compact provides a charter that helps to establish vision, mission, and objectives, behavioral expectations, and a dispute and issue resolution protocol. It is largely a cultural artifact. It is still possible for the relationship of various parties to break down. This may result in litigation, and there are few if any formal mechanisms to force parties to collaborate. Partnering may include the PO/POR and design/delivery team or may be confined to the project delivery team participants. There are often incentives in terms of parties becoming more efficient and hence gaining profit advantage from that though reduced waste, rework, and less administrative effort devoted to protecting positions to prepare for possible litigation. Value engineering workshops may identify savings and these may be shared among parties.
Strategic partnering (Strat. Pntrg.) *PO/POR with delivery team = High* *Within the delivery team = High*	Strategic partnering is an extension to project partnering across a program of work comprising many projects over an extended timeframe. The partners may be a client and contractor and perhaps including selected subcontractors and suppliers, so that a set of protocols are agreed (similar to the above) that may include incentive payments, guaranteed profit margin subjected to open-book scrutiny, and other relational arrangements that build trust and transparency. Relationships develop and all parties in successful strategic partnering arrangements see the value in maintaining these.
Integrated solutions - competitive dialogue (CD) *PO/POR with delivery team = Very High* *Within the delivery team = Varies but is often High*	This is a protocol that is used at the pre-tendering stage to canvass opportunities for a CD and during the tendering stage where the PO/POR and potential contractors have an open discussion about developing a solution in a way that each better understands the other's perspectives, strengths, and weaknesses. This allows wider exploration of options and incentives and improved measures of performance with which to negotiate terms. The outcome of a CD may be a fixed price/time traditional contract, D&C, or other form of procurement, including a project alliance.
Integrated project delivery (IDP) *PO/POR with delivery team = Medium (for IDP Type 1 and 2) and Very High (for IDP Type3)* *Within the delivery team = Very High*	This RBP form evolved out of the Lean Production and Lean Construction concepts (Ballard, 2008). In its manifestation of IDP emphasis on waste reduction, rework and production efficiency has been enhanced to include a focus on relational integration, incentives for collaboration and a behavioral element to bind parties to an explicit set of behavioral protocols (American Institute of Architects - AIA California Council, 2007; Ashraft, 2010; Cohen, 2010). The three levels of collaboration explained by NASF (2010) illustrate a partnering like form of IDP through to an alliance type form. This approach has been used for large and complex projects such as healthcare facilities where speed of delivery was paramount and complexity requires enhanced levels of collaboration and coordination (Cohen, 2010).

Table 10. Relationship Intensity of Various RBP Forms *(Continued)*

RBP Form Name Tag and Relationship focus intensity	Relationship Characteristics
Alliancing (Project, Program, Service or Design Alliance) PO/POR with delivery team = Very High Within the delivery team = Very High	This RBP form can be understood as a highly evolved form of partnering and further advanced form of IPD. It also shares characteristics of SCM but often not as advanced as the Heathrow Airport T5 Agreement form. What principally distinguishes the alliance from Partnering and IDP is that is has structured, well-articulated, and well-understood contractual commitments based on a commercial contract that stipulates how the work to be done will be parceled up and how it will be paid for. An incentive contract that explicitly states gain-sharing and pain-sharing arrangements, explicitly defines KPIs and KRAs and how they will be measured and assessed. And, in contrast to other forms, there is a behavioral contract that explicitly states the nature of the party's behavior, with a no-blame and no-litigation agreement. This is undertaken with explicit protocols for governance and transparency with an open-book approach. Service alliances and program alliances are interesting in that they are similar to framework agreements in some respects, but with greater formality and specificity of commercial and behavioral expectations. Other emerging alliance forms such as design alliances are formed at the pre-tender stage of projects to draw in expertise (similar to Agency MC) and to help develop project procurement delivery strategy.
Early contractor involvement (ECI) PO/POR with design team = Very High Within the delivery team = Varies, refer to Figure 2	This is more of a general term that encompasses many features of MC with design alliances and other interfaces over the project lifecycle, as illustrated in Figure 2 in Chapter 2, as a graphic representation of ECI. A principal feature of collaboration between PO/POR, design team, and ECI project delivery consultant is based in being engaging in constructability or buildability consulting based on a negotiated fee basis.
Framework agreements (FA) PO/POR with framework entity = High Within the delivery team = Varies	Framework agreements are similar to strategic partnering or service alliances in many respects, but are used broadly for design services, construction and project delivery services as well as for maintenance and facilities management. They are similar to these in that a key set of protocols, selection criteria, performance criteria, etc. are established as a framework to apply over an extended time period, but unlike strategic partnering or service alliances (that appear to be generally continuous as a form of in-sourcing resources and expertise), they enable a pool of providers to be available on demand as and when required. In construction and other sectors such as aerospace, first-tier subcontractors may be included in such agreements. In addition, first-tier supply chain members may extend the framework agreement concept deeper to tier 2.

Table 10. Relationship Intensity of Various RBP Forms *(Continued)*

meaning to answer RQ1. This leads us toward a fuller understanding of the KSAEs needed for the various RBP forms. This helps us move toward an answer to RQ3—what specific KSAEs that are required to deliver RBP forms?

Illustrating the intensity and nature of required collaboration provides a solid start to the task of turning our attention to two aspects of answering our research questions RQ1 and RQ3. First identifying the building block elements of generic RBP forms provides us with a model to address the second aspect, linking identified measures to identify KSAEs required for delivering RBP projects.

An RBP Wittgenstein's Family Resemblance Model

Nyström (2005a) developed a useful model for making sense of complex organizational arrangements where project team elements and features are classified into recognizable components that can describe a 'system' or way of working. He applied Wittgenstein's concept of family resemblance to project partnering by emphasising the general components of partnering. The German philosopher Ludwig Wittgenstein had argued "(. . .) that complicated concepts cannot be defined in the traditional way by stating necessary and sufficient conditions. There might not be a single or a small number of features, which are common for all variants of a term and therefore it cannot be defined in the traditional way" (Nyström, 2005a, p. 474). Nyström proceeded to argue that there are complex networks of overlapping similarities among the things that fall under a complex concept. It is an interesting idea, because it lies at the core of meaning and nomenclature based on a number of sufficient and necessary conditions to the question of, what it is to be an "X"? This is particularly salient when there may not be general agreement about what an X may be or where there is a range of interpretations that can be made of X based on sufficient and necessary conditions that can be made explicit in some way. Thus it was valid to use Wittgenstein's family resemblance model in which core attributes or characteristics are surrounded by familiar components that are crystallized from analysis of family resemblances. On the one hand, we can say that at time "t" in geographical location "l" (see **Table 14**) that a particular project may be considered a "partnering" one based on the attributes measures presented in Table 11, Table 12, and Table 13 in a nominalist manner (because people may call the project a partnering one or it may have an artifact such as partnering charter). On the other hand, we can use Wittgenstein's family resemblance concept to describe the project as a form of alliance. One of our participants (A16) who discussed his research study in Sweden, on what was referred to as a partnering project, told us that, on reflection, it was very close to a PA but did not have the artifacts such as a behavioral contract or a no-litigation contract clause but nevertheless the team *acted* as if there were these artifacts. In this way, the Figure 27 model provides a more rational and perhaps more accurate or supportable approach to both globally labelling RBP forms and temporarily doing so as these labels change and adapt over time.

Instead of "family" traits being a particular shaped nose, familiar gate or speech patterns, or other forms of attributes that typifies somebody as likely to belong to a particular family tree Nyström clumped attributes of partnering to be able to analyze the partnering literature and case study data to be able to construct a "flower" analogy with a core ever-present component and "petals" that represent other components that may be present or have been discarded or had not been fully developed. We see flowers with a variety of petal arrangements, yet the genus is usually easily recognisable even if petals are missing. Yeung, Chan, and Chan (2007) used the same logic to study components of project alliances to understand what is specific about alliancing with a focus on the hard (contractual) and soft (relationship-based) elements. We adapt and refine this approach to present our summary analsyis of RBP approaches drawn from the literature we presented in Chapter 2, 3, and 4 of this book, analysis of interview data from participants, and reflection upon our previous and current research data.

Our approach to developing a model was to gather data and make sense of it to be able to refine and distil a discrete set of factors that could be illustrated as "petals" in a Wittgenstein-style model. In doing so, we answer RQ1 in greater depth and with finer granularity than for example was presented in Figure 25. We discussed in Chapter 5 how we conducted the research that led us to our model that describes the fundamental characteristics, the elements, of various RBP forms. We painstakingly analyzed over 500 pages of transcribed interviews of 50 subject matter experts using NVivo10 to develop themes and subthemes that form the elements and sub-elements of a model that answers RQ1 and

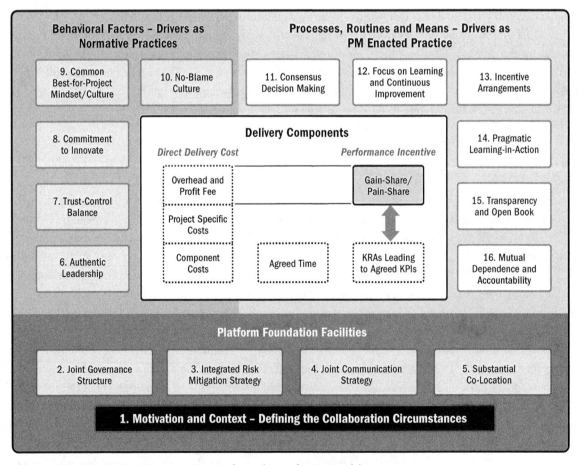

Figure 27. An RBP Wittgenstein's Idea of Family Resemblance

provides a platform for a way in which we can identify the required KSAEs for each element to answer RQ3 and lead to a way to assess the presence and application of the identified KSAEs to be able to address and answer RQ4.

Our form of Wittgenstein's family resemblance model concept is illustrated in Figure 27. To make visualizing and understanding the model less confusing, due to the number of elements or "petals" identified, we grouped the petals into three broad categories. We drew upon and adapted ideas proposed by Jacobsson and Roth (2014), who conceptualize partnering as a potential engagement platform, and by using that concept, they explained how the relationship is structurally and logically based and enabled, and the behaviors that sustain it through what they describe as means, foundations, and factors.

The central core in our model, the *stamen* of the flower, illustrates the project delivery components. These remain stable with some variation in emphasis, for example on the extent of pain and gain sharing. This core element is surrounded by three categories of elements consisting of 16 *petals*. Various combinations of intensity of presence of theses 16 *petals* can be used to explain different forms of RBP. Each RBP form has different characteristics of each petal that fall within a general family resemblance, and when visualized holistically, they can help us identify more specific classes of RBP, forms and so can help us to better anticipate expectations of the various parties to that procurement arrangement.

The delivery component of the project is situated at the core of our Figure 27 model. Delivery success is defined by the PO's defined KRAs. KRAs include cost and time performance but they often include other key results as explained in Chapter 2 and elaborated in Table 8 in Appendix 2 for the sub-element 2.3 "Governance best value strategy through KRAs and KPIs." Performance against KRAs is measured through KPIs For RBP forms, the KPIs are developed based upon the identified benefit that the project is designed to deliver. These KPIs frequently extend beyond traditional cost, time, and fitness for purpose constraints. Differences in the extent and order of collaborative arrangements, as indicated in Figure 25, reflect the extent and manner to which overhead and profit are incentivized (see Chapter 2 discussions relating to project alliances and the range of KPIs and their linkage to performance incentives, or Ross (2003)). The direct-delivery cost component includes direct project specific cost elements such as material, labor, and supply chain input components from suppliers and contractors. The project delivery team's overhead and profit is added to this to form the target outturn cost (TOC). As discussed earlier in Chapter 2, for project alliances in particular, the profit contribution is kept as a separate and discrete "at-risk" fee for service that becomes subject to a pain-share gain-share agreement. For some forms of RBP, the "at risk" profit will be zero, so that all profit goes to the parties individually. The agreement specifies the percentage risk and reward ratio for each participant to the agreement, as well as the percentage of the profit that is at risk. The project is also agreed to be delivered to a set time deadline. Agreed KPIs are used for measuring performance that influence the final quantum and proportion of the pain-share or gain-share at-risk fee for service to be distributed to participants. Surrounding the delivery components core are the 16 "petals" grouped within three clusters or groups of linked factors.

At the base of the Figure 27 model sits five platform foundational facilities that provide infrastructure elements that determines the extent of integration that the RBP form will operate. A core psychological foundational element is the defining motivations and contextual circumstances that shape the logic of the adopted collaborative approach. That base platform element supports the five behavior-shaping factors at the left-hand side of the model that drive normative practices that define the ambience, the workplace cultural sense and feeling experienced by those engaged on the project (for more details on the term ambience refer to Walker and Lloyd-Walker, 2014). These behavioral factors drive six processes, routines, and means factors situated on the right hand side of the model that shape how the RBP form will respond to the platform foundational facility factors.

Figure 27 thus illustrates the "petals" that represent other components that may be present or have been discarded or had not been fully developed for various forms of RBP and change as the various labeled RBP forms change over time and through cultural, geographical, historical, and other contextual influences. We generally label these platform facilities, behavioral factors, and process drivers.

We are now in a position to describe in more depth the other elements of Figure 27 and their sub-elements. Platform foundational facilities comprise the integrating features for collaboration. These are explained in Table 11, with behavioral factors explained in Table 12 and the processes, routines and means explained in Table 13.

Table 11, Table 12, and Table 13 share a common format. The first column contains the main themes, the "petal" factors derived from the NVivo analysis of data into themes and sub-theme nodes. For example the motivation and context of the circumstances impacting upon the procurement choice is presented in Table 11 as element and theme 1. In the the next column, we present the subthemes within each element and we provide a summary description of that subtheme. For example, in Table 11, the sub-element *Best value – motivational focus is on <u>value not lowest cost</u>. Value is expressed in KRAs and KPIs that link to the project purpose. Often, 3BL issues are of high priority in such cases* is presented. The third column contains a suggested measurement scale for the element/theme in general. The scale is fairly course grained ranging from *low* to *high* to be evaluated using an approximation of the descriptor presented for low or high rating of motivation and context. For example, in Table 11, we have suggested low and high ratings as:

Low levels would be related to a *hostile environment* for collaboration. This may be due to lack of conviction of project participants in the value of collaboration within this project's context.

High levels would relate to the procurement choice solution being driven by the acceptance of project participants in the logic of a clear advantage being gained by adopting a focus on a *supportive and collaborative* approach to delivering benefits that align with the values of participants.

A particular project case study being examined can be analyzed and the closeness of the descriptive measures in column three of Table 11 can assessed. We suggest that a five level scale could be deployed with low, medium-low, medium-high and high rating values. This provides a basis for assessing how the factors can be represented in the Figure 27 model to provide a fairly sophisticated visualization of how the RBP form may fit into the accepted categories of RBP.

We now illustrate how the Figure 27 model can be used to visualize what each procurement form may look like and from that to guide the appropriate level of platform facilities, behaviors and means to achieve the project delivery goals and aims represented by the project procurement form. Visualization can be made to gain an appreciation of what is required for a specific RBP type, for example that illustrated in Figure 28 or across RBP forms as illustrated in Table 14.

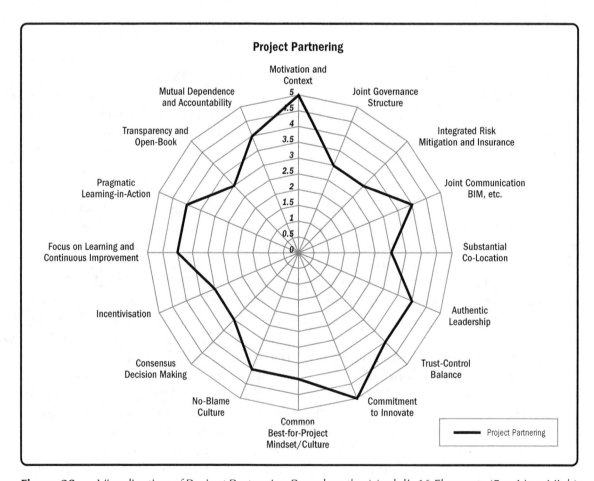

Figure 28. Visualization of Project Partnering Based on the Model's 16 Elements (5 = Very High)

Platform Foundational Facilities – Elements and Themes 1-5	Subthemes from the transcript analysis (see Appendix 2 for more details)	Suggested to be measured by a five-point Likert scale
1. The **motivation and context** of the circumstances impacting upon a procurement choice. This defines a substrate of circumstances that affects the potential degree of possible collaboration.	*Best value* – motivational focus is on value not lowest cost. Value is expressed in KRAs and KPIs that are linked to the project purpose. Often, 3BL issues are of high priority in such cases. *Emergency recovery* – motivation drives a procurement solution that enables recovery from the emergency as quickly and as feasibly as possible. *Experimental* – motivation drives purposeful exploration of options and the ability to learn and reflect upon experience to accumulate valuable knowledge that advances project objectives. *Competitive resource availability environment* – motivation drives a sustainable response to the prevailing competitive environment. Economically buoyant times pose a challenge to POs losing key staff to other employers. In challenging economic times, POs could be obliged by their governments to take advantage of their market position to force project delivery teams to accept contract conditions that may be in the PO's short term but not long term interests. Both conditions impose pressures related to economic times. *Relational rationale* – motivation and context drives the underlying logic of forming and developing relationships with potential project team members to further a longer term interest. Often all parties can benefit from the relationship, perhaps due to high levels of turbulence and change that challenge a BAU approach. *Known risks* – motivation can be triggered by the PO/POR assessing that a particular procurement form appears most appropriate to respond to risk sharing and responsibility that are known, assessable and best managed by the relevant identified participant to be allocated responsibility for those risks. *Unknown risks* – motivation is rooted in a context in which uncertainty requires a response of nurturing deep collaboration and trust between parties within a no-blame environment. There is a need for a psychologically safe environment where all participants can experiment with new approaches to respond to uncertainly and extreme ambiguity using teams with the capacity to rapidly evaluate consequences and outcomes and respond accordingly.	**Low** levels would be related to a hostile environment for collaboration. This may be due to lack of conviction of project participants in the value of collaboration within this project's context. **High** levels would relate to the procurement choice solution being driven by the acceptance of project participants in the logic of a clear advantage being gained by adopting a focus on a supportive and collaborative approach to delivering benefits that align with the values of participants.
2. The level of **joint governance structure**. Having a unified way that each project delivery team party legitimizes its actions through rules, standards and norms, values and coordination mechanisms such as organizational routines, and the way that committees, liaison and hierarchy represents a unified or complimentary way of interacting. This impacts the quality of explicit understanding of how teams should collaborate and communicate.	*Governance processes* – common assumptions and ways of working influences project governance processes and rules. These will vary according to the project procurement delivery form but will be designed to align the strategy, objectives and aims of the project. Process clarity is essential to inform the required behaviors. *Governance structure* – the structure of the entire project team defines how the level of flexibility/rigidity, power and influence and communication symmetry directly influences the workplace culture. The way that a project's overall leadership and management team is constituted impacts upon who has a voice and how they can express ideas, perspectives and concerns. *Governance best value strategy through KRAs and KPIs* – the project output and outcome is influenced by the strategy deployed to define, measure and assess success. The way that these are developed and used impacts upon effective project governance.	**Low** levels would be related to a *laisez faire* approach, where each participating project team has established its own individual stand-alone project governance standards. Little coherence in alignment of the whole project delivery organizational processes and structure is evident, with few explicit expectations about what success looks like and how to define and measure it. **High** relates to an effectively structured, uniform, integrated and consistent set of performance standards that apply across and within the project delivery teams. All participant organizations share a common understanding of how to organize for success and what constitutes valuable project output and outcome success.
3. The extent to which an **integrated risk mitigation strategy** is organized for all parties as part of the client's proactive risk management system. This has an impact upon the quality of explicit understanding of how to collaboratively manage risk and uncertainty and potentially gain advantage from a project-wide insurance policy.	*Risk-sharing conversation* – The conversation about risk sharing; who takes responsibility for any class of, or particular risk. The strategy needs to be coherent to ensure that those best able to manage risk do so in a way that aligns the risk strategy to the project objectives and aims. The nature of these conversations differs in emphasis placed upon means to allocate accountability across project procurement forms. *Risk mitigation actions* – there are a number of ways, ranging from collective to individual, to agree upon and decide how to mitigate risk that vary according to the procurement form. *System integration* – of the project is structured and managed to provide a platform that is based upon the participant's philosophical stance about relationships between teams. Systems can be integrated to cope with risk, uncertainty and ambiguity to respond to a need for a platform to be developed to address these three related but separate concepts.	**Low** levels would be characterized by an immature and confused individual firm-specific risk management approach and poorly defined systemic approaches to deal with uncertainty and ambiguity. **High** levels would be represented by consistent and integrated risk assessment processes being identified, assessed and mitigated against a project-wide and broader systems-wide impact for the project or network in the case of programs of projects.

Table 11.   Wittgenstein's Family Resemblance Elements for Platform Foundational Facilities for RBP *(Continued)*

Platform Foundational Facilities – Elements and Themes 1-5	Subthemes from the transcript analysis (see Appendix 2 for more details)	Suggested to be measured by a five-point Likert scale
4. The level of **joint communication strategy** platforms such as integrated processes and ICT groupware, including building information modeling (BIM) and other electronic forms of communication. While BIM is more prevalent in recent years, past equivalent forms include groupware ICT, sharing drawings and plans between teams. Joint communication facilitates common communication and understanding.	*Common processes and systems* – Project participants need to share a common way of working and a common language and communication approach to avoid misunderstanding that can undermine trust and commitment and consequently undermine effective decision making and action. Bridges and interoperability between systems to cope with a lack of a "one system" are also essential. *Integrated communication platform* – A common ICT platform, including for example common BIM tools can minimize the risk of poor coordination, communication, and misunderstandings between participants.	**Low** levels of joint communication would be characterized by poor quality staff interaction, use of firm-specific rather than project-wide processes and ICT systems, and weak cross-team mechanisms for gaining mutual understanding. **High** levels would be characterized by well integrated processes that are well understood by all participants and advanced communication technologies being used that seamlessly connect all project parties within a particular procurement arrangement.
5. The extent that project teams are **substantially co-located** within easy physical reach of each other. Close proximity facilitates ad hoc and chance encounters to improve building relationships and facilitating common understanding.	*Hierarchal integration mechanisms* – Leaders can inspire motivation toward unity of purpose by physically interacting with individuals in the various levels of an organization. Site visits, meetings held on site, and other ritualistic or practical events that are held in the actual workplace can be very important as a platform for integrated joint action. *Physical co-location* – Project participants can more easily communicate and interact on problem solving, monitoring, and active collaboration when they are in within easy reach of each other. Co-location in a well-considered and conducive environment can facilitate positive interaction.	**Low** levels would be characterized by firm-specific policy determining that disparate teams are physically located in dispersed locations. There may also be a large visibility gap between project leaders and those at the "coal face." **High** levels would be characterized by a project-wide policy that attempts to maximize participant co-location on-site where feasible, including the POR. There would also be high interaction between project leadership groups and the project management and physical delivery team members so that engagement enhances communication and mutual perspective taking.

Table 11. Wittgenstein's Family Resemblance Elements for Foundational Facilities for RBP *(Continued)*

We experimented with this mapping approach and illustrate our results in Figure 28 for a specific project partnering RBP type. This figure shows Element 1, motivation and context rated at 5, indicating the procurement choice solution being driven by the acceptance of the logic of a clear advantage being gained by adopting a high level focus on a *supportive and collaborative* approach to delivering benefits that align with the values of participants. It shows a very high value (5). Several other factors rate medium (3), including joint governance structure, integrated risk mitigation and insurance, incentivization, and consensus decision making.

Graphs such as Figure 28 could be drawn to compare one RBP form with another, or it could be used to design a hybrid RBP project procurement form. Alternatively, this kind of visualization tool can be used as an explanatory tool in benchmarking or project evaluation. Consider an instance of evidence gathered from an audit of a particular project that was designed to be delivered under partnering arrangements but had audit evidence indicated that the appropriate rating for that project was for *low* levels of focus on learning and continuous improvement. Figure 28 and Table 13 suggests that the expectation for this element is *medium* (that is, between low and high). This tool could either prompt useful action to improve the focus or prompt further investigation to re-examine the evidence that led to a *low* rating to ascertain if this is a reasonable judgment.

In this way, the Wittgenstein Family Resemblance Model offers a useful visualization tool for understanding expectations of each project procurement form as well as being a useful benchmarking and auditing tool. We now provide the detailed description of each of the 16 elements.

What do Table 14 and Figure 28 tell us? First, they give us a visualization of identified RBP forms that are known around the world to be compared using the Wittgenstein Family Resemblance concept, adapted to indicate comparative elements in the model presented as Figure 27 and grouped by the order of collaboration indicated in Figure 25.

Behavioral factors driving normative practices—Elements and Themes 6-10	Subthemes from the transcript analysis (see Appendix 2 for more details)	Suggested to be measured by a five-point Likert scale
6. The degree of **authentic leadership**, that is, possessing ethical principled values and consistency of action with espoused rhetoric. This would apply across the project delivery team at every level of team leadership, not only for the project lead person(s) but also the supporting design and supply chain team leaders. It speaks to the project culture.	Authentic leadership is present in designated project leaders who hold institutional or organizational power, but it also applies to "followers" within a collective leadership sense. *Reflectiveness* – Project participants are systems thinkers and often follow a strategic thinking approach about the situational context and know that the situational context is crucial to effective decision making. *Pragmatism* – Project participants get on with the job, are politically astute, and work within constraints or find ethical and sensible ways around these constraints. *Appreciativeness* – Project participants understand the motivations and value proposition of influential stakeholders involved in the project. They are consciously engaged with their team members and exhibit signs of having a high emotional intelligence. *Resilience* – Project participants exhibit adaptability, versatility, flexibility and being persistent when faced with adversity. They are able to effectively learn from experience. *Wisdom* – Project participants have opinions and advice that is valued, consistent, and reliable that others instinctively refer to. Their judgment abilities make their brokering advice crucial. They are perceived as having high levels of integrity based on inner strength of character, knowledge, and experience. *Spirit* – Project participants demonstrate the courage and have sufficient influence and respect to effectively challenge assumptions and often offer radical alternative solutions to resolve complex and difficult situations. *Authenticity* – Project participants demonstrate qualities of being approachable and trustworthy and open to ideas. They encourage and advance collaboration, discussion and new ways of thinking.	**Low** levels are revealed when espoused principled values are not demonstrated in action manifested through a gap between the rhetoric and reality of leading teams. **High** levels demonstrate consistency in espoused and enacted values that are genuinely principled.
7. The **trust-control balance** of representing and protecting the interests of project leaders with that of other genuinely relevant stakeholders while relying on the integrity, benevolence and ability of all project team parties to "do the right thing" in terms of project performance. It is the ability to be able to understand the value-proposition of "the other" project teams and to assess their capacity to deliver the promise while establishing mechanisms to ensure transparent accountability. Trust balance is also about trust in others to suggest improvement and to discuss sensitive (possibly political) issues.	*Autonomy* – Project participants have autonomy to respond to the situational context. Their responsiveness is complicated by institutional and cultural norms that may either restrain their autonomy and therefore their capacity to respond to new initiatives and changes to "plan," or the organizational culture and governance arrangements may leave them with enough autonomy to act somewhat independently. *Forms of trust* – Project participants' capacity to experiment, explore options and take action is advanced or constrained by their leadership teams' perceptions of how various interests are best served. These perceptions are influenced by the nature of that interest, the forms and basis of project participants' and their leaders' level of trust in each other and understanding the impact of assumptions about self-interest and shared interest on trust their levels. *Safe workplace cultures* – Project participants' trust in their leaders and colleagues is often mediated by their perceived treatment in terms of working in a safe psychological, physical, and intellectual environment. *Trust relationship building* – Project participants and their leadership teams engage in varying levels of effort to create a balance in trust and control in which trust with caution is tempered with blind faith.	**Low** balance is demonstrated by extreme naïveté by participants about trusting others implicitly or alternatively by exhibiting high levels of suspicion and/or unreasonable demands for formal and informal control and monitoring that implies a cynical attitude toward trust of others. **High** balance is demonstrated by innate sensibility to juggle transparency and accountability demands with the need for trust with necessary due diligence. It also demonstrates a professional understanding of the nature of project participant accountability constraints and opportunities for resolving and possibly helping resolve institutional paradoxes so that accountability is consistent with accepted responsibility.
8. Commitment to be innovative represents the duality of being willing to be innovative within a structured mechanism to enable and empower people to be innovative. This is closely linked to a project team participants' capacity for learning, reflection, creativity being ambidextrous, and the organization's core values of supporting and rewarding questioning the status quo.	*Innovation types* – Project participants need to understand and adapt to behavioral expectations associated with different types of project procurement forms. They may be engaged in product, process, or behavioral types of innovation within a project or program situational context that could affect how team members' commitment can be initiated and sustained. Balancing exploration and exploitation of innovation, given the procurement form expectation, is important. *Commitment to continuous improvement* – Project participants' purpose for being innovative should be to achieve continuous improvement. The extent to which project participants can be innovative and effect continuous improvement depends upon institutional, governance, and individual motivational and enabling factors. *Testing, prototyping and experimenting* – Project participants' innovative actions are usually manifested by testing, prototyping, and experimentation within the context of having and inquiring, curious, and often skeptical mind.	**Low** commitment levels are manifested by inadequate or incomplete linkage of motivation, ability, and facilitation for innovation within the context of the procurement form. **High** commitment levels are manifested by vision, objectives and desire to be innovative with well-considered instruments to measure and demonstrate innovation, motivation through rewards and incentives and demonstrated high levels of existing absorptive capacity for innovation.

Table 12. Wittgenstein's Family Resemblance Elements for Behavioral Factors for RBP *(Continued)*

Behavioral factors driving normative practices—Elements and Themes 6-10	Subthemes from the transcript analysis (see Appendix 2 for more details)	Suggested to be measured by a five-point Likert scale
9. **Common best-for-project mindset and culture** relates to the focus being placed on value generated in delivering the project compared with objectives of delivering what was explicitly requested or demanded. It is also about the priority of the project outcome taking precedence above all other considerations (despite inherent paradoxes). A major effort is directed at a positive and successful project outcome rather than individual teams being winners or losers.	*Alignment of common goals* – Project participants need to be effectively collaborating to a constructive end through sharing common and aligned goals about best-for-project outcomes and how that delivers VfM. *Outcomes and performance levels* – These should be assessed and judged based upon common best-for-project aligned goals. *Challenging for excellence* – Project participants need to be constantly challenging their level of outcome and performance through effective collaboration toward a constructive evaluation of achieved outcomes and performance. *Value for money reporting* – Project participants need to devise ways to recognize, monitor, and effectively diffuse knowledge about how their performance and workplace culture has impacted VfM on their project or program. This is not about "spin-doctoring" but about making a credible and acceptable case for recognizing achievements. *Recruiting support* – Project participants need to devise ways to effectively recruit support for best-for-project values through an effective PO/POR internal and NOPs recruitment strategy as well as enlisting support for as many members of the project delivery chain as is possible.	*Low* best-for-project mindset levels are manifested by a higher level of priority for individual benefit realization at the potential expense of other project team members and the project owner. *High* best-for-project mindset levels are manifested by a genuine attitude that "we all sink-or-swim together" and a focus on maximizing value to the project (or network in the case of a progam). Contractual arrangements will reinforce pooled gain or pain based on performance measured by KRAs and KPIs.
10. **No-blame culture** relates to the degree to which teams welcome taking responsible accountability for problems as they arise rather than having shirked responsibility in the hope that others take them on who may be vulnerable to being blamed for potential failure. It is also about being "part of the solution" through being part of an overall acceptance of shared-and-several responsibility for understanding. This involves discussing problems in an unprejudiced manner and opening up one's mind to alternative perspectives and seeing issues from multiple perspectives.	*Rationale for a no-blame culture* – Project participants avoiding a blame-shifting culture having felt pain and hardship through past experience of being blamed. They are determined not to repeat the experience and to thus support a no-blame culture. *Facilitating mechanisms for no-blame* – Contractual, behavioral and organizational mechanisms that support the establishment and maintenance of a no-blame culture.	*Low* no-blame culture is manifested by a project participant's high propensity to shift blame from themselves to others. These problems may be attributable to them for unforeseen, unanticipated, or unwanted events that impact adversely upon project delivery. A low no-blame culture is also palpable by a tendency to avoid acknowledging potential problem situations in the hope that blame can be attributed to others. *High* no-blame culture is manifested by a culture of open discussion of problems, unforeseen, unanticipated, or unwanted events that may impact adversely upon project delivery. The purpose of a no-blame culture is to achieve wider team participation in collaboration and collective management of problems and to take responsibility and accountability for developing problem solutions. It may also be manifested by the PO taking ownership of risk elements that other participants are unable to bear, rather than force them to accept accountability for such risks.

Table 12. Wittgenstein's Family Resemblance Elements for Behavioral Factors for RBP *(Continued)*

Second, they supplement and compliment the usefulness of Table 10 as a means to illustrate the intensity of the relationship *between* the PO/POR and project delivery team and the intensity of relationship *within* the project delivery team. Table 11, Table 12, and Table 13 present each of the elements of the Wittgenstein Family Resemblance model illustrated in Figure 27 in a detailed manner and suggests a way to measure them. When applied to each of the applied RBP forms, these measures present a visualization of similarities and differences in the forms from the perspective of those identified measures. Measures indicated in Table 14 are 'Low' = low, *'Med'* = medium, **'High'** = high, 'blnk' = not applicable, uncertain, or highly variable.

It becomes apparent from our order of collaboration clustering of RMP forms indicated in Figure 25 that this could also help us appreciate similar and different properties of the RBP forms. We added to the four orders of collaboration heading Table 14 both CD and ECI as spanning orders 2 to 4 depending on the extent of ECI involvement. Readers may refer to Figure 2 in Chapter 2 for a visualization of ECI potential involvement and CD which are not an RBP form *per se* but a way of conducting negotiations between PO/POR and main project design/delivery entity up

Processes, routines, and means driving normative practices – Elements 11-16	Subthemes from the transcript analysis (see Appendix 2 for more details)	Suggested to be measured by a five-point Likert scale
11. Consensus decision making refers to the extent to which there is total agreement on a decision made at the project strategic and project operational executive level. High levels may require extensive time for discussion, exploration and testing mental models, and this may be against the interest of speedy decisions and action to counter crises. Following Langley et al.'s. (1995) consensus decision making view, this may involve purposefully leaving the means vague while keeping the aims crystal clear, and agreeing to navigate solutions by agreeing on end states rather than developing detailed plans.	*Cultural drivers* – the discussion in Chapter 4 on culture highlighted that some cultures have high-power asymmetry, where it is expected that individuals at higher levels of a hierarchy make decisions and issue orders to those lower in the hierarchy who must accept and act on those decisions. Other cultural dimensions also impact power asymmetry. Uncertainty avoidance leads people to avoid being committed to a risky decision and a collectivist culture encourages, if not requires, that individuals "go along with the crowd" rather than voice concern or opposition to mooted decisions. Some disciplines and workplace settings demand challenges to assumptions, while others demand obedience and discipline. These cultural drivers enhance or impede genuine consensus decision making. *Enablers of consensus* – organizational, structural, as well as behavioral enablers that facilitate and support consensus decision making and action taking. *Inhibitors of consensus* – organizational, structural, as well as behavioral enablers that inhibit and suppress consensus decision making and action taking.	**Low** consensus decision making is manifested by a highly hierarchical project team leader's leadership style under which power and influence determines how decisions are made and where the expected response is on whether decisions are implemented without question or complaint. It is also manifested by a tendency for a domination of top-down directives being issued as edicts. **High** consensus decision making is manifested by a highly egalitarian and collaborative leadership style of project team leaders. Issues and problems requiring a decision develop out of inclusive knowledge sharing and discussion of perspectives, expected intended and unintended consequences, and implications of decisions. High levels of feedback, good or bad, are sought.
12. Focus on learning and continuous improvement refers to providing a compelling projects-as-learning value proposition and the practice of transforming learning opportunities into continuous improvement. It also implies that emphasis on learning KRAs and KPIs should not only be focused on documenting and publicizing lessons learned from projects, but that project teams should value these KRAs and KPIs to be highly ranked as important PM and project outcome success factors.	*Lessons-learned knowledge transfer* – participants should be aware of the mechanisms that projects offer for opportunities for learning. They should be aware of the PO's learning and continuous improvement preferences and needs, how other team members operate, and how to best collaborate with them to learn from the project and to gain technical, process, or interpersonal knowledge. Some projects are specifically established as learning laboratories for radical new innovation or for more methodical incremental improvement. A focus on effective lessons-learned knowledge transfer needs to be designed into a procurement form to avoid lessons learned becoming lessons forgotten or ignored. *Capacity to adapt to new ideas* – participants need to facilitate continuous improvement by prompting learning-oriented ways of thinking and doing. Knowledge transfer, as discussed in Chapter 4 Table 4, is difficult because knowledge is sticky. People who can make the most from continuous improvement are open to the process of "unlearning" and "relearning." Without this adaptive capacity, lessons learned become lessons ignored, and often context is not considered to wisely consider which lessons should be adopted or adapted depending on the way that the new context emerges. *A culture of skills and learning development* – participants need to be developing a culture of organizational and individual learning to facilitate lessons-learned knowledge transfer and provide the environment in which this can effectively take place. This goes beyond training and development at the technical and process level. It also entails enabling participants to perceive and understand context and situation and interconnectedness of elements into a whole so that cause and effect links can be understood to enable intelligent adaptation of lessons learned.	**Low** focus on learning and continuous improvement is manifested by actors within collaborative arrangements, and a network delivering a project being blind to and failing to grasp the potential competitive advantage of applying presented learning opportunities. **High** focus on learning and continuous improvement manifested by actors within collaborative arrangements and a network delivering a project being alert and aware of opportunities for improvement and being successful in grasping competitive advantage through effectively harvesting lessons learned.
13. Incentive arrangements refer to the pain-sharing and gain-sharing agreement. This refers to how the process was instigated and how it operated. Shared accountability and a desire for innovation require a risk and reward mechanism to create an incentive to excel. At one extreme, all profit margins may be quarantined and pooled and subsequently distributed based on a negotiated and agreed pain and gain sharing formula based on total project performance. Alternatively, profit margins may be based solely on individual team performance.	*Incentive arrangements* – Project participants are incentivized to perform at exceptional levels of performance and there is a risk/reward system in place to encourage this. Central to incentive arrangements is developing systematic encouragement for innovation and for benefits of that innovation to be transferred to project participants and then onto their base organizations. Clear KRAs and KPIs are developed to monitor and measure performance. *Managing tension between innovation and incentivization* – participants and project owners need to manage the tension between continuous improvements that keeps raising the performance benchmark and how that is incentivized. It is important to balance providing sufficient incentive and reward for improvement, while avoiding incentive targets being either too easy or too hard, as this may undermine continuous improvement. This also brings in issues about balancing innovation incentivized through a competitive dialogue approach at the front-end of a project before contracts are let, with achieving innovation and improvement by encouraging innovation and continuous improvement progressively throughout the project duration.	**Low** levels of incentivization is manifested by little emphasis being placed upon encouraging parties to agree to place potential profit and gain/pain in a risk/reward arrangement subject to a whole-of-project outcome performance. KRAs and KPIs are absent or rudimentary. **High** levels of incentivization is manifested by much emphasis being placed upon encourage parties to agree to place potential profit and gain/pain in a risk/reward arrangement that is subject to a whole-of-project outcome performance. KRAs and KPIs are well developed, provide stretch and challenge and are sophisticated in their understanding of the project context.

Table 13. Wittgenstein's Family Resemblance Elements for Processes, Routines and Means for RBP *(Continued)*

Processes, routines, and means driving normative practices – Elements 11-16	Subthemes from the transcript analysis (see Appendix 2 for more details)	Suggested to be measured by a five-point Likert scale
14. Pragmatic learning-in-action refers to the active gathering of value through teams collaborating with the strategic aim to learn, and to gain competitive advantage through collective opportunities to learn and adapt. It is about team leaders and members seeing the project as a learning experience, with acceptance that both experimental success and failure requires discussion and analysis. Often, unexpected opportunities arise out of failed experiments through assumptions being re-framed that lead to promising benefits in other contexts.	*Action-learning* – participants as individuals, but more so in groups, undertake action-learning in a number of ways. These range from simply trying out things and experimenting to undertaking complicated modeling and simulation exercises. These activities provide the mechanisms to gain knowledge from action. It remains critical that mechanisms should be in place to capture and make usable, experience, and knowledge gained from action-learning initiatives. *Coaching and mentoring* – another form of pragmatic learning is through coaching and mentoring. This is where experience and insights are shared in a formalized manner through one-on-one interaction between project participants and "wiser" or at least more experienced people who can help their coachees/-mentees to be able to contextualize learning, to refine it through dialogue, and to add value through that knowledge by sharing stories making critical comparisons and exploring meaning and making sense out of that learning.	*Low* pragmatic learning-in-action is manifested by actors within a network delivering a project to fail to translate learning opportunities into actual benefits and competitive action. Failed experiments are punished. *High* pragmatic learning-in-action is manifested by actors within a network delivering a project capitalizing on learning opportunities to achieve competitive action. This can be also assessed by the weight that these actors place on the value of experimentation as a way to see issues and solutions in a new light. Failed experiments are valued for their intellectual stimulation in discovering, for example, a better understanding of cause-effect loops.
15. Transparency and open book processes, routines and practices refer to project participants agreeing to be audited and fully open to scrutiny. Actors within the project network would have confidence that they can trust those inspecting their books not to take advantage of that access and information, and those people doing the audits, due diligence, and inspections must be capable and effective enough to understand the implication of what they inspect. Total transparency and accountability is necessary where the project is undertaken on a cost-plus basis, where the project owner is funding all direct, administrative and management costs. The extent of transparency and accountability is a trade-off between the extent to which the PO plays a "hands-on" or "hands-off" role. There is a fine balance needed between expenditure on direct administrative and management costs and how processes reinforce a trust-but-verify approach.	*Transparency* – the extent to which project participants agree to be fully open about their cost structures, their decision-making process, and their project delivery processes. *Accountability* – the extent to which project participants agree to be fully open to scrutiny, allowing authorized project owner representatives to audit and inspect books, processes, and decision-making rationale.	*Low* transparency and open-book approaches to project delivery intensely protect the security of organizations and individuals to gain access to information about cost structures or the basis of project plans. It is often exemplified by the code words "commercial in confidence." It seeks to hide both good and bad news, but this often results in mistrust that undermines collaboration and opportunities for constructive change. *High* transparency and open-book approaches to project delivery present opportunities for generating trust by clients and other parties that may access that information. It is a confronting notion that many organizations cannot face. It requires the project owner's authorized probity auditors to have free access to their financial books. Thus, confidence in ethical and legal business conduct is necessary to accept this challenge.

Table 13.   Wittgenstein's Family Resemblance Elements for Processes, Routines and Means for RBP *(Continued)*

Processes, routines, and means driving normative practices – Elements 11-16	Subthemes from the transcript analysis (see Appendix 2 for more details)	Suggested to be measured by a five-point Likert scale
16. Mutual dependence and accountability refers to collaboration in projects requiring participants to not only recognize their interdependency but to also honestly respond to a sink-or-swim-together workplace culture when communicating. Governance systems may both support and enhance individual team responsibility and accountability, or alternatively they may inhibit approaches to cross-team collaboration.	*Characteristics of mutual dependency* – various forms of RBP have specific unique characteristics that have a focus on mutual team dependency where they sink or swim together. Teams may or may not perceive themselves to become a temporary single team entity with perceptions about how participants perceive the workplace supports or inhibits a unified team approach to managing the project. *Enhancing enablers of mutual dependency* – participants seek to actively leverage processes, routines, and means to facilitate and sustain collaboration. *Countering inhibitors to mutual dependency* – participants seek to actively counter processes, routines, and means that inhibit and undermine collaboration.	*Low* mutual dependence and accountability refers to an inability or lack of desire to acknowledge the potential value of team interdependence and accountability. Participants follow individualistic paths, possibly at the expense of others, and/or do not support a sink-or-swim-together workplace culture, or they actively undermine that culture. *High* mutual dependence and accountability refers to an ability and keen desire to acknowledge team inter-dependence and accountability in ways that build inter-team trust and commitment through actively enhancing a sink-or-swim-together workplace culture, and to actively counter any actions that may inhibit this culture.

Table 13. Wittgenstein's Family Resemblance Elements for Processes, Routines and Means for RBP *(Continued)*

to the point of tender submission. We include CD in our book, as it is a peculiarly mainland European concept but it is highly relevant to any study of RBP.

We summarize Table 14 in light of our clustering these RBP forms and the rationale that helps explain differences and similarities in Table 15.

Table 14, together with models illustrated in Figure 25, Figure 27, and Figure 28 present the means to suggest and recommend KSAE required for effective performance within the RBP approach. Note that ECI activities are mainly taken prior to and during the tender stage, thus element ratings need to be assessed on the interaction of POR, design team members, and any of the supply chain invited to participate prior to project tender and award. CD negotiations occur at tender through to project delivery decision.

Details of Collaborative Arrangements Skills

Using our analysis of the collaborative forms discussed in Chapter 2 and our categorization illustrated in Figure 25, Figure 26, Figure 27, and Figure 28, we now focus on presenting summary KSAE findings. We only consider procurement forms that require an intense level of collaboration and building sustainable relationships in this book, therefore, we will not be discussing traditional, partially integrated procurement forms, or consortia any further. This despite, as stated in the Chapter 2 section on forms of project procurement, the fact that all procurement forms require building a relationship because projects tend to be long (often many years) and are fraught with uncertainty, so they are not suited to a purely transactional approach.

Collyer (Collyer, 2013; Collyer & Warren, 2009; Collyer, Warren, Hemsley, & Stevens, 2010) studied dynamism in PM, drawing upon interviews, focus groups, and cases from a broad range of complex project types including disaster recovery, space exploration, construction, venture capital, documentary TV/film, and IT. His study spans an interesting range of project experiences and provides one way in which to assess the KSAE required of project teams and individuals. We also arrive at a useful way to address the need for KSAE for various RBP forms through combining ideas proposed about the impact of project dynamism and the environment changing a project and its speed, together with the Cynefin Framework (Kurtz & Snowden, 2003; Snowden, 2002; Snowden & Boone, 2007) discussed in Chapter 3.

Based on our analysis of our study's participant transcripts, reflection upon prior and parallel research in this area that we undertook (see Appendix 1, Table A1 and Table A2 in Section 2), and the literature, we identify four sets

Collaboration Order		1st Order			2nd Order				3rd Order			4th Order	2nd > 4th Order	
RBP Form > Wittgenstein element		D&C	MC	JV	FA	Project Partnering	Strategic Partnering	BOOT PPP/PFI	SCM Normal	DC/P	IPD	Alliancing PA/SA/DA	CD	ECI
Platform	Motivation and context	Med	Med	Med	High	High	High	Med/High	Med	High	High	High		
	Joint governance structure	Low	Low	Med	Med	Med	Med	High	Med	High	Med/High	High		
	Integrated risk mitigation and insurance	Low	Low	Low	Med	Med	Med	Med	Low	High	High	High		
	Joint communication BIM, etc.	Med/High	High	High	Med/High	Med/High	High	High		High	High	High		
	Substantial co-location	Med/High	High	High	Med/High	Med/High	High	High		High	High	High		
Behavior	Authentic leadership				Med/High	Med/High	Med/High			High	High	High	Med/High	
	Trust-control balance		Low/Med	Med/High	Med/High	Med/High	High	Med/High	Low/Med	Med/High	High	High	Med/High	
	Commitment to innovate		Med/High	Med/High	High	High	High	Med/High	Med/High	High	High	High	High	High
	Common best-for-project mindset/culture		High	Med/High	High	Med/High	High	Med/High		High	High	High	High Med/	High
Process	No-blame culture	Low			Med/High	Med/High	Med/High	Med	Low	High	High	High		Med/High
	Consensus decision making	Low	Med	Med	Med/High	Med	Med/High	Med	Low	Med/High	High	High		Med/High
	Incentivization	Low	Low	Low	Med	Med	Med/High	Med/High	Low	High	High	High		
	Focus on learning and continuous improvement	Med/High	Med/High	Med/High	High	Med/High	Med/High	Med/High	Med/High	High	High	High	High	High
	Pragmatic learning-in-action	Med/High	Med/High	Med/High	High	Med/High	Med/High	Med/High	Med/High	High	High	High		High
	Transparency and open-book	Low	Med/High		High	Low/Med	Med/High	Low/Med		High		High		High
	Mutual dependence and accountability	Med	High	Med/High	High	Med/High	High	Med/High	Med/High	High	High	High		High

Table 14.   RBP Forms Mapped to Wittgenstein Model Element Characteristic Measures

of KSAE that are required in varying intensity across the board in RBP. These are technical, PM, business solution, and relational. These are explained more fully below.

Technical KSAE

Technical skills are applied across the spectrum of first to fourth order collaboration in projects, and it is to be expected that high levels of technical skills are required for all procurement forms, including the range of RBP forms that this book focuses upon. Discussion of procurement forms, beginning at the section headed "Focus on Integrated Design and Delivery Procurement Arrangements – Emphasizing Planning and Control" and ending at the Section "Beyond the Iron Triangle Performance Implications" presented in Chapter 2 are highly relevant here. Figure 21 and Table 6 are also particularly relevant. The discussion on complexity in Chapter 3, and in particular Figure 11, informs this section on required KSAE for RBP forms.

RBP Cluster	Main Focus is on:	Within-Cluster Major Differences and Similarities
1st Order Collaboration Modes D&C, MC, and JV *Dominant efficiency and flexibility logic*	The PO/POR establishing an RBP form that adopts a dominant efficiency logic of the individual teams. Collaboration is about creating flexibility. D&C places a single entity responsible for coordination of design and construction to more efficiently translate design into delivery led by a single team leader. MC allows flexibility in packaging main chunks of the work under several contract packages that the MC entity coordinates and manages as an agent to the POR. The way that these are packaged is flexible and efficiency oriented. JVs are groups of contractors (two or more) that combine to offer their specialized resources to maximize project delivery efficiency of the design or delivery or both design and delivery within a single entity to be managed by the POR.	**Similarities:** The focus is on efficiently bringing together the necessary resources to deliver the project. D&C assumes that by integrating the design and delivery lead team that knowledge transfer between the designers and the lead delivery team results in more buildable solutions. MC highlights efficient packaging of the work that can be tendered and let in a flexible manner in terms of timing (fast-tracked) or procurement form (D&C packages, cost reimbursable, fixed price, FA, etc.). A JV has a focus on efficiency through drawing together partners with specific resources and competencies that they can excel at to combine to offer more than they could as individual entities. **Differences:** D&C includes both design and delivery in one package, while for JV, the JV is a single project delivery entity, and for MC, the MC manages a number of separate work package delivery entities that are contractually linked to the PO. The nature of, and need for, POR involvement and relationship with delivery entity varies. For a D&C, the POR deals with one project delivery entity for both design and delivery. For MC and JV, the design and delivery roles are separate. An MC handles the whole project delivery in a pragmatic way using a number of work packages, and is accountable to the POR, and the work package entities have direct contractual accountability to the POR but are accountable for coordination and management control to the MC. For a JV, the JV forms an entity comprised of partners with a stake and obligations that is governed by the JV agreement/contract and is accountable to the POR for project delivery but not project design.
2nd Order Collaboration Modes FA, Partnering (project and strategic), BOOT family PPP/PFI *Dominant process logic for fairness in behaviors and integrated and aligned common purpose*	There is a greater and more explicit focus on collaboration within this cluster, with an emphasis on fairness of treatment of parties and explicit common purpose, often with an agreed project charter. FA have negotiated long-term agreed conditions, protocols for coordination, communication, monitoring and control, and remuneration. Partnering forms have agreed-upon protocols for inter-team working behaviors and responsibilities. The BOOT/PPP/PFI modes integrate entire project delivery, operational, and financing teams, and so the special-purpose vehicle for the project defines the project purpose and alignment of parties within that entity to achieve the purpose.	**Similarities:** There is close collaboration among elements of the supply chain in delivering a project. The collaborative and relational arrangements are explicit and negotiated before project delivery to minimize misunderstanding and negotiation transaction cost. There is an emphasis on fairness in the way that parties can expect to be treated to avoid the transaction cost of conflict and to engender great commitment. FA and partnering alliances agree long-term conditions and protocols to facilitate working together over multiple projects for the same PO and to reduce transaction costs in tendering for projects. BOOT family forms of RBP integrate teams and companies into a special-purpose vehicle to design and deliver the project solution in a way to which each constituent team aligns its objectives. **Differences:** FA and partnering aligns many individual entities through a culture of fair processes and united vision through a project charter. The BOOT family and PPP/PFI entity projects undertake this alignment internally and present a single special-purpose vehicle (SPV) to design, deliver, and operate the facility being delivered. The SPV becomes the PO until that ownership is handed back to the client that commissioned the SPV through the terms of its concession to operate.
3rd Order Collaboration Modes SCM, IPD, DC/P *Dominant logic for common platforms*	These extend the focus applied in 1st and 2nd order modes with the addition of greater intensity of coordination and alignment and use of common platforms. SCM reduces the numbers of sub-contractors and groups them into tiers (1st, 2nd, etc.) that take responsibility for project delivery chunks. The T5 SCM mode took this concept further into deeper integration using a range of common platform elements and including features of the 3rd order of collaboration. IDP uses aspects of SCM developed and evolved from Lean production principles combined with relational behavior and integration principles. DC/P drives deeper into collaboration beyond the 1st tier main contractor participants.	**Similarities:** There is a high level of focus on collaboration through common platforms. Both SCM, in its normal and more intensive form such as the T5 Agreement, and IDP stress use of shared and common approaches and systems. In the case of SCM, there is a rationalization of subcontractors into elemental tiers that take control and responsibility for a common and joint delivery of the project based on logical subsystems of the whole project as an integrated system, common tools, processes, and understanding shape an integration culture focused on the delivery of the subsystems. IDP and DC/P integrates the design team and delivery team via agreed protocols and incentives. **Differences:** SCM is highly delivery focused and while it may take responsibility for elements of design this is more of an operational rather than conceptual design. IDP is more integrative of the design and delivery teams as separate but non-contractually linked entities (such as that found in BOOT/PPP/PFI). IDP moves toward project pain-share and gain-share incentives in their contracts with the PO. There may also be a no-litigation clause in operation and a requirement for close collaboration and agreement on strategic decisions. This contrasts with normal SCM but not with the T5 Agreement which shares more similarities with IDP. DC/P moves further down the supply chain to encourage collaboration and innovation.

Table 15. Major RBP Clusters Similarities and Differences by Order of Collaboration *(Continued)*

RBP Cluster	Main Focus is on:	Within-Cluster Major Differences and Similarities
4th Order Collaboration Modes Project alliancing forms PA/SA/DA *Dominant logic of all parties being committed to all share pain/gain for project incentives as a group rather than individually.*	This form takes the preceding focus on collaboration and common platforms to a higher level and introduces specific explicit and contracted commercial and behavioral elements with a sink-or-swim-together mentality. The defining difference between alliancing and IPD and the T5 Agreement, which are the closest RBP forms to alliancing, is the commitment level of joint and several accountability. There is a specific no-litigation and unanimous-agreement behavioral contract clause to ensure collaboration as a single team, and there is a project single collective insurance policy for the project to ensure collective responsibility and accountability.	**Similarities:** Project, service, and design alliances all share the same triple legs of a contract. They each have a commercial leg of the contract to specify how the cost of direct project resource costs will be reimbursed and what management fee will be placed at risk to agreed performance criteria, and the detail specification of KRAs and KPIs. They have an incentive contract that specifies the pain-sharing and gain-sharing arrangements and conditions. Finally, they have a specific behavioral contract that defines the collaboration form to be expected. **Differences:** A DA takes place before a project will be delivered, and its purpose is to establish the project design and delivery procurement strategy. A project alliance takes place across design, usually after a high-level conceptual design has been agreed upon by the PO as the project outcome objective, through the delivery of a project. An SA is an alliance that crosses the boundaries of multiple projects within a program or portfolio to encompass operation and maintenance, renewal, and capital investment.
CD *Moves beyond a purely efficiency logic to that evident in 2nd to 4th forms in this table*	Competitive dialogue as noted earlier is a collaborative competitive discussion that takes place between a PO/POR and a potential project delivery team to fully understand the scope, possibilities, and limitations of the project brief to provide a proposal that may end up as either a traditional bid or any of the RBP forms indicated in this table.	
ECI *Moves beyond a purely efficiency logic to that evident in 1st to 4th forms in this table*	ECI as illustrated in Figure 2 in Chapter 2 can involve a range of phases of the project with collaboration within MC, FAs to alliancing. It is about providing input on the feasibility of design through practicality of project delivery as an equal party within the project team.	

Table 15. Major RBP Clusters Similarities and Differences by Order of Collaboration *(Continued)*

For many projects, and in particular construction projects, much of the technical task is translating a PO/POR brief into a feasible design solution that is usually delivered in the form of a product. In the case of BOOT/PPP/PFI, however, it is a service that is offered via a concession agreement awarded to a special-purpose vehicle to take that brief and deliver the service. Cognitive and communication skill elements are needed to understand the brief, question and clarify assumptions, translate responses into plans (including visualization and other graphical tools), and then translate a plan into action to deliver the required project outcome. Planning (the design) and doing (delivering) activities require technical KSAE in order to:

1. Understand the objectives and considering opportunities, constraints, and making appropriate decisions to take action based on what is technically feasible.
2. Access and marshaling the necessary resources, tools, and processes to enable technically feasible solutions to be proposed that may be validated and tested.
3. Judge which technical rules, routines, processes, and approaches might impact timing and feasibility of their use.

As Collyer (2013, Table 8.10) has argued, there is a clear set of different application of skills within a static as opposed to dynamic environment. For example, in a static environment, the world is relatively straightforward to predict, whereas in a dynamic environment, the world is difficult to predict. This means that planning and action need a focus on methodical, measured, and consistent approach in the static situation, but agility, ambidexterity, flexibility, and adaptability are needed in volatile and dynamic environments. Figure 29 illustrates a typical project decision-making situation.

Numerous options will present themselves or be presented for consideration from the briefing stage through the design and delivery stages on all projects. As illustrated in Figure 29, there will be a period of instability in knowing what to do, when and how to do it, as various options unfold, emerge, and are considered. Collaboration results in a

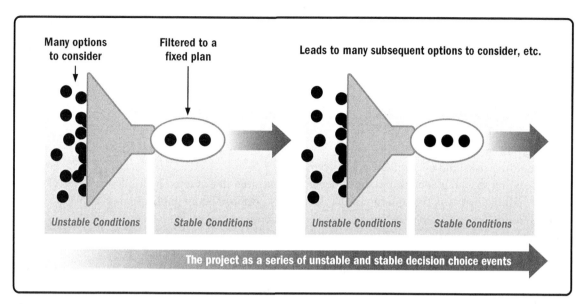

Figure 29. Project Decision Making in Uncertainty

filtering process that explores, tests, and examines alternatives so that a plan that is fixed or frozen can be adopted, and this produces a period of stable conditions when the task direction is clear. The accomplishment and progress of the plan leads to a new situation, such as facing the next part of the project to be addressed, or the need for rework, or the "plan" is found to be no longer functional. The project navigates through a series of islands of stable conditions within a sea of unstable conditions.

Most projects, particularly engineering infrastructure projects, take a long time to develop and deliver and much can change during that time. It is for this reason that such projects are often delivered with aspects, closest to the delivery horizon, having details finalized and frozen during the stable conditions indicated in Figure 29 to allow delivery of those portions, acknowledging that any subsequent changes about what needs to be delivered will result in rework and wastage. This is the price of being flexible to change. However, much of the broad strategy planning can be left with options for refinement and/or change open on these kinds of projects until a decision has to be made. Technical skills that help make sound decisions about when to freeze or keep options open is an important characteristic of the purely technical side of delivering projects. _Managing this tension on purely technical grounds_ is one dimension of the skills required of these types of projects. This can be compared to dynamic situations in which goals and objectives, methods and approaches, politics and agendas may constantly change and fluctuate quite quickly.

Summarizing in simple terms what is meant by **technical KSAE**, we can state that:

- It is about knowing in a practical and pragmatic sense *what* works, *why* it works, *how* it works in various contexts, and *how* it impacts upon other parts of a system, and *where* it can be applied (i.e., in what circumstances, for what purpose), and *when* it should be adopted (timing in relation to impact on other parts of a system).
- Knowledge is not just about what is known. It is also knowledge about what is unknown but knowable (triggering a need to collaborate with others who may know what is unknown), and be aware of what is unknown but is currently unknowable (a form of sixth-sense alertness to unlikely or unusual possibilities).
- Knowledge is both explicit (gained through qualification, study, and accreditation) and tacit (gained through experience, experimentation, and application in a reflective manner).
- Required attributes relate to being pragmatic about the context and having enough sensitivity to understand technical interface issues associated with the technology.
- Experience is not limited to number of years' exposure but is also qualitative in nature in terms of the quality of supervision and mentoring, as well as reflection that took place to position experience firmly within its context.

Project Management KSAE

We tend to associate PM KSAE with aspects of planning and control, coordination, and working with people in teams when delivering projects.

PM KSAE relating to project work can be summarized as including but not being limited to:

- Understanding and analyzing the project context and situation;
- Knowing what tasks/processes can be done;
- Knowing how tasks/processes can be done;
- Understanding risks and consequences involved;
- Understanding interconnections and dependencies about what needs to be done;
- Understanding time, cost, and quality (i.e., in general – performance – implications);
- Understanding and exercising the extent, degree, and depth of room to maneuver;
- Understanding and exercising the optimum or feasible level of planning, monitoring and control to exercise within the environmental context;
- Coordinating activities with other project teams to synergize and ensure the desired outcome is achieved;
- Collaborating with others with and between teams to gather information and marshal knowledge to make valid sensible decisions and to recover from unexpected setbacks; and
- Reflecting upon and learning from experience of both procedural PM aspects and the human interaction aspects, including stakeholders who may have little direct involvement with the project.

1 - Planning and control: Many D&C projects require early freezing of design and planning with acceptance by the PO/POR of the proposed solution—variation of the D&C package after that freezing process results in negotiations about contract variations often requiring extra money, time, and resources. Much energy is expended during these negotiations in making a case, defending a case, and deciding upon "fair" compensation. While gains and losses may be experienced in this process, the managerial energy expended detracts from "getting on with the job." The fiduciary duty of both the PO/POR and project delivery entity is to maximize their advantage and to compromise only to gain longer-term benefit, whether that be in terms of reputation or remuneration.

MC involves high-level coordination and system integration in the same way that D&C does, and JVs require parties to be complementary in their combined KSAEs. FAs partnering and BOOT/PPP/PFI as well as SCM in both "normal" and T5 contexts, together with alliancing, require technical skills with varying emphasis. All these forms require sophisticated PM planning KSAE so that the teams have sufficient information and knowledge about salient issues relating to the way systems can be seen as interrelated components and subsystems. Knowledge about how elements interact and what options exist for their assembly and configuration is vital, as are resource implications, safety, quality of the outcome, and impact upon stakeholders on the way that they are assembled or configured.

Managing risk can be included in this aspect of planning and control. Plans need to take into account risk factors to be viable and pragmatic. The rationale for risk mitigation shapes the procurement choice. For example, D&C draws the design and delivery team under one team leader to maximize design/delivery interface but in a way that the PO/POR hands over most of the responsibility and accountability to that team and take an oversight role. MC (as with ECI) tends to allow the PO/POR to retain accountability and responsibility. With the MC entity, the work packages may be let and managed by the MC as agent to allow the PO/POR great influence and responsibility, and it may also be about timing and bundling up of work packages to suit the project context. ECI usually is similar to MC in that the ECI entity provides valuable advice and knowledge and may or may not be responsible for PM in the form of MC (see Figure 2). In a JV situation, the parties in the JV supply specialized resources and expertise and act in the way specified for planning and control and to assume risk as dictated by the contract form. BOOT/PPP/PFI projects assume all risk and also consider operational risk of the completed project as part of any concession agreement. Partnering, SCM, IDP, and alliancing involves close collaboration, information and knowledge sharing to identify and apportion risk. The CD process involves high level of KSAE in risk aspects to be able to intelligently and constructively identify risk items and negotiate with the PO/POR the risk assumption and mitigation measures that provides best value for money (Hoezen, 2012; Hoezen et al., 2012a).

2 – Collaboration and coordination is necessary to share insights and consolidate technical and PM project expertise for the project delivery entity. Various orders of PM collaboration assume the legitimacy of priority of the other party's consideration quite differently. There needs to be a governance structure (as explained earlier in Chapter 3, and parties need to consider trust and commitment as outlined in Chapter 4). Collaboration is seen as an enabler to reduce transaction costs by minimizing waste bound up in conflict resolution and a narrow self-referential agenda for action.

Collaboration is needed for project teams to gather relevant, salient, and timely information for planning and decision making. Orders of collaboration (refer to Figure 25) suggest varying levels of interaction. First-order collaboration is basically about getting on with the job, the tasks at hand. Collaboration is focused upon teams in the immediate vicinity resolving any issues, whether that is a design problem, preparing plans, resolving translating design into delivery, etc., so there is little collaboration outside those immediately involved. Second-order collaboration involves first agreeing protocols through a FA, partnering agreement, or BOOT/PPP/PFI submission, for example. The terms of those arrangements guide the level and intensity of interaction. The influence of senior management within the organizations but not specifically engaged in the project is highly relevant to organizations engaged in first- and second-order collaboration. D&C, MC, and JV will have incentives to perform well in a project, but this is strictly tempered by the priorities, goals, and aims of the base organization. Naturally they will wish to exercise a professional attitude and approach, but commercial pressures may turn their attention elsewhere unless the procurement agreement has incentives (pain-share/gain-share) that focus their attention more on the project than their other business activities. Similarly, third-order collaboration forms (SCM and IPD) are highly process influenced and common-platform influenced. Collaboration and coordination is also governed and influenced by enabling platforms such as being co-located, sharing a common IT platform, having a common insurance that may require specific collaboration conditions, and the project governance arrangements. For alliancing, the collaboration requirements are clearly spelled out in the alliance agreement and reinforced through the project team selection process and associated KRAs and KPIs.

KSAEs for collaboration and the type types of skill, attribute, etc., was illustrated in Table 6 in detail for project alliances but are also relevant to other orders of collaboration to a varying extent. Table 16 summarizes in simple terms how **PM KSAE** impacts upon the management of projects.

Business Solutions KSAE

These KSAE relate to the business solution focus on a project. Failure of IT projects due to a lack of business knowledge or consideration was identified as a serious flaw in many study reports (for example, Standish, 2003) where a priority on technical excellence has overwhelmed that of delivering a solution that meets the business need. This is particularly true of the need to deliver new products to market before competitors (Collyer et al., 2010; Lindkvist, Söderlund, & Tell, 1998). Further, business does not just mean making a financial return because it also (and in meta-terms) means fulfilling the rationale or need: the business of a hospital is health or a school education, etc.(Artto & Wikström, 2005).

Projects should be based on developing a solution to a particular need (Office of Government Commerce, 2007a; 2007b; Victorian Auditor-General's Office, 2008). Project leaders need to maintain a focus on why the project was sanctioned and approved in the first place. The business case is usually the fundamental document that outlines the rationale for the project and provides insights or specific identification of underlying assumptions and cost/benefit ratio, and this document forms the basis for approval through a gateway system to ensure that the project is a valid solution to a clearly identified problem or situation (Office of Government Commerce, 2007a; 2007b).

The PO/POR should make the vision, aims and objectives of a project crystal clear so that all parties involved know what they should be delivering, its importance, and how their efforts can contribute to a successful outcome (Christenson & Walker, 2003). The project leader and all project team leaders should ensure that the business outcome and its importance is clearly in each team member's mind so that they can visualize their role in the outcome, and that this motivates them to maximize their contribution. It is also important for the business solution to be clearly understood when team members interpret decisions made and what exactly they should be doing. Langley et al. 1995 make the interesting observation that decisions may be sequential and logical, but more often are anarchic with the impetus being driven by reaction to external events or as an iterative sequence. They also note that many complex decisions are iterative, so it is not easy to be clear when a decision was made or if it was remade many times. There are

Characteristic – Highest Focus Levels	Notes on RBP Application
Emphasis on planning and control with high levels of freezing plans	**D&C, MC, JV** – plan and freeze as many "facts" as possible for those aspects that are well known
Role of coordination to fine-tune details	Coordinate to manage interfaces to optimize the plan
Role of collaboration to learn more, converting known-unknown to known	Collaboration to access knowledge, mainly for monitoring and fine-tuning plans
Belief in the validity of "the plan"	Applying skills and expertise to create greater certainty and reliability of a plan
Emphasis on planning and control with high levels of protocol definition, templates with agreed expectations for responsibilities, accountabilities, remuneration, and incentives	**FA, partnering, SCM, IPD DC/P and Alliancing** – planning and control to institutionalize interaction, routines, learning, and a shared knowledge space, and as a means to understand rationale and processes for assigned roles responsibilities and accountabilities
Role of coordination to facilitate collaboration and align objectives, sketch out broad plans, and fine-tune short-term detailed plans	Coordination to manage mutual adjustment, information sharing, risk appropriation, assignment of responsibility and accountability
Role of collaboration to cope with the unexpected, share insights, help resolve unknown-unknown "surprises" toward known-unknowns that can be resolved with more information, knowledge, or time, and to resolve toward known-knowns	Collaboration is the lubricant that allows knowledge and information transfer, and is the glue that binds teams together in joint decision making about issues that impact them
Belief in the validity of "a flexible agreed plan"	Applying skills and expertise to create greater flexibility and guidance for a plan and resilience to respond to the unexpected

Table 16.   PM KSAE Summary of Emphasis by RBP Approach

types of projects where the business case cannot be clearly made or approved because the dynamics of the context changes so radically and frequently that it is difficult to assign identity to a particular decision (i.e., why did decision X subsequently reappear as Y or Z?). Additionally, strategy and decision making is a highly socially interpretive process, and according to Denis et al. (2007, p. 197) ". . .strategy is fabricated by situated and local practices of strategizing using strategic tools and models which are mobilized through tacit and collective knowledge regarding the future of the enterprise." This may be why decisions appear time and again in morphed guises as context and stakeholder pressures change and supply leverage. Having strong business KSAE is important in volatile situations and useful in more stable situations as well to better understand the purpose and *raison d'être* for a project.

In complex and dynamic contexts, the project leader needs to be mindful of not only the project sanction decision and what assumptions, knowledge, and circumstances that it was based upon, but they also need to interpret signals about decisions, non-decisions or partial decisions to judge how to respond. This is why collaboration is essential for complex projects because the project leader needs multiple perspectives with which to triangulate and make sense of the meaning of situations so that appropriate and effective action follows (even if that is inaction in a wait-and-see manner).

Other business KSAE factors come into play for the more intensively collaborative project forms. If we focus on 3rd and 4th order collaboration forms such as T5, IPD, and Alliancing, we see that stakeholder engagement is a vital characteristic. Obvious stakeholders include those that are project-internal such as the supply chain and the many project teams that are brought together to design and deliver a project. Less-obvious stakeholders may be project-external and their influence may have severe impact upon gaining permits, permissions, commitment to the project, and other emotional drivers such as the example of intensive partnering that was required in Sweden for a major rebuild of power transmission lines and facilities over a several-year project (or program of projects) as described by Jacobsson (2011) in his study. In this and other studies of stakeholder management (Aaltonen, 2010; Bourne, 2005; 2011b), it becomes clear that stakeholder management is a critical skill. This skill is not exploitation-focused but focused through collaboration to co-discovery and co-calibration of the project meaning and purpose.

PM politics is often considered as a negative aspect of management that should not be discussed. It has been until recently taboo. However, Machiavelli, one of the most famous early writers on politics and management (Machiavelli & Bull, 1961), had many useful lessons that he imparted that are useful for project managers, and many of these are presented by Lisch (2012). From this seminal source, and from literature on the concept of the value proposition

(Anderson et al., 2006), we see that political agenda are also bound up with what is considered important by the person "being political." Having political skills is seen by Pinto (2000) and others (Bourne, 2005; Crawford & Da Ros, 2002; Geraldi & Adlbrecht, 2007) as being critical and as Peled (2000, p. 28) argues, ". . .there are several steps senior managers can take to improve the political skills of their project leaders. They can provide leaders with courses on the political aspects of project management such as influence, negotiation, and cooperation. They can assign politically skilled mentors to tutor novice project leaders. They can also balance the management skills of a project team. For example, if the designated project leader is technologically strong, the organization can assign to him an analyst whose strength lies in organizational politics."

Several of the attributes identified by Walker and Lloyd-Walker (2011a) and illustrated in Table 6 includes being a reflective systems thinker (Attribute 4, Table 6) to understand and evaluate the context, and to frame strategies that appeals to the value proposition of influential and powerful constituencies while guiding the agenda and action toward fulfilling the project goals and to be sufficiently appreciative (attribute 6, Table 6), with sufficient emotional intelligence to take the perspective of others (Parker et al., 2008). These may be considered as political skills.

Summarizing in simple terms, we can state that **business KSAE** is about:

- Knowing in a practical and pragmatic sense *what* the vision and purpose of the project is so that project managers can focus on ensuring that what needs to get done, is done rather than allowing the project to drift into being what may be technically or aesthetically excellent but fails to deliver what was needed.
- Understanding the business case and rationale in that above context.
- Having sound stakeholder (internal and external) engagement and management abilities beyond "managing through manipulation," but managing through co-calibration of the project outcome.
- Having sufficient political ability to understand the political context and to be able to engage in political activity that is project-centered rather than self-centered so that counterproductive political moves can be deflected, and that politics is used in a positive and fair way to guide and shape the direction in which the project is designed and delivered.
- Reflecting upon and learning from experience gained from a variety of business contexts and demands.

Relational KSAE

We have argued that projects that require an RBP approach tend to be complex and often have an element, if not core feature, of services and product delivery. Remington (2011) stresses the need for high-level relational skills for complex projects, with many examples that she illustrates from an extensive study undertaken on leaders of complex projects in a number of business sectors. And Snowden and Boone (2007) provide concrete advice on leadership and management styles appropriate to projects of varying complexity that were characterized using the Cynefin Framework that we have discussed earlier in this book. Crawford and Pollack (2004, p. 647) argue that "soft methods acknowledge any goal ambiguity, focusing on learning, exploration and problem definition. [. . .] The emphasis then becomes one of negotiation, debate and accommodation." This shifts the emphasis of PM from an iron triangle view of time/cost/quality performance to a far greater scope and depth requiring these "soft skills" and attributes. We illustrate specific relational skills in Figure 21 and in our analysis from our AAA study on profiling excellence in the management of alliance projects (Walker & Lloyd-Walker, 2011c, p. 56–62). These specific KSAEs are provided and explained within the context of PA leadership excellence in Table 6.

These skills form a subset of those KSAE required of the behavioral factors of the Wittgenstein Family Resemblance Figure 27 (factors 5-9) explained in Table 12. They are essential to be able to effectively engage in the processes, routines, and means illustrated as drivers 10-14 in Figure 27 and explained in detail in Table 13. Table 14 illustrates the levels of application of these KSAE across the RBP spectrum. Of particular saliency to focus a discussion on here is that while most if not all of these KSAEs are *useful* across the RBP spectrum, as generally facilitating efficiency through collaborated and coordinated effort, a number of these are *essential* to the higher collaboration forms such as T5 and IDP in the 3rd order RBP forms and for alliancing in the 4th order RBP form.

In all our previous research, in most of the literature cited in this book, and research undertaken for the PMI to write this book, and for a parallel study that we are engaged in as part of an Australian Research Council grant, the terms "trust" and "leadership" are frequently used. It is frustrating that practitioners often loosely use these terms as if everyone shared the meaning of these words and that these terms are fully understood by everyone. We see terms such as "politics" and "being political" as equally prevalent in being loosely used but not explained. When we probed those we interviewed for the meaning of "politics" and "being political," we find that "trust and leadership" is the Holy Grail of PM in general and RBP in particular. We add a further term here, *commitment to innovate*, because our analysis of interviews conducted with academic experts as well as reflective practitioners as part of this study highlighted innovation as a defining priority in 3rd and 4th order RBP forms.

Without laboring points made throughout this book about the need for projects to be viewed as experimental sites of new knowledge generation, it is important to understand that when we study Table 14, for example, that the more collaborative the environment, the more that innovation is evident. We rated FA, project and strategic partnering, T5, IDP, and alliancing as "High" on commitment to innovate. Organizations that engage in FAs generally need to provide proof and demonstrated innovation in their workplace culture and leadership to retain their place in an FA. Innovation commitment is often built into partnering charters and also is the case with the FA. Strategic partnering also usually requires that partners have a continuous improvement demonstrated track record. IPD and T5 as well as alliancing forms required evidence of innovation to exceed BAU levels of performance. Other RBP forms value and appreciate a commitment to innovation, but not as prominently as those indicated in Table 14 to require high commitment to innovate.

To summarize this discussion of **relational KSAE**, we can state the following:

1. **Trust** lies at the core of relationships and, as illustrated in Figure 13, trust is composed of several core constructs. It is essential for people and institutions to have the ability (individual, group, and institutional), benevolence, and authenticity to perform in a trustworthy manner and do what was promised and/or committed. Trust can be monitored-through governance systems that have accountability and responsibility clearly defined and measured but *socially-oriented trust* in which the enforcement mechanisms are social can be potentially a more powerful motivator for being trustworthy.

2. Authentic **leadership** is the overarching enabler and mechanism to allow trust to flourish. This is because authenticity means that words and deeds are matched, and it provides the foundation of ethical and appreciative behaviors to allow the workplace culture to support experimentation, learning, and open transfer and questioning of ideas.

3. A defining difference in RBP forms is the attitude toward BAU. Forms such as D&C, MC, BOOT/PPP/PFI, and SCM seek efficient results, but this may be BAU or marginally better than BAU, whereas other RBP forms demand **innovation** that delivers results beyond BAU. RBP forms such as alliancing, IPD, and T5 have developed

Core Relational KSAE	Associated Terms and Concepts	Comments
Trust	Credibility, ability, ethics, integrity, benevolence, professionalism, predictability, interdependence	Chapter 4 discussed the theoretical background. When we reflect upon an important trust element of the Wittgenstein Family Resemblance Figure 27, we are drawn toward the "defining substrate of motivations and circumstances to collaborate." Some of the most lucid reasons given for high levels of collaboration were a critical requirement for improving on BAU performance. Achieving that demanded collaboration, and for collaboration to be effective, trust is needed to be demonstrated through all the associated terms given here. A striking theme was interdependence that forced people to need to trust each other.
Leadership	Authenticity, systems thinker, wise and reflective, pragmatic, resilient, courage, appreciative, visionary	Clearly, "good" leadership is far beyond compliance to do what is expected as BAU. We found interviewees (and the literature) sought leaders who knew what was needed to be done, had the ability to gather collective wisdom to develop a plan, had the courage to challenge assumptions and resilience to recover when trouble looms, and had the wisdom and pragmatic attitude to recognize poor performance and to react appropriately to overcome that. Further, leaders need to be authentic and match rhetoric with action to remain credible.
Innovative	Challenging norms, out-of-the-box thinking, brave, open minded, playful workplace culture	Being innovative is impossible without trust and sound leadership. Mediocre leaders do not challenge the status quo and so do not set stretch goals that can be understood, aspired to, and trigger plans and ways to be achieved. In our section in Chapter 4 on collaboration frameworks and in particular on organizational learning as well as throughout this book, we stress the need for supportive leadership to help shape and support a workplace culture where experimentation is "safe" and does not result in blame, and that people are facilitated and encouraged to share ideas so that they can continuously improve and perhaps achieve breakthrough innovation. In alliancing, IDP and T5, this was a specified expectation and demand of those RBP forms.

Table 17.   Relational KSAE Summary of Emphasis by RBP Approach

KRAs and KPIs beyond the iron triangle to measure and provide evidence of innovation. Practicing being innovative builds absorptive capacity to become more competent innovators.

4. Relational capabilities also require experience in reflection upon the many facets of people's nature and the circumstances they are placed that affect the way they act and react. Each person and situation must be unique, but common threads emerge about cause-and-effect loops that help explain the way that relationships evolve.

In summarizing the details of KSAE required for RBP forms and how this links to the identified elements in the Wittgenstein model in Figure 27 and subelements in Table 11, Table 12, and Table 13, we developed an additional refinement to these tables by including detailed illustrations in Appendix 2 in Section 2 for each subelement a table that provides the following data:

- description of each subelement to clarify how it fits with its relevant element;
- examples of high-level thinking about that subelement to illustrate how those with the most advanced KSAE may view the purpose of that subelement within the context of the element;
- examples of high levels of KSAE required to perform at the highest level of performance; and
- illustrations of quotes from the SME experts interviewed that illuminate their lived reality of that subelement.

We provide an extract of Appendix 2 here to illustrate the how the analysis of data has delivered a comprehensive and linked detailed exploration of the Wittgenstein model elements, subelements, and the KSAEs required to deliver these sub-elements in Table 18.

Readers who wish to better understand the Wittgenstein Family Resemblance model adapted and developed for RMP options and their associated KSAEs should refer to Section 2 and Tables A7 to Table A22.

Theme and Subtheme	Notes, Examples, and KSAE Quotes
1.5 Relational rationale	RBP forms inherently imply that there is perceived need to create, nurture, and maintain a form of a relationship, the extent of commitment may vary. Some choices may be based upon negative past experiences and the need to overcome problems caused or at least exacerbated by the chosen project procurement form. Other choices are based on positive past experience with use of a specific form of procurement that worked well within that context. Experience can form the basis for rationalizing any given procurement choice within its given context.
Examples of high levels of relational context thinking	• Understanding the causes for past positive or negative experience based on institutional drivers driven by the forms of project delivery contract. • Understanding and appreciating how trust and commitment can be shaped by the form of project delivery procurement and behavioral requirements or habits based on specific project procurement forms. • Understanding the big picture and how a more holistic approach to project delivery may improve value delivered.
High-level KSAE needed for relational needs	• Technical and PM KSAE – High levels relative to the deficit in KSAE that parties wishing to engage in a closer relationship perceive that they need to gain through the relationship. Most likely perceived highly complex projects need a relational approach. • Business solutions KSAE – High levels of ability to understand the value proposition of various parties be able to perceive how the relationship could be of value to the other party(ies) and how to frame a response to that need that can be justified through meeting a sound business case. • Relational KSAE – High levels of ability to be able to visualize broad relationship networks and how value to other party(ies) can be enhanced and how to frame a constructive response to that need.
Illustrative quote	A relational rationale can be based upon filling skills, competence, and knowledge gaps through collaboration in a way that provides sufficient incentive for all involved parties. As P17 and A10 comment:
P17	[relating to a PA] You've got to have something of significance, substance, you know, a hundred million or more. Probably the biggest flag for me really concerns cultural and some of the personalities, far more so than in a normal alliance.
A10	... they've learned through the previous periods that the best way to achieve better outcomes is through greater levels of collaboration, so let's not throw the baby out with the bath water. Let's just turn that around and use that to try and drive costs down by working together. So that's one thing that's come out of it. And another thing that's come out of it is that, to be more efficient from their own point of view of the operations, a lot of the project managers that I interviewed said that they, "Preferred collaborative working. It was more efficient as well as more effective in the long run."

Table 18.   Wittgenstein Model Theme 1: Motivation and Context Extract

Chapter 6 Summary

This chapter summarized our findings. In the section on emerging forms of collaboration terms, we answer research questions 1 and 2: Q1 – What are the fundamental characteristics of emerging relationship-based forms of project procurement? Q2 – Do these forms vary in different parts of the world and, if so, in what way?

We present Table 9 to illustrate these collaboration terms and where they are globally applied. We also illustrated through Figure 25 how these forms integrate the gradation of early contractor involvement, and in Figure 26, which illustrates forms of integration of the PO/POR, the project design team leader and delivery team leader.

We answered research Q3 – What specific skills, attributes and experience required to deliver such projects are currently underdeveloped or missing from traditional project managers' knowledge and skills sets? We did this through first presenting a table of relationship intensity of various identified RBP forms identified from answers to research question 1 and 2 in Table 10 and then developing a model of possible RBP forms in Figure 27. This informed and allowed us to then provide measures of each of the identified elements in Table 11, Table 12, and Table 13. This, in turn, allowed us to map the characteristics of the developed model of possible RBP forms in Table 14, and also to provide analysis and findings on the details of collaborative arrangements with detail discussion of technical, PM, business, and relational KSAE. We also provided an extract from Section 2, Appendix 2, Table A7 as an illustration of the comprehensive analysis undertaken and presented in this book.

We provide specific detailed findings from our interviews with academics, practitioners, and our validation workshop feedback from our study in Appendix 2 because we felt that many readers may find the details cluttering the book so far. Those with an interest in these findings will find Appendix 2 rewarding to read.

CHAPTER 7

Study Conclusions

Chapter 7 Introduction

This chapter present our conclusions for the study. This chapter comprises a section that identifies skills gaps from the current PMI competency framework (PMI, 2007) and suggests how the identified gaps may be bridged. We then discuss and present our assessment of emerging trends in RBP and what we claim may be a way forward. We then discuss what implications this presents for education and skills development. The final section summarizes this chapter and the book.

Mind the Gap! Identifying and Bridging KSAE Gaps

The PMI competency framework (PMI, 2007) is understandably closely linked to the *PMBOK® Guide* (PMI, 2013). However, it still focuses overwhelmingly on the assumption that PM is predominantly a process activity. PM competency is validated using documentation with an emphasis on validity being demonstrated by mechanistic and highly "scientifically proven" evidence. The positivist paradigm is evident throughout the framework. This validation process is dominated by the need for documentary evidence and places "feeling" and "sense" at a nonrecognized level; as if feelings and sense are somehow invalid. There may be some hints of uneasy acceptance that feelings may offer limited credence, but the institution of PM thought has been largely dominated by a rational worldview that is highly deterministic in essence (Bredillet, 2013). It is only recently that this rationalist paradigm has been widely challenged and alternatives have been more generally explored and accepted by PM thought leaders (Bredillet, 2008; Hodgson & Cicmil, 2006; Söderlund, 2004; Winter et al., 2006).

However, PMI has more recently supported PM knowledge creation and the flow of ideas from the disaster recovery and project aid industry sectors in which culture-sensitivity, sensemaking, and empathic characteristics are more highly regarded and considered than in the PM community (Steinfort, 2010). The gap, therefore, in identifying the KSAE needed by project managers who lead the delivery of complex projects is not so much one of managing technical or administrative complexity, but rather in coping with high levels of uncertainty, ambiguity, and even chaos.

The PMI competency framework has not adequately caught up with an emerging emphasis on projects being initiated for non-commercial reasons to reflect emerging and exciting directions of PM that are responding to greater identification with 3BL benefits. The disaster recovery PM sector is one example of this (Ika, Diallo, & Thuillier, 2010; 2012; Steinfort, 2010).

A number of the KSAE's that we have identified, for example in **Table 6** for project and program alliances, are either not mentioned in the PMI competency framework (PMI, 2007) or are given scant attention. The impression that the PMI competency framework gave us (as authors of this book) is that personal competencies are considered in the framework but they are discussed as being generic and universally applicable. For example, the PMI Framework Unit of competency 6.0 Communicating has described as one of its components "6.1 Actively listens, understands, and responds to stakeholders." It suggests as valid evidence that demonstrates this competence as including

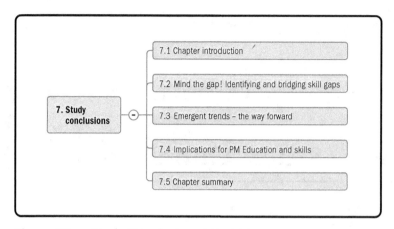

Figure 30. Study Conclusions Mind Map

survey results, documented observations from communication and feedback on empathy (PMI, 2007, p. 26). This is, of course, justified but to communicate for what purpose? In Chapter 4, Table 5, we outlined PM expertise based on work undertaken by Dreyfus and Dreyfus (2005) and Cicmil (2003), and we highlighted in that table the drivers of action by experts and virtuosos. It would be unlikely that an expert of virtuoso PM would painstakingly document evidence such as this before making decisions, because they are more likely to intuitively respond by making a decision without understanding exactly how they came to that decision. Similarly in the discussion on the Cynefin framework (Kurtz & Snowden, 2003; Snowden, 2002) in Chapter 3, and in particular with reference to our Figure 11, it can be appreciated that much decision-making and action-taking by highly skilled project managers is done intuitively, and so documenting evidence to support validating that level of expertise seems both counterproductive and even dangerous. Bredillet (Bredillet, 2013; Bredillet, Conboy, Davidson, & Walker, 2013) observes that practitioners respond in an internal and often difficult to comprehend manner. Books such as the PMI competency framework (PMI, 2007) and this book are necessarily limited because it is so difficult to document feelings, senses, and intangible knowledge. Presentation of research findings in this book should increase our understanding of PM and the KSAE that support excellence, rather than be another prescriptive framework to be slavishly adopted.

We highlighted in Chapter 4 in the Competency Classification section and PMI Competency Framework subsection, that the PMI Framework treats leading, more briefly and in a coarser-grained manner than the authentic leadership characteristics and CMM descriptors presented in the AAA study extract (Walker and Lloyd-Walker, 2011a) illustrated in **Table 6**. The present gap in the PMI Framework content that we can identify relates to the emphasis on 3BL outcomes and the building and maintenance of relationships that support trust and commitment in an RBP context. We do not suggest that all PM attention should now be shifted toward RBP, but we do identify a lack of focus on that form of project delivery and point to very large scale infrastructure project and program delivery in Australasia in particular but also in the U.K., Finland, and the Netherlands that require KSAE that go beyond that which is catalogued in the PMI Competency Framework.

Additional skill sets and attributes that are required for a PA and in other similar RBP forms extend well beyond what is expected of project manager in a BAU setting. It became evident from the data collected in the AAA study, as well as in this study, that a culture of cooperation, collaboration, innovation through cross-team learning, and best-for-project focus drives the need for greater relational management skills, attributes, and experiences. The data suggests that this is evidenced by a high level focus on collaboration, transparency, accountability, engendering an open culture of knowledge sharing, and joint risk/reward absorption, with an emphasis on trust, initiative, breakthrough innovation to achieve outstanding project outcomes, and a set of outcomes that are well beyond the iron triangle of performance. Skills and attributes include greater emphasis on people-management and leadership skills, facilitating a learning environment for innovation to flourish, integrity and authenticity in leadership to allow trust and commitment to flourish, and for governance to rely more on transformational rather than transactional leadership.

The relational KSAEs presented in summary in Chapter 6 Table 17 provide a useful indication of the identified gap in the PMI Competency Framework and helps answer RQ4—how may identified (KSAE) gaps be bridged? Many of these skills—access to knowledge, development of attributes, and acquisition of experience—cannot be obtained through schooling, education providers in a classroom setting, or online training. We suggest that these may be best addressed through greater focus on career development and access to mentoring and coaching opportunities. Specifically, we suggest that higher skill levels require concentrated learning that can be delivered through simulations via workshops or hypothetical case studies that involve an action-learning cycle of planning, acting, reviewing, reflecting, or perhaps reflecting, planning, and then acting, reviewing, and further reflection in a cycle. Mentoring and coaching also has its place. It is necessary for a supportive community of advanced project managers to be established to engage in mentoring, coaching, and knowledge exchange in a community of practice.

We have adapted our conclusions from our work for the AAA study (Walker & Lloyd-Walker, 2011a) in light of the extensive additional research undertaken on the research reported upon here in this study over 2012–2013 as follows.

To summarize the general thrust of our investigations, we can see potential for:

- Closer engagement between project managers and their responsible HRM departments to help identify what they should be doing and what that organization may do to support the project managers career and KSAE development;
- Changes in understanding from traditional HRM practices to practices that better align with temporary organizations composed of multiple firms that collaborate as a single project team;
- Continued use of formal courses and workshops run by education and training providers that are targeted at higher-order relational KSAEs;
- Use of psychometric evaluation tools for project managers to gain a better understanding of their traits, strengths, and weakness in various areas, and for highlighting gaps that may be filled in developing their career paths;
- Use of universities and short-course trainer providers for specific learning that lends itself to a structured approach in enhancing project managers' business and relational KSAEs;
- Closer interaction with professional bodies such as PMI, IPMA, etc., as well as accessing knowledge via their conferences and professional development resources, to allow project managers access to leading-edge research results;
- Developing reflective learning and action learning based protocols for project managers to be able to develop their own careers (including the possibility of masters or PhDs for those willing make long-term learning commitments), and to learn from, and gain better value from, their experience;
- Simulations, hypotheticals, problem-solving interactive workshops, and repositories of difficult case studies on ethical or wicked problem dilemmas typically faced by AMs and;
- Developing a network of mentors and coaches and linking them to a web-based portal that could be dedicated to KSAE enhancement and for this portal to be social networking communities of practice.

Emerging Trends, the Way Forward

The world of project and program management is rapidly changing. We have already discussed changes in mind sets and perspectives of where PM is heading. Readers may also wish to follow up on some very recent papers that show how PM education has evolved. The paper by Bredillet et al. (2013), for example, traces a narrative for Australia that provides a history that is comparable to many other developed countries. The importance of being a reflective practitioner, being able to think deeply and reflect on not just a series of bullet-point lessons learned, but to understand context and changes in context from one situation to another so that lessons learned are used for adaptation and not merely for adoption, is a vital characteristic of KSAE development. Bredillet (2013) suggested that a practitioner who was reflective and reflexive could be termed a PraXitioner. Bredillet's (2013) concept of the PraXitioner is vital to understanding emerging PM trends, and therefore demands placed on the KSAEs that project managers will be expected to have, particularly at the high end of their professional maturity. A PraXitioner truly reflects upon context, pragmatic considerations about means, routines, behaviors, and what is required as a foundation for effective practice. We suggest that in designing a procurement choice to deliver a specific benefit and need that a praXitioner would be able to make sense of our Figure 27. An RBP Wittgenstein's Idea of Family, together with Appendix 2 and Table 6. Three Experiences and Seven Characteristics/Attributes Required of AMs (Source: Walker and Lloyd-Walker, 2011a, p. 12–15) to adapt and customize these guideline features for an appropriate procurement and delivery model that can function within the assumed context.

We already know that project characteristics vary with each industry sector, delivery level configuration, level of complexity, and a host of contextual aspects that we discussed in Chapter 2. We know that project outcomes are steadily moving in emphasis from delivering a product to delivering a service that generates benefit. This trend has been taking us steadily, in terms of the Figure 11. A Johari-Oriented Cynefin Typology of Project Awareness, from Quadrant 1, highly ordered projects, toward Quadrant 4, highly chaotic projects, while most project currently lie in Quadrant 3, complex and somewhat unordered. Our focus on alliance projects in this study is justified because trends in project delivery demands (and in particular the vast need for new and renewed infrastructure projects in our developing global economy), and it was by investigating KSAEs at that project complexity level that enabled us to identify gaps in current PM competencies and to offer guidelines to bridge that gap.

Implications for PM Education and Skills

What does this study and our presented research results imply for the PM discipline and for the vast industry of training and developing project managers and their teams? We can offer some suggestions based on our reflection of the work reported upon here, on the insights of the many highly professional SMEs that we have spoken to, and the views expressed but not yet published by academic colleagues that have generously given us their time to be interviewed about interesting aspects about PM and its KSAEs needed to perform successfully in the emerging context. We also benefited from extensive feedback from our two workshops in the U.K. when we presented preliminary results from our study, and from subsequent comments received from SMEs and other academics on draft versions of this book that we distributed freely as each was written.

One cluster of feedback comments supported our Table 6 and many commented that the identified soft skills were required in BAU as well as the RBP forms of project. We agree, but the models and frameworks we present in Table 6, Figure 25, Figure 27 and in Appendix 2, stress that it is a matter of degree and shaping. The characteristics and quality of these aids also need to be used within context. For example, in Table 6 we highlight several soft skills such as reflectiveness and spirit which can be applied more languidly if time permits in highly ordered BAU projects, but in a situation of chaos they may be employed in short sharp bursts to first act on a hunch (intuition) then rapidly reflect upon emerging consequences and to have the spirit to challenge one's own assumptions and move into an "act, sense, respond" sequence as illustrated in Figure 11 to cope with a chaotic or highly disordered project context. We welcome a praXitioner's judgment on the extent and manner in which our frameworks and models can be effectively applied to be suited to the project context.

Implications for the Project Owner (PO) and POR Education and Skills Development

Another cluster of feedback comments related to whole-of-team view of project delivery. The *Project Manager Competency Development Framework* (PMI, 2007), as with many other guides no doubt, omit to consider the project owner or the POR and the KSAEs that they need to effectively engage in more complex forms of project delivery. Our study did not specifically address this interesting cluster of research questions—what KSAEs **do** PORs have and what KSAEs do they **need** to optimize project outcomes? We interviewed several SMEs who had fulfilled the role of POR, but we did not focus on questions relating to the role of the POR or PO. This opens up possibilities for further research work to answer those questions. In the meantime, we are left with the possibility that some, if not many, project owners and PORs lack technical and PM-based KSAE to be able to effectively discuss options related to the project brief and then later to judge performance levels. For that group of individuals, an effective form of liaison training and development would be necessary. A PO or POR having the same KSAE as a professional project manager would be ideal, because that would enable more complete understanding and perspective taking ability to occur, which should facilitate a more effective exploration of project design and delivery options. This may not be feasible for many organizations, and so facilitating a liaison person with those KSAE could be a viable alternative.

Chapter 4 Figure 21 illustrates KSAEs on an alliance manager taken from our study of AM excellence in the AAA study (Walker and Lloyd-Walker, 2011a). Two skill groups that are generally not seen in the PM world are highlighted there. These are business solutions skills and 3BL and collaborative values skills. A PO or POR could well have high level business solution KSAE's but may not have (if mainly coming from a commercial background) sufficient social and environmental 3BL KSAEs. Bridging that gap could be accomplished through a study program designed more generally to grasp the basics and foundational knowledge and concepts, and be supplemented with advanced level training, coaching, or mentoring.

We cite here P38 who provided an illuminating comment about his experience of being on a number of alliance ALTs. It illustrates how the availability of the most senior managers to be engaged in alliances has become stretched with the increasing number of alliances in the rail infrastructure sector.

> "We had the chief operating officer from [Participant A] or [Participant B] at the time on it, we had a senior guy from [Participant C] on it, the rail manager and so that was my first one and so there you had senior people from organizations and this is, I think, largely what the ALT is good for is accessing back into their business and making a difference. Consistently, every ALT since then has been watered down to the point where you don't have necessarily very senior people or not consistently senior on the ALT and therefore you're just getting a business as usual response because they have to then go back and get approval to do things and getting approval from putting it in the context that they've brought a business, so you don't get what I call special treatment and therefore without the likes of [Project X], we wouldn't have been able to build that without the attention and special treatment, especially from the rail operator. The priority that we got given because the senior by, I think a lot of that's been lost now, so you're not therefore getting a significantly innovative solution".

We can see that as the number and scale of projects delivered move toward the need for a 3rd to 4th order of collaboration, there may be a crisis in KSAE shortage for POs and their PORs. This may be met and accommodated by massive upskilling (which we would expect to be a several-decades program) or greater reliance on project management teams. P38's quote was about the senior leaders and in particular the PORs, being able to make authoritative stable and quick decisions within their home organization to facilitate various demanding aspects of the project. This kind of authority would be very difficult to delegate to a project manager from outside the POR's home organization.

Implications for Project Managers and their Team Members' Education and Skills Development

Regardless of whether the KSAE gaps that we have identified are bridged for project managers and their team participants, or for the project owner and/or POR, the need for technical, project management, business solution, and relational KSAEs is manifest in today's world of increasing complexity and wider systemic 3BL demands. What becomes apparent is that in moving beyond the baseline technical and PM KSAE required for a PMI registered practitioner, and similar qualifications for the IPMA, we see an increasing need for project managers to have business solution and relational KSAE. By business, we refer to accomplishing organizational aims and not for the term business being constrained to a commercial focus. The business of natural disaster recovery projects is to provide or facilitate the reinstatement of a resilient community and its supporting facilities. It is not about replacing what was there with a replica. That type of project requires a great deal of stakeholder engagement to work out what the program of work should entail (Steinfort & Walker, 2011).

Clearly, the implication for PM teams' upskilling for the KSAEs identified in this book is that much of the project delivery needs to be done in the workplace, using skilled and experienced coaches, mentors, and facilitators. We see an important role for universities. This is primarily at the foundational stage where graduate programs of study at graduate certificate, graduate diploma, and masters level delivers project management education and training, but there is evidence to support universities developing doctoral programs to help practitioners develop into praXtitioners (Bredillet et al., 2013; Walker, 2008;). University programs of study are quite long, usually involving studying part-time while working for several years at a masters level and between four to six years at doctoral level. This timeframe is not feasible for the demands of many PM practitioners and their organizations. This is where one-to-one or very small group mentoring and coaching may be a useful KSAE delivery approach. Learning methods should be problem-based and action-learning based to allow what is referred to as Mode 2 learning (MacLean, MacIntosh, & Grant, 2002; Sense, 2005) where experiential and reflective learning is applied to simulated or real experiences to enable individuals to be better prepared for workplace upskilling challenges.

Gathering sufficient quantity and quality of resources has severe implications on coping with the challenge to bridge identified KSAEs gap. Enabling sufficient people-resources presents one dimension, but also there is the demand for high quality learning support materials that includes learning content, tools, and technology as well as physical space for people to meet learn and reflect. Frequently, organizational learning repository resources are not adequately considered. This includes not only lessons-learned-but-forgot issues but also how knowledge and information can best be made available and how a culture of learning can be developed that has been discussed and debated over many years (von Krogh, 1998; von Krogh et al., 2000; Wenger, McDermott, & Snyder, 2002).

Chapter Summary

This chapter wraps up the book. We first identified and articulated what we see is the current gap in KSAE development of PM practitioners. We also highlighted the gap that exists for project owners and their representatives. We proceeded to identify implications for the PM profession, project owners as well as those of us who see ourselves as part of a community of project workers and participants.

Our study involved a significant literature review studying articles, books, government reports, and research study reports. We reread and reflected upon a number of doctoral dissertations in which we have been fortunate enough to have played the role of supervisor or examiner. We also interviewed 14 leading academics in this RBP area and 36 SME practitioners and gathered over 500 pages of transcripts from those interviews. This enabled us to analyze that data using a sensemaking approach and we were able to compare our findings from this study with several other studies that we have been engaged in. We presented draft findings in a validation through exposure process using conference presentations in Australia, the U.K., Iceland, the Netherlands, Ireland, and the U.S. to be able to get international comment and feedback. We also submitted several papers to peer-reviewed journals to gain feedback and to explain our findings within the academic community. We presented findings at two workshops in Oxford and London to an audience of highly experienced complex project and program delivery practitioners. We have taken every opportunity to discuss emerging findings with colleagues from numerous countries, and we found the process of explaining our research approach and our findings strongly crystalized the models and frameworks we have developed or refined from our previous research work in this area.

We present a list of publications accepted and published as late as 2013 in Appendix 1, Table 1. We have also provided details of our interview participants (though intentionally coded IA-nn for interviewed academic 01, 02 etc. and IP-nn for interviewed practitioner) in Appendix 1, Table 2. In Appendix 1, Table 3, we identify and present a summary of the complementary research that has also informed our reflection on the research approach, data, and findings.

Appendix 2 provides details of our findings on the Wittgenstein Family Resemblance model as applied to RBP forms. We present the model again in Figure 1 of Appendix 2, and we then present the Wittgenstein's Family Resemblance Elements for each of the four Figure 1 components with their sub-themes/themes, and a suggested course-grained measurement scale of Low and High for each element. This is followed by details of each element that explains in detail the nature of the subelement/theme as well as examples of high levels of thinking about each subelement/theme, high levels of KSAE, and illustrative quotes from the interview transcripts that support the framework.

We believe that the value that this book contributes to the PM literature is:

- A substantial discussion and presentation in Chapter 2 of PM theory that underpins the study and linked it within a project procurement context;
- A substantial discussion and presentation in Chapter 3 of business theory aspects of RBP that sets the study in context and underpins the study within a project procurement context;
- A substantial discussion and presentation in Chapter 4 of human behavior aspects of RBP that sets the study in context and underpins the study within a project procurement context;
- Table 6 that updates and presents findings from our AAA study of profiling Alliance Manager Excellence to present a model that feedback from practitioners was very enthusiastic to apply to both alliance managers and high-performing project managers working on complex projects;

- Table 9 that presents a current definition of RBP forms as understood in a set of countries in the world. This provides a significant attempt to explain the terms and how the approaches are applied globally;
- Figure 25 that provides a model for categorizing collaboration forms linked to RBP terms generally used globally, together with Table 10 that explains the degree of relationship intensity characteristics to supplement the understanding that readers can gain from Figure 25 and;
- Figure 27, the Wittgenstein's Idea of Family Resemblance model that identifies 16 "petals" or elements that have been grouped into platform foundational, behavioral factors and processes, routines, and means drivers of RBP forms. This, together with Table 11, Table 12, and Table 13, explain in detail what each element and subelement/theme means and how the element may be measured. This provides a visualization model that can be developed through a color-coded table (an example of this is presented in Table 14, with a sample analysis presented in Table 15), or a radar chart for any given RBP configuration, as illustrated in Figure 28. This facilitates better understanding of each element's characteristics, and by using the associated table in Appendix 2 for the element, KSAE and benchmark standards of considering how to best use that element's characteristics to deliver value through the project.

This contribution addresses the research aim to present a body of research work that helps people better understand the various emerging forms of RBP and how to identify what KSAE may be required for any particular RBP form.

This book has several limitations that should be acknowledged. First, we are basing our findings with a culture of accepting the validity of RBP as a means to deliver project value that includes financial gain as only one of several success factors. While we were researching and writing this book between 2012 and 2013, the scale and number of projects delivered using an alliance approach in Australia is declining. Interviewees explain this decline as follows:

- Being a response to state and commonwealth (federal) government changes, with political masters who are mainly concerned with cost and revenue and less enthusiastic about other project performance measures such as community, social capital, and projects as learning vehicles than the governments they replaced;
- A perceived "over-use" of alliances where the rationale for the need and extent of collaboration was not explicitly justified; and
- Some hint of high levels of fatigue by senior management about the commitment and energy required of alliances and the demands made for these projects' ALTs.

Against that backdrop we are seeing increasing use of alliancing in countries such as the U.K., Finland, and the Netherlands and the evolution of the T5 Agreement as a highly collaborative model with high levels of supply-chain integration using common platforms. This RBP form is proving to be one that delivers high levels of value for highly complex projects. The forms of Framework Agreement in the U.K. are very close to program alliances in Australia, though one SME we interviewed felt that FAs seemed to involve less of a sink-or-swim-together mentality and may not gain as much commitment by participants as that of program alliances.

Clearly, this form of procurement has delivered projects with traditional success measures such as the final outturn cost and time while delivering exceptional quality and many other KRA deliverables than appears to be the case for traditionally procured projects, at least in the construction infrastructure sector.

We expect to see the RBP form continuing to evolve but remain as a viable project delivery strategy.

COLLABORATIVE PROJECT PROCUREMENT ARRANGEMENTS
SECTION 2 – APPENDIX 1 AND APPENDIX 2

Derek H. T. Walker, PhD, MSc, Grad Dip (Mgt Sys)
and
Beverley M. Lloyd-Walker, PhD, Grad Cert (Change Mgt AGSM), Grad Dip Info Mgt, Grad Dip Post Sec Ed, BBus

Cite as:

Walker, D. H. T., & Lloyd-Walker, B. M. (2015). *Collaborative project procurement arrangements.* Newtown Square, PA: Project Management Institute.

Appendix 1– Resource Sources

Table A1 details publications arising out of this research project.

Table A1. Validation and Feedback from Publication Sources Developed from this Research

Dissemination event	Citation/Details of Source	Salient comments
Book chapter Book-CH1	Walker, D. H. T., & Lloyd-Walker, B. (2013). Project alliances– A new direction in temporary organisation forms. In Lundin R. & Hällgren, M., *Projects and Temporary Organizations – Theory and Practice*. Copenhagen, Copenhagen Business School Press.	A refined idea from previous conference papers, some of the detail has been discussed earlier in this book in Chapters 2, 3, and 4. The book chapter was peer reviewed.
Journal papers Jour-1	Lloyd-Walker, B., & Walker, D. (2011). Authentic leadership for 21st century project delivery. *International Journal of Project Management, 29*, 383–395.	This paper refined details of a previous paper presented at the EURAM in Rome 2010 and while based upon the AAA research identified in Table 3. It provided an opportunity to reflect upon that work, further journal referee feedback and SME feedback at the start of this present research reported upon here.
Jour-2	MacDonald C, Walker, D.H.T., & Moussa, N. (2013). Towards a project alliance value for money framework. *Facilities, 27*, in press	This paper focuses on the key results of Dr. Charles MacDonald's doctoral thesis. It is highly relevant to this book and Dr. MacDonald was co-supervised by Professor Derek Walker. It provides highly salient expert opinion of the way that value for money can be designed into the PM practice and illustrates required skills needed.
Jour-3	Walker, D. H. T., Lloyd-Walker, B. M., & Mills, A. (2014). Facilitating a no-blame culture through project alliancing. *Project Perspectives, 8*, 58–63.	This paper uses a case study of a major upgrade of a city Arts and Concert Hall complex using an alliance form of project delivery to investigate the project's no-blame culture.
Jour-4	Walker, D. H. T., Lloyd-Walker, B. M., & Mills A. (2013). Enabling construction innovation – the role of a no-blame culture as a collaboration behavioural driver in project alliances. *Construction Management and Economics* (under review for a SI in 2013).	This paper further develops Conf-2 paper (see below) using a case study of a major upgrade of a city Arts and Concert Hall complex, using an alliance form of project delivery to investigate a process improvement innovation.
Conference papers Conf-1	Walker, D. H. T., & Lloyd-Walker, B. M. (2012). *Understanding Early contractor involvement (ECI) Procurement Forms*. Twenty-Eighth ARCOM Annual Conference, Edinburgh, 5–7 September, Smith S., Association of Researchers in Construction Management, 2, 877–887.	These papers were presented in academic conferences and peer reviewed. Further reflection, response to feedback from reviewers and conference participants is leading to journal papers in review, production or being currently written.
Conf-2	Walker, D. H. T., Lloyd-Walker, B. M. and Mills, A. (2013). *Innovation through alliancing in a no-blame culture*. World Building Congress, Brisbane, CIB: 12pp.	This paper focuses on the no-blame culture and its impact upon the delivery of a PA on the Hamer Hall project in Melbourne. Presented in May 2013.
Conf-3	Walker D.H.T., & Lloyd-Walker, B.L. (2013). *Making sense of collaborative forms of relationship based construction procurement*. EPOC. Winter Park, Colorado	This paper draws upon several studies mentioned in this book and provided an opportunity for academic review and feedback by primarily U.S. academics
Conf-4	Walker D.H.T., & Jacobsson M. (2013). Alliancing within a Public–Private Partnership: Consequences and Challenges for Construction Projects. NFF conference Iceland	This paper draws upon a study of a PA within a PPP project and represents a unique case study of a PA and provided an opportunity for review and feedback from Nordic academics.
Practitioner feedback workshop	Validation and feedback presentation to SME practitioners in Oxford and London in October 2013	The U.K. has several decades of experimenting with a range of RBP approaches. The input from these workshops provided clarification of concepts as well as challenging their global interpretation.

Table A2 provides coded details of the interviews undertaken for the research. Coded by academic (IA-Number) and practitioner as (IP-Number) plus name initials.

Table A2.   Interviews with SMEs

Interview Code	Location and date	General topic content - Perspective	Rationale for interview
IA-1 (HV)	Netherlands, 11 June 2012 Face-to-face interview ~1 hour	RBP in the Netherlands, alliances and the CD concept *Procurement forms in general perspective.*	At that time, IA-1 had written a number of academic papers over the previous 3–4 years on this topic and had others in the review and publication process. Discussion of PA and CD trends.
IA-2 (AK) IA-3 (JB) Group interview	Sweden, 14 June 2012 Face-to-face with IA2 and IA3 interview ~30 minutes, I-2 only a further ~60 minutes	Culture, trust, existing RBP and similar projects in Sweden, the CD concept *A trust and service commitment perspective*	Both academic authors have written on project procurement and trust and a service perspective on project delivery
IP-4 (BJ)	France, 19 June 2012 Face-to-face interview ~60 minutes plus further several hours of discussion	RBP in the aircraft industry in France *A lived experience perspective of the aircraft development sector.*	IP-4 is a recently retired executive of a BAE subsidiary and has been deeply involved in the aerospace industry for several decades. This sheds light on aerospace SCM aspects and collaboration.
IP-5 (JL) IP-6 (H) Group interview	Wales, U.K., 26 June 2012 Face-to-face interview ~60 minutes	RBP and framework agreements in U.K. *Consultant to client practitioner perspective*	Both practitioners are deeply involved in the evaluation of and working in framework agreements. IP-5 is managing director of the Welsh subsidiary of a global quantity surveying practice. IP-6 is a senior quantity surveyor (QS) in the practice engaged on framework agreement projects.
IA-7 (MR)	Southern England, U.K., 28 June 2012 Face-to-face interview ~30 minutes	Use of building information modeling (BIM) as a collaborative integrating platform on projects throughout Scandinavia. *Collaboration and BIM perspective*	This provided an interesting and poorly covered aspect of collaboration whose impact is largely understated.
IA-8 (SG)	Southern England, U.K., 28 June 2012 Face-to-face interview ~60 minutes	History of subcontracting and evolution of partnering as a re-integrating mechanism *Collaboration and historical implications perspective*	This provided solid contextual grounding as well as discussion on partnering and other RBP forms.
IA-9 (TP)	Northern England, U.K., 2 July 2012 Face-to-face interview ~1 hour	Case study of a PA in Sydney, Australia, experience of study of PAs over a 10 year period *Innovation and historical PAs evolution perspective*	This academic had studied several PAs closely that were very early adopters in Australia and also has a keen interest in innovation and PAs
IA-10 (HS) IA-11 (SP) IA-12 (PM) Group interview	Southern England, 12 July 2012 Interviews IA-10, IA-11, and IA-12 ~30 minutes 10–11 additional ~30 minutes	Forms of RBP in the U.K., in particular partnering, T5 type supply chain arrangements and impact of trust *Mainly a trust and commitment perspective*	These three academics are widely accepted experts in PM and role of trust and commitment in teams.

(continued)

Table A2.   Interviews with SMEs *(Continued)*

Interview Code	Location and date	General topic content - *Perspective*	Rationale for interview
IA-13 (TB) IA-14 (AD) Group interview	Southern England, 12 September 2012 Face-to-face interviews ~60 minutes	The discussion centered upon the Heathrow T5 Contract form. It was supplemented by a YouTube presentation by IA-13 that was also transcribed for content analysis. *Mainly how T5 worked from a long term research project perspective*	These two academics have written widely about innovation, collaboration and the T5 project.
IA-15 (PL)	Melbourne, Australia, November 2012 Numerous short face-to-face interviews	A visiting Finnish academic who is closely involved in a research project about PAs in Finland *A perspective on newly experimented with PAs in Finland*	This academic was based at RMIT in Australia for 6 weeks and was undertaking research on PAs in Australia to take back lessons learnt to his Finnish clients. We had very useful discussions of varying length over that period about impressions and insights gained from many interviews that he undertook while in Australia.
IA-16 (MJ)	Melbourne, Australia, January 2013 Numerous short face-to-face interviews One 60 minute recorded interview	A visiting Swedish academic who is closely involved in a research project about collaborative temporary organizations in Sweden *A perspective on newly experimented with forms of partnering in Sweden*	This academic was based at RMIT in Australia for 12 weeks and was undertaking research on PAs in Australia to take back lessons learnt to Sweden. We had very useful discussions of varying length over that period about impressions and insights gained from many interviews that he undertook as part of a PhD study into RBP approaches in Sweden.
IP-17 (JR)	Australia, February 2013 Phone interview ~80 minutes	A renowned global expert on PAs *A strong historical perspective on PA formation and maintenance globally*	This practitioner is a pioneer in introducing PAs, has coached numerous PA teams, and has been instrumental in establishing alliances globally.
IP-18 (CS)	Melbourne, Australia, February 2013 Phone interview ~80 minutes	A renowned U.K. global expert on PAs *A strong historical perspective on PA formation and maintenance in the U.K. rail infrastructure in particular*	This practitioner was a pioneer in introducing PAs in the U.K. and has coached numerous PA teams.
IA-19 (SR)	Melbourne, Australia, February 2013 Phone interview ~60 minutes	A renowned academic in the area of RBP approaches from Hong Kong *A strong historical perspective on RBP as well as direct research and publication on the situation in Hong Kong, China, and Japan*	This academic has recently undertaken research into project management in large engineering infrastructure projects in Japan that covered the top tier of contractors. He shared insights from that study as well as providing expert insights on the situation in Hong Kong and to compare that with several Australian project alliances that he had undertaken research on directly as well as through supervision of several PhD candidates.
IP-20 (AP) and IP-21 (FM)	Melbourne, Australia, June 2012 case study for parallel research study on a building PA project. Phone interview ~60 minutes	These SMEs were key PA team members in a building construction (rather than infrastructure engineering) project. *They were able to discuss their project from an alliance manager and facilities manager perspective*	This provided insights into the project culture and how the PA had been used to integrate both early contractor and design team involvement with facilities management to improve operational effectiveness of the completed project.

Table A2. Interviews with SMEs *(Continued)*

Interview Code	Location and date	General topic content - *Perspective*	Rationale for interview
IP-22 (CMacD) IP-23 (PV) IP-24 (JW) IP-25 (DM) IP-26 (JM)	Australia, January, February, and March 2013 Phone interview ~60 minutes each	These SMEs had highly valuable first-hand experience of being senior executives who participated in a PA that was part of a PPP infrastructure project. The PA comprised the two joint-venture construction companies together with the services contractor on a highly complex tunnel fit out that was undertaken as an integrated team. *Interview content reflected upon the nature of this integrated PA team within a traditional D&C delivery of a PPP project.*	IP-22 was the general manager construction of the overall multi-billion dollar infrastructure project. IP-23 was a senior executive from one of the two joint-venture construction companies that were also part of the PPP team. IP-23 had first-hand day-to-day experience of the alliance. IP-24 was with the same construction company and was an executive lead in establishing the alliance. IP-25 was a member of the services contractor also at an executive level. IP-26 was a senior executive from the other party of the two joint-venture construction companies that were also part of the PPP team.
IP-27 (BH)	San Francisco, USA, April 2013 Face-to-face interview ~45 minutes	This SME is an early thought leader and was instrumental in the development of IPD in the U.S.. *Interview content reflected upon the origins and evolution of IPD in the U.S..*	IP-27 had direct personal memory and insights into the formative discussions taking place by project procurement though leaders during the development of the IPD approach and was able to reflect upon nuances of the system and how it evolved to its current application.
IP-28 (GMM)	Brisbane, Australia, June 2013 Phone interview ~60 minutes	This SME holds one of the most senior roles in infrastructure road project delivery in Australia. *Interview content reflected upon the strategic aspects of program alliances from a transport infrastructure perspective.*	This SME has been a project director, ALT and ATM member on project alliances. He contributes data at the strategy level of project delivery.
IP-29 (PN)	Geelong, Australia, July 2013 Face-to-face Interview ~60 minutes	This SME holds one of the most senior roles in infrastructure utility project delivery in Australia. *Interview content reflected upon the strategic aspects of program alliances from a water utilities perspective.*	This SME has been a project director, ALT and ATM member on project alliances. He contributes data at the strategy level of project delivery. He also provide insights into a design alliance case study.
IP-30 (GM)	Melbourne, Australia, August 2013 Phone interview ~60 minutes	This SME holds one of the most senior roles in infrastructure road project delivery in Australia. *Interview content reflected upon the strategic aspects of project alliances from a road infrastructure perspective.*	This SME has been a project director, ALT and ATM member on project alliances. He contributes data at the strategy level of project delivery.
IP-31 (SC)	Geelong, Australia, August 2013 Phone interview ~60 minutes	This SME holds a senior role in infrastructure utility program delivery in Australia. *Interview content reflected upon the operational aspects of program alliances from a water utilities perspective.*	This SME has been a project director, ALT and ATM member on project alliances and also provide insights into a design alliance case study.
IP-32 (SB)	Melbourne, Australia, August 2013 Phone interview ~60 minutes	This SME holds one of the most senior roles in infrastructure road project delivery in Australia. *Interview content reflected upon the strategic aspects of program alliances from a road infrastructure perspective.*	This SME has been a project director, ALT, and ATM member on project alliances. He contributes data at the strategy level of project delivery.

(continued)

Table A2. Interviews with SMEs *(Continued)*

Interview Code	Location and date	General topic content - *Perspective*	Rationale for interview
IP-33 (DC)	Melbourne, Australia, August 2013 Phone interview ~60 minutes	This SME holds a senior role in infrastructure road program delivery in Australia for one of the specialist contractor organizations. *Interview content reflected upon the strategic aspects of program alliances from a road infrastructure perspective.*	This SME has expertise in and for the oversight of a number of maintenance program alliances in several states in Australia. His insights into program alliances from a contractor perspective are invaluable.
IP-34 (MO'D)	Melbourne, Australia, September 2013 Phone interview ~60 minutes	This SME holds a senior role in infrastructure road project delivery in Australia for one of the main contractors. *Interview content reflected upon the strategic aspects of project alliances from a road infrastructure perspective.*	This SME has been a project director, ALT, and ATM member on project alliances. He contributes data at the strategy level of project delivery and also has deep operational management knowledge.
IP-35 (MP)	Melbourne, Australia, September 2013 Phone interview ~60 minutes	This SME has been an alliance Z and general project manager on water utilities projects. *Interview content reflected upon a case study project with a project design alliances element and an ECI with engineer-procurement-construction infrastructure perspective elements.*	This SME has been a project alliance manager and was able to contrast alliance project delivery with an EPC style and also provide insights into a design alliance case study.
IP-36 (PM)	Melbourne, Australia, October 2013 Phone interview ~60 minutes	This SME has been the design manager with a global design engineering firm in a water utilities program alliance for several years. *Interview content reflected upon the operational aspects of program alliances from a water utilities perspective.*	This SME has insights from the design manager perspective within a water utilities program alliance and also provide insights into a design alliance case study.
IP-37 (GC)	Melbourne, Australia, October 2013 Phone interview ~60 minutes	This SME has been the initial alliance manager with a global contracting engineering firm in a water utilities program alliance for several years. *Interview content reflected upon the operational aspects of program alliances from a water utilities perspective.*	This SME has insights from the alliance manager and construction director perspective within a water utilities program alliance.
IP-38 (PW)	Melbourne, Australia, October 2013 Phone interview ~60 minutes	This SME has been the alliance manager with a global contracting engineering firm on several road/rail interface alliances and is currently engaged in a rail project alliance. *Interview content reflected upon the operational aspects of project alliances from a rail and road utilities perspective.*	This SME has insights from the alliance manager and construction director perspective within a rail project alliance within a rail expansion program.

Table A2.   Interviews with SMEs *(Continued)*

Interview Code	Location and date	General topic content - *Perspective*	Rationale for interview
IP-39 (TP)	Melbourne, Australia, November 2013 Phone interview ~60 minutes	This SME has been the alliance manager with a global contracting engineering firm on several road program alliances and is currently general manager, construction. *Interview content reflected upon the operational aspects of project alliances from a water utilities and road perspective.*	This SME has insights from the alliance manager and construction director perspective within a road program alliance.
IP-40 (PG)	Melbourne, Australia, November 2013 Phone interview ~60 minutes	This SME has been the alliance manager with a global contracting engineering firm on several road project and rail program alliances. *Interview content reflected upon strategic and operational aspects of project alliances from a rail and road perspective.*	This SME has insights from the alliance manager and construction director perspective within a road project alliance and a rail program alliance.
IP-41 (BR)	Melbourne, Australia, November 2013 Phone interview ~60 minutes	This SME has been the alliance manager with a global contracting engineering firm on several water program alliances. *Interview content reflected upon strategic and the operational aspects of project alliances from a water perspective.*	This SME has strategic client-side insights from an alliance manager and ALT perspective within a water program alliance as well as the operations of framework agreements in Australia.
IP-42 (SB)	Melbourne, Australia, December 2013 Phone interview ~60 minutes	This SME has been the alliance leadership team representative with a water utilities organization on several program alliances. *Interview content reflected upon strategic and the operational aspects of project alliances from a water perspective.*	This SME has strategic client-side insights from an alliance manager and ALT perspective within a water program alliance.
IP-43 (AH)	Melbourne, Australia, December 2013 Phone interview ~60 minutes	This SME has been the alliance manager with a global contracting engineering firm on several rail program alliances. *Interview content reflected upon strategic and the operational aspects of project alliances from a rail perspective.*	This SME has insights from the alliance manager and construction director perspective within a rail program alliance.
IP-44 (WL)	Melbourne, Australia, December 2013 Phone interview ~60 minutes	This SME has been the alliance manager with a global contracting engineering firm on several rail program alliances. *Interview content reflected upon strategic and the operational aspects of project alliances from a rail perspective.*	This SME has insights from the alliance manager and construction director perspective within a rail project alliance and a rail program alliance.
IP-45 (DdeF)	Melbourne, Australia, December 2013 Phone interview ~60 minutes	This SME has been the alliance manager with a global contracting engineering firm on several water program alliances. *Interview content reflected upon strategic and operational aspects of project alliances from a water perspective.*	This SME has strategic client-side insights from an alliance manager and ALT perspective within a water program alliance as well as the operations of framework agreements in Australia.

(continued)

Table A2. Interviews with SMEs *(Continued)*

Interview Code	Location and date	General topic content - *Perspective*	Rationale for interview
IP-46 (GMcl)	Melbourne, Australia, December 2013 Phone interview ~60 minutes	This SME has been the alliance manager with a global contracting engineering firm on several rail program alliances. *Interview content reflected upon strategic and the operational aspects of project alliances from a rail perspective.*	This SME has insights from the alliance manager and construction director perspective within a rail project alliance and a rail program alliance.
IP-47 (IC)	Melbourne, Australia, December 2013 Phone interview ~60 minutes	This SME has been the HRM manager with a global contracting engineering firm on several water program alliances and a road project alliance. *Interview content reflected upon strategic and the operational HRM aspects of project alliances from a water perspective.*	This SME has insights from the HRM manager perspective within a road project alliance and a water program alliance.
IP-48 (DW)	Melbourne, Australia, December 2013 Phone interview ~60 minutes	This SME has been the project director with a state government on several rail project alliances. *Interview content reflected upon strategic and the operational aspects of project alliances from a rail perspective.*	This SME has insights from the strategic project director client-side perspective within a rail project alliance and a water program alliance.
IP-49 (DdeK)	Melbourne, Australia, December 2013 Phone interview ~60 minutes	This SME has been the design manager on a water project with experience of several water project alliances and D&C projects. *Interview content reflected upon the operational aspects of water alliances and ECI involvement on several water projects.*	This SME has insights from the design manager consultant perspective within a water project and observations from experience of water program alliances.
IP-50 (SP)	Melbourne, Australia, December 2013 Phone interview ~60 minutes	This SME has been the alliance manager and director for a large contractor on several rail program alliances. *Interview content reflected upon strategic and the operational aspects of project alliances from a rail perspective.*	This SME has insights from the strategic and operational perspective within a rail program of project alliances.

Table A3 provides insights from complementary research that we were engaged in that supplements our research for this book.

Table A3. Insights from Complimentary Research Projects

Research Project	Nature of Research	Notes, relevance and linkages
National Museum of Australia PA	Longitudinal study over its construction (completed in 2001) Surveys of participants and embedded researcher for approximately 50% of the time during the late 1999 to March 2001 period.	This project was a pure PA and the first building PA that we were aware of in the world as most PAs had been (and usually are) engineering construction infrastructure projects. The outcome from this research project was significant that included a book, Walker, D. H. T., & Hampson, K. D. (2003) *Procurement strategies: A relationship based approach.* Oxford,:Blackwell Publishing, and many papers including one cited widely in the U.S.–Hauck, A. J., Walker, D. H. T., Hampson, K. D., & Peters, R. J. (2004). Project alliancing at National Museum of Australia–Collaborative *process. Journal of Construction Engineering & Management, 130*(1), 143-153.
Background research for an RBP book published in 2008	Research for the book (Walker & Rowlinson, 2008a) including access to two doctoral theses: 1 - Arroyo, A. C. (2009). The role of the Atlantic Corridor Project as a form of strategic community of practice in facilitating business transformations in Latin America. Doctorate, School of Property, Construction and Project Management. Melbourne: RMIT University. 2 - Davis, P. R. (2006). The application of relationship marketing to construction. PhD, School of Economics, Finance and Marketing. Melbourne: RMIT University.	The book contains 14 chapters that informed literature discussed in Chapters 2, 3, and 4 of this book. Further, it directly drew upon two doctoral theses, Chapters 12 from Arroyo (2009) and 14 from Davis (2006) that one of the authors supervised, and results gained from research undertaken and from case studies researched under the collaborative research center for construction innovation (Chapters 8 and 11). Links to the Doctoral theses: Arroyo - http://researchbank.rmit.edu.au/view/rmit:7891 Davis - http://researchbank.rmit.edu.au/view/rmit:6190
Profiling Professional excellence in alliance management (2010-2011)	We interviewed 10 alliance managers (AMs) of varying experience levels and professional background and each interview took between 1 hour and 1.5 hours in length. Additionally, three managers of AMs were interviewed between 0.5 and 1 hour using the same approach and research tools to provide their perspective of what constitutes excellence in being an AM and how to best attract, retain and develop AMs. Two further validation focus group workshops tookplace. First, in January 2011 with two senior current and former Alliance Leadership Team members for 3 hours. The second took place in early February 2011 with 7 AMs.	The report of the research is available upon request from the Alliancing Association of Australasia on URL http://www.a3c3.org/ the RMIT University research repository or from the authors: Walker, D. H. T., & Lloyd-Walker, B. M. (2011). *Profiling professional excellence in alliance management summary study report.* Sydney: Alliancing Association of Australasia, 36. Walker, D. H. T., & Lloyd-Walker, B. M. (2011). *Profiling professional excellence in alliance management, volume one – Findings and results.* Sydney: Alliancing Association of Australasia, 76. Walker, D. H. T., & Lloyd-Walker, B. M. (2011). *Profiling professional excellence in alliance management, volume two – Appendices.* Sydney: Alliancing Association of Australasia, 98. The report was based on 250+ pages of transcripts and other data that was gathered by both authors of this research. who had all of this at their disposal to contribute toward this book.
Maximizing the value of alliances in delivering infrastructure projects: A mixed methods management study. (2011-2014)	An Australian Research Council (ARC) grant between Queensland University of Technology (QUT) and RMIT University – one of this book's authors is a chief investigator on that project. It involves surveying current PA and other forms of early contractor involvement through an extensive (52 question) survey interview instrument and selected case studies. The second phase of this research involved undertaking case studies of project alliances, a form of design alliance and a series of interviews on program alliances.	This research project directly informs current PA and related activity in Australia for this book and contributed to the literature review chapters 2, 3. and 4. It also allowed informing this book's content with respect to case studies of evolving forms of RBP. The ARC research project allowed direct access to several case studies as well as surveys on the state of the art of PAs and program alliances in Australia undertaken by one of the researchers to provide additional insights for this project and book.

RMIT University

Building 8, Level 8
360 Swanston Street
Melbourne VIC 3001
Australia

GPO Box 2476V
Melbourne VIC 3001
Australia

Tel. +61 3 9925 2230
Fax +61 3 9925 1939
• www.rmit.edu.au

Design and Social Context Portfolio
School of Property Construction and Project Management.

Date 21ˢᵗ May 2012

Dear Sir(s)

Understanding Relationship-Based Project Procurement

My name is Derek Walker. I am managing a research project to develop new knowledge about relationship-based forms of project procurement and the skills needed of project managers for those projects. The project will provide a baseline picture of the various forms of relationship-based project procurement and your participation in this study is crucial. We are undertaking a global literature review of the relevant literature and we will develop from this a typology of relationship-based procurement systems. Our literature data comprises characteristics, cited authors and insights. It has been approved by the RMIT College (DSC) Ethics committee.

The data collection and analysis will be undertaken by RMIT University's School of Property, Construction and Project Management. The main data collection will be done by me and my research associate Dr Beverley Lloyd-Walker, both of us are experienced researchers. In order to successfully gauge the trend in relationship-based project procurement we require some qualitative data from respondents such as you in the form of insights based on your expertise in this area as demonstrated through your publications on this subject.

You have been identified as a researcher who has published on relationship-based project procurement, and is therefore able to provide us with very useful insights into what was reported upon in your studies and what you have subsequently reflected upon relating to those studies. Your details were obtained from papers you have published and our personal knowledge of your work. We only require 20–30 minutes of your time to conduct a telephonic interview about your published work. Professor Derek Walker will contact you on your preferred telephone number at a mutually agreed time. I have attached the kind of questions we intend to ask for your information.

The advantage to participating is that this allows us all to better understand the current state of relationship-based project procurement and its demands upon a range of competencies needed of project managers on this kind of project. You will, if you request, have subsequent access to published reports stemming from the research via industry magazine sources and access indirectly through academic sources.

Your responses **will not** be directly attributable to you or your organisation unless you wish to be cited. You may withdraw at any time, and any unprocessed data may also be withdrawn at your request. RMIT will only reveal summary data in papers which will have no reference to persons, organisations or projects, and as such will ensure anonymity of data. The data and analysis will by used by RMIT to present and publish the findings through research papers and industry magazine or similar publications.

If you are willing to participate in this research, kindly complete and return the attached consent form by email (derek.walker@rmit.edu.au). We look forward to your participation in the survey and thank you in advance for taking part in this important research.

[signature]

Professor Derek Walker

Meta study Interview Instrument

Note participants should feel free to offer examples and insights that can be quoted as qualitative data.

Project Details

Participant Name
Participant contact details: phone
                            Email

About your Paper

We would be interested to know what interesting insights relating to relationship-based procurement forms that you wrote about ended up being omitted that you would like to share with us.

About the context

Can you expand a little more on the global context of your paper? We are trying to compare the concept and construct of various types of relationship-based procurement and so terms you used or context assumed may be perceived differently outside that context. Could you expand on anything that we should know about that issue?

About changes over time

We all know that the research-reporting lifecycle can be quite long and things change from the time of publication. Can you provide us with some updates on how you see things have changed and/or evolved?

About the relevance of findings

We all know that sometimes we only really see the relevance of some of our findings after publication. Is there any added insights you can share with us about your paper that we can include in our meta study?

Case Study Interview Guide

Note: Being an interview guide, the questions are brief and will require some explanation when presenting them to interviewees.

Context:
From what context is this interview undertaken?
Demographics: experience; no. of years in type of business(es), position(s), types of projects.

Fundamental definitional questions

We have presented you with a typology of relationship-based procurement forms that stretches globally in its reach. Different regions use different definitions for each category of procurement form and these legitimately differ with the context. Can you tell us what you feel is reliable and therefore an accurate description in our presentation and where you feel we may be either wrong or where we could fine-tune our categories or descriptions further?
In what way do you feel that these categories vary (in description and content) by region or over time?

Specifically About Team Collaboration, Skills and Attributes

We have presented a capability maturity model that expresses the knowledge, skills, attributes and experience that we propose is needed for each of the categories of relationship-based procurement. Given your expertise in this area, what do you feel is reliable and therefore an accurate description and where you feel we may be either wrong or where we could fine-tune our categories or descriptions further?
How do you feel that the identified knowledge, skills, attributes and experience best be obtained?

Is there anything that you feel we missed that was worth exploring either as part of this study or for future studies?
How do you think the ALT could have improved their performance in terms of barriers and drivers experienced from your perspective?

Case Study Interview Guide – Program Alliance Leaders

Note: Being an interview guide, the questions are brief and will require some explanation when presenting them to interviewees.

Context:
From what context is this interview undertaken?
Demographics: experience; no. of years in type of business(es), position(s), types of projects.

Program Alliance Role questions

What exactly was your role in the programme alliance? Was it a leadership of several concurrent or serial alliances?
How would you say that programme of works alliance procurement process worked?

Program performance questions

How would say this programme met or is meeting its original expectations of strategic intent while fitting in with cost/time/fitness for purpose? How well did you feel that the alliance component KPIs/KRAs were conceptualised and/or had evolved?

Commitment to Best for Project / Best for Client

To what extent do you feel that the ALT and AMT members on the PAs have demonstrated a best for programme attitude across the alliance that you were involved in? Can you provide some examples of how working relationships developed (+ve or −ve) over time?

Value Delivery

To what extent was there a clear statement of value to be generated from this programme arrangement? How was value for money (VfM) expressed? Did it link to any specific strategic KRAs for learning?

Specifically About Team Collaboration – For Program Alliances

How well did the AMT collaborate on this project relative to a business as usual approach? How did the AMT and ALT collaborate in shaping the way the programme delivery took place? To what extent does the collaboration style extend to project teams outside the alliance that were part of your supply chain?

Specifically About the Program Management Culture

To what extent did a 'sink or swim together' attitude prevail? How did this manifest itself?
To what extent did this extend to project teams outside the alliance that were part of your supply chain?
How did the ALT influence the programme culture through their relationship with the AMT for their projects?
Can you name 3 aspects about the workplace culture in this alliance that differentiates it from business as usual experience you have had on past programmes or projects?

Specifically about Innovation on the Program

It is often said that programme alliances spur more innovation than business as usual projects over time. Can you provide any examples of how continuous improvement/innovation was encouraged/facilitated?

<u>**Skills and Attributes**</u>

What specific skills, attributes or experience do you think is needed for alliance programmes that is different to business as usual projects you have experience of?

<u>**Possible Improvements**</u>

How do you think the AMT could have improved their performance in terms of barriers and drivers experienced?

How do you think the ALT could have improved their performance in terms of barriers and drivers experienced from your perspective?

Case Study Interview Guide Project Alliances

Note: Being an interview guide, the questions are brief and will require some explanation when presenting them to interviewees.

Context:

From what context is this interview undertaken?

Demographics: experience; no. of years in type of business(es), position(s), types of projects.

<u>**Fundamental performance questions**</u>

How would say this project met its original expectations of cost/time/fitness for purpose?

If there has been any scope creep in cost time etc. has this been the result of identifying greater value delivery opportunities that explains any cost/time etc creep? (note Charles mentioned something about UGL undertaking some building/civil works where appropriate)

<u>**Commitment to Best for Project / Best for Client**</u>

To what extent do you feel that the ALT and AMT members have demonstrated a best for project attitude? Can you provide some examples?

<u>**Value Delivery**</u>

To what extent was there a clear statement of expected value to be delivered for this project and how was this expressed and recorded in a value statement or record of value generated? How was value for money (VfM) expressed during the bidding process and subsequently through the project delivery phase? Did it link to KRAs for example?

<u>**Specifically About Team Collaboration**</u>

How well did the AMT collaborate on this project relative to a business as usual approach? How did the AMT and ALT collaborate in shaping the way the project delivery took place?

Did the collaboration style extend to project teams outside the alliance that were part of your supply chain?

<u>**Specifically About the Project Culture**</u>

To what extent did the 'sink or swim together' attitude prevail? How did this manifest itself?

To what extent did this extend to project teams outside the alliance that were part of your supply chain?

How did the ALT influence the project culture through their relationship with the AMT?

Can you name 3 aspects about the workplace culture in this alliance that differentiates it from business as usual experience you have had on past projects?

<u>**Specifically about Innovation on the Project**</u>

It is often said that project alliances spur more innovation than business as usual projects. Can you provide 3 examples of how innovation was encouraged and facilitated on this project?

Skills and Attributes

What specific skills, attributes or experience do you think is needed for alliance projects that is different to business as usual projects you have experience of?

Possible Improvements

How do you think the AMT could have improved their performance in terms of barriers and drivers experienced?

How do you think the ALT could have improved their performance in terms of barriers and drivers experienced from your perspective?

Appendix 2

Details of Data Coding for the Wittgenstein Model

We coded the 500+ pages of interview transcripts and took into consideration the documentary (web-based and other company reports case studies etc.) to code the data. Coding transcript data is a sensemaking exercise used in developing concepts using grounded theory (Corbin & Strauss, 1990; Corbin, Strauss, & Strauss, 2008; Strauss & Corbin, 1998). Both researchers perused the data and independently assessed categories and sub-categories that suggested themes and subthemes that fit a logic that emerges from the data. We then compared notes and perceptions and reasoned our choices to agree on the final coding of themes and sub-themes presented below. The following model in Figure 1 represents the themes.

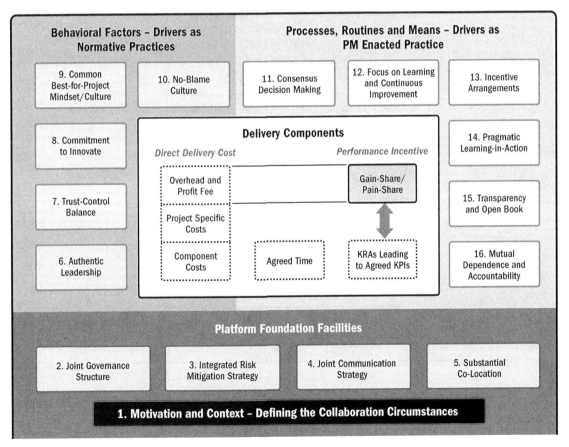

Figure A1.   An RBP Wittgenstein's Idea of Family-resemblance

To make reading this appendix easier for the reader, we have included a duplicate of Section 1, Tables 11, 12, and 13, in Table A4, Table A5, and Table A6. This is followed by detailed discussion of subthemes to each of the 16 themes identified in Figure A1.

Table A4.   Wittgenstein's Family Resemblance Elements for Platform Foundational Facilities for RBP

Platform Foundational Facilities – Elements and Themes 1-5	Subthemes from the transcript analysis (see Appendix 2 for more details)	Suggested to be measured by a five-point Likert scale
1 – The **motivation and context** of the circumstances impacting upon a procurement choice. This defines a substrate of circumstances that affects the potential degree of possible collaboration.	*Best value*—motivational focus is on value not lowest cost. Value is expressed in KRAs and KPIs that are linked to the project purpose. Often, 3BL issues are of high priority in such cases. *Emergency recovery*—motivation drives a procurement solution that enables recovery from the emergency as quickly and as feasibly as possible. *Experimental*—motivation drives purposeful exploration of options and the ability to learn and reflect upon experience to accumulate valuable knowledge that advances project objectives. *Competitive resource availability environment*—motivation drives a sustainable response to the prevailing competitive environment. Economically buoyant times pose a challenge to POs losing key staff to other employers. In challenging economic times, POs could be obliged by their governments to take advantage of their market position to force project delivery teams to accept contract conditions that may be in the PO's short term but not long term interests. Both conditions impose pressures related to economic times. *Relational rationale*—motivation and context drives the underlying logic of forming and developing relationships with potential project team members to further a longer term interest. Often all parties can benefit from the relationship, perhaps due to high levels of turbulence and change that challenge a BAU approach. *Known risks*—motivation can be triggered by the PO/POR assessing that a particular procurement form appears most appropriate to respond to risk sharing and responsibility that are known, assessable and best managed by the relevant identified participant to be allocated responsibility for those risks. *Unknown risks*—motivation is rooted in a context in which uncertainty requires a response of nurturing deep collaboration and trust between parties within a no-blame environment. There is a need for a psychologically safe environment where all participants can experiment with new approaches to respond to uncertainly and extreme ambiguity using teams with the capacity to rapidly evaluate consequences and outcomes and respond accordingly.	**Low** levels would be related to a *hostile environment* for collaboration. This may be due to lack of conviction of project participants in the value of collaboration within this project's context. **High** levels would relate to the procurement choice solution being driven by the acceptance of project participants in the logic of a clear advantage being gained by adopting a focus on a *supportive and collaborative* approach to delivering benefits that align with the values of participants.

Table A4. Wittgenstein's Family Resemblance Elements for Platform Foundational Facilities for RBP *(Continued)*

Platform Foundational Facilities – Elements and Themes 1-5	Subthemes from the transcript analysis (see Appendix 2 for more details)	Suggested to be measured by a five-point Likert scale
2- The level of **joint governance structure.** Having a unified way that each project delivery team party legitimises its actions through rules, standards and norms, values and coordination mechanisms such as organisational routines, and the way that committees, liaison and hierarchy represents a unified or complimentary way of interacting. This impacts the quality of explicit understanding of how teams should collaborate and communicate.	*Governance processes*—common assumptions and ways of working influences project governance processes and rules. These will vary according to the project procurement delivery form but will be designed to align the strategy, objectives and aims of the project. Process clarity is essential to inform the required behaviours. *Governance structure*—the structure of the entire project team defines how the level of flexibility/rigidity, power and influence and communication symmetry directly influences the workplace culture. The way that a project's overall leadership and management team is constituted impacts upon who has a voice and how they can express ideas, perspectives and concerns. *Governance best value strategy through KRAs and KPIs*—the project output and outcome is influenced by the strategy deployed to define, measure and assess success. The way that these are developed and used impacts upon effective project governance.	*Low* levels would be related to a *laisez faire* approach, where each participating project team has established its own individual stand-alone project governance standards. Little coherence in alignment of the whole project delivery organisational processes and structure is evident, with few explicit expectations about what success looks like and how to define and measure it. *High* relates to an effectively structured, uniform, integrated and consistent set of performance standards that apply across and within the project delivery teams. All participant organisations share a common understanding of how to organise for success and what constitutes valuable project output and outcome success
3- The extent to which an **integrated risk mitigation strategy** is organised for all parties as part of the client's proactive risk management system. This has an impact upon the quality of explicit understanding of how to collaboratively manage risk and uncertainty and potentially gain advantage from a project-wide insurance policy.	*Risk-sharing conversation*—The conversation about risk sharing; who takes responsibility for any class of, or particular risk. The strategy needs to be coherent to ensure that those best able to manage risk do so in a way that aligns the risk strategy to the project objectives and aims. The nature of these conversations differs in emphasis placed upon means to allocate accountability across project procurement forms. *Risk mitigation actions*—there are a number of ways, ranging from collective to individual, to agree upon and decide how to mitigate risk that vary according to the procurement form. *System integration*—of the project is structured and managed to provide a platform that is based upon the participant's philosophical stance about relationships between teams. Systems can be integrated to cope with risk, uncertainty and ambiguity to respond to a need for a platform to be developed to address these three related but separate concepts.	*Low* levels would be characterised by an immature and confused individual firm-specific risk management approach and poorly defined systemic approaches to deal with uncertainty and ambiguity. *High* levels would be represented by consistent and integrated risk assessment processes being identified, assessed and mitigated against a project-wide and broader systems-wide impact for the project or network in the case of programmes of projects.
4 - The level of **joint communication strategy** platforms such as integrated processes and ICT groupware, including building information modelling (BIM) and other electronic forms of communication. While BIM is more prevalent in recent years, past equivalent forms include groupware ICT, sharing drawings and plans between teams. Joint communication facilitates common communication and understanding.	*Common processes and systems*—Project participants need to share a common way of working and a common language and communication approach to avoid misunderstanding that can undermine trust and commitment and consequently undermine effective decision making and action. Bridges and interoperability between systems to cope with a lack of a "one system" are also essential. *Integrated communication platform*—A common ICT platform, including for example common BIM tools can minimise the risk of poor coordination, communication, and misunderstandings between participants	*Low* levels of joint communication would be characterised by poor quality staff interaction, use of firm-specific rather than project-wide processes and ICT systems, and weak cross-team mechanisms for gaining mutual understanding. *High* levels would be characterised by well-integrated processes that are well understood by all participants and advanced communication technologies being used that seamlessly connect all project parties within a particular procurement arrangement.

(continued)

Table A4. Wittgenstein's Family Resemblance Elements for Platform Foundational Facilities for RBP *(Continued)*

Platform Foundational Facilities – Elements and Themes 1-5	Subthemes from the transcript analysis (see Appendix 2 for more details)	Suggested to be measured by a five-point Likert scale
5 - The extent that project teams are **substantially co-located** within easy physical reach of each other. Close proximity facilitates ad hoc and chance encounters to improve building relationships and facilitating common understanding.	*Hierarchal integration mechanisms*—Leaders can inspire motivation toward unity of purpose by physically interacting with individuals in the various levels of an organisation. Site visits, meetings held on site, and other ritualistic or practical events that are held in the actual workplace can be very important as a platform for integrated joint action. *Physical co-location*—Project participants can more easily communicate and interact on problem solving, monitoring, and active collaboration when they are in within easy reach of each other. Co-location in a well-considered and conducive environment can facilitate positive interaction.	**Low** levels would be characterised by firm-specific policy determining that disparate teams are physically located in dispersed locations. There may also be a large visibility gap between project leaders and those at the "coal face." **High** levels would be characterised by a project-wide policy that attempts to maximise participant co-location on-site where feasible, including the POR. There would also be high interaction between project leadership groups and the project management and physical delivery team members so that engagement enhances communication and mutual perspective taking.

Table A5. Wittgenstein's Family Resemblance Elements for Behavioural Factors for RBP

Behavioural factors driving normative practices— Elements and Themes 6-10	Subthemes from the transcript analysis (see Appendix 2 for more details)	Suggested to be measured by a five-point Likert scale
6 - The degree of **authentic leadership,** that is, possessing ethical principled values and consistency of action with espoused rhetoric. This would apply across the project delivery team at every level of team leadership, not only for the project lead person(s) but also the supporting design and supply chain team leaders. It speaks to the project culture.	Authentic leadership is present in designated project leaders who hold institutional or organisational power, but it also applies to 'followers' within a collective leadership sense. *Reflectiveness*—Project participants are systems thinkers and often follow a strategic thinking approach about the situational context and know that the situational context is crucial to effective decision making. *Pragmatism*—Project participants get on with the job, are politically astute, and work within constraints or find ethical and sensible ways around these constraints. *Appreciativeness*—Project participants understand the motivations and value proposition of influential stakeholders involved in the project. They are consciously engaged with their team members and exhibit signs of having a high emotional intelligence. *Resilience*—Project participants exhibit adaptability, versatility, flexibility and being persistent when faced with adversity. They are able to effectively learn from experience. *Wisdom*—Project participants have opinions and advice that is valued, consistent, and reliable that others instinctively refer to. Their judgement abilities make their brokering advice crucial. They are perceived as having high levels of integrity based on inner strength of character, knowledge, and experience. *Spirit*—Project participants demonstrate the courage and have sufficient influence and respect to effectively challenge assumptions and often offer radical alternative solutions to resolve complex and difficult situations. *Authenticity*—Project participants demonstrate qualities of being approachable and trustworthy and open to ideas. They encourage and advance collaboration, discussion and new ways of thinking.	**Low** levels are revealed when espoused principled values are not demonstrated in action manifested through a gap between the rhetoric and reality of leading teams. **High** levels demonstrate consistency in espoused and enacted values that are genuinely principled.

Table A5. Wittgenstein's Family Resemblance Elements for Behavioural Factors for RBP *(Continued)*

Behavioural factors driving normative practices—Elements and Themes 6-10	Subthemes from the transcript analysis (see Appendix 2 for more details)	Suggested to be measured by a five-point Likert scale
7 – The **trust-control balance** of representing and protecting the interests of project leaders with that of other genuinely relevant stakeholders while relying on the integrity, benevolence and ability of all project team parties to "do the right thing" in terms of project performance. It is the ability to be able to understand the value-proposition of "the other" project teams and to assess their capacity to deliver the promise while establishing mechanisms to ensure transparent accountability. Trust balance is also about trust in others to suggest improvement and to discuss sensitive (possibly political) issues.	*Autonomy*—Project participants have autonomy to respond to the situational context. Their responsiveness is complicated by institutional and cultural norms that may either restrain their autonomy and therefore their capacity to respond to new initiatives and changes to "plan," or the organisational culture and governance arrangements may leave them with enough autonomy to act somewhat independently. *Forms of trust*—Project participants' capacity to experiment, explore options and take action is advanced or constrained by their leadership teams' perceptions of how various interests are best served. These perceptions are influenced by the nature of that interest, the forms and basis of project participants' and their leaders' level of trust in each other and understanding the impact of assumptions about self-interest and shared interest on trust their levels. *Safe workplace cultures*—Project participants' trust in their leaders and colleagues is often mediated by their perceived treatment in terms of a working in a safe psychological, physical, and intellectual environment. *Trust relationship building*—Project participants and their leadership teams engage in varying levels of effort to create a balance in trust and control in which trust with caution is tempered with blind faith.	*Low* balance is demonstrated by extreme naïveté by participants about trusting others implicitly or alternatively by exhibiting high levels of suspicion and/or unreasonable demands for formal and informal control and monitoring that implies a cynical attitude toward trust of others. *High* balance is demonstrated by innate sensibility to juggle transparency and accountability demands with the need for trust with necessary due diligence. It also demonstrates a professional understanding of the nature of project participant accountability constraints and opportunities for resolving and possibly helping resolve institutional paradoxes so that accountability is consistent with accepted responsibility.
8 – **Commitment to be innovative** represents the duality of being willing to be innovative within a structured mechanism to enable and empower people to be innovative. This is closely linked to a project team participants' capacity for learning, reflection, creativity being ambidextrous, and the organisation's core values of supporting and rewarding questioning the *status quo*.	*Innovation types*—Project participants need to understand and adapt to behavioural expectations associated with different types of project procurement forms. They may be engaged in product, process, or behavioural types of innovation within a project or programme situational context that could affect how team member's commitment can be initiated and sustained. Balancing exploration and exploitation of innovation, given the procurement form expectation, is important. *Commitment to continuous improvement*—Project participants' purpose for being innovative should be to achieve continuous improvement. The extent to which project participants can be innovative and effect continuous improvement depends upon institutional, governance, and individual motivational and enabling factors. *Testing, prototyping and experimenting*—Project participants' innovative actions are usually manifested by testing, prototyping, and experimentation within the context of having and inquiring, curious, and often sceptical mind.	*Low* commitment levels are manifested by inadequate or incomplete linkage of motivation, ability, and facilitation for innovation within the context of the procurement form. *High* commitment levels are manifested by vision, objectives and desire to be innovative with well-considered instruments to measure and demonstrate innovation, motivation through rewards and incentives and demonstrated high levels of existing absorptive capacity for innovation.

(continued)

Table A5. Wittgenstein's Family Resemblance Elements for Behavioural Factors for RBP *(Continued)*

Behavioural factors driving normative practices—Elements and Themes 6-10	Subthemes from the transcript analysis (see Appendix 2 for more details)	Suggested to be measured by a five-point Likert scale
9 - **Common best-for-project mindset and culture** relates to the focus being placed on value generated in delivering the project compared with objectives of delivering what was explicitly requested or demanded. It is also about the priority of the project outcome taking precedence above all other considerations (despite inherent paradoxes). A major effort is directed at a positive and successful project outcome rather than individual teams being winners or losers.	*Alignment of common goals*—Project participants' need to be effectively collaborating to a constructive end through sharing common and aligned goals about best-for-project outcomes and how that delivers VfM. *Outcomes and performance levels*—These should be assessed and judged based upon common best-for-project aligned goals. Challenging for excellence—Project participants' need to be constantly challenging their level of outcome and performance through effective collaboration toward a constructive evaluation of achieved outcomes and performance. *Value for money reporting*—Project participants' need to devise ways to recognise, monitor, and effectively diffuse knowledge about how their performance and workplace culture has impacted VfM on their project or programme. This is not about "spin-doctoring" but about making a credible and acceptable case for recognising achievements. *Recruiting support*—Project participants' need to devise ways to effectively recruit support for best-for-project values through an effective PO/POR internal and NOPs recruitment strategy as well as enlisting support for as many members of the project delivery chain as is possible.	*Low* best-for-project mindset levels are manifested by a higher level of priority for individual benefit realisation at the potential expense of other project team members and the project owner. *High* best-for-project mindset levels are manifested by a genuine attitude that "we all sink-or-swim together" and a focus on maximising value to the project (or network in the case of a progamme). Contractual arrangements will reinforce pooled gain or pain based on performance measured by KRAs and KPIs.
10 - **No blame culture** relates to the degree to which teams welcome taking responsible accountability for problems as they arise rather than having shirked responsibility in the hope that others take them on who may be vulnerable to being blamed for potential failure. It is also about being "part of the solution" through being part of an overall acceptance of shared-and-several responsibility for understanding. This involves discussing problems in an unprejudiced manner and opening up one's mind to alternative perspectives and seeing issues from multiple perspectives.	*Rationale for a no-blame culture*—Project participants avoiding a blame-shifting culture having felt pain and hardship through past experience of being blamed. They are determined not to repeat the experience and to thus support a no-blame culture. *Facilitating mechanisms for no-blame*—contractual, behavioural and organisational mechanisms that support the establishment and maintenance of a no-blame culture.	*Low* no-blame culture is manifested by a project participant's high propensity to shift blame from themselves to others. These problems may be attributable to them for unforeseen, unanticipated, or unwanted events that impact adversely upon project delivery. A low no-blame culture is also palpable by a tendency to avoid acknowledging potential problem situations in the hope that blame can be attributed to others. *High* no-blame culture is manifested by a culture of open discussion of problems, unforeseen, unanticipated, or unwanted events that may impact adversely upon project delivery. The purpose of a no-blame culture is to achieve wider team participation in collaboration and collective management of problems and to take responsibility and accountability for developing problem solutions. It may also be manifested by the PO taking ownership of risk elements that other participants are unable to bear, rather than force them to accept accountability for such risks.

Table A6. Wittgenstein's Family Resemblance Elements for Processes, Routines and Means for RBP

Processes, routines, and means driving normative practices – Elements 11-16	Subthemes from the transcript analysis (see Appendix 2 for more details)	Suggested to be measured by a five-point Likert scale
11 – **Consensus decision making** refers to the extent to which there is total agreement on a decision made at the <u>project strategic and project operational executive level.</u> High levels may require extensive time for discussion, exploration and testing mental models, and this may be against the interest of speedy decisions and action to counter crises. Following Langley et al.'s (1995) consensus decision making view, this may involve purposefully leaving the means vague while keeping the aims crystal clear, and agreeing to navigate solutions by agreeing on end states rather than developing detailed plans.	*Cultural drivers*—the discussion in Chapter 4 on culture highlighted that some cultures have high-power asymmetry, where it is expected that individuals at higher levels of a hierarchy make decisions and issue orders to those lower in the hierarchy who must accept and act on those decisions. Other cultural dimensions also impact power asymmetry. Uncertainty avoidance leads people to avoid being committed to a risky decision and a collectivist culture encourages, if not requires, that individuals "go along with the crowd" rather than voice concern or opposition to mooted decisions. Some disciplines and workplace settings demand challenges to assumptions, while others demand obedience and discipline. These cultural drivers enhance or impede genuine consensus decision making. *Enablers of consensus*—organisational, structural, as well as behavioural enablers that facilitate and support consensus decision making and action taking. *Inhibitors of consensus*—organisational structural as well as behavioural enablers that inhibit and suppress consensus decision making and action taking.	*Low* consensus decision making is manifested by a highly hierarchical project team leaders' leadership style under which power and influence determines how decisions are made and where the expected response is on whether decisions are implemented without question or complaint. It is also manifested by a tendency for a domination of top-down directives being issued as edicts. *High* consensus decision making is manifested by a highly egalitarian and collaborative leadership style of project team leaders. Issues and problems requiring a decision develop out of inclusive knowledge sharing and discussion of perspectives, expected intended and unintended consequences, and implications of decisions. High levels of feedback, good or bad, are sought.
12 – **Focus on learning and continuous improvement** refers to providing a compelling projects-as-learning value proposition and the practice of transforming learning opportunities into continuous improvement. It also implies that emphasis on learning KRAs and KPIs should not only be focused on documenting and publicising lessons learnt from projects, but that project teams should value these KRAs and KPIs to be highly ranked as important PM and project outcome success factors.	*Lessons-learnt knowledge transfer*—participants should be aware of the mechanisms that projects offer for opportunities for learning. They should be aware of the PO's learning and continuous improvement preferences and needs, how other team members operate, and how to best collaborate with them to learn from the project and to gain technical, process, or interpersonal knowledge. Some projects are specifically established as learning laboratories for radical new innovation or for more methodical incremental improvement. A focus on effective lessons-learnt knowledge transfer needs to be designed into a procurement form to avoid lessons learnt becoming lessons forgotten or ignored. *Capacity to adapt to new ideas*—participants need to facilitate continuous improvement by prompting learning-oriented ways of thinking and doing. Knowledge transfer, as discussed in Chapter 4 Table 4, is difficult because knowledge is sticky. People who can make the most from continuous improvement are open to the process of "unlearning" and "relearning." Without this adaptive capacity, lessons learnt become lessons ignored, and often context is not considered to wisely consider which lessons should be adopted or adapted depending on the way that the new context emerges. *A culture of skills and learning development*—participants need to be developing a culture of organisational and individual learning to facilitate lessons-learnt knowledge transfer and provide the environment in which this can effectively take place. This goes beyond training and development at the technical and process level. It also entails enabling participants to perceive and understand context and situation and interconnectedness of elements into a whole so that cause and effect links can be understood to enable intelligent adaptation of lessons learnt.	*Low* focus on learning and continuous improvement is manifested by actors within collaborative arrangements, and a network delivering a project being blind to and failing to grasp the potential competitive advantage of applying presented learning opportunities. *High* focus on learning and continuous improvement manifested by actors within collaborative arrangements and a network delivering a project being alert and aware of opportunities for improvement and being successful in grasping competitive advantage through effectively harvesting lessons learnt.

(continued)

Table A6. Wittgenstein's Family Resemblance Elements for Processes, Routines and Means for RBP *(Continued)*

Processes, routines, and means driving normative practices – Elements 11-16	Subthemes from the transcript analysis (see Appendix 2 for more details)	Suggested to be measured by a five-point Likert scale
13 - **Incentive arrangements** refer to the pain-sharing and gain-sharing agreement. This refers to how the process was instigated and how it operated. Shared accountability and a desire for innovation require a risk and reward mechanism to create an incentive to excel. At one extreme, all profit margins may be quarantined and pooled and subsequently distributed based on a negotiated and agreed pain and gain sharing formula based on total project performance. Alternatively, profit margins may be based solely on individual team performance.	*Incentive arrangements*—Project participants are incentivised to perform at exceptional levels of performance and there is a risk/reward system in place to encourage this. Central to incentive arrangements is developing systematic encouragement for innovation and for benefits of that innovation to be transferred to project participants and then onto their base organisations. Clear KRAs and KPIs are developed to monitor and measure performance. *Managing tension between innovation and incentivisation*—participants and project owners need to manage the tension between continuous improvements that keeps raising the performance benchmark and how that is incentivised. It is important to balance providing sufficient incentive and reward for improvement, while avoiding incentive targets being either too easy or too hard, as this may undermine continuous improvement. This also brings in issues about balancing innovation incentivised through a competitive dialogue approach at the front-end of a project before contracts are let, with achieving innovation and improvement by encouraging innovation and continuous improvement progressively throughout the project duration.	*Low* levels of incentivisation is manifested by little emphasis being placed upon encouraging parties to agree to place potential profit and gain/pain in a risk/reward arrangement subject to a whole-of-project outcome performance. KRAs and KPIs are absent or rudimentary. *High* levels of incentivisation is manifested by much emphasis being placed upon encourage parties to agree to place potential profit and gain/pain in a risk/reward arrangement that is subject to a whole-of-project outcome performance. KRAs and KPIs are well developed, provide stretch and challenge and are sophisticated in their understanding of the project context.
14 - **Pragmatic learning-in-action** refers to the active gathering of value through teams collaborating with the strategic aim to learn, and to gain competitive advantage through collective opportunities to learn and adapt. It is about team leaders and members seeing the project as a learning experience, with acceptance that both experimental success and failure requires discussion and analysis. Often, unexpected opportunities arise out of failed experiments through assumptions being re-framed that lead to promising benefits in other contexts.	*Action-learning*—participants as individuals, but more so in groups, undertake action-learning in a number of ways. These range from simply trying out things and experimenting to undertaking complicated modelling and simulation exercises. These activities provide the mechanisms to gain knowledge from action. It remains critical that mechanisms should be in place to capture and make usable, experience, and knowledge gained from action-learning initiatives. *Coaching and mentoring*—another form of pragmatic learning is through coaching and mentoring. This is where experience and insights are shared in a formalised manner through one-on-one interaction between project participants and "wiser" or at least more experienced people who can help their coachees/mentees to be able to contextualise learning, to refine it through dialogue, and to add value through that knowledge by sharing stories making critical comparisons and exploring meaning and making sense out of that learning.	*Low* pragmatic learning-in-action is manifested by actors within a network delivering a project to fail to translate learning opportunities into actual benefits and competitive action. Failed experiments are punished. *High* pragmatic learning-in-action is manifested by actors within a network delivering a project capitalising on learning opportunities to achieve competitive action. This can be also assessed by the weight that these actors place on the value of experimentation as a way to see issues and solutions in a new light. Failed experiments are valued for their intellectual stimulation in discovering, for example, a better understanding of cause-effect loops.
15- **Transparency and open book processes, routines and practices** refer to project participants agreeing to be audited and fully open to scrutiny.	*Transparency*—the extent to which project participants agree to be fully open about their cost structures, their decision-making process, and their project delivery processes.	*Low* transparency and open-book approaches to project delivery intensely protect the security of organisations and individuals to gain access to information about cost structures or the basis of project plans. It is often exemplified by the code words "commercial in confidence." It seeks to hide both good and bad news, but this often results in mistrust that undermines collaboration and opportunities for constructive change.

Processes, routines, and means driving normative practices – Elements 11-16	Subthemes from the transcript analysis (see Appendix 2 for more details)	Suggested to be measured by a five-point Likert scale
Actors within the project network would have confidence that they can trust those inspecting their books not to take advantage of that access and information, and those people doing the audits, due diligence, and inspections must be capable and effective enough to understand the implication of what they inspect. Total transparency and accountability is necessary where the project is undertaken on a cost-plus basis, where the project owner is funding all direct, administrative and management costs.

The extent of transparency and accountability is a trade-off between the extent to which the PO plays a "hands-on" or "hands-off" role. There is a fine balance needed between expenditure on direct administrative and management costs and how processes reinforce a trust-but-verify approach. | *Accountability*—the extent to which project participants agree to be fully open to scrutiny, allowing authorised project owner representatives to audit and inspect books, processes, and decision-making rationale. | High transparency and open-book approaches to project delivery present opportunities for generating trust by clients and other parties that may access that information. It is a confronting notion that many organisations cannot face. It requires the project owner's authorised probity auditors to have free access to their financial books. Thus, confidence in ethical and legal business conduct is necessary to accept this challenge. |
| 16 – **Mutual dependence and accountability** refers to collaboration in projects requiring participants to not only recognise their interdependency but to also honestly respond to a sink-or-swim-together workplace culture when communicating.

Governance systems may both support and enhance individual team responsibility and accountability, or alternatively they may inhibit approaches to cross-team collaboration. | *Characteristics of mutual dependency*—various forms of RBP have specific unique characteristics that have a focus on mutual team dependency where they sink or swim together. Teams may or may not perceive themselves to become a temporary single team entity with perceptions about how participants perceive the workplace supports or inhibits a unified team approach to managing the project.

Enhancing enablers of mutual dependency—participants seek to actively leverage processes, routines, and means to facilitate and sustain collaboration.

Countering inhibitors to mutual dependency— participants seek to actively counter processes, routines, and means that inhibit and undermine collaboration. | Low mutual dependence and accountability refers to an inability or lack of desire to acknowledge the potential value of team interdependence and accountability. Participants follow individualistic paths, possibly at the expense of others, and/or do not support a sink-or-swim-together workplace culture, or they actively undermine that culture.

High mutual dependence and accountability refers to an ability and keen desire to acknowledge team inter-dependence and accountability in ways that build interteam trust and commitment through actively enhancing a sink-or-swim-together workplace culture, and to actively counter any actions that may inhibit this culture. |

Each theme and subtheme will now be discussed in detail using illustrative quotes to support our findings.

Theme 1 relates to the platform foundational facilities that define the motivation and context circumstances that led to collaboration. Subthemes from Section 1, Table 11, **motivation and context** (refer to Table A4) are now elaborated upon as provided in Table A7.

- The **motivation and context** defines and affects the potential degree of possible collaboration. It answers the fundamental question, why would you use project procurement approach X versus Y?
- Subthemes emerged from the data for **Theme 1 - motivation and context** as follows:
    - 1.1 Best value – the key motivational concept is value, not cost. Value can be expressed well beyond the iron triangle of cost/time/fitness for purpose KPIs to include 3BL issues. These are often of high priority in cases where alliancing is used to achieve social and environmental KRAs;
    - 1.2 Emergency recovery – the motivation is to get a project solution that recovers from the emergency as quickly and as feasibly as possible. KSAEs featuring ambidexiterity and nimbleness to respond to unknowns with high technical performance capacity are key attributes of teams and the procurement method to be chosen for these kinds of project;
    - 1.3 Experimental – the motivation is to purposefully explore options and to be able to learn and reflect on experience to accumulate valuable knowledge to advance the project objectives;
    - 1.4 Competitive resource availability environment – the motivation and context is to respond to the prevailing competitive environment. In time of economic buoyancy, POs are at risk of losing key talent to competitors and other sectors (e.g., public to private sector). It may make sense to capitalise on the opportunity to learn from a public-private sector alliance for key PO employees and NOPs wishing to consolidate that competency to prepare for future PA opportunities. Alternatively, government POs may be tempted in challenging economic times to take advantage of their market position to force project delivery teams to accept more traditional procurement choices with contract conditions that may be subsequently unsustainable. The response could result in defensive actions be taken by parties and a reversion to conflict and a "claims mentality;"
    - 1.5 Relational rationale – the motivation and context here is to form and develop relationships with potential project team members to further a longer-term interest. This may be as stated above in 1.3 to learn from the experience but also may be to gain access to rare and dificult-to-replicate KSAE, so that competitive advantage may be leached to the party seeking the relationship. Often this is a reciprical arrangement in which all parties can benefit from the relationship, perhaps due to high levels of turbulence and change;
    - 1.6 Known risks – this motivation can be triggered by choosing the particular project procurement form to best allocate known risks to participants that can best manage them; and
    - 1.7 Unknown risks – this motivation for basing a procurement choice is rooted in a context in which uncertainty requires deep collaboration, trust between parties, and a no-blame environment in which it is safe for all participants to try new approaches using teams that can rapidly evaluate consequences and outcomes and respond accordingly to overcome risks on a best-for-project basis.

Table A7. Wittgenstein Model Theme 1: Motivation and Context

Theme and Subtheme	Notes, examples, and KSAE quotes
1.1 Best value	Best value means more than value for money (VfM). The narrow view of project delivery success expectations based upon the "iron triangle" of cost/time/fitness for purpose has expanded considerably. Transactionally oriented project procurement forms mainly focus on iron triangle interpretation more rigidly and narrowly to lowest cost and shortest time (bid) and quality or fitness for the purpose of meeting immediate needs. Higher levels of RBP approaches focus more on longer term strategic success. VfM can obtain what the POR asked for but not necessarily what the PO needed or wanted. Higher-order RBP often seeks greater effort and emphasis being placed upon the **purpose** of the project being clear. We see more thought being placed upon coherence in strategy, sustainability, "bigger picture" view of the project outcome, and, increasingly, social responsibility and 3BL considerations.
Examples of high levels of best-value thinking	• Understanding that bid price/time/quality and final cost/time/quality are usually two very different outcomes. • Understanding that output and outcome are also often loosely linked. • Understanding that defining the meaning of value within a context of multiple valid stakeholder interests requires considerable sophistication and wisdom from the POR side and that collaborating with project delivery terms to realise that articulated value requires considerable sophistication and wisdom from the delivery team side through a constructive dialogue to differentiate between what was asked for and what was needed.
High-level KSAE needed for best value outcomes.	• *Technical and PM KSAE* – High levels are required regardless of the project procurement form. Projects characterised by a high levels of known-knowns and known-unknowns (see Chapter 3, Figure 11) may be delivered with a greater level of prescriptiveness and hierarchical "command and control" PM style. Projects characterised by a high level of unknown-knowns and unknown-unknowns (see Chapter 3, Figure 11) may require great levels of flexibility, ambidexterity, stakeholder engagement, openness to new ideas, and perspective taking of both the POR and project delivery team to be capable and effective in collaboration when exploring the viability of best value options. • *Business solutions KSAE* – High levels are required when initially defining and drafting as well as responding to the business case assumptions through project delivery. The main difference in business solutions KSAE requirements between the orders of project collaboration models is the manner in which these are applied to deliver best value as defined by each team member. These skills are focussed internally by each team individually for lower-order collaboration models to enable maximising their benefit whereas for higher order collaboration models, these skills are focussed on best-for-project-value outcomes. • *Relational KSAE* – High levels are required between team members in addition to within teams as the order of collaboration model moves from first to fourth order (see Table 6, soft skills 4 to 10).
Illustrative quotes	Best value is centred upon knowing and articulating what you need, as interviewee P30 said:
P30	. . . if we really want to get value for money as the State, we've really got to put our greatest efforts into putting the business case together because it's our job to help government select the right option for the State in the business case that's value for money and then continue to progress the development of the design from thereafter using an experienced designer and an experienced builder . . .
	In terms of understanding that lowest-bid price is different than final price, TOC P-29 said:
P29	. . . So what would have happened pre alliance is that we would have got a designer to do the design. We put the design out to contractors, they would have quoted on it, we would have accepted a price, and then they would have found all sorts of difficulties in constructing it with all the landfill type issues. . . . So what happened in this particular case is you've got really seasoned constructors in the same room as the designers, so when the designers are trying to design, constructors are going, "well if you've got normal ground conditions you could build it like that but we're going to have all of these other issues we've got to deal with." So by the time you get to the final design and you target it out to cost, there's been a lot of innovation up front in getting to that price.
1.2 Emergency Recovery	There are circumstances where the goal and main objective of a project is to recover after an emergency. This may occur for projects responding to (natural or human-caused) disasters. They may also be a response to a business emergency, such as an accelerated new product delivery or process re-engineering where time-to-market is vital for corporate survival.
Examples of high levels of emergency recovery thinking	• Understanding the scope, scale, and resource demands placed upon the project recovery team. • Understanding risk, ambiguity, and uncertainly inherent in a disaster recovery context. • Managing the process of coping with political, social, and stakeholder issues that will impact the way that the project should proceed.
High-level KSAE needed for emergency recovery outcomes.	• *Technical and PM KSAE* – High levels are required regardless of the project procurement form. • *Business solutions KSAE* – The best response could be simple replacement, but that is unlikely because many disasters occur as a consequence of a chain of events. High-level skills are needed in diagnosing the "real" problems, issues, and challenges, and framing an appropriate response. • *Relational KSAE* – High levels are required, because often discovering the most feasible project solution requires canvassing a wide range of perspectives, and so both the POR and project team participants need high-level relational skills to effectively communicate and take appropriate action.
Illustrative quote	Crisis response is about being nimble, creative, ambidextrous, and committed, as P33 put it:
P33	. . . we're also sitting in a position where we get hit by quite a few crises out there and those guys are able to respond very quickly, engage in the community, get the local workforce to get out there and deliver improvements from things like bushfires and floods.

(continued)

Table A7. Wittgenstein Model Theme 1: Motivation and Context *(Continued)*

Theme and Subtheme	Notes, examples, and KSAE quotes
1.3 Experimental	There are times when a project is triggered by the need to experiment and try something new. Brady and Davies (2004) discuss a class of projects as "vanguard" projects whose prime purpose is co-learning and exploration. These may be to develop completely new stand-alone outcomes or be part of a ramping up of a learning curve for a more production-line approach for new standard-type projects. On other occasions, they may be piloting new products, assemblies, systems, or procedures.
Examples of high levels of experimental thinking	• Understanding the scope, scale and resource demands placed upon the project team in developing the project delivery strategy. • Understanding and managing risk, ambiguity and uncertainly inherent with the novel venture and effectively reflecting to optimise harvesting knowledge gained. • Understanding and managing political, social and stakeholder issues that will impact the way that the project should proceed to ensure successful completion or if necessary abandonment of the experiment.
High-level KSAE needed for experimental outcomes.	• *Technical and PM KSAE* – Particularly high levels are required to ensure a broad repertoire of potential responses to unavoidably frequent unexpected events and outcomes. • *Business solutions KSAE* – High-level cognitive and adaptive skills are needed to sense and pursue opportunities while judging pragmatically how to deal with constraints and limitations to exploiting new knowledge gained. • *Relational KSAE* – High levels are required because these projects often attract unconventional thinkers and this imposes communication challenges.
Illustrative quotes	Large and highly hierarchical organisations may find difficulty with such projects and need to view them as a form of skunkworks or special-purpose organisation. P33 said:
P33	I guess the alliance was formed, [XXX] did a lot of work internally to let their people know that this was a pilot in many respects, they couldn't see a way to lift their standard without changing something about their delivery . . .
	Having a long-term relationship between PO and contractor can be useful for experimenting and piloting new ways to operate and gain advantage from ramping up a learning curve.
P44 from a programme alliance context	. . . on the [XXX] Alliance, we had to put concrete sleepers in, Melbourne to Sydney; and the unit rate at the start of the job was something around the $250 a sleeper, by the end of the job we had got it down to around $160 a sleeper. Now, there were lots of little subtle innovations that took place to drive that price, and that was—is another way of looking at it.
1.4 Competitive resource availability environment	The general competitive environment can impose both opportunities and constraints upon RBP choice from a value for money perspective. In highly buoyant economic times, government agencies and other highly (employment levels and conditions) constrained organisations may form alliance-type arrangement to offer opportunities to key employees to retain and upskill them. In less buoyant economic times, POs may feel that they are in a strong position to demand more of those delivering projects.
Examples of high levels of competitive environment context thinking	• Understanding that the project purpose and aim fit within the current and project delivery period economic and resource availability context to maintain an appropriate balance to match project outcomes demands with available resources. • Understanding and managing opportunities within the realities of the marketplace to avoid behaving as neither victim nor predator.
High-level KSAE needed for competitive environment.	• *Technical and PM KSAE* – High levels of appreciation of the demand and supply ratio of skills and competency availability for the project and their market availability. • *Business solutions KSAE* – Understanding and being able to conduct and effectively communicate the business case strategy for the chosen project delivery approach. • *Relational KSAE* – Effectively managing potential power and influence imbalances.
Illustrative quotes	Two examples follow of alliances established in booming times.
P29 on the rationale to set up a programme alliance	. . . this was all happening at the time of the engineering boom, so if water authorities have got more projects to deliver, that means that the private industry is also going pretty well in terms of consultants and contractors. It becomes a very hot market out there. We were having trouble retaining engineers who wanted to go onto bigger and better things, either within the water industry or in the mining boom, etc. So we had to come up with a strategy that was going to provide the resources both internally and externally to not only delivery the big projects, but our overall program so we set up the [XX] Alliance a bit over four years ago.
P48 on the effort required to attract excellent contractors in booming economic times.	When the government announced the capital program, it was for [XXX], there was about a $7 billion rail program. At exactly the same time they were out for tender for the biggest bridge across the river which was about a billion dollars and they had about $2 billion road program. I had a huge amount of competition for all the A-listers, now all of those contracts were generally hard dollar, with a specific risk profile. What I needed to do was come up with something that had a risk profile which was favourable in terms of the eyes of all the blue-chip companies, so just to attract them to what I was doing.

Table A7. Wittgenstein Model Theme 1: Motivation and Context *(Continued)*

Theme and Subtheme	Notes, examples, and KSAE quotes
1.5 Relational rationale	RBP forms inherently imply that there is perceived need to create, nurture, and maintain a form of a relationship, the extent of commitment may vary. Some choices may be based upon negative past experiences and the need to overcome problems caused or at least exacerbated by the chosen project procurement form. Other choices are based on positive past experience with use of a specific form of procurement that worked well within that context. Experience can form the basis for rationalising any given procurement choice within its given context.
Examples of high levels of relational context thinking	• Understanding the causes for past positive or negative experience based on institutional drivers driven by the forms of project delivery contract. • Understanding and appreciating how trust and commitment can be shaped by the form of project delivery procurement and behavioural requirements or habits based on specific project procurement forms. • Understanding the big-picture and how a more holistic approach to project delivery may improve value delivered.
High-level KSAE needed for relational needs.	• *Technical and PM KSAE* – High levels relative to the deficit in KSAE that parties wishing to engage in a closer relationship perceive that they need to gain through the relationship. Most likely perceived highly complex projects need a relational approach. • *Business solutions KSAE* – High levels of ability to understand the value proposition of various parties ability to perceive how the relationship could be of value to the other party(ies) and how to frame a response to that need that can be justified through meeting a sound business case. • *Relational KSAE* – High levels of ability to be able to visualise broad relationship networks and how value to other party(ies) can be enhanced, and how to frame a constructive response to that need.
Illustrative quotes	A relational rationale can be based upon filling skills, competence, and knowledge gaps through collaboration in a way that provides sufficient incentive for all involved parties. As P17 and A10 comment:
P17	[relating to a PA] You've got to have something of significance, substance, you know, a hundred million or more. Probably the biggest flag for me really concerns cultural and some of the personalities, far more so than in a normal alliance
A10	. . . they've learnt through the previous periods that the best way to achieve better outcomes is through greater levels of collaboration, so let's not throw the baby out with the bath water. Let's just turn that around and use that to try and drive costs down by working together. So that's one thing that's come out of it. And another thing that's come out of it is that, to be more efficient from their own point of view of the operations, a lot of the project managers that I interviewed, said that they, "Preferred collaborative working. It was more efficient as well as more effective in the long run."
1.6 Known risks	Decisions to use a higher or lower intensive RBP form often depends upon the level of perceived complexity relating to known risks—technical, management, political/stakeholder, or for influencing commitment. Managing risks is best deployed by allowing those who can best manage the risk-taking responsibility and be compensated for doing so. This may require purposeful retention of expert staff to retain critical knowledge.
Examples of high levels of known risks context thinking	• Understanding which party is best able to manage known-known risks and who can identify known-unknown risks with the expertise to successfully investigate and then manage these kinds of risk. • Understanding how to best compensate parties for taking responsibility and accountability for those risks. • Understanding how to frame effective risk management through contractual arrangements. • Having the capacity to retain critical KSAE within an organization or ensuring having access to that corporate and individual KSAE.
High-level KSAE needed for dealing with known risks.	• *Technical and PM KSAE* – High levels of ability to identify risks and optimal and effective ways to manage those risks. • *Business solutions KSAE* – High levels of ability to justify the risk management model to be adopted. • *Relational KSAE* – High levels of ability to collaborate and manage people to best develop risk management approaches.
Illustrative quotes	Effective known risk management is about applying excellent KSAE within an appropriate project procurement framework to liberate otherwise dormant energy and commitment to effectively manage those risks. This may involve talent management decisions. As A09 and P28 comment:
A09	. . . if you look at the top-performing companies, they don't downsize. They don't, they find innovation. . . so I mean if you go to Norway it's inscribed in law that you are not allowed to downsize. So you have to find different ways of managing, you have to find different ways of using talent . . .
P28 On known-known and known-unknown risks	Considering all the risk and all those constraints that I spoke about earlier, the alliance was the only one which was going to meet that timeframe that we were tied into and to be able to manage all the risk suitably or appropriately and all the stakeholder and the political issues associated with it. . . . It was a no-brainer, I mentioned one risk we'll go to is just the mines, we didn't even know where the mines were, and we didn't know the extent of them. We found out later on through bloody good luck rather than good management that some of them had methane in just as we were drilling holes. If you did that on a different form of delivery, the first thing that would all be pre-construction works and that would've taken years.

(continued)

Table A7. Wittgenstein Model Theme 1: Motivation and Context *(Continued)*

Theme and Subtheme	Notes, examples, and KSAE quotes
1.7 Unknown risks	Dealing with unknown-known and unknown-unknown risks poses a particular challenge to traditional and low-level RBP forms because high levels of specification inhibits performance through encouraging defensive routines and associated high levels of transaction cost. In this hyper-uncertain and ambiguous context, the POR and project delivery management team members need a system that allows rapid flexibility to adapt to emerging realities with high level collaboration to facilitate maximising access to relevant KSAE to resolve uncertainty.
Examples of high levels of unknown risks context thinking	• Understanding the value of collaboration to identify those who can best contribute to managing unknown risks with the requisite expertise to successfully investigate and then manage these kinds of risk. • Understanding how to best compensate parties for taking responsibility and accountability for those risks. • Understanding how to frame effective risk management through contractual arrangements. • Having the capacity to retain critical KSAE within an organisation or ensuring having access to that corporate and individual KSAE.
High-level KSAE needed for dealing with known risks.	• *Technical and PM KSAE* – High levels of ability to probe think laterally about unknown risks that can be known through making sense of patterns to develop and respond to the risks. High levels of ability to manage unknown-unknown risks through having sufficient KSAE to probe, experiment and rapidly evaluating outcomes and to calibrate risk management on that basis. • *Business solutions KSAE* – High levels of ability to justify the risk management model to be adopted. • *Relational KSAE* – High levels of ability to collaborate and manage people to best develop risk management approaches.
Illustrative quotes	Effective unknown risk management is about maintaining confidence in cross-team collaboration and freedom of action to deal with risks as they emerge. As commented by A16 and P24 :
A16	the major reasons for X doing this is because it is a rural area and it's large distances and it's also on top of mountains and through forests. So it's a big risk and it's hard to get to the places if something happens. If you have one and a half metre of snow, and all of a sudden there are 10 trees falling over and you are about 20-25 kilometres from the nearest road, to where you're supposed to fix that, it's quite problematic.
P24	What would inevitably happen is you would get the tunnellers go through and excavate the tunnel. They hand over to their civil fit-out crew, and at the same time that the civil fit-out crews get access to the tunnel the M&E [mechanical and electrical] subcontractor is also expected to be in there. . . . there's a lot of technology, a lot of integrated equipment that has to be built in the latter stages normally of a project installed, pre-tested, and then commissioned. So it's a massive amount of complicated work at the backend of a project that's on a very tight time curve.

Theme 2 relates to the platform foundational facilities that define how the governance structure evolved and operated. Subthemes from Section 1, Table 11, **joint governance structure** (refer to Table A4) are elaborated upon in Table A8.

- The **joint governance structure** context defines a how common platform governanace characteristics will be incorporated into the project procurement form.
- Subthemes emerged from the data for **Theme 2 - joint governance structure** as follows:
  - 2.1 Governance processes—common assumptions and ways of working will be influenced by project governance processes and rules. These will vary according to the project procurement delivery form but will be designed to align project strategy, objectives, and aims. Process clarity is essential to inform expected behaviours.
  - 2.2 Governance structure—the structure of the entire project team defines such aspects as flexibility/rigidity, power and influence, and communication symmetry. This directly influences the workplace culture. The way that a project overall project leadership and management team is constituted determines who has a voice and how they can express ideas, perspectives, and concerns.
  - 2.3 Governance best value strategy through KRAs and KPIs—the project output and outcome is influenced by the strategy deployed to define, measure and assess success. The way that these are developed and used determines the extent of common understanding and effective project governance.

Table A8. Wittgenstein Model Theme 2: Joint Governance Structure

Theme and Subtheme	Notes, examples, and KSAE quotes
2.1 Processes and rules	Processes rules and routines define the mechanisms by which people agree to relate and work with each other. They can have both formal and informal emphasis and requirements. This aspect of governance can have a major impact on the resulting workplace culture because it sets the tone and expectations of the relationships between teams and individuals.
Examples of high levels of governance process impact thinking	• Understanding that formal rules often set boundaries upon how the informal rules are implemented either to reinforce the intended protocols or to subvert them to get around perceived needless interference with efficiency or effectiveness. • Understanding that output and rules/processes are often closely linked through the culture that they invoke. • Understanding that processes and rules can impose unknown risks and can be used to address known risks through such aspects as communication and escalation protocols for example.
High-level KSAE needed for process and rules design and implementation to enhance the workplace culture	• *Technical and PM KSAE* – High levels of these are required to navigate the limitations and opportunities that processes and rules can have on how problems and opportunities are undertaken. • *Business solutions KSAE* – High levels of these are required to ensure that the desired and designed processes and rules are in place for protection against exploitation and to facilitate opportunities for creative thinking being enhanced. • *Relational KSAE* – High levels of these are required to develop trust in "the system" and how it can be ethically interpreted within the accepted norms and values of project participants and the society in which the project is delivered.
Illustrative quotes	Governance processes and rules are centered upon knowing and articulating how to design a set of process and rules to effectively deal with daily issues in a way characteristic of the project procurement approach. As interviewee A09 said:
A09	. . . design thinking is about bringing people with very different mindsets together, and to deal with problems as a design issue. So typically you'll have design that happens at the front end, you do it and then you might have a bit of design at the end to make it look pretty. The design thinking says the design happens the whole way through, and it's not just the designer that needs to think like the designer, you know? So it's about how you get people together to sort of make sense of problems, and collaborate to create the solution.
	Thinking about how to have rules and flexibility designed into governance rules and procedures can be challenging as P22 and P24 say:
P22	And at times they were able to switch scope between the parties so that they would – say if some civil works were holding up the M & E team, "Well, okay, we'll do those works to make sure that it gets integrated with the work we're doing," and they'll do it rather than just complain about somebody else not doing it. And that kind of flexibility I think was characteristic of the arrangement.
P24	There was work done with our corporate and third party lawyers to draft an initial agreement document but that agreement document evolved quite a bit after the award of the contract. It took a few months to even write down, but with good faith and all the rest of it, the parties started work without the agreement being signed as well.
2.2 Governance structure	The organisational structure and the way that authority and accountability is managed define the way people agree to relate and work with each other. Structures can de designed to be flexible, rigid or something in between these extremes.
Examples of high levels of governance structural impact thinking	• Understanding that governance structure can be designed to provide communication, knowledge, and authority links across project teams, as well as across development phases. • Understanding that a structured way of integrating governance oversight committees and who is accountable for what across the project phases is a vital ingredient of deriving a coherent governance structure. • Establishing and maintaining a common understanding of how the governance structure engages people across project teams so that each person understands what is expected of them, who they are accountable to, and how each level of accountability should behave.
High-level KSAE needed for governance structure to enhance the workplace culture	• *Technical and PM KSAE* – High levels are required to decide what issues can be handled at each of the governance structure levels and which ones should be escalated. This requires both the technical KSAE to deal with this as well as PM KSAE to know how to shape, communicate, and respond to specific issues to be dealt with. • *Business solutions KSAE* – High levels are required to ensure that the desired and designed governance structure facilitates the outcome assumptions made in the business plan. • *Relational KSAE* – High levels are required to ensure that appropriate communication and coordination of effort is delivered to match the governance structures in place and how to effectively use informal structures to support project expected outcomes.

(continued)

Table A8. Wittgenstein Model Theme 2: Joint Governance Structure *(Continued)*

Theme and Subtheme	Notes, examples, and KSAE quotes
Illustrative quotes	Governance structure includes the way, in PAs in particular, that the leadership oversight team provides and facilitates sufficient supervision, support and guidance to the project management team level in order to facilitate the desired and designed-in level of collaboration and coordination of effective action. As P29 says:
P29	They're called project managers, but at the end of the day they were managing contracts. So what we've actually done within the alliance it is very much more that they are project managers and they are involved right from the word go from the design, in terms of the detailed design. So we have a planning area that takes it up to a concept design level . . . and basically we would have a design team, a construction team, but then a project management team over the top. So that project manager would be involved in the project from almost before the project is initiated with the alliance. Would follow through, make sure the design was through and then through to construction. So really taking it from concept design through to handover to the client, which is our operations team.
	In terms of structuring a programme alliance to facilitate upskilling of the PO and for the alliance NOPs to better understand the POR team work methods and culture P32 says:
P32	. . . as part of the agreement we've said that 45% of the office-based staff, being the engineers and the programme managers and so on, needs to be X-PO people. And even the field staff, because we've had some small resource, we want to embed some of our field people in to work alongside your people as well. So we've got about 20 people embedded in that as well.
	In terms of structuring the governance system to provide sufficient "voice" for the project participants to facilitate not only effective decision making but also effective action, P26 says;
P26	I was actually part of the AMT, because I was one of the senior, senior staff members for the project as commissioning manager. The ALT was represented onto by the project director and then two X staff and a couple of staff from Y and Z. So there was an escalation process for matters and things like that, but from an AMT level, to be quite honest, I mean at times the whole AMT probably consisted of about eight to ten people and there was only, at peak, there was only two X staff on that project, on that management team. So you've really got to look at, you've got ask the question about balance on that.
2.3 Governance best value strategy through KRAs and KPIs	Best value is defined through key result areas and key performance indicators and these are part of the project governance overall structure. Their shape and content may be well defined in a business case and then translated into specific KRAs and KPIs through project team collaboration or by the POR through a hierarchical specification. They should effectively translate what the project value and benefit was expected to be delivered and be used to monitor and influence the project output and outcome.
Examples of high levels of best value through KRA/PPI thinking	• Understanding the link between being clear about what success looks like in this context and how it can be defined and measured. • Understanding how to effectively use performance standards to achieve expectations, including how they may be used in any incentivisation strategy. • Establishing and maintaining common understanding of how KRAs guide development of KPIs that promote and facilitate common understanding across project teams of what benefits the project should achieve.
High-level KSAE needed for developing effective KRAs and KPIs	• Technical and PM KSAE – Understanding the technical complexity of KRAs and KPIs and how to specify them practically so that they fulfill their purpose. • Business solutions KSAE – Understanding how they can align business case objectives with delivered outputs and outcomes that minimise unintended negative consequences. • Relational KSAE – How to best engages those who will use these to ensure that they are well designed in terms of being clear, unambiguous, and performable, while still presenting an element of stretch targets to challenge teams to achieve continuous improvement.
Illustrative quotes	In terms of the project team's common standards and values, KRAs and KPIs provide a benchmark measure. As A09 states:
A09	These guys collaborated, but they added uncertainty and ambiguity to it by having complex array of KPIs, viewing industry standards as business as usual, or what they now call "minimum conditions of satisfaction," and saying that we're an alliance and we're special so we shouldn't accept business as usual, so we'll make the industry standards of "excellent" our "business as usual," because we're offering something different.
	In terms of how these were developed in a PA context, P20, P28, and P29 stated:
P20	. . . so the KRAs were initially developed by the owner very early on and massaged to death might I say, you can quote me on that, but finalised at the time of agreeing the TOC as well, so the TOC was really, the value and the scope of work that we landed on in the TOC had to reflect the KRAs that we had for the project and also had to reflect the initial business case of the project, so all of that alignment of value statements and value requirements had to be done at the time of TOC to make sure that what we were putting forward was going to meet the objectives that we had initially planned, but also was going to create that value that we had promised.
P28	Out of the main objectives, the client's objectives and what the client wanted to achieve out of this project fell to the KRAs and the then the KPIs. We had about five or six KRAs

Theme and Subtheme	Notes, examples, and KSAE quotes
P29	…Above normal expectations as well because you've got to keep raising the bar so I think a lot of the alliances, we have our alliance advisors and they had these KPIs but we soon worked out they didn't really mean much to us. You'd end up doing a lot of surveys and all sorts of things so we spent a lot of effort trying to make those KPIs- I think we've achieved it now. Really meaningful and really linked to dollars. If I was doing an alliance again, I wouldn't worry about them terribly much. At the end of the day, if you're delivering the project and delivering it for good dollars' value, everything else has to fit in anyhow in order for you to achieve that, so I'd keep the key result areas and the KPIs very simple.
	And in terms of just what these measures attempt to define, P34 says:
P34	…the KRAs were around reducing congestion, improving safety, improving connectivity. And that improving connectivity is also about access control as well. Then community relations; so a very difficult community that we were living in, and socially very poor, and lastly, the integration with the maintenance regime.

Theme 3 relates to the platform foundational facilities that define how the integrated risk management strategy evolved and operated. Subthemes from Section 1, Table 11, **integrated risk mitigation** (refer to Table A4) are elaborated upon as elaborated upon in Table A9.

- The **integrated risk mitigation** context defines how common assumptions will be incorporated into the project procurement form and how parties will deal with risk.
- Subthemes emerged from the data for **Theme 3 - integrated risk mitigation** as follows:
  - 3.1 Risk sharing conversation—in the beginning there was *the word*. There is always a conversation around sharing risk, who takes responsibility for any class of, or particular, risk. The strategy needs to be coherent to ensure that those best able to manage risk do so in a way that aligns the risk strategy to the objectives and aims of the project. The nature of these conversations differs in emphasis placed upon the means to allocate accountability across project procurement forms.
  - 3.2 Risk mitigation actions—there is a number of ways, ranging from collective to individual, to agree upon and decide how to mitigate risk that very according to the procurement form.
  - 3.3 System integration—the way that the project is structured and managed provides a platform that is based upon the philosophical stance about relationships between teams. Systems can be integrated to cope with risk, uncertainty and ambiguity to respond to a need for a platform to be developed to address these three related but separate concepts.

Table A9.   Wittgenstein Model Theme 3: Integrated Risk Mitigation Strategy

Theme and Subtheme	Notes, examples, and KSAE quotes
3.1 Risk-sharing conversation	Responsibility and manner of accountability has to be decided upon for any project. The nature and quality of the conversation in terms of understanding each party's perspective and respecting each party's obligations provide a defining basis for a specific project procurement form. Conversations reflect the assumptions made relating to the degree of appreciation and validity of information and power asymmetries. Risks are generally known and can be openly discussed, but uncertainty and ambiguity represent shadow conversations where systems need to be designed to address these proactively or reactively as they arise and become risks. The broader conversation should consider both known and unknown risks and their mitigation.
Examples of high levels of risk sharing conversation thinking	• Understanding the risk-taking appetite and ability of all parties including the PO. • Understanding the perspective of various project parties' position on risk and uncertainly accountability and their strengths and limitations in articulating their position and engaging in conversation and negotiation on a risk mitigation platform. • Understanding how to discuss and develop systemic processes and protocols that can be used to address known and unknown risks.
High-level KSAE needed for an effective risk sharing conversation	• *Technical and PM KSAE* – High levels of technical knowledge are needed about potential risk and uncertainty relating to the project inputs and design and delivery processes and how they are connected. • *Business solutions KSAE* – High levels of understanding of how identified and anticipated risk and uncertainties may impact the project business case. • *Relational KSAE* – High levels of perspective taking skills to be able to empathise with other parties sufficiently to help them articulate risks and uncertainties and how these may be addressed.

(continued)

Table A9. Wittgenstein Model Theme 3: Integrated Risk Mitigation Strategy *(Continued)*

Theme and Subtheme	Notes, examples, and KSAE quotes
Illustrative quotes	The degree to which the PO or other parties accept risk varies dramatically with the procurement approach. As interviewee A13 and p17 said:
A13	What they said in T5 "No, we're going to take all the risk because ultimately it comes back to us anyway. We're going to have integrated project teams involving the client and we'll call them partners in our framework agreement, first tier suppliers of work and then the partners will be responsible for pushing this down to their separate owners in the same spirit of that," the spirit of cooperation and so on. In return for this, BAA said "We'll pay you what it costs to build this building, to build this construction rather than having a fixed price because what happens traditionally in construction is that you go in with a low bid, the lowest bidder wins and then you get litigation and you try and get contract variations in order to just be able to make a profit."
P17	So where you have an alliance where the scope of the alliance is to deliver the whole project, and then you have some critical conversations where you have to reach alignment between the owner and non-owner on what risks and opportunities are going to be shared by the alliance participants, and that generally forces a conversation, which is complicated enough, about how do you deal with risks that you don't control.
	This can be contrasted with a citation from (Smalley, Lado-Byrnes, & Howe, 2004, p. 40) which says:
NHS Wales: Construction Procurement Review - Selection of a preferred option for the NHS in Wales, 2004	. . . main contractors' prices will include a "risk allowance." However, this allowance is only to cover the risks that the main contractor may be responsible for. . . . This practice is replicated throughout the supply chain. . . . most clients will include a "contingency" to cover the occurrence of risks that they will be responsible for - primarily, outright variations to the works, "design development" (i.e., design team variations which clients will have to pay for) and events that will entitle the main contractor to compensation under the relevant contractual arrangements. No one is actually identifying and managing the combination of both sets of risks. To do this properly requires the input of all relevant parties (namely the client, main contractors, designers, cost consultants, and probably relevant subcontractors). The occurrence of risks affecting the project are potentially damaging to all parties, but particularly to the client, who will rarely be compensated by liquidated damages or other means for the disruption suffered by late completion and/or disputes about compensation.
3.2 Risk mitigation actions	Taking action to mitigate known and unknown risk involves the process of moving from conversation to action after having taken all necessary preparation steps to obtain political and procedural permission to take the action that was decided upon.
Examples of high levels of risk mitigation actions thinking	• Understanding the contextual opportunities and threats posed by the governance system. • Having an ability to anticipate and prepare for necessary negotiations, including understanding the value proposition of all affected parties. • Being able to visualise and conceptualise innovative solutions to systemic and administrative barriers that may impede optimal risk mitigation solutions that have been identified and agreed upon to implement.
High-level KSAE needed for an effective risk mitigation actions	• *Technical and PM KSAE* - High levels of technical knowledge about the risk impact and effects and how mitigation choices may trigger flow-on effects. • *Business solutions KSAE* - High levels of understanding of the political and energy "cost" and benefit of the mitigation strategy to the business case. • *Relational KSAE* - High levels of cognitive, persuasive, and influencing capacity to discover how to gain team support to advance a mitigation strategy, as well as how to tactically deploy actions to ensure that mitigation actions take place.
Illustrative quotes	Some actions may appear quite radical such as on the T5 project (and this is also more common with PAs) a common platform of project insurance was established. As reported by the National Audit Office (2005, p. 6):
National Audit Office, 2005, p6)	BAA took out project-wide insurance covering loss or damage to property, for injury, for death and also covering professional indemnity. Bulk-buying ensured the cover was in place and was tailored to meet the needs of the project. It reduced the costs of insurance, and avoided wasted effort and duplication on behalf of all the partners.
	Being able to draw a project team around a technical problem that may have far-reaching impact that avoids cost, time, and other social performance measures of project success is another effective risk mitigation strategy deployed in PAs, as P30 stated:
P30	. . . what I'm getting at there is the importance of the avenue of a new line of trees. The importance has come out so much in favor of the retention of the trees that we couldn't deliver [XXX] road extension as we originally planned to do. Wc had to get a permit to remove four elm trees to put a roundabout to form a connection to the [YYY] Freeway. Now in a design and construct environment, we as a client would be facing huge claims from the contractor, being delay, loss of productivity, and all this sort of stuff, but with an alliance—with the cooperative arrangement, we got some excellent advice about planning process and to really further our endeavors to obtain a permit and we didn't face claims as a result. We were basically able to conclude the alliance amicably and pay all fair and reasonable costs without compensating for losses, etc.

Table A9. Wittgenstein Model Theme 3: Integrated Risk Mitigation Strategy *(Continued)*

Theme and Subtheme	Notes, examples, and KSAE quotes
3.3 System integration	The PO and all project participants each exist within their own organisational systems and the project is also subject to its own environmental, economic, political, etc., system. Risk, uncertainty, and ambiguity present challenges when the way that they interact is not well understood. Inevitably, some entity or team needs to build bridges, links, and understanding across multiple system boundaries, so that risks can be mitigated and managed. The level of system integration knowledge and coping mechanisms can be highly influenced by the project procurement form.
Examples of high levels of risk system integration thinking	• Understanding the contextual interaction of each participant in a project and how these interact with the project-external world. • Sourcing the necessary people to explore and map the systems terrain. • Being able to understand how to influence, facilitate and even take action to improve integration of systems that pose risk and uncertainty challenges through providing a common platform of project system interaction to deal with risk.
High-level KSAE needed for effective system integration actions	• Technical and PM KSAE – High levels of technical and administrative knowledge about the systems faced by the project. • Business solutions KSAE – High levels of understanding of the political and of the mitigation strategy to the business case. • Relational KSAE – High levels of cognitive, persuasive, and influencing capacity to discover how to gain team support to advance a mitigation strategy as well as how to tactically deploy actions to ensure that mitigation actions take place.
Illustrative quotes	Systems thinking is quite problematic in most BAU settings because contractors particularly have outsourced so much of the "actual" coalface work. They are good at understanding the supply chain and its strengths and weaknesses, but they often have difficulty in seeing interactions within their own organisations. The frequent disconnect between the bid team and the delivery team leaves gaps, inconsistences, and ambiguities that lead to risk and uncertainty about who is doing what. As A11 illustrates the problem:
A11	One of the things that the literature talks about quite a lot is main contractors being systems integrators, largely because most of them don't produce anything these days. They subcontract everything, and so they have this integrative function linking in with what I was saying earlier from the interviews. One of the things that came out very clearly from all the interviews is that over the project life cycle, all these major contractors have a different system in each of their functions that are not interlinked. So they're not even integrated in their own operations, so business development operates separately from bid management, which operates separately from procurement, from project management and so on, and it's not just in terms of silo thinking. It's in terms, that the systems that they use to conduct their function; the processes, don't interface with each other. . . .So their ability to integrate others is hampered and their ability to put forward value prompt propositions that add value for clients is hampered by their lack of ability to join up their systems internally and provide a seamless content; a seamless service, along those lines.
	As one highly experienced PA director and manager (P34) summed up the way that risks are commonly perceived with a PA road infrastructure project context:
P34	. . . strategy-wise, there were things like the community involvement, cycle access, cross motorway access, so both type for as well as numbers of. And I guess, probably most importantly the landscape—not the landscape but the—yeah, yeah, urban design outcomes met the—had to meet the strategic goals.
	The level of inter-systems complexity can be overwhelming so the approach to leadership in this context may be best suited to the complexity and chaotic situations that Snowden describes in his Cynefin Framework (Kurtz & Snowden, 2003). As P18 describes the U.K. situation for a rail PA form that may have severe project external system impacts:
P18	. . . it's probably more complex here because, if you like, the – it is just a railway. Really we've been with the Victorian railway, and the congestion of places like Kings Cross – there are certain aspects that we're working on with some – alliance. For example, the X alliance. It's not a big project, I think it's about 30 odd million, but basically anything they do has the potential of bringing down the east coast mainland.
	And in terms of the aerospace industry when building new-generation jetliners, P04 stated about system integration of risk (that shares similarities with engineering infrastructure and other PM sector) stated:
P04	Now you then say well, how do put an engine on or landing gear? The air framer, the aircraft manufacture will say, "Okay I have an aeroplane weighing this amount. I want to have two landing gear, and a third on in the middle of the fuselage, this is the design I want to make my aeroplane work." Then he'll go out to the landing gear manufacturers, and as I said there is not a huge number, and say "This is what I want, now how do you," the landing gear manufacturer, "how do you integrate a landing gear on my airplane that would do all these things," specify the weight, the height of the landing gear, etcetera, etcetera. "You tell me how you put that on there and how much it's going to cost me to put that on there." Then you use the expertise of the subcontractors, and once you've selected your subcontractor that's where the integration between, I use the landing gear just as an example, the landing gear to the aircraft. How does it integrate? How it swing and shut in the landing gear bay? It could be the electrical, where do my black boxes sit in the aircraft? How much wiring do I need? The expertise for that little bit is held within the subcontractor. He's got his own aeronautical or electrical engineers who likewise that's his core competency.

Theme 4, **joint communications strategy** (refer to Table A4 above) relates to the platform foundational facilities that define how the joint communications strategy evolved and operated. Subthemes from Section 1, Table 11 are elaborated upon in Table A10.

- The **joint communications strategy** context defines how project participants interact and communicate with each other and how that is affected by the project procurement form.
- Subthemes emerged from the data for **Theme 4 - joint communications strategy** as follows:
    - 4.1 Common processes and systems—Project participants need to share a common way of working and a common language and communication approach if they are to avoid problems of misunderstanding that can undermine trust and commitment, and as a consequence undermine effective decision making and action taking. If they cannot share common processes and systems, then the next best thing is having bridges and interoperability between systems to cope with a lack of a "one system," which is most likely unobtainable for large complex projects with multiple organisations participating.
    - 4.2 Integrated communication platform—A common ICT platform, including, for example, common building information modeling (BIM) tools, can minimise the risk of poor coordination, communication, and misunderstandings between participants.

Table A10. Wittgenstein Model Theme 4: Joint Communication Strategy

Theme and Subtheme	Notes, examples, and KSAE quotes
4.1 Common processes and systems	A key joint communication strategy relates to parties each understanding what is expected of them and how to respond. Terms or language may differ for processes and systems and subsystems. A PO's "hands-off" approach would assume that each participant will handle their business and management processes internally but conform to contractual requirements for progress reporting and use of the POR's standard for accountability processes. By contrast, a highly POR "hands-on" approach such as that for PAS and the T5-type procurement approach would entail common processes be adopted by all participants and even a common bank account for all project-related financial transactions.
Examples of high levels of common process and system thinking	• Understanding the advantages and disadvantages of using common processes and systems. • Having an ability to map system gaps and interoperability to be able to adapt internal systems or negotiate any justifiable and necessary compromises to share system facilities. • Having a sound knowledge of national, regional, and local legislative requirements that may impose challenges on how to conduct project business where the POR processes and system are in conflict with project team participant's legal, business, or ethical obligations.
High-level KSAE needed for effective responding to the need for common process and system integration	• *Technical and PM KSAE* - High levels of technical and administrative knowledge about the processes and systems used in managing the project and how to adapt them as required to meet requirements of the project procurement form being used. • *Business solutions KSAE*- High levels of understanding of the political and business implications to adopting/adapting common processes and systems. • *Relational KSAE*- High levels of cognitive, persuasive, and influencing capacity to negotiate and action any necessary adaption plans to develop the use of common processes and systems.
Illustrative quotes	PORs getting large contractors to adapt their in-house processes and systems can be a challenge. As A07 and P32 states:
A07	X is very active in South America, always been, since the construction crisis in the 1990s in Germany that almost wiped out the whole construction industry at that time. Since then, what they've done is they've replicated the model that they use in Germany, and even though they employ the local supply chain, for instance in Argentina and Brazil and so on, it's not dissimilar to what they would be doing in Germany, and again what you see underlying this is a very, very strong corporate organisation. It's a not a hollowed-out organisation. It's a very strong organisation which has very strong design teams, very strong R&D teams. Sometimes, for instance, it's not unusual for the large German contractors to build their own machinery, to build their own software themselves. They don't outsource that to software developers.
P32	The things where we've really had problems, I think one of the issues was things like getting our financial systems to talk to each other. Contractors' financial systems are set up differently to ours and yet at the end of the day we need the same information, but we probably need different information to what a contractor normally needs, so that's been an issue.

Table A10. Wittgenstein Model Theme 4: Joint Communication Strategy

Theme and Subtheme	Notes, examples, and KSAE quotes
	The reality of most organisations is that their own internal systems do not fully "talk to each other," as A10 and A13 state:
A10	One of the things that came out very clearly from all the interviews is that over the project life cycle, all these major contractors have a different system in each of their functions that are not interlinked. So they're not even integrated in their own operations, so business development operates separately from bid management, which operates separately from procurement, from project management and so on, and it's not just in terms of silo thinking. It's in terms, that the systems that they use to conduct their function; the processes don't interface with each other. Now that's okay; in a sense if you've got a soft system that's overarching, that compensates for that. You see you create your own, as it were alliance along the project life cycle, but none of them have. None of them had at all. So their ability to integrate others is hampered, and their ability to put forward value prompt propositions that add value for clients is hampered by their lack of ability to join up their systems internally and provide a seamless content; a seamless service, along those lines.
A13 on the T5 approach	One of the problems of the fragmented supply chain in construction is that there's lots of opportunities for misinformation and for people not to be working to the same drawings, not working to the same design when changes are made and so on, and so they said "We're just going to have one model that everybody uses, a master model. If changes are made on that, everybody sees those changes" so you don't get this opportunity for misinformation to go through.
4.2 Common communication platform	A key joint communication strategy also relates to parties being able to communicate easily, quickly, and with a suitable audit trail to retrieve documents and message when required. Many projects these days use either the same ICT communication groupware tools or use compatible ones so that interoperability does not present any problems. There is a specific need in high-collaboration project delivery forms, though, for common platforms to ensure that everyone is working with the same data on design and production, and that monitoring and control systems are integrated and interoperable.
Examples of high levels of common communication platform thinking	• Understanding the advantages and disadvantages of using common communication platforms and what they demand in terms of system development and support. • Having an ability to map system gaps and interoperability to being able to adapt internal communication systems, or be able to negotiate any justifiable and necessary compromises in using the POR's or that of a leading NOP. • Having sufficient access to system support to ensure that the risk of system downtime is minimised. • Comprehending and taking action on the necessary requirements for archiving information and data and operability issues associated with legacy data and ICT systems.
High-level KSAE needed for effective responding to the need for a common ICT platform	• *Technical and PM KSAE* – High levels of ICT technical and administrative knowledge about the software and hardware systems used in managing the project and how to adapt them as required by the project procurement form. • *Business solutions KSAE* – High levels of understanding of the political and business implications to adopting/adapting common ICT and other communication systems. Common ICT platform use on projects sparks potential risk issues about ownership rights of information and implicit intellectual property, accuracy, and accountability for errors, discrepancies, and ambiguity. • *Relational KSAE* – High levels of cognitive, persuasive, and influencing capacity to negotiate and act on any necessary adaption plans to develop the use of common communication tools and systems.
Illustrative quotes	One of the more common tools common ICT used in construction and engineering projects is building information modelling (BIM). Recently, the U.K. and Singapore have mandated the use of BIM using a common project team platform on all infrastructure delivery projects. As the U.K. Cabinet Office (2011, p. 14) states:
U.K. Cabinet Office (2011, p. 14)	2.32 Government will require fully collaborative 3D BIM (with all project and asset information, documentation and data being electronic) as a minimum by 2016.
	The T5 project was famous for its use of BIM and integrated systems, as A13 states:
A13	The other thing here we have the single digital model. One of the problems of the fragmented supply chain in construction is that there is lots of opportunities for misinformation and for people not to be working to the same drawings, not working to the same design when changes are made and so on, and so they said "We're just going to have one model that everybody uses, a master model. If changes are made on that everybody sees those changes" so you don't get this opportunity for misinformation to go through.
	Integrated ICT systems are especially needed for programme alliances where a common cluster of organisations enjoy long-term engagement. As P31 observed on a programme alliance:
P31	They link into our portal to get access to a whole heap of system-based stuff. So training information, toolboxes, you know, templates, checklists, procedures, and all that sort of stuff. But not so much, you know, access to programming or estimates or anything like that. We use a cloud-based system called CMO or Compliance Management Office and so through that, they can log on and get hold of all of that information

Theme 5 **substantial co-location** (refer to Table A4) relates to the platform foundational facilities that define how the co-location strategy evolved and operated. Subthemes from Section 1, Table 11 are elaborated upon in Table A11.

- The **substantial co-location** context defines how project participants interact and communicate with each other in terms of physically.
- Subthemes emerged from the data for **Theme 5 – substantial co-location** as follows:
  - 5.1 Hierarchal integration mechanisms—Project participants need to see their leaders. And so site visits, meetings held on site, and other ritualistic or practical events that are held in the actual workplace can be very important as a platform for integrated joint action.
  - 5.2 Physical co-location—Project participants can more easily communicate and interact on problem solving, monitoring and active collaboration when they are in within easy reach of each other. Co-location in a well-considered and conducive environment can facilitate positive interaction and this can enhance communication and perspective taking.

Table A11. Wittgenstein Model Theme 5: Substantial Co-location

Theme and Subtheme	Notes, examples, and KSAE quotes
5.1 Hierarchical integration mechanisms	Leaders can inspire motivation toward unity of purpose by physically interacting with individuals in the various levels of an organisation. On complex multi-organisational participant projects, there is a challenge for the project leadership group to maintain common vision and direction on what the project is expected to deliver and achieve. Individual organisational leaders also need to be visible and to engage with their employees to highlight the need to enthusiastically and effectively support the project vision, aims, and objectives.
Examples of high levels of hierarchical integration thinking	• The overall project leadership team having the ability to understand the need for publicising a common vision, aim, and objectives for the project, but to also take action to ensure that all project participant employees experience "rhetoric" matching "reality." • Openness of the project leadership team to accept the perspectives of others from lower levels in the hierarchy when visiting the worksite or meeting them in other venues. • Understanding the advantages and disadvantages of encouraging an open and low power-distance, low information-asymmetry workplace culture to enhance hierarchical integration opportunities.
High-level KSAE needed for effective hierarchical integration	• *Technical and PM KSAE* - High levels stakeholder engagement skills and sufficient technical KSAE to be able to intelligently interact with others who may have specific technical points to express. • *Business solutions KSAE* - High levels of understanding of the importance of vision and how that is disseminated and effectively turned into action. • *Relational KSAE* - High levels of capacity to communicate and deal with people to perceive and consider their perspective.
Illustrative quotes	In illustrating the need for a project leadership team to be visible and engaging P28 and P33 say:
P28	Each ALT member was a champion for a KRA to get them out there with an AMT member and then that would get them onsite and things like that. It's important that the ALT be onsite as much as possible, be visible, the other thing exhibits the behaviours that the alliance has got and walk the talk with everybody else. We were pretty lucky we had two or three who probably got there weekly, as I said I got there nearly every day, to me that wasn't an issue but to other people it was a big issue because they saw me coming as an ALT representative and the ALT chair. They're all just little bits in helping the culture.
P28	. . . it'd be great to have the ALT more visible onsite, more presence onsite but when you've got general managers, national managers, and company directors on the ALT it's sometimes difficult.

Table A11.   Wittgenstein Model Theme 5: Substantial Co-location

Theme and Subtheme	Notes, examples, and KSAE quotes
P48 in terms of timing of ALT meetings and their frequency and the purpose of them	Initially, every month and then every – about six months into it, it was every three months. In the initial statement it was on every month. Sometimes I held it [ALT meeting] at nine o'clock at night, nine through until two in the morning, it was just depending on getting the diaries synced but we wouldn't have the meeting unless the people that were nominated on the ALT were at that meeting. [question asked] And that would give you the authority to be able to make decisions very quickly? [response] Precisely. There were a couple that we had at four o'clock in the morning.
P33 (program alliance example)	I guess the ALT both sides have been pretty influential in making sure they get down to the ground where the rubber hits the road, so at the depot level and the ALT, AMT too, would conduct, you know, tool box talks with debriefs on results and those sorts of things to the whole workforce. We go about having meetings in different locations, so whether it be [X-depot], [Y-depot], [Z-depot] in the various depots that we maintain in those areas, so our visibility is certainly there.
5.2 Physical co-location	Proximity of access for not only formal meetings but also informal, ad hoc interaction is highly important in facilitating an environment where people can discuss and sort out issues, build trust and effectively communicate as and when required. Co-location, however, does not mean that off-site fabrication cannot occur.
Examples of high levels of physical co-location	• Teams from across the supply chain being located within a common campus that is comfortable, inviting, and a suitable venue for collaboration. • Effective virtual locations in which people can assemble to discuss issues, problems and solutions. Increasingly, this occurs in virtual environments such as in the "second life" software virtual reality tool or through Skype and other similar communication devices. • The development and application of social media is changing conceptions of what being co-located means. These technologies encourage hybrid means of co-location so that essential people that are not able to physically meet in one physical space can join a meeting virtually using social media technology.
High-level KSAE needed for effective physical co-location	• *Technical and PM KSAE* – No specific KSAE are required. • *Business solutions KSAE* – Understanding the importance and value of co-location from a team interaction perspective is useful. • *Relational KSAE* – High levels of capacity to communicate and deal with people to perceive and consider their perspective. This is extremely useful in capitalising on co-location advantages.
Illustrative quotes	Co-location can be critical in resolving issues when rapid response is needed as A16, P20 and P34 say:
A16	. . . a co-location, everything. And signs on the buildings with [Project A], so basically a project or an organisation separate from [X-team] and [Y-team]. And some of the people quit their permanent position in [Y-team] and were hired in the project organisation for the six years that the project should exist
P20	No, I found the ALT, our ALT was willing to climb in and get involved when they needed to, a good example is we, last week we had a little issue with some of the lane conditions on a circular road area, affecting some of the pavement that we have to do out there, and we had an ALT meeting about a week ago and they said, you know we think we want an update on this. I said okay I'll send you an email update and they said no let's catch up, we'll find an hour let's catch up next week, and three out of the five ALT members came down and caught up, and that's the sort of involvement, they're willing to climb in and they're willing to make phone calls if I need them to, so they've been good.
P34	[X-team] collocated as well, had a team that co-located, and again, you have individuals who don't quite get it, but generally quite good about, you know, we're here to get this project completed. Didn't extend, as I said earlier, it sort of overall, to every single team outside the alliance, but certainly to the major ones, we got the collaborative approach working with the major subcontractors.

Theme 6 **authentic leadership** (refer to Table A5 above) relates to the behavioural drivers as normative practices that define how authentic leadership evolved and operated. Subthemes from Section 1, Table 12 are elaborated upon in Table A12. Authentic leadership is present in designated project leaders who hold institutional or organisational power, but it also applies to "followers' within a collective leadership sense.

- The **authentic leadership** context defines how the project leadership team and individuals as participant team leaders interact and communicate with each other in terms of deploying their various sources of power and influence in a way that is perceived as being authentic.
- Subthemes emerged from the data for **Theme 6 – authentic leadership** as follows:
    - 6.1 Reflectiveness—Project participants who are systems thinkers and often follow a strategic thinking approach about the situational context and know that the situational context is crucial to effective decision making.
    - 6.2 Pragmatism—Project participants get on with the job, are politically astute and work within constraints or find ethical and sensible ways to around these constraints.
    - 6.3 Appreciativeness—Project participants understanding the motivations and value proposition of influential stakeholders involved in the project. They are consciously engaged with their team members and exhibit signs of having a high emotional intelligence.
    - 6.4 Resilience—Project participants exhibit adaptability, versatility, flexibility, and being persistent when faced with adversity. They are able to effectively learn from experience.
    - 6.4 Wisdom—Project participants have opinions and advice that is valued, consistent, and reliable that others instinctively refer to. Their judgement abilities make their brokering advice crucial. They are perceived as having high levels of integrity based on inner strength of character, knowledge, and experience.
    - 6.6 Spirited—Project participants demonstrate the courage and have sufficient influence and respect to effectively challenge assumptions and often offer radical alternative solutions to resolve complex and difficult situations.
    - 6.7 Authenticity—Project participants demonstrate qualities of being approachable and trustworthy and open to ideas. They encourage and advance collaboration, discussion, and new ways of thinking.

Table A12.   Wittgenstein Model Theme 6: Authentic Leadership

Theme and Subtheme	Notes, examples, and KSAE quotes
	Authentic leadership is present in designated project leaders who hold institutional or organisational power, but it also applies to "followers" within a collective leadership sense.
6.1 Reflectiveness	Leaders consistently think in systems terms and how the situational context functions within the immediate system and also between and across related systems. This prompts a response to complex and difficult situations to first understand the context and let that guide decision making and action.
Examples of high levels of reflective thinking	• Project team participants having the ability to understand the situation through critical analysis, questioning assumptions, and pattern matching what is known, felt, and observed with how the situation fits useful hypotheses and theories about how the situation should behave within the perceived system and galaxy of systems. • Actively seeking out a range of perceptions about a situation and questioning how relevant these may be in confirming, rejecting, or modifying a working hypothesis or theory of the situation and which contextual aspects are salient. • Having a disposition of confidence to cease action and think and then let reflection guide further decision making and action taking.
High-level KSAE needed for reflection	• *Technical and PM KSAE* - Having sufficient technical KSAE to appreciate the relevance of working hypotheses and theories of situational context to be able to make decisions and take action. Having sufficient PM KSAE to understand dependency and impact of decision making within project constraints and the project vision, aim, and objectives • *Business solutions KSAE* - Understanding the impact of contemplated action on the business case and the project outcome. • *Relational KSAE* - High levels of capacity to communicate and deal with people to gain their perspective in order to frame and test working hypotheses and theories of the situational context.

Table A12. Wittgenstein Model Theme 6: Authentic Leadership *(Continued)*

Theme and Subtheme	Notes, examples, and KSAE quotes
Illustrative quotes	Having an outside view of a situation can be enlightening. An ability to view and perceive a situation as seen with fresh eyes. This reflection was on the construction industry's BAU culture and paradigm. On the subject of non-cognates (that is, people who are in a project team but have little or no technical skills of that situation) A10 said of a conversation with one of his post-graduate students:
A10	One of my students who was non-cognate went to work for a construction company and came back and I can't remember why she came and I said, "What's your observation then? You're now in construction. What do you see?" And she said, "Well it's, what I see is not good. What I see is an industry that's based on kind of incompetency and mediocrity and the systems are there that are self-serving. Various groups are basically just pursuing their own interests and nobody's really interested in the client at all. The client comes second and all of the systems that are in place are about trying to deal with and corrupt the official systems," so she says, "it's a very chaotic industry."
	P30 discussed the ability of project participants who did not have prior PA experience to reflect on how working within a PA context presented challenges to them.
P30	. . . you've got to have people that have got a pretty good degree of experience in the organisation that they represent. That they know their policies, they know their practices and procedures, they know what the intent is and be flexible and agile enough to move into a different team environment which has got a different set of policies potentially, but making sure that they can marry up with the home-based policies so that you're not contravening them.
6.2 Pragmatism	Leaders and team members consistently think in practical terms, what will work, what is effective rather than what is efficient. They are politically astute and conscious of their situational context and use that knowledge and mind set to guide decision making and action.
Examples of high levels of pragmatism thinking	• Project team participants having the ability to make sense of all forms of power and influence to steer decision making and action. Having a technically practical approach. • Having a greater focus on effectiveness over efficiency to win wars rather than win battles.
High-level KSAE needed for pragmatism	• *Technical and PM KSAE* – Having sufficient KSAE to understand the short-term and long-term impact of decisions and action. • *Business solutions KSAE* – Understanding the impact of contemplated action on the business case and the project outcome. • *Relational KSAE* – High levels of capacity to know who to communicate with and how pitch their communication format and message in dealing with people to gain their approval and/ or support to take decisions or actions.
Illustrative quotes	A reflection by P22 on a colleague who led a significant project illustrates the value of scepticism as part of being pragmatic. This is a general quote about that individual.
P22	. . . he is one of those guys who comes across as, you know, the big, gruff, tough project manager, but he's actually a lot more intelligent than he portrays in the first instance and probably a lot smarter than to dismiss something outright, but approaching it with more than a healthy level of skepticism about how valuable this arrangement might be in this circumstance. And on the way that a particular PA was conducted pragmatically, P26 and P21 said:
P26	. . . toward the end it was actually realised that the civil people were better positioned to do these kind of things, so they actually got onto the work and did it. The working relationship on the ground is that people on the ground worked fairly well together.
P21	So what we did as part of the [Project X] influencing the alliance was to actually get an independent theatre planner put on board as well as the acoustician. Now that created a whole lot of tensions with the acoustician but it's actually resulted in a better outcome, and it probably wouldn't have happened if there hadn't been an alliance, because the most efficient and cheapest way to do is just to hire one company to do the lot.
6.3 Appreciativeness	Leaders and team members consistently think about the context and value of others' perspective. Often an idea or suggestion may sound inappropriate or even crazy, but when assumptions and cultural (work or organisational) context is unpacked, the idea can be worked on to provide a novel and innovative solution to an issue. Having the ability and patience to appreciate the validity of the perspective of others is vital to authentic leadership. This is one part of the emotional intelligence (EI) spectrum of KSAE.
Examples of high levels of appreciativeness thinking	• Project team participants making sense of other people's perspective through active listening and also being pragmatic about sources of ideas. • Having a greater focus on effectiveness through being able to appreciate that innovation often begins with novel, unusual, or even crazy-sounding ideas that are explored and developed by people with a multitude of perspectives. • Having sufficient humility to recognise the value of practical knowledge.

(continued)

Theme and Subtheme	Notes, examples, and KSAE quotes
High-level KSAE needed for pragmatism	• *Technical and PM KSAE* – Having sufficient technical and PM baseline KSAE to understand how to respond to insights and ideas offered by others when decision making or planning or taking action. • *Business solutions KSAE* – Understanding the impact of contemplated action on the business case and the project outcome. • *Relational KSAE* – High levels of capacity to communicate and deal with people to encourage contributing ideas and feedback and support to take decisions or actions.
Illustrative quotes	Participant A10, when asked about the role of empathy as an appreciation factor in EI, had the following to say when asked, Do you get any sense that they were good at perception taking?
A10	They could but largely they didn't because they were very task-orientated; they were very task-focused. They were inward-looking, looking at let's just get the job done. Let's just get the functions working properly rather than looking at what the interests of the other parties were; stakeholders or the clients. And in fact, from a marketing perspective but it relates to value, one of the things that came out very strongly is that the value propositions were heavily compromised because they were so inward-looking; so inward-focused.
	P20 commented upon the cross team multi-disciplinary nature of a PA and how it may be improved. She said:
P20	I think the leadership team and the management team has functioned really well, there have been other subgroups within the project that where alliancing behaviour has been harder to infiltrate, and I think there are probably in hindsight some things we could have done differently, that we should have done differently in order to improve that, it's a very multicultural group we've got out here. We have architects, we have builders, we have acousticians, we have [facility users] people, you know, and project managers in the office and they're not people who are always used to working together in the same environment and that sort of smash of cultures in the project office occasionally has been challenging to manage . . .
	And on a different PA, P23 stated:
P23	I think an attitude more than anything, someone that was prepared to sit down and listen to both sides of this team and try and understand what the issues were.
P49 on appreciated "smarts" that the contractor posses	[Contractor X] provided a lot of benefits in the development of the design simply because of their hands-on practical experience in what works and ways and means of building the same system more cheaply but just as effectively. I mean they brought to the table the smarts of the actual constructor and ways of achieving the same result at reduced costs so they were very valuable. We put up various things and they'd say oh no, we tried that over in West Australia and it didn't work and we needed to do this, that, or the other and that really, so you avoid reinventing the wheel and making the same mistakes from their experience.
6.4 Resilience	Resilience, adaptability, versatility, flexibility, and being persistent when faced with adversity characterises this element of ethical leadership and subtheme from the data. Leaders and team members are able to effectively reframe the situation to be able to cope with them, often to advantage.
Examples of high levels of resilience thinking	• Projects seldom, if ever, run to plan. Complex projects such as the infrastructure engineering ones examined in this study provide typical examples where "unknown-unknowns" appear regularly to disrupt plans and action. Apart from environmental (climate, business, or political landscape) challenges, well-planned approaches to address issues may take unexpected turns due to inadequate assumptions being made. • In the IT PM-world, the concept of agile is gaining momentum. In the aid recovery world, there are many examples of the need to be versatile and adaptive, as has been reported upon in a recent PhD thesis (Steinfort, 2010). Steinfort also shows that understanding local culture and context is critical to effective resilience.
High-level KSAE needed for resilience	• *Technical and PM KSAE* – Having sufficient technical and PM baseline KSAE to understand how to respond to complex technology issues and which sets of skills and knowledge to adopt or adapt. • *Business solutions KSAE* – Understanding the impact of the need for resilience to adapt plans and action to meet the business case objectives and the project outcome. • *Relational KSAE* – High levels of capacity to communicate and deal with people to shape and mould their repertoire of KSAE to support being flexible in response to taking decisions or actions.
Illustrative quotes	In terms of a quote from a programme alliance with a set of different challenges and opportunities, two are presented from P33; one relating to resilience about what to do with gains in productivity, and the other about responding to environmental disaster faced by the PO:
P33	. . . what we'd rather do is if we are going ahead of schedule, not pull up stumps and then work out what to do with the left over money is to keep going, to increase scope or keep going basically until you find that you've spent the funds that you'd settled for that particular process. I guess we have done a lot of work in ensuring that if we are working around those gain-share areas that we'd much rather see that money invested in the asset because the more we invest in the asset, the more we save in maintenance costs.

Table A12. Wittgenstein Model Theme 6: Authentic Leadership *(Continued)*

Theme and Subtheme	Notes, examples, and KSAE quotes
P33	. . . but we're also sitting in a position where we get hit by quite a few crises out there and those guys are able to respond very quickly, engage in the community, get the local workforce to get out there and deliver improvements from things like bushfires and floods that could have really hamstrung the bigger organisations for longer. I think from that perspective the working with the AMT and the ALT, so the ALT, if you just go back to the first lot of floods, made a call pretty quickly saying nah, [XXXX programme alliance] is going to deliver all this work, and as a result [XXXX programme alliance] was Johnny-on-the-spot and delivered, organized it, project managed all the work including ensuring that the claims and the bills got paid from the insurer as well to make sure Y [PO] were covered.
	Balancing interests and being flexible, steadfast, and flexible in approaches to issues and contractual ways to facilitate flexibility is illustrated in a case of a PA set within a D&C context. P17 was the project facilitator and stated that:
P17	I think the focus has to be on are the people from the main contractor, who is the equivalent of the owner in this relationship, have they got the maturity, the flexibility, and the leadership qualities to be able to manage the inevitable conflicts of interest that are going to arise between the interests of the overall project and the interests of the alliance that sits within the project. If you've got somebody who's got a very autocratic leadership style, extremely autocratic, who's only going to use this as a way of trying to bully a mechanic and electrical contractor, whoever it is, that's not a good recipe for this working well. It's got to be a relationship between equals.
6.5 Wisdom	Leaders and team members have opinions and advice that is valued their reputation and demonstration of integrity make them valuable as brokers of change, leading innovation and managing challenging complex situations. They have sufficient integrity and sound judgement to realise how to effectively frame and justify questions to be asked and answers provided in decision making and action taking. They also know how and when to close options effectively.
Examples of high levels of wisdom thinking	• Project team participants making sense other people's perspective through active listening and also being pragmatic about sources of ideas. • Project team participants having a greater focus on effectiveness through being able to appreciate that innovation often begins with novel, unusual, or even crazy sounding ideas that are explored and developed by people with a multitude of perspectives. • Project team participants being able to frame and justify changes in direction in response to difficult choices and challenges that can be broadly accepted. • Having the ability to move from divergent exploratory thinking to convergent thinking when settling on a decision and understanding the appropriate response in known-known to unknown-unknown situations (see the Cyefin framework discussion earlier). That is, knowing which questions to ask and which answers to accept as most relevant to the context.
High-level KSAE needed for wisdom	• *Technical and PM KSAE* – Having sufficient technical and PM baseline KSAE to understand how to constructively listen to others. • *Business solutions KSAE* – Understanding the impact on the business case and the project outcome of wise consideration, decision making, and interaction with people. • *Relational KSAE* – High levels of capacity to communicate and deal with people to deal with people to build, develop and maintain, credibility and trust in their decision-making and action-taking approach.
Illustrative quotes	In relation to making sense of others' perspective in order to frame a solution, A11 and P17 state that:
A11	What they really need is for project managers to interface with stakeholders and clients, client departments; whichever they are. Some of those are quite difficult to identify, in the sense that it may be several departments trying to act together and so they're looking for people who will think without the encumbrance of an engineering background. So I think that's why they have recruited non-cognates because they get again better alignment of the client needs, better project definition, and it's not about let's design something based on what's technically feasible. It's about let's design something that really satisfies the needs, and that's what non-cognates are ready to do.
P17 on a PA that was structured with a PPP	I think the focus has to be on are the people from the main contractor, who is the equivalent of the owner in this relationship, have they got the maturity, the flexibility and the leadership qualities to be able to manage the inevitable conflicts of interest that are going to arise between the interests of the overall project and the interests of the alliance that sits within the project.
	In terms of selecting leaders and team managers with sound judgement and integrity in question-framing and decision-making for action, as P18 and P20 said:
P18	. . . what we've put together for alliances is what we call a Right Person Right Job selection process. And so we're – normal project selection would be, "does he have the right technical skills? Does he have the experience? Is he available? Right, give him the job."
P20	. . . I think part of being an alliance manager is about your personal style and it's very important to behave very neutrally and to, I think lead by example as well, I'd like to hope that I do, I'm probably better at interviewing them, but I think the assessment was, I would imagine that I could sort of behave in that neutral impartial way that was going to best for the project, regardless of the issue. It's very important not to be seen to be favouring one side or the other.
	Drawing upon an interview we undertook in another study (Walker & Lloyd-Walker, 2011c, p. 61) interviewee 02 from that study said in relation to this aspect of authentic leadership:

(continued)

Theme and Subtheme	Notes, examples, and KSAE quotes
IV-02	"If you've got people that are absolute stars that can't relate to other members within the team, then you've really got to get rid of them because they're going to be counterproductive. . . . I think they would have to be a person who you would obviously respect for their ability, for their experience, for their technical capability and someone that could relate to people. If they don't relate to people, then any one of those things could ring alarm bells. But I think really one of the things I've learnt is that you must respect your client and you must respect the people that are members of your team. If you don't give that respect, you can't expect to receive it. That is not such an easy task at times."
	And in terms of knowing what questions to ask and how to respond to answers in convergent and different thinking terms, IV-06 in that study said:
IV-06	So the level of technical detail I don't need to be across, but I do need to be able to ask sensible questions about it, if we're in a pricing discussion or something like that. Somebody is saying "we need X tonnes of rock to do this" – I have to have a bit of enough knowledge to say "that seems like a lot," or "that doesn't seem enough," or at least knowing that I should ask the question about the volume. . . . I probably have less onus on me to actually be able to ask some of those challenging questions, because you've already got 10 people with that level of technical knowledge who are doing all of that. And then it becomes more about encouraging those 10 people to do the challenging, and use their expertise in perhaps a slightly different way than they might be useful, which is getting everything out on the table.
6.6 Spirited	Leaders and team members demonstrate the courage and have sufficient influence and respect to effectively challenge assumptions and often offer radical alternative solutions to resolve complex and difficult situations.
Examples of high levels of courage and spirit thinking	• Project team participants being unafraid to express opinions, feedback, views on plans and action and in contributing ideas. • Project team participants having sufficient EI and KSAE to frame views constructively yet firmly so that they are effectively considered and valued. • Project team participants being committed to challenging BAU and to actively seek continuous improvement and best-for-project outcomes through persuasive argument.
High-level KSAE needed for courage and spirit	• *Technical and PM KSAE* – Having sufficient technical and PM baseline KSAE to feel confident in voicing views, feedback and contributions to decision making and action. • *Business solutions KSAE*– Understanding the impact of spirited challenges and stretch targets on the business case and the project outcome. • *Relational KSAE*– High levels of capacity to build trust and confidence that people can voice their opinions, perspectives and ideas and that these contributions are valued.
Illustrative quotes	Reinforcing the need for independent and critical thinkers who have the courage and sprit to provide challenge assumptions and open divergent thinking.
A09	Intrepeneurs, yeah. So they were seen as mavericks, but they were playing with these issues of value, so the idea of public value versus private value, and so they opened themselves up as explorers, but they also opened themselves up as threats to the organisation.
P22	. . . you needed to have people at the senior level sufficiently enlightened to be able to say, "Well, if we're going to achieve and extraordinary result, and we need to achieve an extraordinary result to make this program, we can't do it in the same way we've done these things before."
P18	And so the guy, just around about 40, basically after [XXX alliance], his career just took off. He had a lot of courage. Another thing that really stuck in my mind with working with him, he made the suggestion that, "I think this is the right thing for my industry, I think it's the right thing for my company. If my company don't approve of me, they can sack me. Let's do it"
	On an interesting aspect of timidity and reticence, as opposed to courage and spirit, by A10
A10	. . .but the body language; which was what was used to measure in this case, was very defensive and it looked - and I didn't analyse the—it was filmed; the evidence was filmed. I didn't sift through the evidence but what my colleague suggested was that they were defensive, as if to protect their professional standing. Not quite the same as reputation but they wanted to protect their professional position and stance; standing in the team, rather than necessarily contributing to what was best for the team or the coalition as a whole.
6.7 Authentic, trustworthy and open	Project participants demonstrate qualities of being approachable and trustworthy and open to ideas. They encourage and advance collaboration, discussion, and new ways of thinking. This is impacted upon by the national and organisational culture within which the project is delivered as well as by the characteristics of the various project team participants.
Examples of high levels of authenticity thinking	• Project team participants mindfully behaving in a way that demonstrates that they have considered their actions' impact on others. • Project team participants appearing genuinely enthusiastic about achieving best-for-project outcomes. • Project team participants being trustworthy and effective in championing collaboration.

Table A12.   Wittgenstein Model Theme 6: Authentic Leadership *(Continued)*

Theme and Subtheme	Notes, examples, and KSAE quotes
High-level KSAE needed for authenticity	• *Technical and PM KSAE* – Having sufficient technical and PM baseline KSAE to be accepted and respected. • *Business solutions KSAE*– Understanding the impact of authentic leadership on the business case and the project outcome. • *Relational KSAE*– High levels of capacity to build trust and confidence in people to enable the building of mutual trust and respect.
Illustrative quotes	Reflecting on the competitive dialogue approach that illustrates the need of the POR to be, or at least appear to be, authentic when negotiating with competing project delivery teams. A01 says:
A01	The tension between transparency and competition and trying that indeed some confidential information about that you as a party work on certain innovations come in public, that's really, that's a problem. . . . The supplying parties do not give complete transparency because of the fear that, yes, that they will give some of their innovations away.
	Examples of national and workplace culture influences on perception of authenticity and trust, as expressed by A02 and A16:
A02	Because what we have here is you also have a working culture where there's not so much distance between superiors and the people who do the work. . . .the transport administration, the infrastructure projects they have, they have projects with Swedish contractors and with German contractors primarily. And they say that there is a big difference in dealing with the Germans. . . . because Swedish, we have a consensus culture which can be extremely frustrating for other people and sometimes also for Swedes as well. But there are so many discussions and everybody has to agree. But what happens in those discussions, they take an endless long time, but after a decision is reached it's generally agreed upon by people and it's implemented, while perhaps if you make a decision at an early, somebody high up in the organisation makes a decision at an early stage, you then have to kind of communicate and sell it within the organisation. So it's kind of, so they said that [German contractor X] got angry at the [Swedish project owner authority Y] and they say that you want discussions, discussions, discussions, and we want decisions, decisions, decisions.
A16	You realise quite early, after a few months, that we need to be humble and we need to have a dialogue with everyone and need to spend time on creating a good working relation, not just between [Swedish project owner authority A] and [Swedish contractor B] within the project organisation, but with every subcontractor, because they are representing us with the land owners.
	On organisational and professional group cultures, A10 said:
A10	Whether it really did or not, the actors thought that where emotional intelligence was higher, there were greater levels of collaboration and again, [UK PO A] have this pro-collaborative approach. And so, in particular, one of the two contractors was much better at collaborative working in terms of displaying emotional intelligence than the other one. The client [UK PO A] were pretty good on some dimensions but not very good on others; for example, transparency. The engineers were actually pretty lousy at it. They were actually quite a negative factor, which is perhaps not what one would think from an engineer; particularly from that engineer, but it was the case.
	On balancing being open and collaborative and shielding others from information that may have a temporary but not permanent negative effect in order to maintain trust and collaboration within and between teams, P21 said:
P21	I think so and it's not about being secretive or manipulative, when you were saying before about patience and then one things that I've really learnt is to shut up on some things they're not actually— sometimes you've got to let things play out a bit and that's sort of been the way I've always managed and behaved, but you need to let things play out a little longer.
	The behavioural contract in PAs can contribute to a climate of trust and collaboration, as P28 stated:
P28	I got called a few times, we're building a bloody big complex project and there's always going to be robust discussions and a lot of heat in these discussions, but as long as people are respectful of the other people's opinion, acknowledge it and are willing to listen. The charter of the behaviours which come out are the most important things, so calling behaviours is very important.

Theme 7, the **trust-control balance** (refer to Table A5), relates to the behavioural drivers as normative practices that define how the balance between trust and control evolved and operated. Subthemes from Section 1, Table 12 are elaborated upon in Table A13.

- The **trust-control balance** context defines how the project leadership team balances representing and protecting the interests of the POR with that of other genuinely relevant stakeholders, while relying on the integrity, benevolence and ability of all project team parties to "do the right thing" in terms of project performance. They need to understand the value proposition of "the other" project teams and to assess their capacity to deliver the promise while establishing mechanisms to ensure transparent accountability.
- Subthemes emerged from the data for **Theme 7 – trust-control balance** as follows:
  - 7.1 Autonomy—Project participants' situational context may be complicated by institutional and cultural norms that restrain their autonomy and therefore their capacity to respond to new initiatives and changes to "plan," and appear to be weak and poorly trusted by their leaders. In contrast, their organisational culture and governance arrangements may leave them with enough autonomy to act somewhat independently.
  - 7.2 Forms of trust—Project participants' trust in their leaders and vice versa is often mediated by perceived forms and basis of that trust, together with notions of self-interest and shared interest as well as the nature of that interest. Reliance on project participants' capacity to experiment, explore options and take action may be advanced or constrained by their or their leadership teams' perceptions of how various interests are best served.
  - 7.3 Safe workplace cultures—Project participants' trust in their leaders is often mediated by their perceived treatment in terms of a working in a safe psychological, physical, and intellectual environment.
  - 7.4 Trust relationship building—Project participants, and their leadership teams, engage in varying levels of effort to create a balance in trust and control in which trust with caution is tempered with blind faith.

Table A13.   Wittgenstein Model Theme 7: Trust-Control Balance

Theme and Subtheme	Notes, examples, and KSAE quotes
7.1 Autonomy	Being relied upon to have the capacity to make agreements or to take agreed action can be enhanced or constrained by the cultural context, governance requirements, and perceptions of each party's power and influence.
Examples of high levels of autonomy thinking	• Project team participants mindfully demonstrating consideration of their and others' constraints or opportunities to make commitments and deliver on promises. • Project team participants understanding the nature and limits of each other's power and influence. • Project team participants' capacity to renegotiate their level of autonomy in terms of a trust and control balance perspective. • Project team participants being able to initiate scope changes based on changes in information relating to value achievable from any scope or scale changes.
High-level KSAE needed for autonomy of trust thinking	• *Technical and PM KSAE* – Having sufficient technical and PM KSAE to understand their limits of autonomy or capacity to negotiate changes in autonomy within the project procurement context with particular attention to an holistic workplace safety perspective. • *Business solutions KSAE* – Understanding the purpose and logic of their present level of autonomy in terms of the situational business dynamics. • *Relational KSAE* – High levels of capacity to build and maintain trust and confidence in people to enhance mutual trust and respect.
Illustrative quotes	Participant A02 reflects on cultural implications of autonomy due to power distance and collectivism dimensions. In particular, culture within infrastructure sectors is illustrated (see Table 3 in Chapter 4).
A02	. . . another issue is that the German people have to go back to their bosses all the time and ask for permission about everything, while Swedish people can be more, kind of, they can make decisions and they can check, perhaps check afterwards or they have kind of, they have some autonomy to make decisions on their own based on their expert areas. So it's easier, shorter decision routes in the Swedish culture. But what's interesting is that also the Germans when they have been working in these projects, they think that it is a very good way of working, so they perceive it as a way of working which is much better than their traditional way, and they are able to adapt, it just takes a bit longer time for them. So it's not impossible.

Table A13. Wittgenstein Model Theme 7: Trust-Control Balance *(Continued)*

Theme and Subtheme	Notes, examples, and KSAE quotes
A02	. . . they have a tradition, especially I think in the road area, not so much in the rail—they are more centralised—but in the road area it's very decentralised so you can't really tell any road person what to do. They want to decide for themselves . . .
	On relating to the issue of gaining autonomy through a PA to be able to make commitments supported by the governance system and the organisation's hierarchy to make scope changes that achieve better project outcomes, P23 and P34 say:
P23	I guess one of the big advantages of having the alliance was that we had an alliance manager who had to become intimately familiar with the whole M&E scope and what the challenges were for the M&E team, etc., and had some influence in the project management, the bigger project, and had some influence in what they did. Whereas [Participant X] is the subcontractor wouldn't be able to influence the civil work at all, the alliance manager was able to influence it in some ways to the benefit of the alliance, for the M&E scope.
P34	So we were directed not to—I know, I know—we extended the scope of the project. So the project stopped at, you know, chainage zero say, and that out beyond chainage zero there was a couple of hundred metres of really poor alignment and bridge that probably didn't have much more than 10 years in it. So we sort of felt pretty strongly about it all, what's the point of delivering 110 kilometre-an-hour facility, with 100-year design life bridges, and 40-year design life pavement, and butt it up to something that's going to be dead in 10 years. So we suggested the client that we ought to do that, and [we] did. And that was pretty good going because that was fairly late in the process, and we needed to really hustle, so we did concurrent design construction, and that gave the designers a headache and the constructors a headache, but it was just something that needed to happen.
7.2 Forms of trust	Project participants' trust in their leaders and vice versa is often mediated by perceived procurement forms. This perception forms the basis of that trust together with evaluation of self-interest and shared interest and appreciation of the nature of that interest.
Examples of high levels of trust forms thinking	• Understanding how various project procurement forms either assume or specify accountability and transparency "behavioural" requirements of trust for the project procurement context. Understanding that self-interest trust with legal and highly procedural control mechanisms reinforce that trust concept and may operate in one context, while social trust may better apply in another in which norms and longer-term reputational impact is more salient. • Appreciating the various underlying concepts of what trust means so that project participants can share a common understanding of what differences in meaning can be attributed to trust. • Project team participants accepting the validity of trust-with-caution as being a valid balance of unreservedly expecting the other party(ies) to deliver on commitments and basing their accountability monitoring requirements with inflexibly demanding adherence to signed contract conditions.
High-level KSAE needed for trust forms thinking	• *Technical and PM KSAE* – Having high levels of understanding and knowledge of the concept of behaviour trust and verification through accountability and its implications for the project procurement form as an effective governance measure. • *Business solutions KSAE* – Having high levels of ability to respond appropriately to the trust-control balance specified or implied by the procurement form to achieve long term business success. • *Relational KSAE* – Having high levels of interpersonal KSAE needed to match social interaction with the appropriate behaviours to generate and maintain trust.
Illustrative quotes	Relating to the nature of and basis for trust, and potential opportunistic behaviours to illustrate the need to understand participants interest and motivation, A10, P06, and P23 state that:
A10	. . . if each party's looking at their own interest. If I trust you, I'm going to get something out of it. If you trust me, you're going to get something out of it. We sense that's what's going to go on and then we get a classic win-win. . . Ultimately, in self-interested trust you'll get classic win-win. In contrast to game theory, an enhanced level of trust is more of the social orientation, where you say, "Well if I look after the interests of the other party, I will benefit from that; either in the short or in the long run." So you're not looking first of all at your own interests. You're looking at their interest first and then you hope, you believe, and that's the level of vulnerability, if you like; you believe that it's possible that they will look after yours. You don't know that they will and it's then a question of collecting the evidence through iterative exchanges and through iterative contact in relationships to see whether that's what's happening. Now all the companies I interviewed [across the spectrum of procurement forms, including PA-like forms] were looking at trust in terms of self-interested trust. None had really gone to socially orientated trust at all [refer to Chapter 4 for types of trust theoretical discussion].
A10	. . . my thought has mainly been from the inside of those relationships but there's the external aspect; those looking from the outside, those excluded from those relationships. Is that a good thing? And is it, even though it may be good for the project, is it good over a programme of projects, over a framework? We don't know. No one's looked at that, so that would be the first point about an omission; an area that hasn't really been considered.
P06	The biggest issue of all of this is when the contractor wants to maximise his return on any project he's dealing with, and that's what you're also fighting against.

(continued)

Table A13.   Wittgenstein Model Theme 7: Trust-Control Balance *(Continued)*

Theme and Subtheme	Notes, examples, and KSAE quotes
P23	. . . the main contractor is really only interested in the date and wants whatever resources are necessary to be thrown on the project, whereas the M&E subcontractor has to protect their position and make sure that they can show a profit at the end of the day. So therefore they're lining up, recording bullets that they could fire, etc., to make sure they don't fall way behind on the financial side.
	Contrasting opportunistic behaviour with positive trust aspects on an extremely complex Nordic project characterised by high collaboration levels under uncertainty A16 says:
A16	And when I did some of the interviews in the beginning with a few of the guys working, they said, "To be honest, we don't really know what it's all about, but we trust them, so hope it works out."
7.3 Safe workplace cultures	Project participants' trust in their leaders is often mediated by their perceived treatment in terms of a working in a safe psychological, physical, and intellectual environment. All infrastructure engineering projects have an emphasis on a physically safe workplace but a safe psychological and intellectual workplace is also essential to foster trust and innovation.
Examples of high levels of safe workplace culture thinking	• Understanding that a physically safe workplace culture emphasises the importance of not exposing people to risk of physical injury. • Understanding that a psychologically safe workplace culture emphasises the importance of not exposing people to risk of feeling inferior, inhibited, and constrained in a particular behavioural direction. • Understanding that an intellectually safe workplace culture emphasises the importance of allowing people to challenge ideas and to offer even crazy suggestions that could be refined and developed, so it inhibits inhibition to experiment and make mistakes that can be learnt from.
High-level KSAE needed for safe workplace cultures	• *Technical and PM KSAE* – High levels of understanding and knowledge of the implications of technology and methods on potential risk of injury. • *Business solutions KSAE* – High levels of understanding of the advantages and disadvantages of physical, psychological and intellectual health of workplace environments to achieving long term business success. • *Relational KSAE* – High levels of interpersonal KSAE to communicate and influence others about the value of creating and maintaining appropriate behaviours to balance trust and control of the workplace environmental conditions.
Illustrative quotes	Concern for employees' health and well-being on-site has been well established to encourage employees on-site to trust their employers to not cause them physical harm. This has been extended to office workers for the same reason, and as P28 states:
P28	The focus on safety is something I've never seen before, we set benchmarks in safety, we'll work that in the training or putting people through those trainings. I'm 40 years in the game and I've been used to dropping off onsite and walking up and down where you feel like it. Those days are gone, you've got to sign on, sign off . . .
P28	The safe spine initiative, I don't know if you heard of that one where they do all the exercises and things. Before people start work in the morning they do 10 minutes of stretching exercises and they do them at the end of evening, or just after lunch and things like that.
	Relating to the nature of psychological workplace safety, two quotes illustrate different aspects. In the first, A10 discussed power relationships and supportive safe collaborative environments, and in the second, P34 talks about a potential sexual harassment situation.
A10	[Organisation X] and that was about trust or the lack of it between the project sponsors and the project managers and there were quite low levels of trust between those two roles; the people occupying those roles in that organisation. And they have a project management framework that's supposed to again, facilitate collaborative working with their contractors. Well if you haven't got high levels of trust internally, it's going to be very difficult to inject good levels of trust to facilitate collaborative working with your contractors, so they may be a strong client in some ways but they're weak in that way for sure.
P34	. . .and I warned him once, twice, and the third time I said no. And as it turned out, he was one of the corridor gossipers as well, he and another girl who was on the AMT, would put around all sorts of weird and wonderful rumours and stories, and just crap, outside the AMT. And I guess I—you know, I guess we all turned a blind-eye to it, but didn't realise that the problem there was how the AMT was perceived by the rest of the team, like the wider team, and these people were representing poorly to the wider team. So we needed to correct that and correct it quickly, and we did. A number of things happened that made— get corrected.
	Intellectual safety to be able to creatively think and express ideas as a contribution is critical to innovation. A09 in discussing this aspect of trust to be different states:

Theme and Subtheme	Notes, examples, and KSAE quotes
A09	I think the solution lies in design thinking, because design thinking is about bringing people with very different mindsets together and to deal with problems as a design issue. So typically you'll have design that happens at the front end, you do it and then you might have a bit of design at the end to make it look pretty. The design thinking says the design happens the whole way through, and it's not just the designer that needs to think like the designer, you know? So it's about how you get people together to sort of make sense of problems, and collaborate to create the solution.
7.4 Trust relationship building	Project participants' and their POR engage in varying levels of effort in creating a balance in trust and control in which trust with caution is tempered with blind faith. Trust relationship building requires thinking about the types of trust as well as creating safe environments.
Examples of high levels of relationship building	• Establishing protocols and culturally acceptable norms through a behavioural charter so that people understand what the norms are. • Actively establishing processes and training to strengthen people skills to allow people to understand each other's perspective. • Rewarding high relationship building and maintenance mechanisms being effectively deployed. • Demonstrating integrity and ethical dealing to support confidence in building sound relationships between and within project teams.
High-level KSAE needed for relationship building	• *Technical and PM KSAE* – High levels of understanding of tools and techniques for building trust across and within teams. • *Business solutions KSAE* – Participants need high levels of understanding of the advantages and disadvantages of various trust building approaches and how that impacts upon business success. • *Relational KSAE* – High levels of interpersonal and cultural appreciation KSAE are needed to effectively deploy and maintain relationship building processes.
Illustrative quotes	Participant A01 stated in relation to the Competitive Dialogue process, an aspect that related to integrity and ethics in terms of dealing confidentially with bidding parties that is salient to the nature of trust building that:
A01 on the Competitive Dialogue	So in principle the information given to one party, to one supplying party, you have to give to the other supplying party but there is discretion by giving certain information to one supplying party, also we said - what's the English word? You also give maybe certain - what do you call it? Certain confidential information because when you answer a certain question of this party, you may be also - and make it transparent that you answered this question and give this answer - you also maybe give some information to other parties about what type of innovation they're working on.
	And others interviewed contributed comments that are salient to behaviours that support trust.
A13 on the T5 project agreement	As I said, it was a code of behaviour really about how you were going to work together and it would always return to that T5 Agreement if there were any debates or any problems that arose. The emergence complexity, well, partly the reimbursable contracts dealt with that, so you've got unexpected things happening but they'd still pay you what it costs to sort those out.
A19 on Chinese cultural norms	Well, you've got to bear in mind that the guanxi works in China in a command economy. It's all about policy drives decision-making or whatever, whereas in Japan it's still actually—you would describe it as an open or market economy. So within the market economy, these relationships make, if you like, business much easier, much simpler, do you understand?
P17 on PAs where one team bids and others not part of the bid team deliver the project.	Well, there is an amount of trust, but a lot of people go into these relationships and you might call it trust, but also in many cases it's blind faith and not really thinking it through, because the individuals involved at that stage, their focus, they'll be heroes if they win the job, then they're out of it. And so, they'll do whatever they want to do to try and win the job, then it's somebody else's problem when they've won the job to make it work. That's a heightened risk when you're building in as part of your bid your half-billion-dollar alliance that relies on your delicate network of relationships to make it work properly, and you don't even know who's going to be involved in those relationships.
	And in relationship to trust building throughout the project delivery phase:
P28	We did a lot of work with coaching and mentoring and did a lot of health checks, especially early and just seeing how the health was going, we spent especially the combined AMT/ALT going through those surveys with a fair bit of rigour just to try and see what the issues are.
P30	I'm really impressed with the way people get out of their normal organisational roles into a team environment with strangers, they've quickly formed strong relationships and they're sharing information and work with each other very well to get the very best outcomes for the project objective.
P34	Well yeah, forming relationships, maintaining relationships, understanding that a relationship doesn't look after itself, you have to actually work at it, ensuring that you're recognising performance and rewarding performance, making sure that other people within your relationship are aware of people's performance and the effect on those people of those rewards, so encouraging better performance, so all of those things go to a more self-aware team.

Theme 8 **commitment to innovation** (refer to Table A5) relates to relates to the behavioural drivers as normative practices that define how commitment to innovation evolved and operated. Subthemes from Section 1, Table 12 are elaborated upon in Table A14.

- The **commitment to innovation** context represents the duality of project participants being willing, and able, to be innovative. This requires a structured mechanism to enable and empower people to be innovative. This is closely linked to a project team participants' capacity for learning, reflection, creativity being ambidextrous, and the organisation's core values of supporting and rewarding questioning the *status quo*.
- Subthemes emerged from the data for **Theme 8 – commitment to innovation** as follows:
  - 8.1 Innovation types—Project participants need to understand and adapt to behavioural expectations associated with different types of innovation (product, process, or behavioural) within a project or programme situational context that may affect how team member's commitment can be initiated and sustained.
  - 8.2 Commitment to continuous improvement—A vital element of innovation in a project setting is to achieve continuous improvement. The extent to which project participants can be innovative and effect continuous improvement depends upon institutional, governance, and individual motivational and enabling factors.
  - 8.3 Testing, prototyping, and experimenting— Project participants' innovative actions are usually manifested by testing, prototyping and experimentation within the context of having an inquiring, curious, often sceptical mind.

Table A14.   Wittgenstein Model Theme 8: Commitment to Innovation

Theme and Subtheme	Notes, examples, and KSAE quotes
8.1 Innovation types	Project participants need to understand and adapt to behavioural expectations associated with different types of innovation (product, process, or behavioural) within a project or programme situational context that may affect how team members' commitment can be initiated and sustained.
Examples of high levels of thinking about innovative forms of project procurement	• Project participants understand that various project procurement approaches assume or specify specific "behavioural" that directs or at least strongly influences their capacity and motivation to initiate and sustain innovation. PAs and programme alliances have firmer and more specific behavioral contract clauses that require collaboration, whereas other forms of RPB such as partnering set aspirational agreements and expectations without firm measures of innovation or rewards for innovation. • Project participants have a sophisticated and deep understanding of underlying concepts of drivers and inhibitors of innovation. • Project team participants understand that innovation can be initiated across the project life cycle from project definition to project handover, and how forms of collaborative engagement can be designed to be quarantined to specific phases, for example, with ECI forms and design, project and programme alliances.
High-level KSAE needed for choosing effective innovation forms to encourage innovation commitment	• *Technical and PM KSAE* - High levels of technical understanding of the process and required behaviours of innovation and its diffusion in terms of procurement choice. • *Business solutions KSAE* - High levels of understanding of the drivers and inhibitors of innovation, understanding business process, and how to identify value chains, and how innovation may impact long-term business success. • *Relational KSAE* - High levels of interpersonal KSAE to communicate and influence others about creating workplace environmental conditions required to enhance commitment for innovation and effective continuous improvement.
Illustrative quotes	The Competitive Dialogue requires short-listed contractors to consider innovative approaches to the design and construction of a facility to be effective in both the short and long term. As A01 states:
A01 on a product innovation	… also it was more also about how do you organise your maintenance programme, what type of asphalt would you use, what—that was a very important issue for the ministry for how many maintenance days, what's the planning of your maintenance in relation to the type of asphalt that you use on the road; is it under—do you put some asphalt on the road and do you have only 1-10 years sort of big maintenance project or each year a few days maintenance. That trade-offs—that was very important because it was one of the major and ambitious tunnels in Netherlands so the number of days that it would be closed or how did you organise the maintenance of this tunnel during the next 30 years was a very important issue during this procurement issue and discussion.
On a process technology innovation	Use of BIM as an innovation was shown to be readily accepted in this illustration that hints at cultural factors that influence innovation motivation that were discussed in detail in Chapter 4. A07's quote also shows how liberating this [person] found the innovation to be and how that motivated him.

Table A14.   Wittgenstein Model Theme 8: Commitment to Innovation *(Continued)*

Theme and Subtheme	Notes, examples, and KSAE quotes
A07 on cultural factors impacting innovations of any type	Finnish people . . .are very quiet people normally, but one thing that I notice is they're very open to any kind of new solutions and this chap has never criticised anything that he was using. He said this is wonderful, it's got its own limitations and so on and so on, but actually it has enabled me to do this and that and he was demonstrating on a construction site how he can order with the click of a mouse a component that is going to be installed where they were building the new coffee roasting factory and it automatically triggered the whole supply chain to actually produce that component.
	This next example illustrates the thought processes behind the decision to use a PA approach on a project they studied in depth and how that project required rethinking how to measure performance and how it required a specific workplace culture. The second quote illustrates an innovation developed out of that project. As A09 states:
A09 on a philosophical stance for innovation	And you are seeing this sort of idea of design thinking, which is quite common now, this idea or concept of design thinking, but you are seeing the design thinking applied to an organisation or to a social problem. Essentially, how are we going to meet the Olympics, how are we going to clean the harbour up in time and build a 20km tunnel when our closest estimates where we took seven years to do a similar project in California? And how are we going to involve a complex array of stakeholders, give them a say in how it's designed but no accountability? And so it went against all the ideas of. . . resource-base, views of the firm, if you look at those sorts of ideas, it went against all those ideas that you collaborate to reduce uncertainty. Because these guys collaborated, but they added uncertainty and ambiguity to it by having complex array of KPIs, viewing industry standards as business as usual, or what they now call "minimum conditions of satisfaction," and saying that we're an alliance and we're special so we shouldn't accept business as usual, so we'll make the industry standards of "excellent" our "business as usual," because we're offering something different.
A09 on technology innovation	Yeah, process innovation, but also product innovation. The invention of, you know, a CAD system where they were different colour-coded lines representing gas pipes, water pipes, electricity pipes and so on. So typically you'd have like a radio that would go over them, where they developed a system that could tell the difference between the three. And this is the innovation through that project. You know, totally reducing the level of dust from cutting concrete, for example, one of the most riskiest parts of construction . . .

Another great innovation which has gone global is trenchless technology, so trenchless drilling . . . It's a little tunnel outside people's houses so you don't disrupt the community. So people can get in and out of their houses, you don't block the road, and you just pop it down one side, it comes out the other end, then. . . so they developed those sorts of technologies. And this came out through their commitment to their KPIs to community, for example. So those KPIs didn't just become ways of managing or control, they became points of innovation they got you to think differently about what you do. |
| | Other examples from more RBP types follow: |
| A13 on the T5 project procurement form | You had incentives to innovate so if you did things faster or quicker or better than the benchmarking, then you could make more profit. Adjusting time logistics also helped this emergence stuff. So if there was any problem that arose, you could deal with it by not putting those stuff on-site and stopping other work being done. |
| A16 on the Nordic form of partnering | And they're trying to do that but the thing was it worked really well in summer time, but as fast—as soon as it got a bit cold it didn't work. So they tried a few different alternatives, and they had that one and they had another big machine that they shipped over and tried . . .

And also, actually, having the flexibility to work around obstacles. So there was quite a lot of ad hoc discussion with land owners.

. . . commitment to innovate, that is, I would say, partly a behavioural thing, but partly a process or routine driver thing. That's my understanding. For example, if we take this trying to find innovative ways of using other types of machines, this chain saw thing, that was—they tried to establish that from more a normative way of top-down decision of, "Well, let's found processes to make this more effective and implement this." And that was an agreement between the partners. But when it wasn't fruitful for the project as a whole, and the subcontractors didn't really think, "Well, why should we use this?" It wasn't really part of the behavioural factors. I think - I would say that this is more a bottom-up driven thing, and this is more a top-down, or possible to implement more top-down. |
| P31 on innovations in a programme alliance context | It's, you know, smart design. So examples would be like a pump station usually has a round wet well and then a valve chamber on the outside. The designs have come up with sort of integrates that all into one sort of construction rather than two separate ones. So that generates savings. Other examples are [utility organisation X] up to this point has only built steel tanks. We've sort of really challenged the standards and brought in concrete tanks and, you know, saving millions of dollars on projects that way sort of thing. So challenging standards is another area as well. |
| **8.2 Commitment to continuous improvement** | Project participants' purpose for being innovative should be to achieve continuous improvement. The extent to which project participants can be innovative and effect continuous improvement depends upon institutional, governance, and individual motivational and enabling factors. Motivating to achieve continuous improvement depends upon institutional, governance, and individual motivational and enabling factors. |

(continued)

Table A14. Wittgenstein Model Theme 8: Commitment to Innovation *(Continued)*

Theme and Subtheme	Notes, examples, and KSAE quotes
Examples of high levels of thinking about commitment to continuous improvement	• Project participants understand that effective sustainability can only be achieved through continuous improvement and having sound mechanisms to capture and diffuse innovation from lessons learnt. • Project participants have a sophisticated and deep understanding of underlying concepts of what drives or inhibits continuous improvement. • Project team participants deeply understand and can adopt and adapt mechanisms for encouraging the diffusion of continuous improvement.
High-level KSAE needed for continuous improvement commitment	• *Technical and PM KSAE* – High levels of technical understanding of tools and processes and how these can be continuously improved and how these impact upon and are impacted by other project systems and project external systems. • *Business solutions KSAE* – High levels of understanding of driver and inhibitor processes for continuous improvement and how innovation impacts long term business success. • *Relational KSAE* – High levels of interpersonal KSAE are needed to communicate and influence others about the workplace environmental conditions required to enhance commitment for effective continuous improvement and its diffusion.
Illustrative quotes	P29 made a point about continuously improving KRAs and KPIs as form of process innovation, continuous improvement. He also illustrates how continuous improvement is also a balance of discarding processes, after duly considering their context, that fail to deliver value, and as he states:
P29	To me, that's one of the key learning's out of our whole alliance and unfortunately we're not going to get to do another one. To me that's where the real value could be added to anyone else going down the alliance path. We spent a lot of time and brainpower improving those KPIs to something that really means something.
P29	To give you an example, it specified that when all these different management plan documents had to be put together and we soon realised that they didn't actually add any value, and yet we'd paid for them so very much we were on the process mapping path and that has been much more effective. So the alliance is extremely good for delivering the programme.
	Use of value engineering as a continuous improvement tool was discussed by P23
P23	On this project, there were value engineering workshops and the like where they were constantly looking for better ways to deliver the project, and those workshops would involve alliance team members and people outside the alliance because it was often the situation where you were trying to find the best solution, project-wise—not necessarily just best for the alliance - but best for the overall project.
	And on continuous improvement through learning on similar elements in a tunnel fit out PA, P22 observed that:
P22	Two things happened, I suppose. One is there's a natural learning curve anyway on these projects, there always is. Irrespective of whether it's an alliance or any other delivery method, it's just a matter of fact that when you have 30 repetitive processes, obviously later on you work out how to do it. And they had put an awful lot of thought, an awful lot of pre-planning, into how they were going to pre-fabricate and do all sorts of things to try and advance the program. In the subsequent section of the eastern section, and certainly the central section, they managed to achieve quite remarkable program gains there in order to bring it in when they did, and I just can't see with a traditional form of contract they would have ever got there in the time they did.
8.3 Testing, prototyping, and experimenting	Project participants' innovative actions are usually manifested by testing, prototyping, and experimenting within the context of having an inquiring, curious, and often sceptical mind.
Examples of high levels of thinking about prototyping and experimenting	• Project participants understand the value of trial and error and are not inhibited, by the project governance system or workplace cultural norms, to experiment. • Project participants have a sophisticated and deep level scientific approach to effectively experiment with prototypes and simulations. • Project team participants have the capacity that when it appears to be appropriate, they can argue for, and influence, an argument for experimentation.
High-level KSAE needed for prototyping and experimenting	• *Technical and PM KSAE* – High levels of understanding project systems and project external systems and the technology involved in prototyping and modelling. • *Business solutions KSAE* – Participants need high levels of understanding limitations of a model versus the "real" situation and context and how this impacts upon long-term business success. • *Relational KSAE* – High levels of interpersonal KSAE are needed to communicate and influence others to support experimentation.

Table A14. Wittgenstein Model Theme 8: Commitment to Innovation *(Continued)*

Theme and Subtheme	Notes, examples, and KSAE quotes
Illustrative quotes	A02 drew attention to the value of adapting existing knowledge while designing new processes in an experimental fashion. She says:
A02	But this city tunnel project they say that now it was important for us to develop our own guidelines. Because if you are involved in developing something you learn it, yes and then it implements itself, instead of taking something that somebody else has developed and train people in it. They prefer to do it the other way round.
	A09 comments about common managerial attitudes to perceived risk of experimenting.
A09	And it comes down to the issues of improvisation, you know. But see, there's an interesting. . . whenever you talk about improvisation, if you go into a company and talk about improvisation – which I do a lot – they think you're crazy, because what they think is what you're talking about is letting go of everything you know.
	A13 made some interesting points about the T5 project. British Airports had a distinct policy of not trying something new, yet they required subcontractors to do a lot of off-site prototyping to experiment with potential new (in terms of scale and complexity) approaches and products.
A13	So they proved in these experiments that you could put a car park in there, put a car park in there, put a car park in there using the same design. The idea was design once, build many times and then you'd get improvements in terms of productivity and in terms of cost. They did lots of this pre-assembly, they tried these things before, pre-off-site testing and as I mentioned before they had this policy of not adopting untested technologies and that was one of the problems with the reporting of it. They said "This is another one of those IT disasters because they've just introduced this big bang IT system" but actually it wasn't true. They had been tested elsewhere before they were put in here.
A13	The fifth element of this, off-site pre-assembly tests. Because of this problem about one entrance and the restrictions getting onto the site and no laydown space, they had to come up with alternative arrangements and what they did they created off-site two consolidation areas. One at Colnbrook where they had a railway line going in bringing steel, concrete, and a lot of prefabrication of all the steel and concrete cages and prefabricated concrete panels, which were then brought onto site already partly manufactured. The other part of that was testing, because you didn't want to have unexpected things happen on the construction-site you'd test the method of construction off-site before you brought anything on-site. So again it's about learning. Make your mistakes off-site so when you come on-site you can do things right. And the last element in this system was the adjusted time logistics and again this is really to deal with this problem of having no laydown areas and having just one entrance to the thing.

Theme 9 **common best-for project mindset and culture** (refer to Table A5) relates to behavioural drivers as normative practices that define how a best-for-project mindset and culture evolved and operated. Subthemes from Section 1, Table 12 are elaborated upon in Table A15.

- **Common best-for-project mindset and culture** relates to the focus being placed on value generated in delivering the project compared with objectives of delivering what was explicitly requested or demanded. It is also about the priority of the project outcome taking precedence above all other considerations (despite inherent paradoxes). Major effort is directed at a project win outcome rather than individual teams being winners or losers.
- Subthemes emerged from the data for **Theme 9 – Common best-for-project mindset and culture** as follows:
  - 9.1 Alignment of common goals—Project participants' need to be effectively collaborating to a constructive end through sharing common and aligned goals about best for project and how that delivers value for money.
  - 9.2 Outcomes and performance levels—These should be assessed and judged based upon common best-for-project aligned goals.
  - 9.3 Challenging for excellence—Project participants' need to be constantly challenging their level of outcome and performance through effective collaboration toward a constructive evaluation of achieved outcomes and performance.
  - 9.4 Value for money reporting—Project participants' need to devise ways to recognise, monitor, and effectively diffuse knowledge about how their performance and workplace culture has impacted value for money on their project or programme.
  - 9.5 Recruiting support—Project participants' need to devise ways to effectively recruit support for best-for-project values through an effective PO/POR internal and NOPs recruitment strategy, as well as enlisting support for as many members of the project delivery chain as is possible.

Table A15.   Wittgenstein Model Theme 9: Common Best-for-project Mindset and Culture

Theme and Subtheme	Notes, examples, and KSAE quotes
9.1 Common aligned goals	Project participants need to be effectively collaborating to a constructive end by sharing commonly aligned best-for-project goals and how that delivers best value. The project outturn cost (the end of project cost) should represent best value to meet profit and other benefit expectations of participants to motivate and set a culture of collaboration to those ends.
Examples of high levels of thinking about common aligned goals	• Project participants understand the value and limitations of commonly aligned goals and how to achieve that alignment in both explicit and implicit terms. • Project participants realise that goals are context-constrained and are that they are not afraid to challenge, review, and recalibrate goals when the context changes. • Project team participants deeply understand the process of developing and recalibration of goals (as expressed as KRAs and KPIs) and realignment when this process is required.
High-level KSAE needed for common aligned goals	• *Technical and PM KSAE* – High levels of understanding of tools and processes and how to review and influence goal recalibration. • *Business solutions KSAE* – Participants need high levels of understanding of the purpose and limitations of goals and their alignment impacts upon long term business success. • *Relational KSAE* – High levels of interpersonal KSAE are needed to communicate and influence others about their own goals that may need to be reviewed and recalibrated to be aligned with those of the project's aims and goals. PORs, in particular, need to understand the motivational and commercial drivers of participants and the strengths and weaknesses of their organisational culture.
Illustrative quotes	The fundamental purpose of the whole project requires goals to be fully understood and to be aligned with how the project can be actually delivered. P17 makes a point about process performance that is elaborated upon in the following quote. P20 comments on best-for-project culture and thinking, and P29 comments on refining and clarifying common goal aspects.
P17	. . . the scope of the alliance is to deliver the whole project, and then you have some critical conversations where you have to reach alignment between the owner and non-owner on what risks and opportunities are going to be shared by the alliance participants, and that generally forces a conversation, which is complicated enough, about how do you deal with risks that you don't control. . . .one of the key conversations that we had in setting this up was that exact issues that just arose is about the scope of work, and back at the start we talked at length about that in one of the workshops, about why limit this to the mech and elec. And what we did is we actually opened it up so that the scope of the target cost included the civil works to be carried out by [participant 1 and 2]. That was one of the little breakthroughs we had in the commercial setup.
P20	. . . the KRAs were initially developed by the owner very early on and massaged to death, might I say, you can quote me on that, but finalised at the time of agreeing the TOC as well, so the TOC was really, the value and the scope of work that we landed on in the TOC had to reflect the KRAs that we had for the project and also had to reflect the initial business case of the project, so all of that alignment of value statements and value requirements had to be done at the time of TOC to make sure that what we were putting forward was going to meet the objectives that we had initially planned, but also was going to create that value that we had promised.
P29	It's a lot easier getting information and all working together, so I've got to say that's been an extremely positive experience and there's been no—I can honestly say I haven't seen any sort of real drivers to produce fat TOCs, fat target outturn costs that gives more gain share to the designer and to the contractor. I think what actually happens with a programme alliance is after awhile you work out the sweet spot in terms of what is really going to meet everyone's expectations, and you all work toward that and that has been very positive.
9.2 Outcomes and performance levels	These should be assessed, judged and be based upon agreed common best-for-project aligned goals. Performance is a multi-dimensional concept, and each project has its own drivers and context that influences the balance of output and outcome measures. Once realistically usable measures are in place, they can be linked to performance monitoring, decision making, and incentivisation arrangements. It's important to think of performance holistically.
Examples of high levels of thinking about best-for-project outcomes and performance	• Project participants understand the value of not just what was asked for by the POR but by what the POR found difficulty in articulating and what the POR actually meant to ask for. • Project participants understand how to effectively elicit information from the POR to clarify and explore aspects of the project business case and brief to clarify ambiguous or uncertain stated output and outcome requirements. • Project team participants deeply understand the process of developing and recalibrating goals (as expressed as KRAs and KPIs) to enable effective performance targets to be set that are express best-for-project outputs and outcomes.
High-level KSAE needed for best-for-project outcomes and performance	• *Technical and PM KSAE* – High levels of understanding tools and processes and how to review and influence refinement of the brief to squeeze out as much uncertainty and ambiguity as possible to lay foundations for excellent best-for-project decision making. • *Business solutions KSAE* – High levels of understanding of the purpose and limitations of goals and their alignment impacts upon long term business success. • *Relational KSAE* – High levels of interpersonal KSAE to communicate and influence others about how to develop a best-for-project culture.

Table A15. Wittgenstein Model Theme 9: Common Best-for-project Mindset and Culture *(Continued)*

Theme and Subtheme	Notes, examples, and KSAE quotes
Illustrative quotes	Outcomes and outputs are different concepts. Project outputs can be more tangible and thus more easily recognised and measured. Outcomes imply longer term impact and a broader set of end-states. This can include what the POR did not ask for but really wanted. Articulating these to enable linking them to success measures is important. P34 discusses some of these wider articulated outcomes as well as outputs, and P30 provides a quote about how a PA delivered better results than could have been achieved using a different procurement approach.
P34	It was very clear that they had a safety concern, they had traffic flow concern, they had connectivity and stakeholder concerns, as well as design integration with maintenance concerns, so they were basically the five KRAs.
	But very loose in the document, well enough defined, it was clear that that was their intent, they needed performance in those areas. And then the evolution of the KPIs associated with each of those KRAs, yeah it took—I don't know how many alliance guys you've talked to, but you can spend a long time with the detail of the KPIs, and I guess we spent a fair bit on [PA X], and realised, you know, we nearly got to the end of the project before we actually defined what it was we were measuring. So on [PA Y] we spent probably six months, the first six months, when we weren't really building much anyway, we were just basically preparing design and doing a bit of early works, and then about at the end of six months, they'd evolved enough that we said "Right, stop, that's what they're going to be, we'll measure them like that." And I think there might have been a couple of tweaks during the four years, but they weren't significant tweaks. They were just some oh shit moments where we thought; oh we're not measuring that properly because of such and such. So yeah, they evolved fairly quickly and became quite stable quite early.
P30	I mean think about what it is you're trying to achieve and mitigate the risk as best you can and the way it's progressing there is that we did achieve the objective at getting started early and we have delivered almost in slightly under the target out turn cost—less than one per cent I think is how it's shaping up under target out turn cost—and we've achieved all the things that were expected in the scope of the work and with huge traffic management challenges on that project as you'd expect, and it's something that we underbid actually. The traffic management has turned out to be a lot more expensive than we all thought. Now in a design and construct environment, you can see what could happen, couldn't you? The contractor is facing these huge bills for traffic management then you start cutting corners and they start switching off listening to the client who is persisting about the importance of continuing to manage traffic as efficiently as we possibly can but they'll just switch off. I hear you but I'm sorry I'm bleeding over here, I can't deliver on excellent traffic management. That's what tends to happen in a D&C procurement model. I'm really pleased again to hear that the alliance model has been able to achieve the client's objective and the alliance partners have made a reasonable financial gain out of it but not over the top.
9.3 Challenging for excellence	Project participants' within a PA context are required to be constantly challenging their level of outcome and performance through effective collaboration toward a constructive evaluation of achieved outcomes and performance. This provides a fission of uncertainty because it encourages project leaders to keep raising the bar of expectations of team performance and what can be achieved while team members use a bottom-up approach through reflecting upon and questioning assumptions and work approaches to rise above business-as-usual expectations. The PA approach can be contrasted with lower levels of project design and delivery collaboration intensity, where the main focus is on providing what was specifically requested.
Examples of high levels of thinking for challenging for excellence	• Project participants understand the value of reflection on assumptions underpinning work methods and design elements. They contemplate and act upon how to achieve continuous improvement and innovation that generates sustainable outcome improvement. • Project participants understand the distinction between efficiency and effectiveness, product and service, output and outcome. They also can distinguish between unnecessary "gold-plating" and "lean" project outputs and find a realistic balance in their approach. • Project team participants effectively apply a process of developing and recalibrating goals (as expressed as KRAs and KPIs) to improve best-for-project outputs and outcomes.
High-level KSAE needed for challenging for excellence	• *Technical and PM KSAE* – High levels of understanding of tools and processes and how to review and influence accepted BAU approaches to lay foundations for excellent best-for-project decision making and action taking. • *Business solutions KSAE* – Participants need high levels of understanding of the purpose and limitations of goals and to avoid unnecessary "gold-plated" solutions or needlessly "lean" ones that may have driven out requisite variety for innovation. • *Relational KSAE* – High levels of interpersonal KSAE are needed to inspire and influence others about how to develop a best-for-project culture through challenging for excellence.
Illustrative quotes	Challenging assumptions to be innovate has its risks if it is not within a culture that protects challenging orthodoxy and rewarding innovation. The Competitive Dialogue (CD) process and dual TOC PAs suffer the same risks in terms of exposing very bright ideas before being officially accepted as being part of the project team. As A01 discussed in relation to a CD situation:

(continued)

Table A15. Wittgenstein Model Theme 9: Common Best-for-project Mindset and Culture *(Continued)*

Theme and Subtheme	Notes, examples, and KSAE quotes
A01	. . . one of the very radical ideas but it was so radical that they were afraid that certain dialogue information would become public that that type of process—well you call it, is it innovation—but that approach would become, yes, would become public for the other parties, for the competitors. And also it was more also about how do you organise your maintenance programme, what type of asphalt would you use, what—that was a very important issue for the ministry for how many maintenance days, what's the planning of your maintenance in relation to the type of asphalt that you use on the road; is it under—do you put some asphalt on the road and do you have only 1–10 years sort of big maintenance project or each year a few days maintenance? That trade-offs—that was very important because it was one of the major and ambitious tunnels in Netherlands so the number of days that it would be closed or how did you organise the mainte-nance of this tunnel during the next 30 years was a very important issue during this procurement issue and discussion.
	Being prepared to challenge assumptions and offer radical ideas has its own constraints. In terms of needing political and well as technical skills, A09 made a good point that is similar to P21's observation on a very different project context:
A09	. . . the one thing I can see that was really strong is this desire to do something different, and the willingness for people to take on significant battles, even to their own detriment. To put a number on it - and I'm not saying this is what it is, but just to put a number—I would say 80% of the battle is political, and we don't pay enough attention in projects. . .
P21	I've experienced it, but being right in the middle of it and constantly being confronted by things that you need to try and correct in terms of an architect's view of the world and how things should operate and the builders view of the world and how things should operate. It's tough but I think that we are able, traditionally in projects I know—theatre buildings and theatres and renovations of theatres—is that areas that suffer the most are the end product which is actually the operational capacity of the building which actually delivers the product and they're the things that are most easily cut, and so I've worked with a lot of people in this project to make sure that that hasn't happened so we're going to come out with a really good technical result for the staging and a really good result in things operational relating to food and beverage and things like that.
9.4 Value for money reporting	Project participants' need to devise ways to recognise, monitor, and effectively diffuse knowledge about how their performance and workplace culture has impacted value for money on their project or programme.
Examples of high levels of thinking for value for money reporting	• Project participants understand the distinction between cost and value and therefore how to best frame stakeholders' value proposition in what really counts as value for them. • Project participants understand the how stakeholders may visualise value for money (VfM) so that they can articulate it an explicit and unambiguous way. • Project team participants effectively apply a process of reporting in a meaningful yet simple way best-for-project outputs and outcomes that clearly identify VfM.
High-level KSAE needed for reporting value for money	• *Technical and PM KSAE* - High levels of understanding of tools and processes and how to identify, measure, and communicate VfM. • *Business solutions KSAE* - Participants need high levels of understanding of the purpose and limitations of influential project stakeholders' value proposition that leads to effectively articulating VfM in terms that these stakeholders can understand. • *Relational KSAE* - High levels of interpersonal KSAE are needed to effectively identify, define and communicate VfM in terms that influential stakeholders can understand.
Illustrative quotes	Reporting VfM entails more than dryly cataloguing how the project has delivered benefits that are appreciated, valued, and "count." It requires an element of inspirational communication to develop a reporting format that motivates influential stakeholders to fully recognise what has been delivered. However, there still seems to be difficulty in the POR and NOPs identifying specific VfM examples to adequately demonstrate this element of success. Two aspects of VfM reporting emerged from the data. One set of quotes relates to initial business case justification of VfM. Envisaging VfM is sometimes captured by KRAs and operation-alised through KPIs.
P34	The value for money case here was reducing congestion, improving traffic flows, reducing the poor safety record, or improving the poor safety record. You know, realignments that were more—that suited the traffic, I guess better, because what was there before was pretty ordinary. . . . improving access provisions, so all of those things go to the value—statement of value I guess, but [client/owner X] trying to encapsulate that in a statement, well no, not really. We prepared a quarterly value for money report, and we reported—and I haven't gone through all the elements of value, but they were probably the main ones. And we'd report on how we were going against each of them, comparing that to the business case that [client/owner X] put together to justify the project.
P17	. . . when we're dealing with the public sector, everyone is walking on eggshells about value for money and probity, et cetera, and what I find in the private sector is people make much more rapid decisions and they're far more empowered; if they think that they'll get the best deal by negotiating on a sole-source basis with one player, that's what they'll do

Table A15. Wittgenstein Model Theme 9: Common Best-for-project Mindset and Culture *(Continued)*

Theme and Subtheme	Notes, examples, and KSAE quotes
P20	. . . the value and the scope of work that we landed on in the TOC had to reflect the KRAs that we had for the project and also had to reflect the initial business case of the project, so all of that alignment of value statements and value requirements had to be done at the time of TOC to make sure that what we were putting forward was going to meet the objectives that we had initially planned, but also was going to create that value that we had promised.
P28	once you've made a decision in that selection then it's a priority consideration in the selection because they all lead to the value for money, how you manage your risk, how do you manage the scope, how you manage your time. To me, that's the end of the argument or the discussion because in selecting that form of delivery you have picked the best value-for-money delivery method. I know later we put up value-for-money reports and things like that, but to me, when they talk about value for money, once the decision's been made which form of delivery you use to me that's the end of the discussion, but some people don't agree with me.
	The second aspect is about post-project or during-project VfM reporting that may be undertaken to articulate broad VfM results.
P30	. . . there's also a requirement that when you reach practical completion of your alliances that the client needs to prepare a value-for-money report to demonstrate what has been achieved. With doing that, I've been reflecting on my experience that these sort of reports tend to pop out at the end of the alliance work when teams are being disbanded and the knowledge capture is extremely difficult because all those with the wisdom about the value that we've delivered, have departed. So trying to bring it all together and collated to form a great value-for-money report becomes very problematic. And I've been saying to the recent alliances that I'm in and they get it, and six months out before the end I really made an issue of it, and I get lots of people promising me that we're in the throes of developing and we've got a framework and we've drafted something up, and I keep saying "I want to see it," guess what happens? It doesn't come. It's a low priority from the team's perspective and again becomes a very difficult task at the end to pull it together. Having said that, though, the quality of the value-for-money reports is improving. Some years ago there wasn't a requirement, I don't think, to prepare value-for-money statements, although treasuries now ask from us a report on value for money for each of the alliances we've undertaken.
P30	So we're in the process of collating these value for money reports and feeding them up to treasury who I'm sure will go through them very closely and be coming back with lots of questions about who decided to make this change event? Who gave authority for this? Why did you need to have this change event? All those sorts of questions I'm sure will come back. Now that doesn't worry me because we've got processes here with all of our contracts that with delegations of authority, you cannot change scope of work without getting approval of the chief executive. In variations you've always got to put a value-for-money statement in there, to demonstrate that it's been properly considered it is value for money before we tick it off anyway. So it doesn't worry me, it's just that again people might be frightened by the number of change events, the nature of them, without really understanding them. And also importantly I think it's good to have value for money reports but the other thing we're insisting on is having lessons learnt which feeds into value for money. The lessons-learnt workshops are proving to be really good value to reflect on how we've gone, where were the areas for improvement, and what should we continue to do in the future. I think they're tremendously valuable forums.
9.5 Recruiting support	Project participants' need to devise ways to effectively recruit support for best-for-project values through an effective PO/POR internal and NOPs recruitment strategy as well as enlisting support for as many members of the project delivery chain as is possible.
Examples of high levels of thinking for recruiting support	• Project participant organisations hire on the basis of technical excellence as being baseline BAU expectations, and business and interpersonal collaboration skills as providing a defining edge. • Project participant organisations understand the value proposition of their employees to encourage their support and enthusiasm to work within an alliance. • Project participant organisations understand that they need to provide strong KSAE development initiatives and programmes to attract and retain rare talent. • Project team participant organisations understand and effectively manage the transition of team members entering and leaving an alliance so that they remain energetic and motivated and that they are willing and keen to remain working within an alliance context.
High-level KSAE needed for recruiting support	• *Technical and PM KSAE* – High levels of understanding of recruitment, development and retention processes, and how to apply them in recruiting teams with a best-for-project mind set. • *Business solutions KSAE* – Participant organisations' HRM staff need high levels of understanding and the value of knowledge, skills, and experience gained by their employees while on an alliance to the base organisation. • *Relational KSAE* – High levels of interpersonal KSAE are needed to effectively engage and communicate with staff who become, in many ways, expatriate staff embedded in the alliance but will at some stage return to their base organisations.
Illustrative quotes	The manner in which staff is recruited with a best-for-project mindset/culture can be illustrated at three levels. The first level is selecting and recruiting the entire NOPs team.

(continued)

Theme and Subtheme	Notes, examples, and KSAE quotes
P18	We're trying to put together a process for selection that is ruled up and rigorous and gives us the best chance of getting the best group of people together into an alliance. So we've got that ongoing tension. What's happened now is we've probably, in terms of the winning criteria, there's probably about 20/21% is based on behaviour, and that's behaviour we assess in two-day workshops. And a big lot of the people who work for us are GPs or charted psychologists and things like that, and they carry that [the team assessment for selection] out. So I suppose there's only about three of us with project-type backgrounds. Most come from psychology-type backgrounds, but very practical. They've worked on business for most of their careers. With a heavier emphasis on that, we use the personality profiling to help us select members—not as effectively as members of the project alliance board, because sometimes there isn't a choice when the supplier does need to have a certain person in there. But what we do with that personality profile, they all have the profile done, they have one-to-one feedbacks, and then we have a session where we look at the dynamics of the group. And that's taken through by one of the psychologists in terms of the differences in how people do things and how they will behave and how we have to manage that inside the project alliance board. And we do the same with inside the alliance leadership team. And then there's a series of workshops, because what we're doing in the [PO X] situation is we're treating it as a change management programme, because we're having to change from a traditional mindset to an alliancing mindset, with all the appropriate tools that go with that.
P28	. . . in selecting the alliance we spent a lot of time in picking what we felt was the best team, the right team at the right place at the right time. We spent a lot of time looking at the people that they were putting up and the cultures of the organisations in knowing that we have to bring six different organisations together, six different cultures, and there was a lot of mainly gut feeling on how it would work and things like that. We went to the market and we had the majors in one group, we had the designers in one group, and we had the second-tier players in another group. We were really focussing on the culture of the people, their availability to hit the ground running as soon as we appointed them. The other thing which we focussed on was trying to give the second tier a bit of an opportunity of playing with the majors and we achieved that by having both [NOPs A and B] in it.
P31 recruiting for a programme alliance	One of the benefits for [PO X] is that [PO X] has been able to retain some pretty good employees, particularly, I mean the market's softened right up now, but during a time when there was some pretty tight competition for resources, it gave [PO X] employees a really good opportunity to work in the semi-private sector type environment, but have the comfort of working for a government organisation—if that makes sense. So [PO X] has got some—well I mean the [PO X] employees within the alliance sort of rate pretty much equally with, you know, the [NOP A], [NOP B] employees and I don't think [PO X] would have been able to hold onto them over the last five years if there wasn't this opportunity, I would say.
	The second level is at the POR level internally. The manner in which the PO selects its internal POR staff is summed up as follows:
P29 recruited for a programme alliance	So basically because the other thing to keep in mind is that this was all happening at the time of the engineering boom, so if water authorities have got more projects to deliver, that means that the private industry is also going pretty well in terms of consultants and contractors. It becomes a very hot market out there. We were having trouble retaining engineers who wanted to go onto bigger and better things either within the water industry or in the mining boom, etc. So we had to come up with a strategy that was going to provide the resources both internally and externally to not only delivery the big projects, but our overall programme so we set up the [PO X] Alliance a bit over four years ago. Basically to deliver those smaller type projects that have built up in the order of 90–100 million dollars' worth of a year within a project. So in the order of 15-25 projects a year that we had to deliver. So it was about coming up with a methodology to deliver the programme. Secondly, it was about trying to provide opportunities to retain our staff, but also to secure external resources rather than have to compete all the time.
P30 who was a POR ALT member	I really wasn't sure what I was in for. I'd heard a little bit from [person X] about what they're like and that, but that was from a distance, so to speak. But yeah, dropping into them it was interesting and I think I made a comment to one or two alliances that it would have been good if there was some induction for new ALT members, that's something that I found we haven't been really good at. So it's a really sharp introduction into what is the alliance and this is where we're at so far. So a bit of an induction would have been good, in my opinion so I was up a steep learning curve. I was just sort of overwhelmed at the beginning, too, with the Section of information that was coming.
	The third level is the way that second tier participants who are outside the alliance but working as suppliers and subcontractors using more traditional procurement forms are expecting or being encouraged to work within the collaboration framework of an alliance.
A13 reflecting on studies and observation of the T5 project in operation	. . . the T5 Agreement worked because BAA was unusual because they were the client and owner and operator, but they were also working as the project manager for the whole project as what we call a systems integrator. They were pulling everything together and they were the first-tier suppliers who were involved in this T5 Agreement. The second-tier suppliers were a number of contractors who would support the first-tier suppliers were part of the T5 Agreement and supposed to use the same spirit of this agreement in the way that they managed their subcontractors.

Table A15. Wittgenstein Model Theme 9: Common Best-for-project Mindset and Culture *(Continued)*

Theme and Subtheme	Notes, examples, and KSAE quotes
P28 on how the alliance affected all other site workers.	That commitment has got to be acknowledged from the organisation, we never lost anybody that we wanted to keep unless they resigned from the organisations. We did a lot of inductions and things like that for supply chain, we induced about ten thousand people but there was always a focus in the inductions on our culture, our safety requirements, what's expected of those people. When they were onsite, they were seen to be a part of a team and they were expected to exhibit the behaviours as the rest of the team.
P33's contrasting experience	I think realistically the collaboration is really between [Org X] and [Org Y]. I don't necessarily see subcontractors that the alliance would engage see a need or some sort of different incentive to perform the job differently because of collaboration approach. I think they understand that [Org Y] has the [Org X] hat on or that in that area there is a slightly different hat on; it's like state government with a bit of a private edge and they require different outcomes and they're going to be hotter on the safety and those sort of things, but also focused on delivery, focused on getting things done quickly and to standard and making that happen. I don't see a lot of flowing out of the collaboration culture into other subbies necessarily, they're all pretty hungry out there and they want to make sure that they get a chance to work on the alliance because that's a pay cheque. They know that if they work, they get consistency, they get the same focused aim day in, day out, there are no loss or they don't need to guess at where they are in the process.

Theme 10, **no-blame culture** (refer to Table A5) relates to the behavioural drivers as normative practices that define how a no-blame culture evolved and operated. Subthemes from Section 1, Table 12 are elaborated upon in Table A16.

- **No-blame culture** relates to the focus being placed on creating and maintaining a culture with its supporting mechanisms to eliminate the attribution of blame and "finger-pointing."
- Subthemes emerged from the data for **Theme 10 – No-blame culture,** which fell into two categories. The first is about blame and reasons for it—about a rationale for a no-blame culture. The second is about mechanisms that support the creation and maintenance of a no-blame culture. These two categories can be summarised as follows:
  - 10.1 Rationale for a no-blame culture—Project participants avoiding a blame shifting culture having felt pain and hardship through past experience of being blamed, and therefore determined not to repeat the experience and to thus support a no-blame culture, or having experienced the positive side of a no-blame culture.
  - 10.2 Facilitating mechanisms for no-blame— contractual, behavioural, and organisational mechanisms that support the establishment and maintenance of a no-blame culture.

Table A16. Wittgenstein Model Theme 10: No-blame Culture

Theme and Subtheme	Notes, examples, and KSAE quotes
10.1 Rationale for a no-blame culture	Project participants embracing a no-blame culture and avoiding blame shifting as a result of two sets of drivers. First, having felt pain and hardship through past experience of being blamed and therefore, being determined not to repeat the experience and to thus support a no-blame culture. Second, having experienced positive benefits as a result of working within a no-blame culture.
Examples of high levels of thinking about the rationale for a no-blame culture	• Project participants being able to reflect upon past experiences of the harm triggered by a blame culture and identifying and understanding how those behaviours developed and were supported by the workplace or prevailing community culture. • Project participants being able to reflect upon past experiences and understanding the advantage of working within a no-blame culture and identifying that and understanding how those behaviours developed and were supported. • Project participants being able to develop alternative mechanisms to those that produce and nurture a blame-culture. This may include linking collaborative consensus decision-making to shared pain/gain based on project performance (as opposed to individual participant team performance) along with a no-litigation contract clauses and other support measures that enhance participants taking shared responsibility and accountability for all project outcomes rather than those only directly affecting them.
High-level KSAE needed for understanding the rationale for, and implementation of, a no-blame culture	• *Technical and PM KSAE* – High levels of understanding of tools and processes and their advantages and limitations to be able to judge *when* to agree or disagree with others and how to negotiate, through adopting a constructive dialogue with others, and shape solutions that all can agree upon and take responsibility and accountability for. • *Business solutions KSAE* – Participants need high levels of understanding of the relative transaction cost of lack of collaboration and disputation, as often is present within a BAU. They need to understand how a no-blame culture environment may save transaction costs. • *Relational KSAE* – High levels of interpersonal KSAE are needed to communicate with others and to influence others and be influenced by them to achieve a no-blame culture.

(continued)

Table A16. Wittgenstein Model Theme 10: No-blame Culture *(Continued)*

Theme and Subtheme	Notes, examples, and KSAE quotes
Illustrative quotes	A core part of the no-blame culture is centred on the right (and propensity) for parties to sue each other in most contract forms, and how for some procurement forms this right is given up in exchange for elimination of the need for litigation. The following quotes on two separate projects in Australia illustrate this aspect. The first is where A09 discusses how an alliance was considered but the project ended up as a joint venture agreement that attempted a watered-down version of an alliance because of a reluctance to accept any form of no-litigation and no-blame culture. The second was illustrated with quotes from P17 and P25 about the rationale for subsequently forming an alliance between two organisations on a project.
A09 illustrates how half-measures do not seem to work and that	One of the projects we were going to look at is the cross-city tunnel, and we went there for an interview and we were talking to the guys and then they just clamped up, you know, went away and decided not to do it as an alliance, they decided to do it as a . . . just a joint venture. I mean, the results speak for itself – it's a dismal result. Over budget, got sued by residents and businesses, and traffic didn't flow through the tunnel. The old industry, the old ways of doing things, are entrenched, and it's very hard to change that, and you find a group of people who work on innovative forms of contracting or organisation forms that once these finish they expect you to go back to old ways of doing things, and they don't cope, and slowly they give up, lose hope and just become indoctrinated into the old system. So these people that could have potentially transformed an industry have become like everyone else.
P17 on . . . the essence of effective alliancing as producing a no-blame culture	. . . it's always been my belief that in order to facilitate that you have to create at least predominantly a commercial framework where you remove the run points and create a commercial reason why it actually makes sense to collaborate and direct your energies toward understanding and working together, rather than directing your energies toward pointing the finger. And I have seen examples of people who in other contexts are quite dictatorial and quite hard-nosed, when put into a context where you've changed the rules and they've actually been quite effective, because what they realise is that now my interests are served by working with these people to solve a problem, because our fates are entwined. There's no point in blaming. So I think it's a combination of creating the right commercial and contractual context, coupled with having those kind of leadership qualities of people who inherently are more authentic, they have better skills at empathy and understanding, but are nonetheless still driven toward a commercial outcome.
P25	. . . [Project X] was still underway and there was an enormous amount of conflict occurring on [Project X] between the M&E contractor in the tunnel and the civil contractor, which was basically us. And I'm talking serious conflict, so the parties were more or less at war from a contractual point and a commercial point of view, but even worse than that, the project was suffering a time lag because the parties were very misaligned.
	. . . And so what was happening on [Project X] is the project director would just go "Look, I've got to get my civil works done," so they would just go and do things in there that were detrimental to the M&E contractor. Then that would result in a claim from the subcontractor that sort of went on. There was a guy who I was trying to negotiate the contract with. His name was [xxxx], who was telling me the [Org A] side of the story on [Project X]. And he said "Look, without you listening to just your guys in isolation, how about I take you down to [Project X] and show you what's happening from my point of view?" And I could see, because I had no bias in this, the [Org B] guys I talked to just hated [Org A]. They just thought they were incompetent. Then when I met with the [Org A] guys and they showed me some of the photos of what had happened, even historically, you could see, the whole thing, it was just a bunfight inside the tunnel. Everybody was trying to get access and they weren't necessarily deciding on what were the best priorities in terms of the best outcome from the project. They were all just looking after their own personal interests and definitely we were getting a substandard outcome.
	P06 provides a useful insight about the D&C approach from a client's perspective. In this quote, it is clear that there is litigation going on but between the designer and constructor participants in a D&C contract. The client gains from the arrangement but the D&C parties do not. There is no evidence of collaboration between the client and D&C consortium and so potential gains are not considered. The no-blame culture is absent here in contrast to the alliance examples.
P06	Well it was the way the whole system used to be run and it didn't help the client, because it was all cleared up at the end, they didn't know what their commitment was. You finished on site and a big claim turned up and no one knew it was coming your way and it was obviously a financial mess. But the market place has virtually turned away from traditional contracts, you get the odd one, but design and build has just become more and more, you know, the norm. And we've just finished the [Project x], which is a very, very sophisticated building . . . so there was lots and lots of issues of not having it constructed properly. We went design and build in the end, and the reason we went design and build because we felt the design team couldn't actually produce the information in sufficient time and quality, not to have a claim by the contractor. And that was proven to be the case, so what happened was the client had a budget of 22 ½ million, we delivered the project for 22 ½ million, it was late because of late receipt of design information, and the claim right is the contractor against the consultant, not the contractor against the client, because of the poor performance of the professional team, the architects, and the engineers. As far as the client is concerned, they're tickled pink because they didn't have any more money, and I was actually there this morning and said if you'd gone down that old route, you'd be sat here with a massive claim thinking where am I going to get this two or three million pounds from disruption and everything else and how am I going to pay it. And all we're talking about now is a few defect acoustic doors, okay which is an issue but nothing like it could have been.

Table A16.   Wittgenstein Model Theme 10: No-blame Culture *(Continued)*

Theme and Subtheme	Notes, examples, and KSAE quotes
10.2 Facilitating mechanisms for no-blame	Central to support mechanisms for the establishment and maintenance of a no-blame culture is a need for genuine collaboration to enable participants to gain a more accurate understanding of the perspective and problems faced by each party to the collaboration and an ability to use that knowledge to generate creative win-win problem solutions. Developing consensus decision making (discussed in theme 11) also helps develop a no-blame culture because with it becomes illogical to allocate blame to others for a decision that one is a party to. Having a binding no-litigation agreement helps to bolster trust because there is greater confidence in parties sharing an interest, and this is further reinforced by having agreed fair pain/gain sharing arrangements tied to a project rather than individual team performance.
Examples of high levels of thinking abo-49p0.968ut facilitating a no-blame culture	• Project participants being able to affectively identify with other parties' perspectives and to empathise with them to understand issues and challenges they are grappling with. • Project participants being able to effectively collaborate to find and implement win-win problem solutions that meet best-for-project outcomes while meeting reasonable needs of each participant. • Considering how to best share responsibility and accountability for decisions that all parties are affected by or can influence to enable fair and just decision action outcomes.
High-level KSAE needed for facilitating a no-blame culture	• *Technical and PM KSAE* – High levels of understanding of tools and processes and how each party can collaborate to help develop synergistic decision making and action outcomes. • *Business solutions KSAE* – Participants need high levels of understanding of how to frame mechanisms that engender a no-blame culture. • *Relational KSAE* – High levels of interpersonal KSAE are needed to communicate with others and to influence others and be influenced by them to achieve a no-blame culture.
Illustrative quotes	Central to developing mechanisms supporting a no-blame culture is intense collaboration and consensus decision making, through truly being able to appreciate multiple perspectives on issues and challenges to be overcome.
A02 on the Nordic cultural propensity for inclusive decision making	They say that yeah, there is somewhat of a cultural clash for us, because we Swedish we have a consensus culture which can be extremely frustrating for other people and sometimes also for Swedes as well. But there are so many discussions and everybody has to agree. But what happens in those discussions, they take an endless long time, but after a decision is reached it's generally agreed upon by people and it's implemented, while perhaps if you make a decision at an early, somebody high up in the organisation makes a decision at an early stage, you then have to kind of in communicate and sell it within the organisation.
P20 on the mechanisms used on an Australian alliance project. This quote illustrates collaborative decision making structures, impact of co-location and aspects of authentic leadership.	Because the management team was quite balanced in terms of perspective, then it meant that we were able to have a robust discussion at the management team level. Then if we couldn't come to an agreement with the management team, then it would go to the leadership team, I would present it to the leadership team for approval, but honestly we didn't have to have the leadership team get involved in more than 10 of these things, and there have been hundreds over the course of the project, so much things have been able to be managed by the management team. The other thing I would do differently, just by chance, the way the project office is laid out, it's mostly square, there's this though, where do you think the architects are? . . . up in that corner. . . Even just the little thing about the positioning of people makes a difference, yeah, so if I had it to do again I would have integrated it into the office. When you're sitting in a meeting talking about ductwork above a seating array, you need to understand enough of it to understand the problem and understand what's needed, what needs to be tweaked in order to solve the problem, not from a technical perspective but who do you need to involve, who do you need to move or who needs to move in order to solve the problem and who's going to have to compromise and how are we going to get to that compromise and all of that.
A13 discusses the U.K. T5 Agreement and how risk treatment impacts collaboration.	. . . the client bears the risks. This is the kind of traditional approach to risk which is that the client dumps the risk down onto the contractor, the contractor dumps it down onto their subcontractors and so on. So all the way down you're getting risk dumped down. What they said in T5 "No, we're going to take all the risk because ultimately it comes back to us anyway. We're going to have integrated project teams involving the client and we'll call them partners in our framework agreement, first-tier suppliers of work and then the partners will be responsible for pushing this down to their separate owners in the same spirit of that," the spirit of cooperation and so on. In return for this, BAA said "We'll pay you what it costs to build this building, to build this construction rather than having a fixed price because what happens traditionally in construction is that you go in with a low bid, the lowest bidder wins and then you get litigation and you try and get contract variations in order to just be able to make a profit.

(continued)

Table A16.   Wittgenstein Model Theme 10: No-blame Culture *(Continued)*

Theme and Subtheme	Notes, examples, and KSAE quotes
Also he discusses the impact of the contractual relationships with behavioral requirements to foster collaboration and no-blame	So an interesting way of controlling costs is to pay what it costs. All of this was written down in a novel kind of contract and they called it Handbook T5 Agreement. The handbook is a big fat thing and it gave details of how you're going to work in this kind of an environment right from the top in great detail, and each of the contractors was given this and asked to read it. If they agreed to that code of conduct, to working in that way, they would sign it and it became a contract and that's how they operated this thing. So basically what they were doing was social engineering in a way, trying to change the behaviour of years and years of behaviour in the construction industry, collaborative works, integrated project team working partly.
P37 on a no-blame culture within a programme alliance in Australia	. . . when we say things like no-blame, that doesn't mean that you can't challenge. So we really—so part of our induction was saying, look, it's alright to challenge somebody, it's alright to say look, you've stuffed that up, as long as you do that in a respectful manner. So we did spend time, and we did this without facilitation. We started with facilitators, and then we thought, look, we could probably try this ourselves. But we really tried to just induct people into what was required, but at the same time, have the courage or the strength to actually challenge it when things weren't right. So as I say, I know that there's two or three that had to go because I had to challenge them and say, look, and after a couple of times say this isn't working. But most of the times when you challenge them and say, look, that type of behaviour is—standing up and saying bloody designers are hopeless and they're always late with designs, and they've got no concept of budget and—that behaviour is unacceptable. It's unacceptable because—not because I say so, but because it doesn't align with our behaviours, we're all one team, we've got—we all share an equal role. So reminding people that the designer is part of the overall project and the overall programme performance, not just in getting his IFT drawings out. His performance is also linked to the overall project. He's part of the team. It's an integrated team. So we really did spend quite a lot of time trying to induct and train people of that. We would do things like fortnightly communication workshops where we really tried to build that team spirit and break down that design and construct thing. I suppose the other was that it comes back to the culture of the team. So the things that we thought of made up a culture of systems, symbols and procedures. So things like badging.

Theme 11, **consensus decision making** (refer to Table A6) relates to the processes, routines and means that facilitate and enable decisions to be made in a consensual manner. Subthemes from Section 1, Table 13 are elaborated upon in Table A17.

- **Consensus decision making** relates to the extent to which there is total agreement on a decision made at the strategic and project executive level.
- Subthemes emerged from the data for **Theme 11, consensus decision making.** These fell into three categories. The first is about participants' cultural drivers of the decision-making process. The second subtheme relates to enablers of consensus decision making. The third relates to inhibitors of consensus decision making. These can be summarised as follows:
  - 11.1 Cultural drivers—the discussion in Chapter 4 on culture highlighted that some cultures have levels of high power asymmetry where it is expected that individuals at loftier levels of a hierarchy make decisions and issue orders to those lower down in the hierarchy who must accept and action those decisions. Other cultural dimensions also impact power asymmetry. Uncertainty avoidance leads people to avoid being committed to a risky decision and a collectivist culture encourages, if not requires, that individuals "go along with the crowd" rather than voice concern or opposition to mooted decisions. Some disciplines and workplace setting demand challenges to assumptions, while others demand obedience and discipline. These cultural drivers enhance or impede genuine consensus decision making.
  - 11.2 Enablers of consensus—there are a number of organisational structural as well as behavioural enablers that facilitate and support consensus decision making and action taking.
  - 11.3 Inhibitors of consensus—there are a number of organisational structural as well as behavioural enablers that inhibit and suppress consensus decision making and action taking.

Table A17.   Wittgenstein Model Theme 11: Consensus Decision-making

Theme and Subtheme	Notes, examples, and KSAE quotes
11.1 Cultural drivers	Taking into account national and organisational cultural theory discussed in Chapter 4, we focus here on power distance, uncertainty avoidance, and collectivist/individualist cultural dimensions, though these can be seen to also be linked the other cultural dimensions such as masculine/feminine with regard to behaviours and attitudes to diversity and inclusivity and to some extent concepts of time (short-term or long-term). Cultural orientation drives behaviours and that, in turn, affects the extent to which decision making is consensus driven or command-and-control driven.
Examples of high levels of thinking about the cultural drivers	• Participants expect that those with relevant expertise to contribute opinion and discussion input do so regardless of their place within a hierarchy. • Participants welcome assumptions being challenged and are careful to consider a range of perspectives when making decisions. • Participants are respectful of others' perspective but assertively argue their points of view to arrive at a balanced conclusion. • Participants expect that a consensus will emerge from a meaningful debate and that consensus-driven decisions will be more effectively actioned when they are not afraid to raise the issue of reviewing a consensus-based decision if they believe that the basis, context and underlying assumptions for those decisions have changed.
High-level KSAE needed for effective cultural drivers	• *Technical and PM KSAE* – High levels of technical and PM competence should be demonstrated and offered to contribute to all relevant decision-making discussions. • *Business solutions KSAE* – High levels of understanding longer-term business impacts of decisions being considered on the home base organisation and project. • *Relational KSAE* – High levels of ability to communicate, comprehend the perspective of others, and to effectively negotiate.
Illustrative quotes	National cultural traits are highlighted by interviews with people with experience in Nordic countries, where there is a high emphasis on consultation and consensus in decision making.
A02	. . . there is somewhat of a cultural clash for us, because we Swedish we have a consensus culture which can be extremely frustrating for other people and sometimes also for Swedes as well. But there are so many discussions and everybody has to agree. But what happens in those discussions, they take an endless long time, but after a decision is reached it's generally agreed upon by people and it's implemented, while perhaps if you make a decision at an early, somebody high up in the organisation makes a decision at an early stage, you then have to kind of in communicate and sell it within the organisation. . . . . another issue is that the German people have to go back to their bosses all the time and ask for permission about everything, while Swedish people can be more, kind of, they can make decisions and they can check, perhaps check afterwards, or they have kind of, they have some autonomy to make decisions on their own based on their expert areas. So it's easier, shorter decision routes in the Swedish culture. But what's interesting is that also the Germans, when they have been working in these projects, they think that it is a very good way of working, so they perceive it as a way of working which is much better than their traditional way, and they are able to adapt, it just takes a bit longer time for them. So it's not impossible.
A16	Especially when talking to these people that were involved in the projects and others around, they—I mean their interpretation of what partnering is—I mean if I put it this way, the word "partnering" the Swedish translation of that have a meaning of its own, which is similar to partnering—the American expression. But I think the interpretation and it—for the people that aren't involved in partnering on a daily basis, they base their understanding on what partnering is through what the word partnering means. So I found that talking to a lot of people they didn't use or they didn't talk about the same thing as partnering. And looking at the procurement or the agreement in this case, no one involved in the project, I think this is just—read about the definition of what partnering is and what partnering should be. They just decided that we need some collaborative way of working and let's call is partnering, and then negotiated what it should be.
A19 discussing Japanese contractors working in the Middle East	So culture is actually a major moderating force and it's the thing that most companies forget, and the Japanese forgot when they went abroad. You know, you can't do that. . . . the problem is that gave them a serious problem, in terms of—they—you know, they say that basically all their business is based on trust. It is the case in Japan, but it's not the case when they end up working in the Arab states, where they get ripped off and don't get paid. So it's a totally different ballgame out there. This is what they're struggling to, I think, come to terms with, but they have to learn to work in those environments and they have to get themselves project management systems.
And on China A19 says:	Well, I mean you're stuck within an institutionalised system and I think the issue with that is it's—everything changes, not by individuals but by policy. Policy is what drives the—if you like, the company or the organisation or whatever. It's not individuals. That's quite difficult for westerners to get their head around.

(continued)

Theme and Subtheme	Notes, examples, and KSAE quotes
11.2 Enablers of consensus	Structural and organisational elements are important beside culture as an enabler or inhibitor. The way that governance is designed has great impact, the roles that people play in various committee or decision-making board levels, and protocols used that govern how meetings will be conducted, all affect how consensus decisions can be enabled or inhibited.
Examples of high levels of thinking about enablers of consensus	• Participants ensure that organisations are structured to facilitate communication between hierarchical and discipline levels within the project. • Participants are mindful about national and organisational/discipline cultural norms and expectations to ensure that they design mechanisms to open up dialogue and challenging assumptions to ensure that each party to a decision is allowed to work through any difficulties in understanding broader perspectives. • Participants understand the value of face-to-face as well as electronic meetings to allow trust and commitment to "grow" and be sustained to result in ease of consensus-based decision making.
High-level KSAE needed to enable consensus	• *Technical and PM KSAE* – High levels of technical and PM competence should be demonstrated and offered to design governance mechanisms that facilitate consensus of decision making. • *Business solutions KSAE* – High levels of understanding the value of trust and social capital to be gained and grown from consensus in decision making. • *Relational KSAE* – High levels of ability to communicate, comprehend the perspective of others, and to effectively reach consensus in decision making.
Illustrative quotes	Two aspects are illustrated here for enabling consensus decision making. P20 explains how the structure of the AMT and ALT can facilitate consensus decision making. P28 talks about how consensus works for setting KPIs, which are important for agreed performance.
P20 on structural aspects:	Construction manager, design manager and basically client interface manager, the user interface manager, so if you want to go to corporate hats you have someone from the architect, someone from the builder and one of the clients in the AMT throughout the project. So that's been consistent, some of the people have changed, but [X] used to be in the AMT previously. But the roles of the people in the AMT has been consistent and it's been a small AMT all the way through. Then we have a mixed group of people that we call key managers who are that next layer of people with key responsibilities within their lives.
And P20 later describing how a bottom-up and top-down approach led to a consensus decision.	. . . we had done a design for the air conditioning which absolutely didn't work because there was, one entity had gone off and done it themselves and it came back on the table and it just, it wouldn't work, we couldn't actually fit it in the ceiling, kind of a problem. So, we went back and we, for it to be about getting this design right because it had to fit in the ceiling, it had to have enough capacity to blow enough air on the people to make them comfortable, and it had to be quiet enough so that the acoustics were, the acousticians were happy so it had to please the architects, the engineers and the acousticians in this, and we were desperate time-wise to get this result, it went for weeks trying to get resolved. How it finally got resolved is that we had a number of sort of group sessions and we'd get to what we thought was a solution and we'd get just shy of the solution and then we'd find a major problem, and in the end, the acoustician, who was not a party to the alliance, but who happens to be a mechanical engineer by trade, before he was an acoustician, said I'm going to take the plans home over the weekend and I'm going to solve this and I'll come back on Monday with a proposal that meets the mechanical engineering criteria and the acoustical criteria. He was sure he could do this if, you know, it was a classic examples of too many cooks in the stew, so he said, let me go away on the weekend, let me think about this, I'll come back on Monday, we'll meet first thing on Monday and I'll propose a solution, and he did and it worked, and it's in and it works and we did our commissioning and it works beautifully.
P28 on setting protocols to facilitate consensus including how at the group level targets and KPIs were set	We did spend a lot of time early in developing the AMT/ALT relationship and we had a lot of dual meetings for a while, especially trying to set the ground rules and early in the project we'd focus on the culture and that. For four weeks or something like that and times of adversity like that pulled people together, we reset all our targets, we took it on the management team to refocus people and set where we're going. Call it the second half that we were into or the third quarter of the football analogies and things but it just built stronger and stronger.

Table A17.   Wittgenstein Model Theme 11: Consensus Decision-making *(Continued)*

Theme and Subtheme	Notes, examples, and KSAE quotes
P31 on a program alliance that illustrates the mechanism of collaboration, negotiation, and refining mutual understanding	I think there's enough of a driver within, you know, the three organisations working in the alliance to want to do well with what [PO X], the client, sees as key results areas without having to incentivise them. And supervising then places a whole sort of requirement on [PO X] to be able to prove that they're actually getting real value for money in paying for those KPIs, so it really influences the way the KPIs are developed. So I think if you are able to free up the KRA, KPI framework from incentivisation, rather have that sort of amount in an agreed sort of fixed margin, it would reduce a lot of unnecessary effort in trying to sort of come up with KPIs that can be justified to pay money against.
	And on the strength of "formerly mere subcontractors" having a real voice in decision making P24 highlighted that:
P24	Another example there was the alliance manager was a programme maker, rather than a D&C contractor being a programme taker. That's a big difference. So we had a proper voice at the table on overall project planning decisions. That was quite an important aspect.
	An enabler of consensus is having both the people that can make authoritative decisions empowered to do so, as well as the procurement choice structure that enables that. P38 says:
P38	. . . especially from a client perspective because [Project A] was a classic for that. We closed down the railway line, [Line P and Line Q] for four weeks and during that time [PO X] was having trouble with their Siemens trains braking, so they had all these trains on the [Line P and Line Q] side of our site and they were all being nicely serviced and everything and the ones on the city side couldn't get serviced and they were being taken out of service because of their braking problem. I think it was about day 13 they said they need to get six of the trains from the outer network, if you like, to the inner network and within three days we'd totally changed our program, our sequence of works and dragged the trains through on skeleton track by diesel train and by day 17 and they got them through and that helped their broader business. There's no need for correspondence, it's all just a meeting, talked about the practicalities of it, whereas with D&C you'd be looking at all the claims and setting yourself up to put some sort of delay claim in and all that, so it cuts all that out . . .
11.3 Inhibitors of consensus	While inhibitors are mainly the reverse of enablers, a notable inhibitor to consensus is a feeling of participants being coerced or railroaded into a decision without sufficient time, information, or credibility of voice to be heard and considered. Lack of motivation to commit the energy and intellectual effort to arrive at consensus can be an inhibitor, as noted in the discussion of decision making and chaos and complexity in Chapter 3 (Figure 11), as opposed to complicated situations. There are times when there is a need of rapid action and reflection in which consensus decision making is not viable.
Examples of high levels of thinking about inhibitors of consensus	• Participants ensure that organisations avoid being poorly resourced and structured to facilitate communication between hierarchical and discipline levels within the project. • Participants avoid being poorly mindful about national and organisational/discipline cultural norms and expectations to ensure that they design mechanism to open up dialogue and challenging assumptions to ensure that each party to a decision is allowed to work through any difficulties in understanding broader perspectives. • Participants avoid misunderstanding or ignoring the value of face-to-face as well as electronic meeting to allow trust and commitment to be "grown" and sustained that may result in ease of consensus in decision making.
High-level KSAE needed for avoiding inhibiting consensus	• *Technical and PM KSAE* - High levels of technical and PM competence should be demonstrated and offered to design governance mechanisms that facilitate consensus of decision making. • *Business solutions KSAE*- High levels of understanding the value of trust and social capital to be gained from consensus in decision making. • *Relational KSAE*- High levels of ability to communicate, comprehend the perspective of others, and to effectively reach consensus in decision making.

(continued)

Table A17. Wittgenstein Model Theme 11: Consensus Decision-making *(Continued)*

Theme and Subtheme	Notes, examples, and KSAE quotes
Illustrative quotes	A10 had some interesting things to say about research on non-alliance, but framework and partnering type delivered projects where consensus decision making was not required. Several comments were made worth highlighting, the first being about trends away from RBP. He also makes an interesting point about the role of trust in commitment and non-coercive consensus agreement. These were on non-alliance but notionally RBP projects.
A10 Relating to a focus by the PO on cost reduction as a prime consideration	The other aspect, which relates to the interviews I've been doing with four major contractors and the starting point for this was not procurement. It was actually marketing and business development, and the primary question is: to what extent has the post-2008 credit crunch changed marketing business development practices? And there are a couple aspects behind that. The first is that we've seen the demise of formal partnering arrangements with the post-Egan and post-Egan agendas in the U.K. We're seeing more or less the demise to that and anecdotally, the rise of cost drivers, rather than trying to lever the better value. . . . cost drivers would seem to suggest perhaps the demise of relationship marketing growing—it's never really been established, but growing in construction and perhaps reining back to more the price-driven transactional marketing mix approach.
This is interesting as it indicates collaboration intent but full consensus is being compromised by a high focus on cost reduction over value consideration.	One was that, in order to achieve the better value for money and that particularly through cost reduction, was through collaboration. That they've learnt through the previous periods that the best way to achieve better outcomes is through greater levels of collaboration, so let's not throw the baby out with the bath water. Let's just turn that around and use that to try and drive costs down by working together. So that's one thing that's come out of it. And another thing that's come out of it is that, to be more efficient from their own point of view of the operations, a lot of the project managers that I interviewed, said that they, "Preferred collaborative working. It was more efficient as well as more effective in the long run." So they were still pursuing that road and they believe that it was better for achieving the cost outcomes and therefore efficiencies for the company itself. So there's a lot of collaborative practices still being conducted on a more informal basis; by major contractors and largely on major projects. . . . all the companies I interviewed were looking at trust in terms of self-interested trust. None had really gone to socially-orientated trust at all.
On the role of trust	A paper I gave at [Conference name about an organisation using Framework Agreements] . . . was about trust or the lack of it between the project sponsors and the project managers, and there were quite low levels of trust between those two roles, the people occupying those roles in that organisation. And they have a project management framework that's supposed to, again, facilitate collaborative working with their contractors. Well, if you haven't got high levels of trust internally, it's going to be very difficult to inject good levels of trust to facilitate collaborative working with your contractors, so they may be a strong client in some ways but they're weak in that way for sure.
And ability to take the perspective of the other parties	They were inward-looking, looking at let's just get the job done. Let's just get the functions working properly rather than looking at what the interests of the other parties were; stakeholders or the clients. And in fact, from a marketing perspective, but it relates to value, one of the things that came out very strongly is that the value propositions were heavily compromised because they were so inward-looking, so inward-focused.
Commenting on engineers in the above case study and indicators on a lack of non-coercive consensus	. . .but the body language; which was what was used to measure in this case, was very defensive and it looked—and I didn't analyse the—It was filmed; the evidence was filmed. I didn't sift through the evidence but what my colleague suggested was that they were defensive, as if to protect their professional standing. Not quite the same as reputation but they wanted to protect their professional position and stance; standing in the team, rather than necessarily contributing to what was best for the team or the coalition as a whole.
	A lack of ability of participants to make authoritative decisions when required can inhibit consensus-based decision making. Those unable to do this may not be incapable of doing so but simply may not have sufficient authority to commit to a decision. An example of this was given in a PA context relating to the seniority levels of ALT members.
P38	. . . I think all the projects that had a rail component, but two of them were road authority and the other two for the Department of Transport, but I think what's happening now probably all of them had the rail operator involved, but I think [PO X] probably has got so many projects on the go now, you're not getting any special treatment, as I was saying we had a [Project A] and even [Project B] and so you're getting this middle manager, then you've got to stand in line with all the other projects that [PO X] is involved in. . . . and then what you're finding that they're just going back to their business and their business is giving a business-as-usual response or requirement back and so they don't have a lot of pull. I'm just thinking even, so [Project C] we had chief operating officer and his made the project's goal from the rail operator. Then on [Project D], that had gone down a notch, a general manager and his first guy and by the time we got to [Project E], you're literally having middle management on the ALT.

This summary of Theme 12, **focus on learning and continuous improvement** (refer to Table A6) relates to the processes, routines, and means that facilitate and enable learning and continuous improvement. Subthemes from Section 1, Table 13 are elaborated upon in Table A18.

- **Focus on learning and continuous improvement** relates to the extent to which there is total agreement on a decision made at the strategic and project executive level.
- Four categories of subthemes that emerged from the data for **Theme 12 focus on learning and continuous improvement.** The first is about participants' capability for adapting to new ideas, being open and enthusiastic about learning new things, and new approaches to their work. The second subtheme relates to the process of lessons-learnt absorption and transfer within and between teams. The third relates to the culture of skills and learning development.
- The fourth relates to tensions inherent between innovation and incentivisation procedures. These can be summarised as follows:
  - 12.1 Lessons-learnt knowledge transfer—participants should be aware of the mechanisms that projects offer for many opportunities for learning about the PO's preferences and needs, how other team members operate, and how to best collaborate with them and to learn from the project to gain technical, process, or interpersonal knowledge. Some projects are specifically established as learning laboratories for radical new innovation or for more methodical incremental improvement. A focus on effective lessons-learnt knowledge transfer needs to be designed into a procurement form to overcome lessons learnt becoming lessons forgotten or ignored.
  - 12.2 Capacity to adapt to new ideas—participants need to facilitate continuous improvement by prompting new ways of thinking and new ways of doing. Knowledge transfer as discussed in Chapter 4 Table 4 is difficult because knowledge is sticky. People who can make the most from continuous improvement are open to the process of "unlearning" and "relearning." Without this adaptive capacity, lessons learnt become lessons ignored, and often context is not considered to wisely consider which lessons should be adopted, or adapted depending on the way that the new context emerges.
  - 12.3 Culture of skills and learning development—participants need to be developing a culture of organisational and individual learning to facilitate lessons-learnt knowledge transfer and provide the environment in which this can effectively take place. This goes beyond training and development at the technical and process level. It also entails enabling participants to perceive and understand context and situation so that cause-and-effect links can be understood to enable intelligent adaptation of lessons learnt to occur.

Table A18.   Wittgenstein Model Theme 12: A Focus on Learning and Continuous Improvement

Theme and Subtheme	Notes, examples, and KSAE quotes
12.1 Lessons-learnt transfer	Participants should be aware of the mechanisms that projects offer for many opportunities for learning about the PO's preferences and needs, how other team members operate, and how to best collaborate with them and to learn from the project to gain technical, process, or interpersonal knowledge. Some projects are specifically established as learning laboratories for radical new innovation or for more methodical incremental improvement. A focus on effective lessons-learnt knowledge transfer needs to be designed into a procurement form to overcome lessons learnt becoming lessons forgotten or ignored.
Examples of high levels of thinking about lessons learnt being transferred	• Participants understand the purpose and aim of the project so that they can adapt to new ideas and better direct their focus on effective rather than purely efficiency continuous improvement. • Participants understand and are able to effectively frame lessons learnt within the context of the project and the socio-political environment in which the project is delivered. • Participants understand the value proposition of those who may benefit to be familiar with lessons learnt about the projects performance and challenges faced to enable continuous improvement to take place.
High-level KSAE needed for effective cultural drivers	• *Technical and PM KSAE* – High levels of technical and PM competence in being able to know the underlying context and assumptions about existing technology and what is new so that lessons learnt can be framed and documented in a way that makes transfer of these more effective. • *Business solutions KSAE* – High levels of understanding longer-term business impacts of gains and improvements made from lessons learnt and how best bring these back into the base organisation from the project setting. • *Relational KSAE* – High levels of communication and empathic ability to align learning styles with the context and content of lessons learnt.

(continued)

Table A18.   Wittgenstein Model Theme 12: A Focus on Learning and Continuous Improvement *(Continued)*

Theme and Subtheme	Notes, examples, and KSAE quotes
Illustrative quotes	In terms of aiming for standard approaches so that people are familiar with what has been best practices, A02 observed of a government agency that there was an appetite for standardisation through best practice models being promoted. This quote illustrates the value of all project participant teams having a clear idea of how each other works and how they make decisions and act on decisions made. It illustrates the challenge of coming up with a lessons-learnt process that is meaningful to all parties involved in a project and that can enable people to see the need to adapt to new ideas and reframing ideas where existing technology is changing.
A02	. . . you perhaps have to create some common culture and way of acting early on which kind of has to be continuously nurtured in some way. So and they also have this idea of handbooks and processes, they say in Transport Administration . . . we should have the same way of working, in all our projects, they haven't had that but they think it would be good to have the same way of working and the consultants, contractors say that it would be good if the Transport Administration worked in the same way in all projects. Because as it is now it's probably more similarity between how the different contractors work and how the consultants work than it is between the different parts of the Transport Administration.
	In terms of processes for capturing lessons learnt, the effectiveness of this process varies across projects that our respondents were familiar with. It was generally far from satisfactory, even in project alliances where there should be documented evidence of innovation and continuous improvement, as P24 and P30 observed:
P24	There were certainly things tried and investigated, but they weren't logged. They probably just stayed in the heads of the people who were involved.
P30	The national guidelines require value-for-money statements to be prepared in advance of going to the market place to form an alliance. So the client needs to be very clear about what is the value for money and then we deduce a whole big document on value for money before we proceeded to select partners or potential partners for the [X] and [Y] rail grade separations. And there's also a requirement that when you reach practical completion of your alliances that the client needs to prepare a value-for-money report to demonstrate what has been achieved. With doing that, I've been reflecting on my experience that these sort of reports tend to pop out at the end of the alliance work when teams are being disbanded and the knowledge capture is extremely difficult because all those with the wisdom about the value that we've delivered have departed. So trying to bring it all together and collated to form a great value-for-money report becomes very problematic. And I've been saying to the recent alliances that I'm in and they get it, and six months out before the end I really made an issue of it and I get lots of people promising me that we're in the throes of developing and we've got a framework and we've drafted something up, and I keep saying "I want to see it," and guess what happens? It doesn't come. It's a low priority from the team's perspective and again becomes a very difficult task at the end to pull it together. Having said that, though, the quality of the value-for-money reports is improving. Some years ago there wasn't a requirement, I don't think, to prepare value-for-money statements, although treasuries now ask from us a report on value for money for each of the alliances we've undertaken.
P49 on one of the Road Authorities that had a reasonable system of documenting lessons learnt.	[PO X] has quite a commitment to, I guess, end-of-project reporting which is collecting information about key benefits, key risks, key achievements, risk and innovation and breakthroughs and a few other categories like that, and that we surveyed for key people who were responsible for all of these areas, whether it's design innovations. We had a design register of 30 or 40 innovations or something, these are major breakthroughs that we made at different stages to substitute a different material that gave a better performance in these conditions, or it might be a constructability improvement by lowering a gantry by this method you could produce the amount of disruption of traffic flow, that sort of thing.
12.2 Adapting to new ideas	Capacity to adapt to new ideas—participants need to facilitate continuous improvement by prompting learning-oriented ways of thinking and doing. Knowledge transfer as discussed in Chapter 4 Table 4 is difficult because knowledge is sticky. People who can make the most from continuous improvement are open to the process of "unlearning" and "relearning." Without this adaptive capacity, lessons learnt become lessons ignored, and often context is not considered to wisely consider which lessons should be adopted or adapted depending on the way that the new context emerges.
Examples of high levels of thinking about adapting to new ideas	• Participants understand the mechanisms of reducing the "stickiness" of knowledge to facilitate transforming knowledge awareness into action. • Participants understand the importance of context when applying lessons learnt from one situation to another and can effectively learn, unlearn, and relearn to accommodate adaptation to changed contexts. • Participants understand the value proposition of those who may benefit from applying lessons learnt and reward those who are responsible for contributing this knowledge accordingly—this would usually entail non-financial forms of acknowledgement and reward that encourages the process of effectively documenting lessons learnt.
High-level KSAE needed for adapting to new ideas	• *Technical and PM KSAE* – High levels of technical and PM competence in effectively being able to adopt/adapt and apply knowledge. • *Business solutions KSAE* – High levels of understanding longer term business impacts of effectively benefiting from knowledge. • *Relational KSAE* – High levels of communication and empathy ability to gain insights and knowledge from others and to be able to reframe personal knowledge.

Table A18. Wittgenstein Model Theme 12: A Focus on Learning and Continuous Improvement *(Continued)*

Theme and Subtheme	Notes, examples, and KSAE quotes
Illustrative quotes	Adapting existing knowledge perhaps in a quite different context is discussed by A02. Also, A09 had some observations about unlearning and relearning and the challenges of some people in the industry accepting the value of improvisation through adapting knowledge. A10 draws out the strength of non-cognates (people in leadership or senior manager roles who are not from the dominant disciplines engaged in a project) in seeing lessons learnt and collaboratively shared knowledge differently.
A02	But this city tunnel project, they say that now it was important for us to develop our own guidelines. Because if you are involved in developing something you learn it, yes and then it implements itself, instead of taking something that somebody else has developed and train people in it. They prefer to do it the other way round.
A09 on improvisation	And it comes down to the issues of improvisation, you know. . . . whenever you talk about improvisation, if you go into a company and talk about improvisation—which I do a lot—they think you're crazy, because what they think is what you're talking about is letting go of everything you know. . . . And that's not what improvisation is. It's like a jazz musician, you know, a jazz musician who's learnt how to play his or her instrument since they were the age of three, so they know the limits they can take this instrument. A jazz guitarist know exactly the sound that guitar will make, what every fret will make, what every note will do by bending the head of the guitar, you know, what clicking his fingers on it will do, so he knows that instrument inside out, but they're still able to improvise with other musicians and create new music that is not. . . that can't replicated.
And also on the concept of "design thinking" being free to adopt and adapt knowledge	I mean this is a real challenge for us, and this is where I think the solution lies in design thinking, because design thinking is about bringing people with very different mindsets together, and to deal with problems as a design issue. So typically you'll have design that happens at the front end, you do it and then you might have a bit of design at the end to make it look pretty. The design thinking says the design happens the whole way through, and it's not just the designer that needs to think like the designer, you know? So it's about how you get people together to sort of make sense of problems, and collaborate to create the solution.
A10	I think that's why they have recruited non-cognates, because they get, again, better alignment of the client needs, better project definition, and it's not about let's design something based on what's technically feasible. It's about let's design something that really satisfies the needs, and that's what non-cognates are ready to do. . .
	Continually challenging assumptions and context of past lesson learnt, P33 states in reference to a programme alliance setting where continuous improvement is a critical KRA.
P33	I guess innovation is always about challenging, and whenever you innovate, you need to challenge the current paradigms, so we've set about creating and being part of a maintenance alliance that has the opportunity to run for 10 years and you'd like think in three to five, 10, over the last three years and certainly over the next 10 that you'd be able to look back and say we are a lot more efficient in delivery than we were to start.
12.3 Culture of learning and skills development	Participants need to be developing a culture of organisational and individual learning to facilitate lessons-learnt knowledge transfer and provide the environment in which this can effectively take place. This goes beyond training and development at the technical and process level. It also entails enabling participants to perceive and understand context and situation so that cause-and-effect links can be understood to enable intelligent adaptation of lessons learnt to occur.
Examples of high levels of thinking about a culture of learning and skills development	<ul><li>Participants understand the variety of learning models that suit various people.</li><li>Participants understand the importance of context when applying lessons learnt from one situation to another, and can effectively establish mechanisms to suit the people-learning context.</li><li>Participants carefully ensure that the workplace is a "safe" place to learn from a physical sense (experimentation, simulation, for example) and from a psychological perspective (able to make mistakes without retribution, provided that there is learning from the mistake etc.).</li><li>Participants understand the value proposition of those who may benefit from learning new skills and discovering new approaches.</li></ul>
High-level KSAE needed for a culture of learning and skills development	<ul><li>*Technical and PM KSAE* – High levels of technical and PM competence in effectively being able to design learning events that generate new knowledge.</li><li>*Business solutions KSAE* – High levels of understanding longer-term business impacts of effectively benefiting from knowledge.</li><li>*Relational KSAE* – High levels of communication and empathy ability to design and deliver learning and skills enhancement events to reflect the learner's needs and learning approach preferences.</li></ul>

(continued)

Theme and Subtheme	Notes, examples, and KSAE quotes
Illustrative quotes	P36 talked about how they actually used a lessons-learnt software tool and how it has affected the team's working approach. It illustrates what they did but does not strongly link back into a rationale for the approach. P31 also had a similar story about creating a learning environment for hands-on work learning:
P36	But from a lessons point of view, our focus this year is really, at the back end of the alliance, is to gather our lessons and incorporate them into our new projects, but incorporate them into the systems that are transferring to all the three alliance partners really, but primarily to [PO X]. So we've actually got that fairly bedded in now in that we run a, we've got an overall lessons register and there's been a fair bit of work put into development. We've got, particularly, a guy in our alliance that is very good at developing these systems, so we've got an overall register now that we're using, where we put project lessons. And then we've also got what's, a thing called CMO which allows us then to track them. So we've got a good process now where, and we do a, each project we do a workshop at the end of each project and we bring a member of each of the different teams, stakeholder approvals, design, construction, project management, and the planning team from [PO X] now comes along, and we bring them all together for what's typically a two-hour meeting, and we go through the project from the referral phase through to the commissioning phase and say well, what were the lessons? Positive, negative, what were the lessons? And we capture then and then we say, we look at them and say well, can we change any of our systems, our specifications, our standard drawings? We've got design guides which really relate to the operation requirements on various different disciplines so we're then really feeding these back in. We've got an extensive flowchart system which is really one of the innovations I see in what we've done, and with 25 years of consulting experience I can tell you that, I quite often always talk about well, let's learn our lessons in consulting and then build them into the next project. But it's quite hard because you've got to have management and motivation and it takes time and effort to bring that all in together, and just an alliance atmosphere is a unique opportunity because you've got all the team members there and get everyone committed to it, and we're really starting to see that happening. So it's one of the big advantages, I think, and the positives that's come out of the alliance. And that's coming from a designer's perspective, so you've got to keep in mind that I'm a designer, so I always focus on those design improvement areas.
P31	They saw that as an opportunity to bring someone like [Alliance Participant A] down into the region, impart [Alliance Participant A]'s key . . . capabilities on contractors in the region so that when the alliance leaves, [PO as participant] is left with a set of contractors that are really good at not only putting pipes in the ground, but their safety systems are first class, their quality systems, their environmental systems – all that sort of stuff that goes around that comes from a tier-one contractor. So a lot of the focus for us is getting the contractors on board on a lump sum, but then also working with them to build their capabilities. So all our sort of systems are designed to be shared. So, you know, all our project management, environmental safety, our quality systems are available on a portal that any contractor that works with us can download, put their branding on, and use sort of thing. So quite a few of the contractors use the alliance as an opportunity to build their business to the next level and, you know, obtain certification, you know, expand the type and range of clients that they can go for – all that sort of stuff.
	P18 is a practitioner who is involved in alliance team and individual selection and also in coaching and training. His comments about team and individual selection illustrate which attributes of alliance participants are most highly valued.
P18	. . .we're trying to put together a process for selection that is ruled up and rigorous and gives us the best chance of getting the best group of people together into an alliance. So we've got that ongoing tension. What's happened now is we've probably, in terms of the winning criteria, there's probably about 20/21% is based on behaviour, and that's behaviour we assess in two-day workshops. And a big lot of the people who work for us are GPs or charted psychologists and things like that, and they carry that out. So I suppose there's only about three of us with project-type backgrounds. Most come from psychology-type backgrounds but very practical. They've worked on business for most of their careers. With a heavier emphasis on that, we use the personality profiling to help us select members—not as effectively as members of the project alliance board, because sometimes there isn't a choice when the supplier does need to have a certain person in there. But what we do with that personality profile, they all have the profile done, they have one-to-one feedbacks, and then we have a session where we look at the dynamics of the group. And that's taken through by one of the psychologists in terms of the differences in how people do things and how they will behave and how we have to manage that inside the project alliance board. And we do the same with inside the alliance leadership team. And then there's a series of workshops, because what we're doing in the [PO X] situation is we're treating it as a change management programme, because we're having to change from a traditional mindset to an alliancing mindset, with all the appropriate tools that go with that.

This summary of Theme 13, **incentive arrangements** (refer to Table A6 above) relates to the processes, routines, and means that facilitate and enable incentive arrangements to function effectively. Subthemes from Section 1, Table 13 are elaborated upon in Table A19.

- **Incentive arrangements** relate to the processes, routines, and behavioural and normative practices that facilitate and enable incentives to encourage excellence in performance.
- Two categories of subthemes emerged from the data for **Theme 13 – incentive arrangements.** The first is about the mechanism themselves, and the second is how any tension between innovation and incentivisation is managed These can be summarised as follows:
  - 13.1 Incentive arrangements—Project participants are incentivised to perform at exceptional levels of performance, and there is a risk/reward system in place to encourage this. Central to incentive arrangements is developing systematic encouragement for innovation and for that innovation to be transferred to project participants and then onto their base organizations.
  - 13.2 Tension between innovation and incentivisation—participants and project owners need to manage the tension between continuous improvement that keeps raising the BAU benchmark and how that is incentivised. It is important to balance providing sufficient incentive and reward for improvement while avoiding incentive targets being neither too easy nor too hard to undermine continuous improvement. This also brings in issues about the single versus dual TOC approach and how much innovation capacity is held back in a dual/ competitive TOC approach, and how the competitive dialogue approach works in practice or indeed how it could be improved.

Table A19   Wittgenstein Model Theme 13: Incentive arrangements

Theme and Subtheme	Notes, examples, and KSAE quotes	
13.1 Incentive arrangements	This refers to the pain-sharing and gain-sharing arrangements, how the process was instigated, and how it operated. Shared accountability and a desire for innovation require a risk-and-reward mechanism to create an incentive to excel.	
Examples of high levels of thinking about pain-sharing and gain-sharing agreements	• Participants understand the nuances of the incentive pain/gain sharing philosophy, the value of trust and commitment that a risk/reward arrangement entails, and how best to effectively leverage the agreement to achieve best for projects outcomes. • Participants understand consequences associated with the manner in which negotiations take place and how that affects participant positions, for example, single versus dual TOC processes and how that impacts upon identifying innovation during any negotiation phase. • Participants understand how to balance pain and gain incentives to maximise the positive effects of potential innovation.	
High-level KSAE needed for managing the incentive arrangements	• *Technical and PM KSAE* – High levels of technical and PM competence in effectively understanding the technical requirements of what is being negotiated in terms of risks, uncertainties, and potential innovation and process improvements. • *Business solutions KSAE* – High levels of understanding longer-term business impacts of building capacity to negotiate at this level. • *Relational KSAE* – High levels of communication and empathy ability to successfully and effectively build confidence, trust, and commitment through negotiation.	
Illustrative quotes	The U.K. Design for Life Framework Agreements appear to be fairly straight forward in the risk/reward framework, as P05 and P06 outlines:	
P05	. . . essentially the contractors are target cost, so the SCP [Supply Chain Partner] signs up to a sum of money to deliver the job including all the design work and that's what you have to do. If he delivers that job for less than the target cost, he gets a portion of the difference. However in the design for life, if you go over, it's 100% pain, so it's up to them now to keep within that cost. (Interviewer's question) Okay so that's where the profit and gain- and pain-sharing arrangements are agreed and then they just sort of work of that sort of fee arrangement? (P05 response) All of that's agreed, at a framework level, so there's nothing for the client to negotiate, really, with the SCP, all they've got to do really is appoint them and let them get on with it. . . . the contractors' target cost, so the SCP signs up to a sum of money to deliver the job, including all the design work, and that's what you have to do. If he delivers that job for less than the target cost, he gets a portion of the difference. However, in the design for life, if you go over, it's 100% pain, so it's up to them now to keep within that cost.	

(continued)

Table A19   Wittgenstein Model Theme 13: Incentive arrangements *(Continued)*

Theme and Subtheme	Notes, examples, and KSAE quotes
P06 points out impact of the timing of the agreement.	But the other issue is that economic circumstances should also reflect what choice you make in your contract selection. Because in today's marketplace, people are cutting their throats to get work, it's that competitive. If you've got a framework that you know is four years old and was agreed in the boom times and you've done nothing about it, and you carry on with it, you're paying well, well over the odds.
	P17 illustrates how flexible these arrangements for pain/gain sharing are, as well as scope of works within the agreement, in relation to an innovative project alliance that was structured within a D&C contract in turn within a PPP.
P17	. . . what we did is we actually opened it up so that the scope of the target cost included the civil works to be carried out by [NOP A and B]. That was one of the little breakthroughs we had in the commercial setup. And what that did, we talked about this in advance, we wanted to create an environment where there wasn't such a kind of a silo mentality about the scope of work, you know, and that it was just the mechanical and electrical scope and work.

. . . And the terms of compensation are all full open book sharing, 50/50 with some time KPIs and a few other use of the target outturn cost. |
	We also cite two examples now from a programme alliance. The first is where P31 explained the TOC formation and pain/gain sharing arrangements and how it worked in practice across many projects in a programme. This is important because on programme alliances overall, value for money is vital. This illustrates managing the tension of VfM with a reasonable gain-share incentive. The second is on a road alliance for capital expenditure and maintenance, where P32 explains the operation in practice after several years of experience of the programme alliance.
P31	So the way the commercial model works, so if I just take [Participant A] as an example. They get a fixed margin on works done. So X% sort of paid on all works done. But then there's the top-up from KRA performance and top-up from under run on projects or the profit on individual projects. So the target additional top-up is very well understood by everyone in the alliance, and I guess we target on individual projects for at least a Y% under run, which is what [Contractor A] needed to top their margin up. And we very much understand if we go over an 8% under run, [Program owner] really starts questioning value-for-money. So we all understand our sweet spot by sort of between X-8% under runs on projects and that's, you know, the zone where everyone is happy sort of thing. So the good thing with a programme is there's a lot of swings and roundabouts on individual projects. So you have projects that have big over runs and big under runs, but overall the programme—we try and manage it so it's achieving that sort of Y-8% under run.
P32	We started off we had a set of KPIs and there's some performance gain share/pain share in this. The KPIs we've had from the outset were probably a bit too clunky, a bit too detailed, a bit too labour intensive, so we're currently looking at reviewing those to simplify those and better target the KPIs. Interestingly, we set the KPIs in terms of what behaviours we wanted to drive, we've found those behaviours were there at the outset anyway and indeed they haven't really achieved anything significant in their own right. And from the contractor's point of view, the first couple of years they've had a performance gain share and they've actually decided as a show of good faith to reinvest that in the road. So they've actually spent their profit on doing more road works because they see that as reducing the maintenance costs in the long term, best for their network. Which is a really good indication of their commitment. But it puts into focus what are these KPIs.
13.2 Tension between innovation and incentivisation	Participants and project owners need to manage the tension between continuous improvement that keeps raising the BAU benchmark and how that is incentivised. It is important to balance providing sufficient incentive and reward for improvement while avoiding incentive targets being neither too easy nor too hard to undermine continuous improvement. This also brings in issues about the single versus dual TOC approach, and how much innovation capacity is held back in a dual/competitive TOC approach, and how the competitive dialogue approach works in practice, or indeed how it could be improved.
Examples of high levels of thinking about managing the innovation incentivisation tension	• Participants understand the nuances of the impact of stretch target's measures on motivation to improve the effectiveness of incentives for innovation and continuous improvement. • Participants understand how to effectively negotiate improvement targets and KPIs that minimise harmful unintended consequences flowing from innovation and risk acceptance. • Participants understand how to be flexible in reviewing and amending how KRAs are operationalized into KPI stretch targets to fit performance, and any administrative burden in their implementation that may reduce enthusiasm to innovate and improve.
High-level KSAE needed for managing the innovation incentivisation tension	• *Technical and PM KSAE* – High levels of technical and PM competence in effectively being able design learning KPIs and stretch targets. • *Business solutions KSAE* – High levels of understanding of the longer-term business impacts of effectively benefiting from continuous improvement and how to embed that within the organisation while minimising lost sunk costs in legacy systems and facilities. • *Relational KSAE* – High levels of communication and empathy, ability to recognise and obviate unintended negative consequences of stretch targets and to ensure that there are open channels for project management teams to negotiate and fine tune KPIs.

Theme and Subtheme	Notes, examples, and KSAE quotes
Illustrative quotes	In response to a question about how the TOC was developed and any games being played to deliberately produce a "soft TOC" (i.e., one that has lots of hidden contingency "fat" in it), P20 stated that:
P20	The commercial framework is a little bit different than sort of typical alliances and there's not a lot of upside for coming in way under budget or that sort of thing, so it kept people focused at the time of TOC, I think, on genuine best-for-project behaviours. TOC is the time when you can tend to see people retreating to sort of stereotypical behaviours and really, for the most part, people were very good. I was surprised actually. But you know, from time to time you will see a little bit of that, but for the most part, people have been surprisingly good, actually, for me. I haven't been involved in an alliance before, so maybe that's just expected and maybe we're less than others, so I don't have anything to compare it to, but I guess compared to what I expected at the beginning, I would say that people have been able to behave pretty well in a best-for-project manner.
	And in response to the PA example we had where there was only a 50/50 profit-at-risk model used rather than 100% profit-at-risk, P25 states:
P25	. . . we ended up having this element of the margin that was protected. There was always this danger that they'd go "Oh well, if worst comes to worst, at least we'll make the $20 million that's guaranteed. We might not make the 40, but we'll make the 20." Then they'd lose interest, so that was the problem. And that's the danger with any alliance, of course, is that when the margin's completely gone then it just becomes cost, so you've got to avoid that, but ideally if you're aligned, then it won't happen. So that was probably the main improvement.
	The process of operationalizing the KRAs into meaningful KPIs that can be useful in a pain- and gain-sharing arrangement requires a fine balance of avoiding be over-specific and yet being demonstratively accountable, especially with respect to gains from perceived soft KPIs. P45 had some useful observations, including this one.
P45	If I use the KRAs as an example, so they define the KRAs which then get converted, then we get a bunch of KPIs associated with that, and the KPIs that are generally thought up are I think good KPIs, they're relevant KPIs, and then what happens is that they realise these KPIs are difficult to measure and when I say difficult to measure, I mean two things. One, from an administration point of view, they're time-consuming but they're really hard to defend in front of Treasury when you're giving out money based on the performance of a KPI, so then they start to alter the KPI, either the—so that they can get something that they've got robust measurement against, and then all of a sudden what you're capturing or measuring is not really meeting the intent of your KRA, so one of the KRAs that we had for one of the alliance was value for money, like value for money was a KRA.

This summary of Theme 14, **pragmatic learning-in-action** (refer to Table A6) relates to the processes, routines and means that facilitate and enable learning within the project and between the project and the participant's organisations to function effectively. Subthemes from Section 1, Table 13 are elaborated upon in Table A20.

- **Pragmatic learning-in-action** refers to the active gathering of value from collaboration with the strategic aim to learn and to gain competitive advantage through opportunities to learn and adapt.
- Two categories of subthemes emerged from the data for **Theme 14 – a focus on pragmatic learning.** The first is about the mechanism themselves and the second is how any tension between innovation and incentivisation is managed. These can be summarised as follows:
  - 14.1 Action-learning—participants as individuals but more so in groups, undertake action-learning in a number of ways from simply trying out things and experimenting to complicated modelling and simulation exercises. These provide the mechanisms to gain knowledge from action. It remains critical that mechanisms should be in place to capture and make usable experience and knowledge gained from action-learning initiatives.
  - 14.2 Coaching and mentoring—another form of pragmatic learning is through coaching and mentoring. This is where experience and insights are shared in a formalised manner through one-on-one interaction between project participants and "wiser," or at least more experienced, people who can help their coachees/mentees to be able to contextualise learning, to refine it through dialogue, and to add value through that knowledge by sharing stories, making critical comparisons, and exploring meaning and making sense out of that learning.

Table A20. Wittgenstein Model Theme 14: A Focus on Pragmatic Learning-in-Action

Theme and Subtheme	Notes, examples, and KSAE quotes
14.1 Action-learning	Action learning is about team leaders and members seeing the project as a learning laboratory, and there needs to be acceptance that both experimental success and failure requires discussion and analysis. Often unexpected opportunities arise out of failed experiments where they are being reframed and have led to encouraging benefits in other contexts.
Examples of high levels of thinking about action-learning.	• Participants understand the role that reflection, dialogue and debate has in learning-by-doing and the value of action learning as a critical part of continuous improvement and innovation. • Participants understand the importance of action learning within projects and being able to face paradoxes and challenges as experiences to learn from through learning with others. • Participants understand the value of the two conversations of action learning. The first being the internal conversation with oneself that models, reasons, predicts and anticipates results from action. The second is the external conversation of clarification with others, where concepts, plans and actions are explained in a peer-review environment so that clarity of explanation and rationale is extracted from this process. • Participants understand who may benefit from action learning and how to engage them.
High-level KSAE needed for action learning	• *Technical and PM KSAE* – High levels of technical and PM competence in effectively being able to design and participate in action learning, including the use of simulation, modelling and experimentation. • *Business solutions KSAE* – High levels of understanding the longer-term business advantage of gaining absorptive capacity from action learning, experimentation, and modelling. • *Relational KSAE* – High levels of communication and empathy ability to be able to effectively participate in action learning and be able to communicate lessons learnt.
Illustrative quotes	In Europe there is extensive use of what is called the Competitive Dialogue (CD), in which participants negotiating to undertake a project is engaged in a series of in-depth interviews and exploration of the project's scope, scale, and complexity with the project owner. This CD, in effect, produces a series of simulations through what-if questions and through the dialogue investigating and modelling innovative practices that may be deployed. This illustrates one form of action learning. A01 explained this process and provided a useful illustration:
A01	. . . also it was more also about how do you organise your maintenance programme, what type of asphalt would you use, what—that was a very important issue for the ministry for how many maintenance days, what's the planning of your maintenance in relation to the type of asphalt that you use on the road; is it under—do you put some asphalt on the road and do you have only 1–10 years sort of big maintenance project or each year a few days maintenance. That trade-offs—that was very important because it was one of the major and ambitious tunnels in Netherlands so the number of days that it would be closed or how did you organise the maintenance of this tunnel during the next 30 years was a very important issue during this procurement issue and discussion.
	Other forms of action learning are to reflect on practices and try to document them and to systematically develop process and procedures from knowledge gained that is the fine-tuned, enhanced and updated within and based upon practice. As A02 states:
A02	But this city tunnel project, they say that now it was important for us to develop our own guidelines. Because if you are involved in developing something you learn it, yes and then it implements itself, instead of taking something that somebody else has developed and train people in it. They prefer to do it the other way round.
	A13 in his discussion about his team's longitudinal research into the Heathrow T5 programme of work made the following comments about experimentation and prototyping as a form of action learning:
A13 on pre-assembly testing and off-site works	The fifth element of this, off-site pre-assembly tests. Because of this problem about one entrance and the restrictions getting onto the site and no laydown space, they had to come up with alternative arrangements, and what they did, they created off-site two consolidation areas. One at Colnbrook where they had a railway line going in bringing steel, concrete, and a lot of prefabrication of all the steel and concrete cages and prefabricated concrete panels, which were then brought onto site already partly manufactured. The other part of that was testing because you didn't want to have unexpected things happen on the construction site, you'd test the method of construction off-site before you brought anything on-site. So again it's about learning.
And on simulation and modelling	Make your mistakes off-site so when you come on-site you can do things right. And the last element in this system was the adjusted time logistics and again this is really to deal with this problem of having no laydown areas and having just one entrance to the thing. What they did was they took some software that had been used in the car industry and adapted it. I can't remember what they called it but basically what happened every day there is a plan of how much work you're going to do, and the materials are called on-site for that amount of work that you're going to do.

Theme and Subtheme	Notes, examples, and KSAE quotes
	A16 observing an engineering projects in remote parts of Sweden in terms of flexibility and experimentation to try out different approaches makes some salient points, and it also reinforces the need for a no-blame culture to be flexible and solve problems:
A16	They tried some new - they had, from North America, this huge—it looks like a huge chainsaw that you put on a big machine that goes through and kind of cuts like a chainsaw in the dirt. Similar to the ones that you use when you do tunnels, but it's not going around, you have a chainsaw. . . . it worked really well in summer time, but as fast—as soon as it got a bit cold it didn't work. So they tried a few different alternatives, and they had that one and they had another big machine that they shipped over and tried . . . . . . actually, having the flexibility to work around obstacles. So there was quite a lot of ad hoc discussion with landowners also. If you had a path that was decided and all of a sudden they realised that there were rocks . . . They just had discussions along the way and say, "Would it be okay for you if we go around this one? If we go to the edge there. It takes us. . . we go around during the day, it takes a week to go across" and have an informal agreement and then putting in all the documents when they already did it. And taking the risk of with the appeals and everything, but if it went through they are already past that.
	Finally, to leave this subtheme with a practitioner quote, the impact of increasing a group's absorptive capacity to embed action-learning outcomes into their business model is illustrated by P36 with two relevant aspects as follows. The first is about the way that insights from action learning can be captured and used as an organisational learning tool, and the other aspect is the impact that this kind of learning can have on organisations.
P36 on a useful tool for action-learning lessons-learnt capture.	. . .rather than fill that in the form and saying, "I went out and inspected it," and how we track our SQE, our safety, quality, and environment inspections, and what's happening out on site, they're all done through iPads now. So they go out on site and use an iPad and these link either remotely to, back into our office or when they come back into WiFi zone that all their reports, and all that automatically get loaded up, and CMO is a software package that's been developed, that's been, the last 12 months we've been developing it. . . . And so with our lessons, what we're doing is we have all these lessons, of course, then you get actions out of it. So we do all this workshop, we're doing all these discussions and then there's actions. People, we're saying well, we need to get these actions incorporated into our systems, our tools, everything that we use. So the team has to do that.
And on the impact of action learning leading to increased absorptive capacity and becoming more innovative	I was out on site last week and talking to a contractor that, I probably worked with 20 years ago that's been a long-term pipeline contract during, in the western part of Victoria and they've actually gone, they've done a number of projects with the Alliance now, so they've gone through this learning curve and enhanced their systems and their tools, and the comment that was given to me is that they're now there, they're actually using these systems and tools to win work that they weren't winning before with larger and higher tier companies and contractors, and that the feedback they're getting is wow, this is really good stuff. This is better than what some of the other contractors have got. So it's part of business development. That contractor is actually from the growth through doing the alliance work, has really moved their business into another level.
14.2 Coaching and mentoring	This is where experience and insights are shared in a formalised manner through one-on-one interaction between project participants and 'wiser' or at least more experienced people who can help their coachees/mentees to contextualised learning, to refine it through dialogue and to add value through that knowledge by sharing stories, making critical comparisons, and exploring meaning and making sense out of that learning. Coaching occurs when individuals are assigned an experienced coach who can help them perceive their thought processes and actions more clearly, and steps them through scenarios and simulations of how particular issues, challenges, and problems can be addressed. Mentoring is more general and can help individuals to see decision-action in a more holistic light and how their career and personal/professional development can be enhanced through access to wise advice.
Examples of high levels of thinking about coaching and mentoring.	• Participants understand the role and advantages that coaching and mentoring can have to help them confront and overcome immediate challenges and difficulties, with the coach drawing answers out of them through a reflective dialogue and mentors providing some sound advice to do their job and how they can effectively identify and use the services available. • Participants understand the political environment they confront and have the ability to source political advice and to enhance their political skills to handle situations where the solution is political and not technical or administrative. • Participants understand how they can coach and mentor their colleagues or to identify suitable coach and mentor resources for them.
High-level KSAE needed for coaching and mentoring	• *Technical and PM KSAE* – High levels of technical and PM competence in effectively being able to design and participate in a coaching and mentoring initiative to develop project/programme staff to help them achieve and perhaps exceed their potential. • *Business solutions KSAE*– High levels of understanding longer-term business advantages of coaching and mentoring on people's ability to excel in their job. • *Relational KSAE*– High levels of communication and empathy ability to be able to effectively initiate and maintain a coaching and mentoring initiative for identified staff.

(continued)

Table A20. Wittgenstein Model Theme 14: A Focus on Pragmatic Learning-in-Action *(Continued)*

Theme and Subtheme	Notes, examples, and KSAE quotes
Illustrative quotes	Two examples of coaching are presented. First, A09 brought up a useful point about political astuteness in dealing with important stakeholders from research undertaken on a seminal PA in Australia. His comment is about skills required to handle stakeholders in complex situations. This is typical example of the kind of KSAE that may be required, is rare, and may need expert help that a coach or mentor could provide for somebody facing this situation. Second is a quote from P28 about a PA that he was an ALT member on.
A09	. . . it's about a certain level of political astuteness. This is where [wise person X] was a really intelligent political player and he asked the right political questions of the alliance. So he'd say "if the auditor-general comes to you and says 'you have said this, this, and that,' what are you going to say to him, because this is what you've just promised in this meeting room," right? And they go. . . they don't know how to answer, because they're not politically. . . these are engineers. What would an engineer know? You imagine an engineer, the sorts of engineers that you and I would know, talking to 12 hippies who actually aren't really hippies, they are not in my backyard [NIMBY syndrome people] and they look like hippies, but they're fathers and they're husbands and they're wives or barristers and QCs and. . . right? And this engineer's got to tell them why they're going to go for a cheaper carbon scrubber next to their school for the tunnel. How's that engineer going to start that conversation?
P28	The client was very much an active and respected member of the AMT so there was no railroading of the client or anything like that. They spent a lot of time, they did their own training and mentoring, and even to the end of the project or probably halfway through the project, they brought on their own personal coach just to individually challenge each other. Not really the AMT as a team, but she spent a lot of time just challenging the individuals themselves. I found this lady quite confronting in her style, but they seemed to grow and really continued to grow right throughout the project. Most of them have been promoted and gone on to more senior leadership roles in their home organisations or other organisations out of it, because by the end of it they were a really strong business group.
	In terms for discussions about a *need* for mentoring and or/coaching that was not provided but would have been useful to be provided, P30 made the following comments:
P30	I inherited some alliances when I became executive director of major projects having come from road safety. So some alliances were already live and it was part of my role to step into those alliances in taking over from [person X], and [person X] moved into the chief operating officer role, so he started to step back from his role in alliances and I took over. I really wasn't sure what I was in for. I'd heard a little bit from [person X] about what they're like and that, but that was from a distance, so to speak. But yeah, dropping into them it was interesting, and I think I made a comment to one or two alliances that it would have been good if there was some induction for new ALT members, that's something that I found we haven't been really good at. So it's a really sharp introduction into what is the alliance, and this is where we're at so far. So a bit of an induction would have been good in my opinion so I was up a steep learning curve. I was just sort of overwhelmed at the beginning, too, with the Section of information that was coming.

This summary of Theme 15, **transparency and open-book** (refer to Table A6) relates to the processes, routines, and means that facilitate transparency and an open-book access by PO/POR-authorised personnel. Total transparency and accountability is necessary where the project is undertaken when a cost-plus basis variant of procurement form is adopted—in other words, when the PO funds all direct, administrative, and management costs and TOC are based upon these costs. The extent of transparency and accountability is a trade-off between the extent to which the project owner pays direct administrative and management costs and reinforces the trust-but-verify approach to a highly hands-on role by the project owner. Subthemes from Section 1, Table 13 are elaborated upon in Table A21.

- **Transparency and open-book** refers refer to project participants allowing themselves to be audited and fully open to scrutiny.
- Two categories of subthemes emerged from the data for **Theme 15 – transparency and open-book.** The first is about the transparency and all the mechanisms and protocols that this involves for various parties to be open and transparent, particularly about costs. The second is about being accountable and the processes and systems that ensure that companies and systems can be audited to demonstrate that the aims of the procurement choice system are not being abused and fulfil governance commitments as agreed. These can be summarised as follows:
  - 15.1 Transparency—the extent to which project participants agree to be fully open about their cost structures, their decision-making processes and their project delivery processes.
  - 15.2 Accountability—the extent to which project participants agree to be fully open to scrutiny, allowing authorised project owner representatives to audit and inspect books, processes, and decision-making rationale.

Table A21.   Wittgenstein Model Theme 15: Transparency and Open-Book

Theme and Subtheme	Notes, examples, and KSAE quotes
15.1 Transparency	The extent to which project participants agree to be fully open about their cost structures, their decision-making process, and their project delivery processes.
Examples of high levels of thinking about transparency.	• Participants understand the importance of the role that transparency plays in building trust and mutual commitment toward clear project goals and aims. • Participants understand the rationale of transparency in demonstrating that opportunistic behaviour is not occurring, particularly when developing a TOC or project duration forecast. • Participants understand and can justify the rationale for open book in terms of reduced transaction costs associated with verifying proprietary information and data. • Participants are clear in their intentions and approaches, and understand the level of trust propensity of others they deal with, and they think deeply about how they can assure the project owner and other project partners that their processes and communication forms support gaining and maintain credibility and trust in them.
High-level KSAE needed for transparency.	• *Technical and PM KSAE* – High levels of technical and PM competence relating to identifying, defining, and measuring all project aspects requiring transparency. • *Business solutions KSAE* – High levels of business integrity and application of governance measures to assure openness and transparency. • *Relational KSAE* – High levels of communication and empathy ability to be able to effectively create and maintain high trust levels.
Illustrative quotes	In developing the TOC for a project in Sweden, A16 stated that his observation of a massively complex project to scope that was highly uncertain and difficult to scope and estimate cost/time, but the project had an immovable completion date. After unsuccessfully trying to tender the project, the project owner ended up deciding upon a highly integrated form of partnering between the project owner and a main contractor.
A16 on openness and transparency in dealing with stakeholders	But it worked quite well and one of the things I realised that was extremely important was the dialogue that the project organisation had with all the stakeholders. You realise quite early, after a few months, that we need to be humble and we need to have a dialogue with everyone and need to spend time on creating a good working relation, not just between [PO X] and [Contractor A] within the project organisation, but with every subcontractor. . . I didn't mention that, but every subproject, one of these routes that was sent as an order to the project organisation, after they'd done the mapping and all the negotiation and so on, they calculated the cost of it, on the basis of how the land might look and how much distances was and so on and so on? And then they decided that the budget for it, in an agreement between world partners in the project, just saying, "Okay, let's agree that this will cost $1.6 million." And after that they had a gain share or pain share of plus/minus five per cent from that negotiated. So they knew that we need to negotiate this as close as possible to what we think it will be, and it wasn't a "you and I" or "we and them" relationship, it was, "We need to try to figure out how close or how much this will cost."
	In terms of the BAU approach with transparency about costs in an open-book approach, P06 observes a potential problem with this:
P06	But the problem that you've got with these things is the dodges, then they have the contract says 2 ½% main contractors' discount, but they may have a side deal with a letter that you never see that gives 5%. There's all those sorts of issues.
	Apart from financial transparency, an important element of transparency is clarity of understanding between people and organisations.
P17	So where you have an alliance where the scope of the alliance is to deliver the whole project, and then you have some critical conversations where you have to reach alignment between the owner and non-owner on what risks and opportunities are going to be shared by the alliance participants, and that generally forces a conversation, which is complicated enough, about how do you deal with risks that you don't control.
	And in taking an example that started as a design alliance then went into the delivery phase as a competitive tender based on a TOC a negotiated fixed-fee profit margin with negotiations after the contractor was on board to explore innovations and cost reductions, P35 stated that:

(continued)

Table A21.   Wittgenstein Model Theme 15: Transparency and Open-Book *(Continued)*

Theme and Subtheme	Notes, examples, and KSAE quotes
P35	I'm not party to how [PO X] assessed our tender to them, but in the development of our price that they accepted for the construction phase that was all open book and fully scrutinised by the independent estimator. It was a select tender, if you like, competitive-based and [PO X] was involved in all of those processes. So they were fully informed and advised as to who we went to tender, they saw the tender documents go out, the prices come back and then after the submission of our lump sum price they had full visibility on how the price was developed. . . . another thing that I would say was well considered in the development of the contract and its framework was that the construction wasn't to start until the project was adequately, or rather not adequately, but well-defined and we knew, [Contractor A] knew, that there would be very little opportunity for variation or increased scope. So there was a lot of effort put into accurately defining and pricing the project. So straight away after the turning out of the $92 million budget cost, we did a value engineering workshop where we're looking for innovation as well as adjustments to specification to bring the price down, and that process went for probably nearly three months to revisit the design and reduce the cost. Through that process there were lots of things that were done to reduce the price.
Design for Life U.K. Framework agreement	In the Design for Life U.K. Framework agreement document it states that: Without clarity of agreed sensible margins, separated from the cost element of the "price," the elements of cost can never be fully identified so that effort can be focused on reducing each in turn until the lowest cost is arrived at without affecting the target margin. So, the best practices by which costs can be managed, ideally on an open book basis, are rarely implemented and, even when they are attempted, run into the difficulty that the industry simply has no cost data on which to work other than "rates" which are inadequate for the purpose.
15.1 Accountability	The extent to which project participants agree to be fully open to scrutiny allowing authorised project owner representatives to audit and inspect books, processes, and decision-making rationale.
Examples of high levels of thinking about accountability	• Participants understand the importance of the role that accountability plays in building trust and mutual commitment toward clear project goals and aims. • Participants understand the rationale of accountability in demonstrating that opportunistic behaviour is not occurring. • Participants are clear in their intentions and approaches and demonstrate high levels of integrity about decisions and actions they take.
High-level KSAE needed for accountability	• *Technical and PM KSAE* – High levels of technical and PM competence relating to understanding how to best demonstrate and communicate what they do, so that decisions and actions can be intelligently challenged and questioned to prompt improvement and beneficial innovation. • *Business solutions KSAE* – High levels of business integrity and application of openness and transparency to engender trust and confidence. • *Relational KSAE – High* levels of communication and empathic ability to be able to effectively demonstrate their decisions and actions to prompt evaluation and questioning that may lead to improvement and beneficial innovation.
Illustrative quotes	In an example from a water utilities programme alliance the respondent was questioned about how extraordinary events were dealt with, for example major floods or bushfires, etc. The answer provided some insights about open-book interpretation of "facts and figures" as well as what may constitute and extraordinary event.
P42 on a programme alliance	. . . there's a provision for extraordinary events so at the end of every year, in the wash-up of the budget, they can identify and they don't necessarily have to be big expensive one-off events, they're encouraged to not just look for big one-offs that they go, well that's extraordinary, it's more about the event itself and whether it was an extraordinary event and unexpected, and the partner companies shouldn't be punished for something that was completely unpredicted or unpredictable in a normal year. So there is a provision to negotiate that and back it out of the calculation for whether there is a pain share or a gain share. To be honest, that's quite a difficult exercise because obviously they will put lots of things on the table that they think are unpredictable, and so it comes down to how skilled everyone is at negotiating and providing substantiation and then governance for how you divvy that up. So that's part of my job is the governance of it all and documenting and providing evidence and so what I've been doing is encouraging, as I work with the alliances, encouraging them to consider throughout the year what might be extraordinary, rather than waiting until the end of the year and getting the evidence together at the time. It's much harder in August next year to be thinking about something that happened in August this year.

Table A21. Wittgenstein Model Theme 15: Transparency and Open-Book *(Continued)*

Theme and Subtheme	Notes, examples, and KSAE quotes
P20 illustrates how expectations for accountability were made clear from the outset of the project.	There was documentation of expectations early on and also at the time of TOC, but I think value has been achieved less by trotting out a statement and then matching the statement more with the process that we followed, particularly for developing the TOC. But also with the culture that we created in the alliance, I think we made it very clear, very early on that this wasn't a sort of cashed-up kind of operation that we're, that you know things will be scrutinised and we will be evaluating whether things are worth, whether it's worth spending money on things, and I really am glad that we did that early on, I know there was a fair bit of grumbling from some of the people in the office about, what do you mean we're not going to have this, we always have this perk or that perk or whatever, what do you mean you're scrutinising this cost; well, we are, and we have to because we don't have a lot of money, and that sort of culture though starts to pervade people's thinking, and it means that when they're considering variation requests from subcontractors are the things that are keeping things in perspective. So from a perspective of value, I think, yeah at the end of this project when we're having to prove to Treasury, yes we've achieved value for money, I'm very confident about that.
P30 on accountability to produce VfM reports to demonstrate value	The national guidelines require value-for-money statements to be prepared in advance of going to the marketplace to form an alliance. So the client needs to be very clear about what is the value for money and then we deduce a whole big document on value for money before we proceeded to select partners or potential partners for the [Project X] and the [Project Y]. And there's also a requirement that when you reach practical completion of your alliances, that the client needs to prepare a value-for-money report to demonstrate what has been achieved.
	In terms of transparency and benchmarking, P48 had something very interesting to say about the value of a highly sophisticated and knowledgeable PO/POR who had intimate knowledge about what questions to ask and therefore how transparency could have a deep, rather than shallow, value and meaning.
P48	Well, in terms of value for money, I had three or four guys in the development of each of the TOCs, I had three or four guys in my group which were generally accounting for the rest of the jobs on the program, all the hard dollar jobs, so I used them to benchmark each of the TOCs in through about four or five different stages in the development of the TOCs, in terms of all the hourly rates and man-hours per job and all the direct costs, so I benchmarked that all the way through to the development of the TOC, so that when we came to the – so when the final TOC was presented to the ALT, I had a whole lot of benchmarks for the ALT to look at and compare when we were going through the TOCs, because the ALT, it would have been the first time a lot of those guys have ever done anything like that before in their lives, so I took them away for about four days and just gave them my feelings in terms of the prices to expect in terms of rates, overhead - erection of overhead per kilometre, weighing of civil works per kilometre, so they all had these fundamental breakdowns in their minds when they went into the TOC review. Now we had two TOCs on two of the projects with the program presented to us within about three months of each other, we accepted the first one and rejected the second one.

This summary of Theme 16, **mutual dependency and accountability** (refer to Table A6) relates to the processes, routines, and means that facilitate and enable mutual dependency and accountability, Subthemes from Section 1, Table 13 are elaborated upon in Table A22.

- **Mutual dependency and accountability** refers to collaboration in projects requiring participants to not only recognise their interdependency but to also honestly respond when communicating.
- Subthemes emerged from the data for **Theme 16 – mutual dependency and accountability.** These fell into three categories:
    - 16.1 Characteristics of mutual dependency—various forms of RBP have specific unique characteristics that have a focus on mutual dependency to degree, that is, the extent to which teams sink-or-swim-together. Teams may or may not perceive themselves becoming a temporary single team entity, with perceptions about how participants perceive the workplace support or inhibit a unified team approach to managing the project. This subtheme is more descriptive in illustrating the ambience with perceptions about how participants perceive the workplace to them and others.
    - 16.2 Enhancing enablers of mutual dependency—participants seek to actively leverage various processes, routines, and means to facilitate and sustain collaboration.
    - 16.2 Countering inhibitors to mutual dependency—participants seek to actively counter various processes, routines, and means that inhibit and undermine collaboration.

Table A22.   Wittgenstein Model Theme 16: Mutual dependency and accountability

Theme and Subtheme	Notes, examples, and KSAE quotes
16.1 Characteristics of mutual dependency	Characteristics that shape the way that participants feel toward one another in collaborating, trusting, and committing to each other and their teams in a way that makes them dependent and integrated rather than working as independent and autonomous groups, teams, and individuals. Mechanisms that shape how participants are integrated to influence the extent to which they collaborate and are mutually bound in action-consequence loops.
Examples of high levels of thinking about mutual dependency characteristics.	• Participants can identify and understand how structures, processes, and behaviours they encounter produces a workplace ambience that drives or inhibits their mutual dependency and collaboration, and the degree to which they take accountability for the impact of their actions upon one another. • Participants empathise with fellow participants and any difficulties they may face, and seek out ways in which to ease that burden within limitations and constraints of the RBP approach while remaining committed to promote joint best-for-project outcomes. • Participants clearly understand the impact that others may have on their capacity to deliver best-for-project outcomes and what they need to do to ensure that they can jointly deliver to or beyond project KRAs.
High-level KSAE needed for mutual dependency characteristics.	• *Technical and PM KSAE* – High levels of technical and PM competence relating to understanding dependency interfaces and interconnectivity of participant actions. • *Business solutions KSAE* – High levels of business integrity and systems knowledge to be able to appreciate business/technical/ PM interfaces and interaction. • *Relational KSAE* – High levels of ability for communication and empathy to be able to effectively gain mutual understanding between teams and individuals of their interdependency and how they can best sink or swim together.
Illustrative quotes	A01 raised a point about trade-offs in a lifecycle cost context, but it is applicable to mutual dependency. That project required a build and maintain solution and so the capital cost and running costs were then entwined and interdependent. This illustration is useful for understanding that characteristic of mutual dependency. It also shows that the project owner had a responsibility and duty for a project solution that illustrates what happens when there is a tradeoff in scope and cost between project owner and project delivery team.
A01	. . . they tried to introduce your new type of asphalt that needed hardly any maintenance but was very expensive. So that was a sole discretion, the trade-off between product and number of maintenance days that that was so in this competitive dialogue for the tunnel project also. . . . But the rail, yes, authority is in principle responsible, yes, for they are responsible that the maintenance will be well organised by the markets.
	The rationale behind project teams realising their project interdependencies and necessary trade-off of interests is illustrated by the following quotes about project characteristics:
P20	Any sort of discussions are very important because while at the end of the day whatever decision we make, we've all got to own it and we've all got to, you know, the cost impact or the time impact or the quality impact or the design impact, whatever way the decision goes, in that instance everybody wears that and there is that sort of collective view, but it's important, I think, that everyone brings their own perspective to those discussions too. So it's not sort of groupthink, that's not what it's about.
P22	I think it's part of a no-blame culture and it's part of the fact that they were in it together. And at times they were able to switch scope between the parties so that they would—say if some civil works were holding up the M&E team, "Well, okay, we'll do those works to make sure that it gets integrated with the work we're doing," and they'll do it rather than just complain about somebody else not doing it. And that kind of flexibility, I think, was characteristic of the arrangement.
	Another characteristic of mutual dependence is branding of a single project delivery team and the way that it binds people together into a "project tribe."
P28	. . . we spent a lot of time in making sure that we were just seen as one entity and they were part of that entity until they left the alliance. Even little things, like you were never allowed to drive a car which had one of your home organisations . . . Had a symbol on it, you wear the same clothes all the time, you have the same thing, we had a lot of pressure in making sure that everybody was part of that entity and felt that they were one entity, and it was one culture in developing that culture. . . . It was sink or swim, it was forming a team which had a really challenging job which motivated itself.
P29	You could go into our alliance office, so at the peak we had in our alliance office about 90 people and I could tell you, you couldn't pick who was from the parent companies. It was very much an integrated model, so we spent a lot of effort in terms of building the team. And that's worked extremely effectively.

Theme and Subtheme	Notes, examples, and KSAE quotes
16.2 Enhancing enablers of mutual dependency	Specific mechanisms and processes that shape the way that participants feel toward one another in collaborating, trusting, and committing to each other and their teams in a way that makes them dependent and integrated, rather than working as independent and autonomous groups, teams and individuals.
Examples of high levels of thinking about enhancing enablers of mutual dependency.	• Participants understand how structures, processes and behaviours that they encounter result in mutual dependency, encouraging collaboration and accountability for the impact of their actions upon one another. • Participants support and leverage enabling structures, processes, and behaviours that they encounter that result in mutual dependency encouraging collaboration and accountability for the impact of their actions upon one another.
High-level KSAE needed for enhancing enablers of mutual dependency.	• *Technical and PM KSAE* – High levels of technical and PM competence relating to actively enhancing structures, processes and behaviours that enable interdependency and interconnectivity (sink or swim together) of participant actions. • *Business solutions KSAE* – High levels of business integrity and systems knowledge to be able to enhance business/technical/PM advantages to interdependency interaction (sink or swim together) of participant actions. • *Relational KSAE* – High levels of communication and empathy ability for teams and individuals to be able to effectively enhance a sink-or-swim-together collaborative mode of working.
Illustrative quotes	One enabler of a sink or swim together is recognition of the challenge of highly complex interfaces and the ability to develop mechanisms, structures, and methods of collaborating to effectively enhance collaboration.
P23 on how complexity drove a sink-or-swim-together attitude.	Typically a tunnel might be commissioned in the last two or three months, but the sheer size of this particular tunnel required us to start commissioning six months out, and that meant six months out while we're still building some of it, so again not the luxury of stopping work and then handing over to the commissioning team. These were some, I suppose, of the input drivers for looking at smarter models.
P23 added that	. . . so we have the alliance manager and I guess one of the big advantages of having the alliance was that we had an alliance manager who had to become intimately familiar with the whole M&E [mechanical and electrical] scope and what the challenges were for the M&E team, etc., etc., had some influence in the project management, the bigger project, and had some influence in what they did. Whereas [X] is the subcontractor wouldn't be able to influence the civil work at all, the alliance manager was able to influence it in some ways to the benefit of the alliance, for the M&E scope. I think if we talk about this particular alliance, it was set up because of those risks that we talked about in the start where we had traditionally the M&E contractor coming in conflict with the civil contractor, working in that confined space at the same time. I think it solved a lot of those issues reasonably well in that we had a team that was working as one. The smaller party in that team, [X]—there was a pain/gain formula but they had limited exposure so they could comfortably provide the resources needed to get the job done without constantly going back into the contractual mode. We had an alliance manager who could exert some influence over the overall project, giving M&E a voice that they wouldn't have had under a subcontract model. So for those reasons I think it worked reasonably well.
P26, discussing the same project, says:	The way the job was set up with all the support, some of the people finishing works into the M&E fit-out of the tunnel, but I mean, toward the end it was actually realised that the civil people were better positioned to do these kind of things, so they actually got onto the work and did it.
	And on the driver or enhancer of having a team with a culture attuned to collaboration and sink or swim -together. Strong authentic leadership traits seem to be one enabler, the ability to guide and serve the team that delivers the project.
P28 says	You had the disciplines of the alliance leader, you've got the clients representative, you've got the construction, you've got the design interface manager, and you've got your business manager, your quality person and the safety person. It wasn't a big AMT, but it was very, very focussed and they were very, very visible onsite, and they were always around at a number of activities we had. They were expected to be there, but they just did that as part of being proud members of the team. We were very lucky in getting some really high-quality people in the AMT.
	One aspect of a sink-or-swim-together arrangement is to get the project in the first place. In this quote from P48, he recalls how an unsuccessful proponent team responded to the need to pull together, to pool all intellectual effort for innovation, and to arrive at a feasible proposal.
P48 on a dual TOC bid process	The second TOC [PA X] ever presented the ALT was rejected, so they were absolutely deflated and I said "We're not expecting business as usual, we expect you to go away, we expect you to be clever, and we expect you to come up when the bloody price is right and be innovative," so they went away and spent a month on it, and they came back and they'd stripped $100 million out of it and we got the right price and the right approach. That had a big impact on the way the place worked, particularly the management; the alliance management team.

(continued)

Theme and Subtheme	Notes, examples, and KSAE quotes
P34 makes the valid point about the AMT composition that:	So certainly that's one of the pillars of an alliance agreement, we're all in this together, and we had a charter, we put ourselves together and made up a charter. Again, you know the pragmatic constructors didn't see the point of sitting down for a day and coming up with a charter, because they knew what would be on it anyway. It didn't take long though to convince them that the purpose wasn't to get the charter; the purpose was to sit down for the day together. So we did that, and one of the key points in the charter was everyone's in this together, we all win, we all lose together. Again, how it manifested itself, well how it didn't—the sort of the other way around, again, no siloing. Siloing sort of raised its head early, but we cleaned that up fairly quickly with structural changes, and made sure that we had a good spread across all disciplines, or across all teams, sub-teams within the alliance. So that worked to reinforce that whole sink-or-swim-together attitude.
P36 on a programme alliance observes:	I think the sink or swim question, we were pretty strong from the beginning, strong leadership, so the alliance manager. . . . we were always thinking of [PO X] as a client, but it was more the whole attitude of working together was like, almost like a business unit. Here's our KPIs, here's our goals, here's what we're moving toward and it was, all the discussion was around that. So I think if that's directed from alliance management and then particularly from your alliance manager then that's, it really starts there.
16.3 Countering inhibitors of mutual dependency	Generally these are the reverse of the 16.2 enablers. However, they are more about processes, structures, and attitudes or workplace culture that tends to foster individualism over collectivism so that teams may each feel high committed to a best-for-project outcome, but their interpretation and meaning of this is purely based on *their personal* view of performance and of their performance and not on how *their* actions contributes to or hinders the *whole team's performance*.
Examples of high levels of thinking about countering inhibitors of mutual dependency.	• Participants understand how structures, processes, and behaviours that they encounter result in mutual dependency, encouraging collaboration and accountability for the impact of their actions upon one another, and make a special effort to ensure that their actions and performance is in synch with other participants, and that they do not undermine the performance of others as a consequence of their individually focussed performance. • Participants understand that a sink-or-swim-together culture is mutually beneficial and provides valuable social capital to work together as a single focussed integrated team, and that they should be on guard to identify and remedy any structures, processes, and actively counter behaviours that inhibit a sink-or-swim together project delivery culture.
High-level KSAE needed for countering inhibitors of mutual dependency.	• *Technical and PM KSAE* – High levels of technical and PM competence relating that actively inhibit the impact of structures, processes and behaviours that promote participant actions of interdependency and interconnectivity (sink or swim together). • *Business solutions KSAE* – High levels of business integrity and systems knowledge to be able to counter actions that inhibit interdependency interaction (sink or swim together) of participant actions business/technical/PM. • *Relational KSAE* – High levels of communication and empathy ability for teams and individuals to be able to effectively counter systems and actions that inhibit a sink-or-swim-together collaborative mode of working.
Illustrative quotes	One potential inhibitor of a sink-or-swim-together workplace culture is often the processes, policies, performance and reward incentives, etc., that act as barriers to people looking out for each other and to collaborate freely to achieve best long-term and sustainable value. This may be a legacy of systems used by participants in a project that cannot be harmonised, or it may be simply that participants cannot fully comprehend the impact that their operating procedures and processes has on other participants and how it inhibits collaboration.
A10 on a study into marketing within an RBP context and a series of firms' representatives that had been interviewed.	It's in terms that the systems that they use to conduct their function; the processes don't interface with each other. Now that's okay; in a sense if you've got a soft system that's overarching, that compensates for that. You see you create your own, as it were, alliance along the project life-cycle but none of them have. None of them had at all. So their ability to integrate others is hampered, and their ability to put forward value prompt propositions that add value for clients is hampered by their lack of ability to join up their systems internally and provide a seamless content; a seamless service, along those lines. . . . for example, the procurement managers would source things from the supply chain against technical criteria; like responsible sourcing or performance criteria in use or price. But all of those decisions will bear no relationship at all to say what the business development had understood about the client needs, and they weren't connected. So they couldn't develop an aligned value proposition at all at bid stage, and most of them weren't talking to the bid managers either. So the ability to alliance well with others, it doesn't mean it doesn't work but what I am saying—after a fashion—but what I am saying is that if you want to have alliances that help to maximise value, that's hampered by the lack of alliance, the lack of integration internally within each contractor organisation.

Table A22.   Wittgenstein Model Theme 16: Mutual dependency and accountability *(Continued)*

Theme and Subtheme	Notes, examples, and KSAE quotes
P21 discusses a tension of resources available to be in a team and experience needed, etc., to overcome	. . . when you come from a culture at the [Project X] which has been for the last 10 years of collaboration, teamwork and actually, and theatre actually operates on the spot and people think it's not particularly soft, it's pretty tough, it's pretty hard to get results. You've got less money and you don't have money to throw around, so therefore there's a lot of fairly sophisticated behaviours and things that happen in theatre to get the very clever outcomes that we see which, and I'll keep on trying to say, is that it's just a very different, lots of different cultures in there and trying to get them operating together. So it's been, I think it's been the best way to go having an alliance, but I think it's been really hard and I think we've underestimated how much. I think our teams would have been too small, everybody probably says that, but there's only been through the thick of it all there's only really three, four of us trying to, I mean, corral all that stuff that's going on.
P26 on the implications of reporting "bad news" that needs to be known	I mean we started off commissioning on construction that was incomplete, and it took quite an amount of work in order to convince people further up the tree that the construction work actually wasn't complete, that the only way we could end progressing was by actually taking on the incomplete construction work, and when you start reporting all sorts of the associated numbers in relation to completing work, you can imagine the attention that that starts drawing, when you start exceeding various critical numbers you've put forward, if you know what I'm saying.
	Finally, countering hubris by a PO/POR or NOP may be essential for a sink-or-swim-together situation. P48 provides a colourful quote relating to a rail programme alliance consisting of multi-billion dollar investments.
P48	. . . Technical reasons, operations reasons, a whole bunch of reasons, so we had to go back and tell our client they were wrong from day one and that took some balls from the ALT.

. . . Well, that original discussion that we had with [PO], that they don't know everything, so we managed that as best we could and from there on in, we invited someone from [PO] to be on the ALT, so we then had buy-in from them as well, and we educated them on the basis from what railways are all about. It absolutely opened their eyes. |

References

Aaltonen, K. (2010). *Stakeholder Management in International Projects*. PhD Dissertation, Department of Industrial Engineering and Management, Espoo, Helsinki University of Technology.

Aaltonen, K., & Kujala, J. (2010). A project lifecycle perspective on stakeholder influence strategies in global projects. *Scandinavian Journal of Management, 26*(4), 381–397.

Aaltonen, K., & Sivonen, R. (2009). Response strategies to stakeholder pressures in global projects. *International Journal of Project Management, 27*(2), 131–141.

Abrahamson, E. (1996). Management Fashion. *Academy of Management Review, 21*(1), 254–285.

Ahola, T. (2009). Efficiency in project networks: The role of inter-organizational relationships in project implementation. PhD, *Department of Industrial Engineering and Management*. Espoo, Helsinki University of Technology.

Ahola, T., Laitinen, E., Kujala, J., & Wikström, K. (2008). Purchasing strategies and value creation in industrial turnkey projects. *International Journal of Project Management, 26*(1), 87–94.

Akintoye, A., Beck, M., & Hardcastle, C. (2003) *Public-Private Partnerships: Managing Risks and Opportunities*, Oxford, Blackwell Science Ltd.

Alliancing Association of Australasia (2010). (ECI): A practical overview, Australian collaboration insight series. Sydney, Australia, Alliancing Association of Australasia: 31.

Alliance Association of Australasia (2012). Collaboration where it matters: In planning and design, Sydney: 13pp.

Alliancing Association of Australasia (2008). Case study: The Pacific Link Alliance Tugun Bypass Project, Sydney, NSW, Alliancing Association of Australasia: 8.

Alliancing Association of Australasia (2010). Case Study 'us'–Utility Services Alliance Sydney, NSW, Alliancing Association of Australasia: 7.

Alsop, R. J. (2004). Corporate reputation: Anything but superficial – the deep but fragile nature of corporate reputation. *Journal of Business Strategy, 25*(6), 21–29.

Alvesson, M. (2000). Social Indentity and the problem of loyalty in knowledge-intensive companies. *Journal of Management Studies, 37*(8), 1101–1124.

Amabile, T. M., & Kramer, S. J. (2007). Inner work life. *Harvard Business Review*. 85(5), 72–83.

American Institute of Architects–AIA California Council (2007) *Integrated project delivery: A guide*, Sacramento, CA.

Anderson, J. C., Narus, J. A., & van Rossum, W. (2006). Customer value propositions in business markets. *Harvard Business Review, 84*(3), 90–99.

Anvuur, A., & Kumaraswamy, M. (2008). Better collaboration through cooperation. In Smyth H., & S. Pryke, *Collaborative relationships in construction: Developing frameworks and networks* (pp. 107–128). Chichester, U.K.; Malden, MA: Wiley-Blackwell.

Anvuur, A. M., Kumaraswamy, M. M., & Mahesh, G. (2011). Building relationally integrated value networks (RIVANS). *Engineering, Construction and Architectural Management, 18*(1), 102–120.

APM (2006) *APM Body of Knowledge*, 5th edition, APM, London.

Aranda-Mena, G., Crawford, J., Chevez, A., & Froese, T. (2009). Building information modelling demystified: Does it make business sense to adopt BIM? *International Journal of Managing Projects in Business, 2*(3), 419–433.

Arroyo, A., & Walker, D. H. T. (2008). Business Transformation Through an Innovative Alliance. In Walker D. H. T., & S. Rowlinson, *Procurement Systems–A Cross Industry Project Management Perspective* (pp. 423–444). Abingdon: Oxon, Taylor & Francis.

Arroyo, A. C. (2009). *The Role of the Atlantic Corridor Project as a Form of Strategic Community of Practice in Facilitating Business Transformations in Latin America*. Doctorate, *School of Property, Construction and Project Management*. Melbourne, RMIT University.

Arroyo, A. C., & Walker, D. H. T. (2009). *A Latin American Strategic Organisational Transformation Project Management Experience: The Motivation to Transform Business*. In Bredillet C., & Middler. C., European Academy of Management EURAM: Renaissance & Renewal in Management Studies, Liverpool, May 11–14: 20pp.

Artto, K., & Kujala, J. (2008). Project Business as a Research Field. *International Journal of Managing Projects in Business, 1*(4), 469–497.

Artto, K., Kujala, J., Dietrich, P., & Martinsuo, M. (2008). What is project strategy. *International Journal of Project Management, 26*(1), 4–12.

Artto, K. A., & Wikström, K. (2005). What is project business? *International Journal of Project Management, 23*(5), 343–353.

Ashcraft, H. W. (2010). The IPD Framework, Contract Briefing Note. San Francisco, CA: Hanson Bridgett LLP.: 26pp.

Ashkanasy, N. M., Trevor-Roberts, E., & Earnshaw, L. (2002). The Anglo cluster: Legacy of the British empire. *Journal of World Business, 37*(1), 28–39.

Atkinson, R. (1999). Project management: Cost, time and quality, two best guesses and a phenomenon, its time to accept other success criteria. *International Journal of Project Management, 17*(6), 337–342.

Auditor-General of the Australian National Audit Office (2000). Construction of the National Museum of Australia and the Australian Institute of Aboriginal and Torres Strait Islander Studies, Audit Report. Canberra, Australia, Australian National Audit Office,34, 1999–2000.

Augustine, S., Payne, B., Sencindiver, F., & Woodcock, S. (2005). Agile project management: Steering from the edges. *Communications of the ACM, 48*(12), 85–89.

AusAID (2005). AusGuide–A guide to program management; 3.3 The Logical Framework Approach, Canberra, Commonwealth of Australia, AusAID: 39.

Australian Constructors Association (1999). Relationship contracting–Optimising project outcomes. Sydney: Australian Constructors Association.

Baccarini, D. (1996). The concept of project complexity–A review. *International Journal of Project Management, 14*(4), 201–204.

Baccarini, D. (1999). The logical framework method for defining project success. *Project Management Journal, 30*(4), 25–32.

Bachmann, R., & Inkpen, A. C. (2011). Understanding Institutional-based trust building processes in inter-organizational relationships. *Organization Studies, 32*(2), 281–301.

Bakker, R. M., Cambré, B., Korlaar, L., & Raab, J. (2011). Managing the project learning paradox: A set-theoretic approach toward project knowledge transfer. *International Journal of Project Management, 29*(5), 494–503.

Ballard, G. (2008). The lean project delivery system: An update. *Lean Construction Journal*. 1–19.

Barnett, A. M. (1998/9). The many guises of a project manager. *The Australian Institute of Building Papers, 3*(1), 119–134.

Barrett, P., & Stanley, C. (1999) *Better Construction Briefing*, Oxford, UK, Blackwell Science Ltd.

Beheshti, H. M. (2006). What managers should know about ERP/ERP II. *Management Research News, 29*(4), 184–193.

Bennett, J., & Jayes, S. (1995) *Trusting the Team*, Reading, UK: Centre for Strategic Studies in Construction, The University of Reading.

Bennis, W. G., & O'Toole, J. (2005). How business schools lost their way. *Harvard Business Review, 83*(5), 96–104.

Bentley, C. (2010) *Prince 2 : A practical handbook.* Oxford; Boston: Butterworth-Heinemann.

Berggren, C., & Söderlund, J. (2008). Rethinking project management education: Social twists and knowledge co-production. *International Journal of Project Management, 26*(3), 286–296.

Bing, L., Tiong, R. L. K., Fan, W. W., & Chew, D. A. S. (1999). Risk management in international construction joint ventures. *Journal of Construction Engineering and Management, 125*(4), 277–284.

Bleeke, J., & Ernst, D. (1993) *Collaborating to Compete–Using Strategic Alliances and Acquisitions in the Global Marketplace.* New York: John Wiley.

Bontis, N., Crossan, M. M., & Hulland, J. (2002). Managing an organizational learning system by aligning stocks and flows. *Journal of Management Studies, 39*(4), 437.

Bosch-Rekveldt, M., Jongkind, Y., Mooi, H., Bakker, H., & Verbraeck, A. (2010). Grasping project complexity in large engineering projects: The TOE (Technical, organizational and environmental) framework. *International Journal of Project Management, 29*(6), 728–739.

Bourne, L. (2005). *Project relationship management and the stakeholder circle.* Doctor of Project Management, Graduate School of Business. Melbourne: RMIT University.

Bourne, L. (2011a). Advising upwards: Managing the perceptions and expectations of senior management stakeholders. *Management Decision, 49*(6), 1001–1023.

Bourne, L., & Walker, D. H. T. (2005). Visualising and mapping stakeholder influence. *Management Decision, 43*(5), 649–660.

Bourne, L. M. (2009) *Stakeholder Relationship Management,* Farnham, Surrey, UK: Gower.

Bourne, L. M., Ed. (2011b). *Advising upwards–A framework for understanding and engaging senior management stakeholders.* Farnham, Surrey, UK: Gower.

Bourne, M. (2008). Performance measurement: Learning from the past and projecting the future. *Measuring Business Excellence, 12*(4), 67–72.

Bradley, G. (2010) *Benefit Realisation Management.* Aldershot, UK: Gower.

Brady, T., & Davies, A. (2004). Building project capabilities: from exploratory to exploitative learning. *Organization Studies, 25*(9), 1601–1621.

Brady, T., & Davies, A. (2010). From hero to hubris–Reconsidering the project management of Heathrow's Terminal 5. *International Journal of Project Management, 28*(2), 151–157.

Brady, T., Davies, A., Gann, D., & Rush, H. (2007). Learning to manage mega projects: the case of BAA and Heathrow Terminal 5. *Project Management Perspectives, XXIX,* 33–39.

Brady, T., Davies, A., & Gann, D. M. (2005). Creating value by delivering integrated solutions. *International Journal of Project Management, 23*(5), 360–365.

Bredillet, C. (2013). A Discourse on the non-method. In Drouin N., R. Müller, & Sankaran, S., *Novel Approaches to organizational project management research–Translational and transmormational* (pp. 56–94). Koege, Denmark: Copenhagen Business School Press.

Bredillet, C. N. (2008). Mapping the dynamics of the project management field: Project management in action (part 1). *Project Management Journal, 39*(4), 2–4.

Bredillet, C. N., Conboy, K., Davidson, P., & Walker, D. (2013). The getting of wisdom: The future of PM university education in Australia. *International Journal of Project Management, 31*(8), 1072–1088.

Bredin, K. (2008). People capability of project-based organisations: A conceptual framework. *International Journal of Project Management, 26*(5), 566–576.

Bredin, K., & Söderlund, J. (2006). HRM and project intensification in R&D-based companies: A study of Volvo Car Corporation and AstraZeneca. *R&D Management, 36*(5), 467–485.

Bredin, K., & Söderlund, J. (2011a). The HR quadriad: a framework for the analysis of HRM in project-based organizations. *International Journal of Human Resource Management, 22* (10), 2202–2221.

Bredin, K., & Söderlund, J. (2011b) *Human resource management in project-based organizations.* Basingstoke, UK: Palgrave Macmillan.

Bresnen, M. (2003). *The Seven deadly paradoxes of partnering (seven deadly sins?).* TG23–Culture in Construction: International Conference on Professionalism in Construction–Culture of High Quality, Hong Kong, 27–28 October, Fellows R.: 1–15.

Bresnen, M., & Marshall, N. (2000). Building partnerships: case studies of client-contractor collaboration in the UK in construction industry. *Construction Management and Economics, 18*(7), 819–832.

Bresnen, M., & Marshall, N. (2011). Projects and partnerships institutional process and emergent practice. In Morris P. W. G., Pinto, J. K., & Söderlund, J., *The Oxford Handbook of Project Management* (pp. 154–174). Oxford: Oxford University Press.

Brockbank, W. (1999). If HR were really strategically proactive: Present and future directions in HR's contribution to competitive advantage. *Human Resource Management, 38*(4), 337–352.

Brookes, N. J., Morton, S. C., Dainty, A. R. J., & Burns, N. D. (2006). Social processes, patterns and practices and project knowledge management: A theoretical framework and an empirical investigation. *International Journal of Project Management, 24*(6), 474–482.

Bygballe, L. E., dewulf, G., & Levitt, R. (2013). *The impact of relational contracting on flexibility in health care projects*. in Carrillo P. and P. Chinowsky, eds., Proceedings of Engineering Project Organization Conference, Devil's Thumb Ranch, Colorado, July 9–11, 2013, 14pp.

Carroll, A. B. (1991). The pyramid of corporate social responsibility: Toward the moral management of organizational stakeholders. *Business Horizons, 34*(4), 39–48.

Cavaleri, S. (2008). Are learning organizations pragmatic? *The Learning Organization.* 15(6), 474–485.

Chan, A. P. C., Chan, D. W. M., & Ho, K. S. K. (2003). An empirical study of the benefits of construction partnering in Hong Kong. *Construction Management & Economics, 21*(5), 523–533.

Chen, L., Manley, K., & Lewis, J. (2012). The learning capability of construction organisations engaged in collaborative contracting. Brisbane: Alliance Project research Groupt, Queensland University of Technology: 19pp.

Cherns, A. B., & Bryant, D. T. (1984). Studying the client's role in construction management. *Construction Management and Economics, 2*(2), 177–184.

Chhokar, J. S., Brodbeck, F. C., & House, R. J. (2008) *Culture and leadership across the world: the GLOBE book of in-depth studies of 25 societies*. Mahwah, N.J.: Lawrence Erlbaum Associates.

Christensen, C. M., & Overdorf, M. (2000). Meeting the challenge of disruptive change. *Harvard Business Review, 78*(2), 66–76.

Christenson, D. (2007). *Using vision as a critical success element in project management*. Doctor of Project Management, DPM, School of Property, Construction and Project Management. Melbourne, RMIT.

Christenson, D., & Walker, D. H. T. (2003). *Vision as a critical success factor to project outcomes*. 17th World Congress on Project Management, Moscow, Russia, June 3–6: On CD-ROM.

Christenson, D., & Walker, D. H. T. (2004). Understanding the role of "vision" in project success. *Project Management Journal, 35*(3), 39–52.

Cicmil, S. (2003). *From instrumental rationality to practical wisdom*. PhD. Leicester, SImon de Montfort University.

Cicmil, S. (2006). Understanding project management practice through interpretative and critical research perspectives. *Project Management Journal, 37*(2), 27–37.

CIDA, C. I. D. A. (1993a) *Building best practice in the construction industry–A practitioner's guide*. Sydney: Commonwealth of Australia.

CIDA, C. I. D. A. (1993b). *Project performance update–A report on the time and cost performance of australian building projects completed 1988–1993*. Sydney: CIDA.

CIDA, C. I. D. A. (1994). *Two steps forward, one step back–Management practices in the australian construction industry*. Sydney: Construction Industry Development Agency.

CII (1996). *The partnering process–Its benefits, implementation, and measurement*. Austin, Texas: CII, Bureau of Engineering Resources, University of Texas at Austin.,CII Source Document 102–11.

CIIA, C. I. I. o. A. (1995). *Benchmarking engineering and construction–Review of performance and case studies*. Adelaide: CIIA and University of South Australia.

Clark, I., & Colling, T. (2005). The management of human resources in project management-led organizations. *Personnel Review, 34*(2), 178–191.

Coase, R. H. (1937). The nature of the firm. *Economica, 4*, 386–405.

Cobb, C. G. (2011) *Making sense of agile project management balancing control and agility*. Hoboken, NJ: John Wiley & Sons.

Cohen, J. (2010) *Integrated project delivery: Case studies*. Sacramento, CA: American Institute of Architects (AIA)–AIA California Council.

Cohen, W. M., & Levinthal, D. (1990). Absorptive capacity: A new perspective on learning and innovation. *Administrative Science Quarterly, 35*(1), 128–152.

Collyer, S. (2013). *Managing dynamism in projects–A theory-building study of approaches used in practice*. PhD, University of Queensland Business School. Brisbane: University of Queensland.

Collyer, S., Warren, C., Hemsley, B., & Stevens, C. (2010). Aim, fire, aim—Project planning styles in dynamic environments. *Project Management Journal, 41*(4), 108–121.

Collyer, S., & Warren, C. M. J. (2009). Project management approaches for dynamic environments. *International Journal of Project Management, 27*(4), 355–364.

Commission of the European Communities (1996). Green Paper, Public Procurement in the European Union: Exploring the Way Forward–Communication adopted by the Commission on 27th November 1996 on the proposal of Mr. Monti. Brussels: Commission of the European Communities, 59.

Conforto, E. C., & Amaral, D. C. (2009). Evaluating an agile method for planning and controlling innovative projects. *Project Management Journal*, *40*(3), 1–8.

Cooper, R. G. (2005) *Product leadership : pathways to profitable innovation.* New York: Basic Books.

Cooper, R. G., Edgett, S. J., & Kleinschmidt, E. J. (1997). Portfolio management in new product development: Lessons from the leaders–I. *Research Technology Management*, *40*(5), 16–28.

Corbin, J. & Strauss, A. (1990). Grounded Theory Research: Procedures, Canons, and Evaluative Criteria. *Qualitative Sociology. 13* (1): 3.

Corbin, J. M., Strauss, A. L., & Strauss, A. L. (2008) *Basics of qualitative research : Techniques and procedures for developing grounded theory.* Los Angeles, CA: Sage Publications Inc.

Crawford, L., & Da Ros, V. (2002). Politics and the project manager. *Australian Project Manager*, *22*, 20–21.

Crawford, L., Morris, P., Thomas, J., & Winter, M. (2006). Practitioner development: From trained technicians to reflective practitioners. *International Journal of Project Management*, *24*(8), 722–733.

Crawford, L., & Pollack, J. (2004). Hard and soft projects: A framework for analysis. *International Journal of Project Management*, *22*(8), 645–653.

Crawford, P., & Bryce, P. (2003). Project monitoring and evaluation: a method for enhancing the efficiency and effectiveness of aid project implementation. *International Journal of Project Management*, *21*(5), 363–373.

Creswell, J. W. (2009) *Research design : qualitative, quantitative, and mixed methods approaches.* Thousand Oaks, CA: Sage Publications.

Crossan, M. M., Lane, H. W., & White, R. E. (1999). An organizational learning framework: from intuition to institution. *Academy of Management Review*, *24*(3), 522–537.

Dahlsrud, A. (2008). How corporate social responsibility is defined: An analysis of 37 definitions. *Corporate Social Responsibility and Environmental Management*, *15*(1), 1–13.

Dainty, A. R. J., Cheng, M.-I., & Moore, D. (2005). A comparison of the behavioral competencies of client-focused and production-focused project managers in the construction sector. *Project Management Journal*, *36*(2), 39–49.

Dal Gallo, L., O'Leary, S., & Louridas, L. (2009). Comparison of integrated project delivery agreements. San Francisco: Hanson-Bridgett, 10pp.

Das, T. K. (2005). Deceitful behaviors of alliance partners: Potential and prevention. *Management Decision*, *43*(5), 706–719.

Das, T. K., & Teng, B.-S. (1998). Between trust and control: Developing confidence in partner cooperation in alliances. *Academy of Management Review*, *23*(3), 491–512.

Davenport, T. H., & Glaser, J. (2002). Just-in-time delivery comes to knowledge management. *Harvard Business Review*, *80*(7), 107–111.

Davies, A., & Brady, T. (2000). Organisational capabilities and learning in complex product systems: Towards repeatable solutions. *Research Policy*, *29*(7–8), 931–953.

Davies, A., Gann, D., & Douglas, T. (2009). Innovation in megaprojects: systems integration at london Heathrow Terminal 5. *California Management Review*, *51*(2), 101–125.

Davies, A., & Hobday, M. (2005) *The business of projects managing innovation in complex products and systems.* Cambridge: Cambridge University Press.

Davies, A., Hobday, M., & Prencipe, A. (2005) *The business of systems integration.* Oxford: Oxford University Press.

Davis, P. R. (2006). *The application of relationship marketing to construction.* PhD, School of Economics, Finance and Marketing. Melbourne: RMIT University.

Davis, P. R., & Love, P. E. D. (2011). Alliance contracting: adding value through relationship development. *Engineering Construction & Architectural Management*, *18*(5), 444–461.

Davis, P. R., & Walker, D. H. T. (2008). Case study–Trust, commitment and mutual goals in alliances. In Walker D. H. T., & Rowlinson, S, *Procurement systems–A cross industry project management perspective* (pp.378–399). Abingdon, Oxon: Taylor & Francis.

Debourse, J.-P., & Archibald, R. D. (2011a). *Project managers as senior executives Volume 1–Research results, advancement model, and action proposals.* Newtown Square, PA: Project Management Institute.

Debourse, J.-P., & Archibald, R. D. (2011b). *Project managers as senior executives: Volume 2—how the research was conducted: Methodology, detailed findings, and analyses.* Newtown Square, PA: Project Management Institute.

DeFillippi, R. J., & Arthur, M. B. (1998). Paradox in project-based enterprise: The Case of film making. *California Management Review, 40*(2), 125–139.

Denis, J.-L., Langley, A., & Rouleau, L. (2007). Strategizing in pluralistic contexts: Rethinking theoretical frames. *Human Relations, 60*(1), 179–215.

Department of Infrastructure and Transport (2011). *National alliance contracting guidelines guide to alliance contracting. department of infrastructure and transport A. C. G.* Canberra: Commonwealth of Australia, 168.

Department of Treasury and Finance Victoria (2010). *The practitioners' guide to alliance contracting.* Melbourne: Department of Treasury and Finance, Victoria, 161.

Dessler, G., Griffiths, J., & Lloyd-Walker, B. M. (2007). *Human Resource Management.* Frenchs Forest, NSW, Australia: Pearson Education Australia.

Doherty, S. (2008). *Heathrow's T5 History in the making.* Chichester: John Wiley & Sons Ltd.

Doz, Y. L., & Hamel, G. (1998). *Alliance advantage–The art of creating value through partnering.* Boston: Harvard Business School Press.

Dreyfus, H. L., & Dreyfus, S. E. (2005). Expertise in Real world contexts. *Organization Studies, 26*(5), 779–792.

Dreyfus, S. E. (2004). The five-stage model of adult skill acquisition. *Bulletin of Science Technology And Society, 24*(3), 177–181.

Dyer, J. H., Cho, D. S., & Chu, W. (1998). Strategic supplier segmentation: The next "best practice" in supply chain management. *California Management Review, 40*(2), 57.

Dyer, J., H., & Nobeoka, K. (2000). Creating and managing a high-performance knowledge-sharing network: The Toyota case. *Strategic Management Journal, 21*(3), 345–367.

Dyer, J. H., & Singh, H. (1998). The relational view: Cooperative Strategy and sources of interorganizational competitive advantage. *Academy of Management Review. 23*(4), 660–679.

Egan, J. (1998). *Rethinking construction–The report of construction task force.* London: Department of Environment, Transport and the Regions.,ISBN 1851120947, pp. 38.

Egan, J. (2002). Accellerating change. Rethinking construction, Report. London, Strategic Forum for Construction,ISBN 1 898671 28 1, 44.

Ehrgott, M., Reimann, F., Kaufmann, L., & Carter, C. R. (2011). Social Sustainability in selecting emerging economy suppliers. *Journal of Business Ethics, 98*, 99–119.

Eisenhardt, K. M. (1989). Agency theory: an assessment and review. *The Academy of Management Review, 14*, 57–74.

Eisenhardt, K. M., & Tabrizi, B. N. (1995). Accelerating adaptive processes: Product innovation in the global computer industry. *Administrative Science Quarterly, 40*(1), 84–110.

Ekstedt, E., Lundin, R. A., Söderholm, A., & Wirdenius, H. (1999). *Neo-industrial organising: Renewal by action and knowledge formation in a project-intensive economy.* London: Routledge.

Elkington, J. (1997). *Cannibals with forks.* London: Capstone Publishing.

Emerson, C. (1983). The outer word and inner speech: Bakhtin, Vygotsky, and the internalization of language. *Critical Inquiry, 10*(2), 245–264.

Eppler, M. J., & Sukowski, O. (2000). Managing team knowledge: Core processes, tools and enabling factors. *European Management Journal, 18*(3), 334–341.

Eriksson, P. E. (2010a). Improving construction supply chain collaboration and performance: A lean construction pilot project. *Supply Chain Management: An International Journal, 15*(5), 394–403.

Eriksson, P. E. (2010b). Partnering: what is it, when should it be used, and how should it be implemented? *Construction Management and Economics, 28*(9), 905–917.

Ezulike, E. I., Perry, J. G., & Hawwash, K. (1997). The barriers to entry into the PFI market. *Engineering Construction and Architectural Management, 4*(3), 179–193.

Faisal, M. N. (2010). Analysing the barriers to corporate social responsibility in supply chains: An interpretive structural modelling approach. *International Journal of Logistics: Research and Applications, 13*(3), 179–195.

Firestone, J. M., & McElroy, M. W. (2004). Organizational learning and knowledge management: The relationship. *Learning Organization, 11*(2), 177–184.

Firestone, J. M., & McElroy, M. W. (2005). Doing knowledge management. *Learning Organization. 12*(2), 189–212.

Fitzgerald, P. (2004). Review of Partnerships Victoria Provided Infrastructure, Final Report to the Treasurer. Melbourne: Growth Solutions Group, 42.

Flyvbjerg, B. (2009). Survival of the unfittest: Why the worst infrastructure gets built and what we can do about it. *Oxford Review of Economic Policy*, 25(3), 344–367.

Frederiksen, L., & Davies, A. (2008). Vanguards and ventures: Projects as vehicles for corporate entrepreneurship. *International Journal of Project Management*, 26(5), 487–496.

Gann, D. (2001). Putting academic ideas into practice: Technological progress and the absorptive capacity of construction organizations. *Construction Management and Economics*, 19(3), 321–330.

Gareis, R. (1989). Management by projects: The management approach for the future. *International Journal of Project Management*, 7(4), 243–249.

Gareis, R., & Hueman, M. (2007). Maturity models for the project oriented company. In Turner J. R, *Handbook of Project Management* (pp. 183–208). Aldershot, UK: Gower,.

Geraldi, J. G., & Adlbrecht, G. (2007). On faith, fact, and interaction in projects. *Project Management Journal*, 38(1), 32–43.

Gil, N. (2009). Developing cooperative project client-supplier relationships: How much to expect from relational contracts? *California Management Review*, 51(2), 144–169.

Gilbert, C., & Bower, J. L. (2002). Disruptive change–When trying harder is part of the problem. *Harvard Business Review*, 80(5), 95–101.

Glaser, B. G., & Strauss, A. L. (1967). *The Discovery of grounded theory : Strategies for qualitative research*. New York: Aldine Pub. Co.

Goleman, D., Boyatzis, R. E., McKee, A., & Buntine, A. (2002). *The leadership repertoire; emotional intelligence: leadership competencies*. London: Little Brown.

Gottlieb, S. C., & Jensen, J. S. (2012). Making sense of partnering: discourses, governance and institutional change. *Engineering Project Organization Journal*, 2(2), 1–16.

Gratton, L., & Ghoshal, S. (2003). Managing Personal human capital: New ethos for the 'volunteer' employee. *European Management Journal*, 21(1), 1–10.

Green, S. (1999a). Partnering: The Propaganda of corporatism. *Journal of Construction Procurement*, 5(2), 177–186.

Green, S. D. (1999b). Partnering: The Propaganda of Corporatism? In Ogulana, S. O., *Profitable Partnering in construction procurement* (p. 735). London, E & FN Spon.

Green, S. D., Fernie, S., & Weller, S. (2005). Making sense of supply chain management: a comparative study of aerospace and construction. *Construction Management and Economics*, 23(6), 579–593.

Grimsey, D., & Graham, R. (1997). PFI in the NHS. *Engineering Construction and Architectural Management*, 4(3), 215–231.

Grix, J. (2002). Introducing students to the generic terminology of social research. *Politics*, 22(3), 175–186.

Groysberg, B., & Lee, L.-E. (2009). Hiring stars and their colleagues: Exploration and exploitation in professional service firms. *Organization Science*, 20(4), 740–758.

Gwynne, P. (1997). Skunk works, 1990s-style. *Research Technology Management*, 40(4), 18–23.

Hampson, K. D., Peters, R. J., Walker, D. H. T., Tucker, S., Mohammed, S., Ambrose, M., & Johnston, D. (2001). Case study of the Acton Peninsula development, government research report. Canberra, Canberra: Department of Industry, Science and Resources, Commonwealth of Australia Government, 515.

Hancock, D. (2010) *Tame, messy and wicked risk leadership/* Farnham, UK: Gower.

Hansen, M. T., & Birkinshaw, J. (2007). The innovation value chain. *Harvard Business Review*, 85(6), 121–130.

Hansen, M. T., Nohria, N., & Tierney, T. (1999). What's your strategy for managing knowledge? *Harvard Business Review*, 77(2), 106–116.

Hartmann, A., Davies, A., & Frederiksen, L. (2010). Learning to deliver service-enhanced public infrastructure: balancing contractual and relational capabilities. *Construction Management & Economics*, 28 (11), 1165–1175.

Heidemann, A., & Gehbauer, F. (2011). The way towards cooperative project delivery. *Journal of Financial Management of Property and Construction*, 16(1), 19–30.

Henderson, L. S. (2005). Reflecting on Athens 2004: What we can learn about modern project management from ancient Olympian archetypes. *Organization Development Journal*, 23(4), 10–19.

Hertogh, M., Baker, S., Staal-Ong, P. L., & Westerveld, E. (2008) *Managing large infrastructure projects–Research on best practices and lessons learnt in large infrastructure projects in europe*. Baarn, Netherlands: Osbourne B.V.

Highsmith, J. A. (2004) *Agile project management : Creating innovative products*, Boston, MA, Addison-Wesley.

HM Treasury and Infrastructure UK (2013). Infrastructure procurement routemap: A guide to improving delivery capability. London, UK,ISBN 978-1-909096-56-1, 49pp.

Hobday, M., Davies, A., & Prencipe, A. (2005). Systems integration: A core capability of the modern corporation. *Industrial and Corporate Change*, *14*(6), 1109–1143.

Hobday, M., Rush, H., & Tidd, J. (2000). Innovation in complex products and system. *Research Policy*, *29*(7–8), 793–804.

Hodge, G. A. (2004). The risky business of public–private partnerships. *Australian Journal of Public Administration*, *63*(4), 37–49.

Hodgson, D., & Cicmil, S. (2006) *Making projects critical*. Basingstoke, UK: Palgrave MacMillan.

Hoezen, M. (2012). The competitive dialogue procedure: Negotiations and commitment in inter-organisational construction projects. PhD. Enschede, the Netherlands, University of Twente.

Hoezen, M., Van Rutten, J., Voordijk, H., & Dewulf, G. (2010). Towards better customized service-led contracts through the competitive dialogue procedure. *Construction Management & Economics*, *28* (11), 1177–1186.

Hoezen, M., Voordijk, H., & Dewulf, G. (2012a). Contracting dynamics in the competitive dialogue procedure. *Build Environment Project and Asset management*, *2*(1), 6–24.

Hoezen, M., Voordijk, H., & Dewulf, G. (2012b). Formal and informal contracting processes in the competitive dialogue procedure: A multiple-case study. *Engineering Project Organization Journal*, *2*(3), 145–158.

Hoffmann, T. (1999). The meanings of competency. *Journal of European Industrial Training*, *23*(6), 275–286.

Hofstede, G. H., Hofstede, G. J., & Minkov, M. (2010) *Cultures and organizations: Software of the mind: Intercultural cooperation and its importance for survival*. New York: McGraw-Hill.

Holyoak, K. J., & Thagard, P. (1997). The analogical mind. *American Psychologist*, *52*(1), 35–44.

Holzer, B. (2008). Turning stakeseekers into stakeholders: A political coalition perspective on the politics of stakeholder influence. *Business Society*, *47*(1), 50–67.

Hosmer, L. T. (1994). Why be moral? A different rationale for managers. *Business Ethics Quarterly*, *4*(2), 191–204.

Hosmer, L. T. (1995). Trust: The connecting link between organizational theory and philosophical ethics. *The Academy of Management Review*, *20*(2), 379–403.

House, R., Javidan, M., Hanges, P., & Dorfman, P. (2002). Understanding cultures and implicit leadership theories across the globe: An introduction to Project GLOBE. *Journal of World Business*, *37*(1), 3–10.

House, R. J., Hanges, P. J., Javidan, M., Dorfman, P. W., & Gupta, V. (2004) *Culture, leadership, and organizations– The GLOBE study of 62 societies*. Thousand Oaks, CA: Sage Publication Ltd.

Howell, D., Windahl, C., & Seidel, R. (2010). A project contingency framework based on uncertainty and its consequences. *International Journal of Project Management*, *28*(3), 256–264.

Huemann, M. (2010). Considering human resource management when developing a project-oriented company: Case study of a telecommunication company. *International Journal of Project Management*, *28*(4), 361–369.

Huemann, M., Keegan, A., & Turner, J. R. (2007). Human resource management in the project-oriented company: A review. *International Journal of Project Management*, *25*(3), 315–323.

Hutchinson, A., & Gallagher, J. (2003). Project alliances: An overview. Melbourne: Alchimie Pty Ltd, Phillips Fox Lawyers, 33.

Ika, L. A., Diallo, A., & Thuillier, D. (2010). Project management in the international development industry: The project coordinator's perspective. *International Journal of Managing Projects in Business*, *3*(1), 61–93.

Ika, L. A., Diallo, A., & Thuillier, D. (2012). Critical success factors for World Bank projects: An empirical investigation. *International Journal of Project Management*, *30*(1), 105–116.

Imai, M. (1986) *Kaizen: The key to Japan's competitive success*. New York: McGraw-Hill.

Jackson, B. (1997). Designing projects and project evaluations using the logical framework approach. Gland, Switzerland: International Union for the Conservation of Nature and Natural Resources, the IUCN, 16.

Jacobbson, M., & Roth, P. (2014). Partnering Projects as Engagement Platforms. *Construction Management and Economics*. in press.

Jacobsson, M. (2011). Samordningens dynamik: om samordningens samspel och förändring i ett interorganisatoriskt anläggningsprojekt. PhD, Umeå University, Faculty of Social Sciences, Umeå School of Business and Economics *(USBE)*. Umeå, Sweden: Umeå University.

Jarvenpaa, S. L., Knoll, K., & Leidner, D. E. (1998). Is anybody out there? Antecedents of trust in global virtual teams. *Journal of Management Information Systems, 14*(4), 29–65.

Järvinen, A., & Poikela, E. (2001). Modelling reflective and contextual learning at work. In Antonacopoulou, E. P., Jarvis, P., Andersen, V., Ellkjaer, B,. and Hoyrup, S., *Learning, Working And Living: Mapping the Terrain of Working Life Learning*, (pp. 282–289). Houndmills, Basingstoke, Hampshire ; New York: Palgrave Macmillan.

Järvinen, A., & Poikela, E. (2006). The Learning process in the work organization: From theory to design. In Antonacopoulou, E. P., Jarvis, P., Andersen, V., Ellkjaer, B,. and Hoyrup, S., *Learning, working and living: Mapping the terrain of working life learning* (pp. 170–187). Houndmills, Basingstoke, Hampshire; New York: Palgrave Macmillan.

Javidan, M., Stahl, G. K., Brodbeck, F., & Wilderom, C. P. M. (2005). Cross-border transfer of knowledge: Cultural lessons from Project GLOBE. *Academy of Management Executive, 19*(2), 59–76.

Jewell, M., & Walker, D. H. T. (2005). Community of practice perspective software management tools: A UK construction company case study. In Kazi, A. S., *Knowledge Management in the Construction Industry: A Socio-Technical Perspective.* (pp. 111–127). Hershey, PA: Idea Group Publishing.

Johannes, D. S. (2004). Joint venture contracting relationships between foreign and local contractors in the construction and engineering industry of Hong Kong: Implications of understanding collaborative practice. PhD, School of Management. Melbourne: RMIT University.

Jones, D. (2001). Keeping the options open: Alliance and other forms of relationship contracting with government. *Building and Construction Law, 17*(3), 153–163.

Judgev, K., & Thomas, J. (2002). Project management maturity models: The silver bullets of competitive advantage? *Project Management Journal, 33*(4), 4–14.

Kang, S.-C., & Snell, S. A. (2009). Intellectual capital architectures and ambidextrous learning: A framework for human resource management. *Journal of Management Studies, 46*(1), 65–92.

Kaplan, R. S., & Norton, D. P. (1992). The balanced scorecard–Measures that drive performance. *Harvard Business Review, 70*(1), 171–179.

Kaplan, R. S., & Norton, D. P. (1996). Using the balanced scorecard as a strategic management system. *Harvard Business Review, 74*(1), pp. 75-85.

Kaplan, R. S., & Norton, D. P. (1998a). Putting the balanced scorecard to work. In *Harvard Business Review on Measuring Corporate Performance* (pp. 147–181). Boston, MA: Harvard Business School Publishing.

Kaplan, R. S., & Norton, D. P. (1998b). Using the Balanced scorecard as a strategic management system. In *Harvard Business Review on Measuring Corporate Performance* (pp. 183–211). Boston, MA: Harvard Business School Publishing.

Kaplan, R. S., & Norton, D. P. (2000). Having Trouble with your strategy? Then map it. *Harvard Business Review, 78*(5), 167–76.

Kaplan, R. S., & Norton, D. P. (2004a). How strategy maps frame an organization's objectives. *Financial Executive, 20*(2), 40–45.

Kaplan, R. S., & Norton, D. P. (2004b). Measuring the strategic readiness of intangible assets. *Harvard Business Review, 82*(2), 52–63.

Kaplan, R. S., & Norton, D. P. (2004c) *Strategy maps converting intangible assets into tangible outcomes.* Boston: Harvard Business School Publishing.

Khalfan, M. M. A., & McDermot, P. (2006). Innovating for supply chain integration within construction. *Construction Innovation: Information, Process, Management, 6*(3), 143–157.

Khalfan, M. M. K., & Maqsood, T. (2012). Supply chain capital in construction industry–Coining the term. *International Journal of Managing Projects in Business, 5*(2), 300–310.

Klakegg, O. J. (2010). Governance of major public investment projects in pursuit of relevance and sustainability. PhD, Faculty of Engineering Science and Technology, Department of Civil and Transport Engineering. Trondheim: Norwegian University of Science and Technology.

Klakegg, O. J., Williams, T., & Magnussen, O. M. (2009). *Governance frameworks for public project development and estimation.* Newtown Square, PA: Project Management Institute.

Klakegg, O. J., Williams, T., Walker, D. H. T., Andersen, B., & Magnussen, O. M. (2010). *Early Warning Signs in Complex Projects.* Newtown Square, PA: Project Management Institute.

Knights, D., & O'Leary, M. (2005). Reflecting on corporate scandals: The failure of ethical leadership. *Business Ethics: A European Review, 14*(4), 359–366.

Kogut, B. (1988). Joint ventures: Theoretical and empirical perspectives. *Strategic Management Journal, 9*(4), 319–332.

Kolb, D. A. (1984) *Experiential learning : Experience as the source of learning and development.* Englewood Cliffs, NJ: Prentice-Hall.

Koskinen, K. U. (2008). Boundary brokering as a promoting factor in competence sharing in a project work context. *International Journal of Project Organisation and Management, 1*(1), 119–132.

Koskinen, K. U. (2009). Project-based company's vital condition: Structural coupling. An autopoietic view. *Knowledge and Process Management, 16*(1), 13–22.

Koskinen, K. U. (2010) *Autopoitic knowledge systems in project-based companies.* London: Palgrave Macmillan.

Koskinen, K. U. (2012). Organizational Learning in Project-based companies: A process thinking approach. *Project Management Journal, 43*(3), 40–49.

Koskinen, K. U., & Aramo-Immonen, H. (2008). Remembering with the Help of personal notes in a project work context. *International Journal of Managing Projects in Business, 1*(2), 193–205.

Koskinen, K. U., & Pihlanto, P. (2006). Competence transfer from old timers to newcomers analysed with the help of the holistic concept of man. *Knowledge and Process Management, 13*(1), 3–12.

Koskinen, K. U., Pihlanto, P., & Vanharanta, H. (2003). Tacit knowledge acquisition and sharing in a project work context. *International Journal of Project Management, 21*(4), 281–290.

KPMG (1998). Project alliances in the construction industry, literature review. Sydney, NSW Department of Public Works & Services,7855-PWS98-0809-R-Alliance.

Kulik, C., & Bainbridge, H. (2006). HR and the line: The distribution of HR activities in Australian organisations. *Asia Pacific Journal of Human Resources, 44*(2), 240–256.

Kulik, C. T., & Perry, E. L. (2008). When Less is more: The effect of devolution on HR's strategic role and construed image. *Human Resource Management, 47*(3), 541–558.

Kurtz, C. F., & Snowden, D. J. (2003). The new dynamics of strategy: sense-making in a complex and complicated world. *IBM Systems Journal, 42*(3), 462(22).

Laan, A., Voordijk, H., & Dewulf, G. (2011). Reducing opportunistic behaviour through a project alliance. *International Journal of Managing Projects in Business, 4*(4), 660–679.

Lahdenperä, P. (2012). Making sense of the multi-party contractual arrangements of project partnering, project alliancing and integrated project delivery. *Construction Management and Economics, 30*(1), 57–79.

Langley, A. (1995). Between "paralysis by analysis" and "extinction by instinct". *Sloan Management Review, 36*(3), 63–76.

Langley, A., Mintzberg, H., Pitcher, P., Posada, E., & Saint-Macary, J. (1995). Opening up decision making: The view from the black stool. *Organization Science, 6*(3), 260–279.

Langley, A. N. N., Smallman, C., Tsoukas, H., & Van De Ven, A. H. (2013). Process studies of change in organization and management: Unveiling temporality, activity, and flow. *Academy of Management Journal, 56*(1), 1–13.

Latham, M. (1994). *Constructing the team.* Final Report of the Government/Industry Review of Procurement and Contractual Arrangements in the UK Construction Industry. London: HMSO.

Lawler III, E. E. (2001). The era of human capital has finally arrived. In Bennis W., Spreitzer, G. M., & Cummings, T. G., *The Future of Leadership–Today's Top Leadership Thinkers Speak to Tomorrow's Leaders* (pp. 14–25). San Francisco: Jossey-Bass.

Lawrence, P. R., & Lorsch, J. W. (1967) *Organization and environment: Managing differentiation and integration.* Boston, MA: Harvard University.

Lawrence, T. B., Mauws, M. K., Dyck, B., & Kleysen, R. F. (2005). The politics of organizational learning: Integrating power into the 4I framework. *Academy of Management Review, 30*(1), 180–191.

Lechler, T., & Byrne, J. C. (2011) *The Mindset for Creating Project Value.* Newtown Square, PA: Project Management Institute.

Legault, M.-J. (2005). *Differential gender effects of project management and management by project on skilled professionals.* Reformulating Industrial Relations in Liberal Market Economies: Proceedings of the Canadian Industrial Relations Association (CIRA) Conferences: 41st Conference Concord, Canada, Devine K. S., & Grenier, J.-N. CIRA & Captus Press, 105–124.

Legault, M.-J., & Chasserio, S. (2012). Professionalization, risk transfer, and the effect on gender gap in project management. *International Journal of Project Management, 30*(6), 697–707.

Lenard, D. J., Bowen-James, A., Thompson, M., & Anderson, L. (1996) *Partnering–Models for Success.* Adelaide, Australia: Construction Industry Institute Australia.

Lenfle, S. (2008). Exploration and project management. *International Journal of Project Management, 26*(5), 469–478.

Lenfle, S., & Loch, C. (2010). Lost roots: How project management came to emphasize control over flexibility and novelty. *California Management Review, 53*(1), 32–55.

Leonard-Barton, D. (1992). Core capabilities and core rigidities: A paradox in managing new product development. *Strategic Management Journal, 13*(S1), 111–125.

Leonard-Barton, D. (1995) *Wellsprings of knowledge–Building and sustaining the sources of innovation.* Boston, MA: Harvard Business School Press.

Leonard, D., & Rayport, J. F. (1997). Spark innovation through empathic design. *Harvard Business Review, 75*(6), 102–113.

Leonard, D., & Sensiper, S. (1998). The role of tacit knowledge in group innovation. *California Management Review, 40*(3), 112–132.

Leonard, D., & Straus, S. (1997). Putting your company's whole brain to work. *Harvard Business Review, 75*(4), 110–121.

Levinthal, D. A., & March, J. G. (1993). The myopia of learning. *Strategic Management Journal, 14*(S2), 95–112.

Lewicki, R. J., Tomlinson, E. C., & Gillespie, N. (2006). Models of interpersonal trust development: Theoretical approaches, empirical evidence, and future directions. *Journal of Management, 32*(6), 991–1022.

Lindgren, M., & Packendorff, J. (2006). What's New in new forms of organizing? On the Construction of gender in project-based work. *Journal of Management Studies, 43*(4), 841–866.

Lindkvist, L., Söderlund, J., & Tell, F. (1998). Managing product development projects: On the significance of fountains and deadlines. *Organization Studie, 19*(6), 931–951.

Lingard, H., Brown, K., Bradley, L., Bailey, C., & Townsend, K. (2007). Improving employees' work-life balance in the construction industry: Project alliance case study. *Journal of Construction Engineering and Management, 133* (10), 807–815.

Lingard, H., Wakefield, R., & Cashin, P. (2011). The development and testing of a hierarchical measure of project OHS performance. *Engineering, Construction and Architectural Management, 18*(1), 30–49.

Lisch, R. (2012) *Ancient wisdom for modern management: Machiavelli at 500.* Farnham, UK: Gower.

Lloyd-Walker, B., & Walker, D. (2011). Authentic leadership for 21st century project delivery. *International Journal of Project Management, 29,* 383–395.

Lloyd-Walker, B. M., Lingard, H., & Walker, D. H. T. (2008). Project procurement and the quest for talent. In Walker D. H. T., & Rowlinson, S., *Procurement Systems–A Cross Industry Project Management Perspective.* (pp. 311–357). Abingdon, Oxon: Taylor & Francis.

Locke, K. D. (2001) *Grounded theory in management research.* London; Thousand Oaks, CA: Sage Publications.

Lönngren, H.-M., Rosenkranz, C., & Kolbe, H. (2010). Aggregated construction supply chains: Success factors in implementation of strategic partnerships. *Supply Chain Management: An International Journal, 15*(5), 404–411.

Lopez-Cabrales, A., Valle, R., & Herrero, I. (2006). The contribution of core employees to organizational capabilities and efficiency. *Human Resource Management, 45*(1), 81–109.

Love, P. E. D., Edwards, D. J., Irani, Z., & Walker, D. H. T. (2009). Project pathogens: The Anatomy of omission errors in construction and resource engineering project. *IEEE Transactions On Engineering Management, 56*(3), 425–435.

Lovitt, M. R. (1997). The new pragmatism: Going beyond Shewhart and Deming. *Quality Progress, 30*(4), 99–106.

Luft, J., & Ingham, H. (1955). *The Johari window, a graphic model of interpersonal awareness.* Proceedings of the western training laboratory in group development, Los Angeles: UCLA.

Lundin, R. A., & Söderholm, A. (1995). A theory of the temporary organization. *Scandinavian Journal of Management, 11*(4), 437–455.

Luo, Y. (2007). The independent and interactive roles of procedural, distributive, and interactional justice in strategic alliances. *Academy of Management Journal, 50*(3), 644–664.

Luria, A. R. (1973) *The working brain: An introduction to neuropsychology.* New York: Penguin.

Lynn, G. S., & Akgün, A. E. (2001). Project visioning: Its components and impact on new product success. *The Journal of Product Innovation Management, 18*(6), 374–387.

MacDonald, C. C. (2011). Value for money in project alliances. DPM, School of Property, Construction and Project Management. Melbourne: RMIT University.

Machiavelli, N., & Bull, G. (1961) *The prince.* Harmondsworth, Mddx.: Penguin Books.

MacLean, D., MacIntosh, R., & Grant, S. (2002). Mode 2 management research. *British Journal of Management, 13*(4), 189–207.

Manchester Business School (2009a). Study on voluntary arrangements for collaborative working in the field of construction services–Main Report Part 2: Best Practice Guide and Case Studies, Research Report. Manchester: Manchester Business School, 87.

Manchester Business School (2009b). Study on voluntary arrangements for collaborative working in the field of construction services–Main Report Part 3: Country Reports, Research Report. Manchester: Manchester Business School, 198.

Manchester Business School (2009c). Study on voluntary arrangements for collaborative working in the field of construction services–Part 1: Main Report, Research Report. Manchester: Manchester Business School, 166.

Maqsood, T., Finegan, A., & Walker, D. H. T. (2006). Applying project histories and project learning through knowledge management in an Australian construction company. *The Learning Organization, 13*(1), 80–95.

March, J. G. (1991). Exploration and exploitation in organizational learning. *Organization Science: A Journal of the Institute of Management Sciences, 2*(1), 71.

Martinsuo, M., & Ahola, T. (2010). Supplier integration in complex delivery projects: Comparison between different buyer-supplier relationships. *International Journal of Project Management, 28*(2), 107–116.

Masterman, J. W. E. (1992) *An Introduction to building procurement systems.* London: E & FN SPON.

Masterman, J. W. E. (2002) *An introduction to building procurement systems.* London: Spon.

Mathews, O., & Howell, G. (2005). Integrated project delivery an example of relational contracting. *Lean Construction Journal, 2*(1), 46–61.

Matten, D., & Moon, J. (2008). "Implicit" and "explicit" CSR: A conceptual framework for a comparative understanding of corporate social responsibility. *Academy of Management Review, 33*(2), 404–424.

Matthews, J., Pellew, L., Phua, F., & Rowlinson, S. (2000). Quality relationships: Partnering in the construction supply chain. *International Journal of Quality & Reliability Management, 17*(4), 493–510.

Maturana, H. R. (1999). The organization of the living: A theory of the living organization. *International Journal of Human-Computer Studies, 51*(2), 149–168.

Mayer, R. C., Davis, J. H., & Schoorman, F. D. (1995). An integrated model of organizational trust. *Academy of Management Review, 20*(3), 709–735.

McCarthy, A., Darcy, C., & Grady, G. (2010). Work-life balance policy and practice: Understanding line manager attitudes and behaviors. *Human Resource Management Review, 20*(2), 158–167.

McGeorge, W. D., & Palmer, A. (2002) *Construction management new directions–Second edition,* London:Blackwell Science.

McKenna, D. G. (2010). Adjudicating an ill-defined problem from a system development/project management perspective: Utilizing a knowledge management overlay model. PhD, School of property, Construction and Project Management. Melbourne: RMIT University.

McKenna, D. G., & Walker, D. H. T. (2008). *Knowledge management and knowledge transfer in a dynamic project environment – A case study.* Defining the future of project management, Warsaw, 13–16 July, Andrews E., PMI, 16 pp.

Meyer, J. P., & Allen, N. J. (1991). A Three-component conceptualization of organizational commitment. *Human Resource Management Review, 1*(1), 61–89.

Meyer, J. P., & Herscovitch, L. (2001). Commitment in the workplace: Toward a general model. *Human Resource Management Review, 11*(3), 299–326.

Meyer, J. P., Paunonen, S. V., Gellatly, I. H., Goffin, R. D., & Jackson, D. N. (1989). Organizational commitment and job performance: It's the nature of the commitment that counts. *Journal of Applied Psychology, 74,* 152–156.

Meyer, J. P., Stanley, D. J., Herscovitch, L., & Topolnytsky, L. (2002). Affective, continuance, and normative commitment to the organization: A meta-analysis of antecedents, correlates, and consequences. *Journal of Vocational Behavior, 61*(1), 20–52.

Mills, A., & Harley, J. (2010). Alliance performance and perception survey in public sector infrastructure–2010, Sydney, Alliance Association of Australasia: 17pp.

Mingers, J. (2003). A classification of the philosophical assumptions of management science methods. *The Journal of the Operational Research Society*, 54(6), 559–570.

Mitchell, R. K., Agle, B. R., & Wood, D. J. (1997). Toward a theory of stakeholder identification and salience: Defining the principle of who and what really counts. *Academy of Management Review*, 22(4), 853–886.

Morgan, D. L. (2007). Paradigms lost and pragmatism regained: Methodological implications of combining qualitative and quantitative methods. *Journal of Mixed Methods Research*, 1(1), 48–76.

Morris, P. W. G. (2011). A Brief history of project management. In Morris P. W. G., Pinto, J. K., & Söderlund, J., *The Oxford Handbook of Project Management* (pp. 15–36). Oxford: Oxford University Press.

Morris, P. W. G., & Geraldi, J. (2011). Managing the institutional context for projects. *Project Management Journal*, 42(6), 20–32.

Morris, P. W. G., & Jamieson, A. (2004) *Translating corporate strategy into project strategy: realizing corporate strategy through project management*. Newtown Square, PA: Project Management Institute.

Morris, P. W. G., Jamieson, A., & Shepherd, M. M. (2006). Research updating the APM Body of Knowledge 4th edition. *International Journal of Project Management*, 24(6), 461–473.

Morris, P. W. G., & Lock, I. C. A. (2004). *Knowledge creation and dissemination (organizational learning) in project-based organizations*. PMI Research Conference 2004, London, 12–14 July, Slevin D. P., Cleland, D. I., and Pinto, J. K., PMI, CD-ROM Disk, 1–17.

Morwood, R., Pitcher, I., & Scott, D. (2008) *Alliancing, a participant's guide–real life experiences for constructors, designers, facilitators and clients*. Brisbane: AECOM.

Mosey, D. (2009) *Early contractor involvement in building procurement: Contracts, partnering and project management*. Oxford: Wiley-Blackwell.

Müller, R. (2009) *Project governance*. Farnam, Surrey, UK: Gower.

Müller, R., Andersen, E. S., Kvalnes, Ø., Shao, J., Sankaran, S., Turner, J. R., Biesenthal, C., Walker, D. H. T., & Gudergan, S. (2012). *The interrelationship of governance, trust and ethics in temporary organizations*. PMI Research Conference, Limerick, Ireland, July 15–18, Project Management Institute, 29pp.

Müller, R., Andersen, E. S., Shao, J., Kvalnes, Ø., Turner, J. R., Sankaran, S., & Walker, D. H. T. (2011). Governance, trust and ethics; A study on the interrelationship of governance, trust and ethics in temporary organizations, intermediate research report. Oslo, Norway BI, 40pp.

Murray, M., & Langford, D. A. (2003) *Construction reports 1944–98*. Oxford: Blackwell Science. Ltd.

Murray, P. (2004) *The saga of Sydney Opera House : The dramatic story of the design and construction of the icon of modern Australia*. New York: Spon Press.

Nahapiet, J., & Ghoshal, S. (1998). Social capital, intellectual capital, and the organizational advantage. *Academy of Management Review*, 23(2), 242–266.

Naoum, S. (2003). An overview into the concept of partnering. *International Journal of Project Management*. 21(1), 71–76.

NASF, COAA., APPA, AGC and AIA, (2010). Integrated project delivery for public and private owners, standard. Integrated Project Delivery For Public and Private Owners, 40pp, a joint industry-association publication, available from http://www.aia.org/ipd.pdf.

National Audit Office (2001). *Modernising Construction*. London, Comptroller and Auditor General.

National Audit Office (2005). *Case Studies. Improving Public Services Through Better Construction*. London, Comptroller and Auditor General, 51.

National Audit Office (2009). The National Offender Management Information System, Audit. London, Comptroller and Auditor General, 41.

NBCC (1989). *Strategies for the reduction of claims and disputes in the construction industry–No dispute*. Canberra: National Building and Construction Council.

Nogeste, K. (2004). Increase the likelihood of project success by using a proven method to identify and define intangible project outcomes. *International Journal of Knowledge, Culture and Change Management*, 4, 915–926.

Nogeste, K. (2006). Development of a method to improve the definition and alignment of intangible project outcomes with tangible project outputs. Doctor of Project Management, DPM, Graduate School of Business. Melbourne: RMIT.

Nonaka, I., & Konno, N. (1998). The concept of 'Ba': Building a Foundation for knowledge creation. *California Management Review*, 40(3), 40.

Nonaka, I., & Takeuchi, H. (1995) *The Knowledge-Creating Company*. Oxford: Oxford University Press.

Nonaka, I., Toyama, R., & Konno, N. (2001). SECI, *Ba* and leadership: A Unified model of dynamic knowledge creation. In Nonaka I., & Teece, D., *Managing Industrial Knowledge–creation, Transfer And Utilization* (pp. 13–43). London: Sage.

Norrie, J. (2008) *Breaking through the project fog: How smart organizations achieve success by creating, selecting and executing on-strategy projects*. Toronto: John Wiley & Sons Canada, Ltd.

Norrie, J. L. (2006). Improving results of project portfolio management in the public sector using a balanced scorecard approach. Doctor of Project Management, School of Property, Construction and Project Management. Melbourne: RMIT University.

Nyström, J. (2005a). The definition of partnering as a Wittgenstein family-resemblance concept. *Construction Management and Economics, 23*(5), 473–481.

Nyström, J. (2005b). Partnering; definition, theory and the procurement phase. Licentiate, School of Architecture and the Built Environment. Stockholm: Royal Institute of Technology (KTH).

Nyström, J. (2007). Partnering: definition, theory and evaluation. PhD, School of Architecture and the Built Environment. Stockholm: Royal Institute of Technology (KTH).

Oaks, G. (2008) *Project reviews, assurance and governance*. Aldershot, UK: Gower Publishing Ltd.

Office of Government Commerce (2007a) *Gateway review workbooks*. London: The Stationery Office (TSO).

Office of Government Commerce (2007b) *Managing successful programmes*. London: The Stationery Office (TSO).

Office of Government Commerce (2007c) *The OGC Gateway™ process–A manager's checklist*. London: The Stationery Office (TSO).

Ogunlana, S. O., Ed. (1999). *Profitable Partnering in Construction Procurement*. Series Profitable Partnering in Construction Procurement. London: E & FN Spon.

Othman, R., & Hashim, N. A. (2004). Typologizing organizational amnesia. *The Learning Organization, MCB University Press, 11*(3), 273–284.

Owen, G., & Merna, A. (1997). The private finance initiative. *Engineering Construction and Architectural Management, 4*(3), 163–177.

Packendorff, J. (1995). Inquiring into the temporary organization: New directions for project management research. *Scandinavian Journal of Management, 11*(4), 319–333.

Parent, R., Roy, M., & St-Jacques, D. (2007). A systems-based dynamic knowledge transfer capacity model. *Journal of Knowledge Management, 11*(6), 81–93.

Parker, S. K., Atkins, P., & Axtell, C. (2008). Building better work places through individual perspective taking: A fresh look at a fundamental human process. *International Review of Industrial and Organizational Psychology, 23*, 149–196.

Paulk, M. C., Curtis, B., Chrisses, M. B., & Weber, C. V. (1993). Capability maturity model, version 1.1. *IEEE Software, 10*(4), 18–27.

Peansupap, V. (2004). An Exploratory approach to the diffusion of ict innovation a project environment. PhD, School of Property, Construction and Project Management. Melbourne: RMIT University.

Peansupap, V., & Walker, D. H. T. (2005a). Diffusion of information and communication technology: A community of practice perspective. In Kazi A. S., *Knowledge Management in the Construction Industry: A Socio-Technical Perspective* (pp. 89–110). Hershey, PA: Idea Group Publishing.

Peansupap, V., & Walker, D. H. T. (2005b). Factors affecting ICT diffusion: A case study of three large australian construction contractors. *Engineering Construction and Architectural Management, 12*(1), 21–37.

Peansupap, V., & Walker, D. H. T. (2006). Information communication technology (ICT) implementation constraints: A construction industry perspective. *Engineering Construction and Architectural Management, 13*(4), 364–379.

Peansupap, V., & Walker, D. H. T. (2009). Exploratory factors influencing design practice learning within a Thai context. *Engineering, Construction and Architectural Management, 16*(3), 238–253.

Peel, S., & Inkson, K. (2004). Contracting and careers: Choosing between self and organizational employment. *Career Development International, 9*(6), 542–558.

Peled, A. (2000). Politicking for success: The missing skill. *Leadership & Organisation Development Journal, 21*(1), 20–29.

Perks, H., & Halliday, S. V. (2003). Sources, signs and signalling for fast trust creation in organisational relationships. *European Management Journal, 21*(3), 338–350.

Perminova, O., Gustafsson, M., & Wikström, K. (2008). Defining uncertainty in projects–A new perspective. *International Journal of Project Management*, *26*(1), 73–79.

Pettigrew, A., Whittington, R., Melin, L., Sánchez-Runde, C., van den Bosch, F. A. J., Ruigrok, W., & Numagami, T. (2003) *Innovative Forms of Organizing*. Thousand Oaks, CA: Sage.

Pinto, J. K. (2000). Understanding the role of politics in successful project management. *International Journal of Project Management*, *18*(2), 85–91.

Pitsis, T. S., Clegg, S. R., Marosszeky, M., & Rura-Polley, T. (2003). Constructing the olympic dream: A future perfect strategy of project management. *Organization Science*, *14*(5), 574–590.

PMI (2003) *Organizational project management maturity model (OPM3) knowledge foundation*. Newtown Square, PA: Project Management Institute.

PMI (2006a) *The standard for portfolio management*. Newtown Square, PA: Project Management Institute.

PMI (2006b) *The standard for program management*. Newtown Square, PA: Project Management Institute.

PMI (2007) *Project management competency development (PMCD) framework*. Newtown Square, PA: Project Management Institute.

PMI (2008) *A guide to the project management body of knowledge (PMBOK® guide)* – Fourth edition. Newtown Square, PA: Project Management Institute.

PMI (2013) *A guide to the project management body of knowledge (PMBOK® guide)* – Fifth edition. Newtown Square, PA: Project Management Institute.

Polanyi, M. (1997). Tacit knowledge. In Prusak L., *Knowledge in Organizations–Resources for the Knowledge-Based Economy* (pp. 135–146). Oxford: Butterworth-Heinemann.

Porter, M. E. (1985) *Competitive advantage: Creating and sustaining superior performance*. New York: The Free Press.

Prahalad, C. K., & Hamel, G. (1990). The core competence of the corporation. *Harvard Business Review*, *68*(3), 79–91.

Prahalad, C. K., & Ramaswamy, V. (2004a). Co-creating unique value with customers. *Strategy & Leadership,*, *32*(3), 4–9.

Prahalad, C. K., & Ramaswamy, V. (2004b). Co-creation experiences: The next practice in value creation. *Journal of Interactive Marketing*, *18*(3), 5–14.

Prahalad, C. K., & Ramaswamy, V. (2004c) *The future of competition–Co-creating unique value with customers*. Boston MA: Harvard Business School Press

Putnam, R. D. (1995). Bowling alone: America's declining social capital. *Journal of Democracy*, *6*(1), 65–78.

Radosavljevic, M., & Bennett, J. (2012) *Construction management strategies–A theory of construction management*. Chichester, West Sussex UK: Wiley-Blackwell.

Raelin, J. A. (2007). Toward an epistemology of practice. *Academy of Management Learning & Education*, *6*(4), 495–519.

Regan, M., Smith, J., & Love, P. E. D. (2011). Impact of the capital market collapse on public-private partnership infrastructure projects. *Journal of Construction Engineering and Management*, *137*(1), 6–16.

Remington, K. (2011) *Leading complex projects*. Aldershot, UK: Gower.

Remington, K., & Pollack, J. (2007). *Tools for complex projects*. Aldershot, UK: Gower.

Rezania, D., & Lingham, T. (2009). Coaching IT project teams: A design toolkit. *International Journal of Managing Projects in Business*, *2*(4), 577–590.

Rittel, H. W. J., & Webber, M. M. (1973). Dilemmas in a general theory of planning. *Policy Sciences*, *4*(2), 155–169.

Rogers, E. M. (2003) *Diffusion of innovation*. New York: The Free Press.

Ross, J. (2003). *Introduction to project alliancing*. Alliance Contracting Conference, Sydney, 30 April 2003, Project Control International Pty Ltd,

Rousseau, D. M., Sitkin, S. B., Burt, R. S., & Camerer, C. (1998). Not so different after all: A cross-discipline view of trust. *Academy of Management Review*, *23*(3), 393–405.

Rowlinson, S., & McDermott, P. (1999) *Procurement systems A Guide to Best Practice in Construction*. London: E&FN Spon.

Rowlinson, S., & Walker, D. H. T. (2008). Case study–Innovation management in alliances. In Walker D. H. T., & Rowlinson, S., *Procurement Systems–A Cross Industry Project Management Perspective* (pp. 400–422). Abingdon, Oxon: Taylor & Francis.

Rowlinson, S., Walker, D. H. T., & Cheung, F. Y. K. (2008). Culture and its impact upon project procurement. In Walker D. H. T., & Rowlinson, S., *Procurement Systems–A Cross Industry Project Management Perspective* (pp. 277–310). Abingdon, Oxon: Taylor & Francis.

Ruuska, I., Ahola, T., Artto, K., Locatelli, G., & Mancini, M. (2011). A new governance approach for multi-firm projects: Lessons from Olkiluoto 3 and Flamanville 3 nuclear power plant projects. *International Journal of Project Management*, *29*(6), 647–660.

Ruuska, I., Artto, K., Aaltonen, K., & Lehtonen, P. (2009). Dimensions of distance in a project network: Exploring Olkiluoto 3 nuclear power plant project. *International Journal of Project Management*, *27*(2), 142–153.

Scase, R. (2001). *Britain in 2010: The changing business landscape.* London: Capstone.

Scheepers, R., Venkitachalam, K., & Gibbs, M. R. (2004). Knowledge strategy in organizations: Refining the model of Hansen, Nohria and Tierney. *Journal of Strategic Information Systems*, *13*(3).

Schein, E. H. (2004). *Organisational culture and leadership.* San Francisco: Jossey Bass.

Schindler, M., & Eppler, M. J. (2003). Harvesting project knowledge: A review of project learning methods and success factors. *International Journal of Project Management*, *21*(3), 219–228.

Schön, D. A. (1983). *The reflective practitioner–How professionals think in action.* Aldershot, UK: BasiAshgate ARENA.

Selvin, A. M., Buckingham Shum, S. J., & Aakhus, M. (2010). The practice level in participatory design rationale: studying practitioner moves and choices. *Human Technology: An Interdisciplinary Journal on Humans in ICT Environments*, *6*(1), 71–105.

Sense, A. J. (2003). Learning generators: Project teams re-conceptualized. *Project Management Journal*, *34*(3), 4–12.

Sense, A. J. (2005). Cultivating situational learning within project management practice. PhD, Macquarie Graduate Shool of Management. Sydney: Macquarie University.

Sense, A. J. (2007) *Cultivating learning within projects.* New York: Palgrave MacMillan.

Shalin, D. N. (1992). Critical theory and the pragmatist challenge. *The American Journal of Sociology*, *98*(2), 237–279.

Shelley, A. (2007) *The organizational zoo: A survival guide to workplace behavior.* Connecticut, USA: Aslan Publishing.

Shelley, A. (2011). Creative metaphor as a tool for stakeholder influence. In Bourne, L. M., *Advising Upwards– A Framework for Understanding and Engaging Senior Management Stakeholders* (pp. 271–296). Farnham, Surrey, UK: Gower.

Shelley, A. (2012). Metaphor as a means to constructively influence behavioural interactions in project teams. PhD, School of Property, Construction and Project Management. Melbourne: RMIT University.

Shenhar, A., & Dvir, D. (2007) *Reinventing project management : The diamond approach to successful growth and innovation.* Boston: Harvard Business School Press.

Shenhar, A. J. (2001). One size does not fit all projects: Exploring classical contingency domains. *Management Science*, *47*(3), 391–414.

Shenhar, A. J., Dvir, D., Levy, O., & Maltz, A. C. (2001). Project success: A multidimensional strategic concept. *Long Range Planning*, *34*(6), 699–725.

Shenhar, A. L., & Dvir, D. (2004). How Projects differ, and what to do about it. In Morris, P. W. G., & Pinto, J. K., *The Wiley Guide to Managing Projects* (pp. 1265–1286). New York: Wiley.

Sidwell, A. C., & Ireland, V. (1989). An international comparison of construction management. *The Australian Institute of Building Papers*, *2*(1), 3–12.

Sidwell, A. C., & Mehertns, V. M. (1996). *Case studies in constructability implementation.* Adelaide: Construction Industry Institute Australia.

Slaughter, E. S. (1998). Models of construction innovation. *Journal of Construction Engineering and Management*, *124*(2), 226–231.

Small, J. M. (2009). The emergent realities of project praxis in socially complex project environments. Doctor of Project Management, DPM, School of Property, Construction and Project Management. Melbourne: RMIT.

Small, J. M., & Walker, D. H. T. (2011). Providing structural openness to connect with context: Seeing the project entity as a human activity system and social process. *International Journal of Managing Projects in Business*, *4*(3), 389–411.

Smith, C. (2007). *Making sense of project realities : Theory, practice and the pursuit of performance.* Aldershot, UK: Gower Publishing Ltd.

Smith, C., & Winter, M. (2010). The craft of project shaping. *International Journal of Managing Projects in Business*, *3*(1), 46–60.

Smyth, H. (2006). Measuring, developing and and managing trust in relationships. In Pryke, S., & Smyth, H., *The Management Of Complex Projects : A Relationship Approach* (pp. 97–120). Boston: Blackwell Pub.

Smyth, H., & Edkins, A. (2007). Relationship management in the management of PFI/PPP projects in the UK. *International Journal of Project Management*, *25*(3), 232–240.

Smyth, H. J. (1999). Partnering: practical problems and conceptual limits to relationship marketing. *International Journal of Construction Marketing*, *1*(2), 1–14, online version http://www.brookes.ac.uk/other/conmark/IJCM/issue_02/010202.pdf.

Smyth, H. J., & Morris, P. W. G. (2007). An epistemological evaluation of research into projects and their management: Methodological issues. *International Journal of Project Management*, *25*(4), 423–436.

Snowden, D. J. (2002). Complex acts of knowing: paradox and descriptive self-awareness. *Journal of Knowledge Management*, *6*(2), 100–111.

Snowden, D. J., & Boone, M. E. (2007). A Leader's framework for decision making. *Harvard Business Review*, *85* (11), 69–76.

Sobek, D. K., Liker, J. K., & Ward, A. C. (1998). Another look at how Toyota integrates product development. *Harvard Business Review*, *76*(4), 36–49.

Söderlund, J. (2004). On the Broadening scope of the research on projects: A review and a model for analysis. *International Journal of Project Management*, *22*(8), 655–667.

Söderlund, J. (2010). *Knowledge entrainment and project management: Understanding project management as knowledge integration under time pressure*. IPMI Reserach Conference 2010, Washington, July 11–14, Messikomer C., PMI, 23pp.

Söderlund, J. (2012). *Organization of human resources in a project-based economy: Towards an analytical framework*. EURAM 2012, Project Organising General Track, Rotterdam, Netherlands, 6th-8th June, Gemünden H. G., & J. R. Turner, Erasmus University, 13pp.

Spear, S. (2004). Learning to lead at Toyota. *Harvard Business Revie*, *82*(5), 78–86.

Spear, S., & Bowen, H. K. (1999). Decoding the DNA of the Toyota production system. *Harvard Business Review*, *77*(5), 97–106.

Standish (1994). The chaos report (1994). Company research report. Dennnis, MA, 14.

Standish (2003). Latest Standish Group CHAOS Report Shows Project Success Rates Have Improved by 50%, http://www.standishgroup.com/press/article.php?id=2, March 25

Steinfort, P. (2010). Understanding the antecedents of project management best practice-lessons to be learned from aid relief projects. PhD, School of Property, Construction and Project Management. Melbourne: RMIT University.

Steinfort, P., & Walker, D. H. T. (2011). *What enables project success: Lessons from aid relief projects*. Newtown Square, PA: Project Management Institute.

Stewart, R. A., & Mohamed, S. (2001). Utilizing the balanced scorecard for IT/IS performance evaluation in construction. *Journal of Construction Innovation*, *1*(3), 147–163.

Stewart, W. E. (2001). Balanced scorecard for projects. *Project Management Journal*, *32*(1), 38–53.

Strauss, A. & Corbin, J. (1998). *Basic of Qualitative Research*, Thousand Oaks, CA: Sage publications Inc.

Storck, J., & Hill, P. A. (2000). Knowledge diffusion through strategic communities. *Sloan Management Review*, *41*(2), 63–74.

Sundbo, J. (1997). Management of innovation in service. *Service Industries Journal*, *17*(3), 432–455.

Sveiby, K. E. (1997). *The new organizational wealth: Managing and measuring knowledge-based assets*. San Francisco: Berrett-Koehler Publishers, Inc.

Sweeney, S. M. (2009). Addressing market failure: Using transaction cost economics to improve the construction industry's performance. PhD, Dept. of Civil and Environmental Engineering. Melbourne: University of Melbourne.

Sydow, J., Lindkvist, L., & DeFillippi, R. (2004). Project-based organizations, embeddedness and repositories of knowledge: Editorial. *Organization Studies*, 1475–1489.

Szulanski, G. (1996). Exploring internal stickiness: Impediments to the transfer of best practice within the firm. *Strategic Management Journal*, *17* (Winter special Issue), 27–43.

Szulanski, G. (2003). *Sticky Knowledge barriers to knowing in the firm*. Thousand Oaks, CA: Sage Publications.

Tan, K. C. (2002). A comparative study of 16 National Quality Awards. *The TQM Magazine*, *14*(3), 165–171.

Teigland, R. (2000). Communities of practice at an internet firm: Netovation vs on-time performance.In Lesser E., Fontaine, M. A., and Slusher, J. A., *Knowledge and Communities* (pp. 151–178). Boston: Butterworth-Heinemann.

Testi, J., Sidwell, A. C., & Lenard, D. J. (1995). Benchmarking Engineering and Construction–Winning Teams. Adelaide: CIIA and University of South Australia,5.

The World Bank (2005). *The Logframe handbook–A Logical framework appraoch to project cycle management.* Washington, DC: The World Bank.

Thiry, M. (1997). *Value management practice.* Newtown Square, PA: Project Management Institute.

Thiry, M., & Deguire, M. (2007). Recent developments in project-based organisations. *International Journal of Project Management, 25*(7), 649–658.

Thomke, S. (2001). Enlightened experimentation–The new imperative for innovation. *Harvard Business Review, 79*(2), 66–75.

Thompson, P. J., & Sanders, S. R. (1998). Partnering continuum. *Journal of Management in Engineering–American Society of Civil Engineers/ Engineering Management Division, 14*(5), 73–78.

Thorsdottir, T. (2001). Merging organizational culture: lessons for international joint ventures. In Tayeb, M. H., *International Business Partnership: Issues and Concerns.* New York: Palgrave.

Treacy, M., & Wiersema, F. (1993). Customer intimacy and other value disciplines. *Harvard Business Review, 71*(1), 84–93.

Trompenaars, F. (1993). *Riding the waves of culture: Understanding cultural diversity in business.* London: Economics Books.

Trompenaars, F., & Hampden-Turner, C. (2004). *Managing people : Across cultures.* Chichester, England: Capstone.

Trompenaars, F., & Prud'homme, P. (2004) *Managing change across corporate cultures.* London: Piatkus.

Tsai, W., & Ghoshal, S. (1998). Social capital and value creation: The role of intrafirm networks. *Academy of Management Journal, 41*(4), 464–476.

Tulley, S. (1998). How Cisco mastered the net. *Fortune, 4* (138), 207–209.

Turner, J. R. (2000). Do you manage work, deliverables or resources? *International Journal of Project Management, 18*(2), 83–84.

Turner, J. R. (2006). Towards a theory of project management: The nature of the project governance and project management. *International Journal of Project Management, 24*(2), 93–95.

Turner, J. R., & Cochrane, R. A. (1993). The goals and methods matrix: coping with projects with ill-defined goals and/ or methods of achieving them. *International Journal of Project Management, 11*(2), 93–102.

Turner, J. R., Müller, R., & Dulewicz, V. (2009). Comparing the leadership styles of functional and project managers. *International Journal of Managing Projects in Business, 2*(2), 198–216.

Turner, N. (2011). The management of ambidexterity – An intellectual capital perspective. PhD, School of Management. Bath: University of Bath.

Turner, R. (2007). Determining the impact of emotional intelligence in project management as a measure of performance. Doctor of Project Management, School of Property, Construction and Project Management. Melbourne: RMIT.

Turner, R., Huemann, M., & Keegan, A. (2008). Human resource management in the project-oriented organization: Employee well-being and ethical treatment. *International Journal of Project Management, 26*(5), 577–585.

Turner, R., & Lloyd-Walker, B. (2008). Emotional intelligence (EI) capabilities training: Can it develop EI in project teams? *International Journal of Managing Projects in Business, 1*(4), 512–534.

Tuulenmäki, A., & Välikangas, L. (2011). The art of rapid, hands-on execution innovation. *Strategy & Leadership 39*(2), 28–35.

Uher, T. (1999). Partnering performance in Australia. *Journal of Construction Procurement, 5*(2), 163–176.

Ulrich, D. (1997). HR of the future: Conclusions and observations. *Human Resource Management, 36*(1), 175–179.

Ulrich, D. (1998). Intellectual capital = competence x commitment. *Sloan Management Review, 39*(2), 15–26.

van de Ven, A. H. (1986). Central problems in the management of innovation. *Management Science, 32*(5), 590–607.

van Eijnatten, F. M., & Putnik, G. D. (2004). Chaos, complexity, learning, and the learning organization: towards a chaordic enterprise. *The Learning Organization, 11*(6), 418–429.

van Marrewijk, M. (2003). Concepts and definitions of CSR and Corporate sustainability: between agency and communion. *Journal of Business Ethics, 44*(2), 95–105.

Vargo, S., & Lusch, R. (2008). Service-dominant logic: Continuing the evolution. *Journal of the Academy of Marketing Science, 36*(1), 1–10.

Vargo, S. L., & Lusch, R. F. (2004). Evolving to a new dominant logic for marketing. *Journal of Marketing*, *68*(1), 1–17.

Victorian Auditor-General's Office (2008). Investing smarter in public sector ICT. Melbourne, 68.

von Hippel, E. (1990). "Sticky Information" and the locus of problem solving: Implications for innovation. *Management Science*, *40*(4), 429–439.

von Hippel, E., Thomke, S., & Sonnack, M. (1999). Creating breakthrough at 3M. *Harvard Business Review*, *77*(5), 47–57.

von Krogh, G. (1998). Care in knowledge creation. *California Management Review*, *40*(3), 40–54.

von Krogh, G., Ichijo, K., & Takeuchi, H. (2000) *Enabling knowledge creation*. Oxford: Oxford University Press.

von Krogh, G., Nonaka, I., & Rechsteiner, L. (2012). Leadership in organizational knowledge creation: A Review and framework. *Journal of Management Studies*, *49*(1), 240–277.

Vorakulpipat, C., & Rezgui, Y. (2008). An evolutionary and interpretive perspective to knowledge management. *Journal of Knowledge Management*, *12*(3), 17–34.

Vygotskii, A. L. (1986). *Thought and language*. Cambridge, MA: MIT Press.

Walker, A. (1993). *Project management in construction*. London: Blackwell Science.

Walker, C., & Smith, A. J. (1995). *Privatised Infrastructure–The BOT approach*. London: Thomas Telford.

Walker, D. H. T. (1996). The contribution of the construction management team to good construction time performance–An Australian experience. *Journal of Construction Procurement*, *2*(2), 4–18.

Walker, D. H. T. (1998). The contribution of the client's representative to the creation and maintenance of good project inter-team relationships. *Engineering and Architectural Management*, *5*(1), 51–57.

Walker, D. H. T. (2004). The Knowledge advantage (k-adv) unleashing creativity and innovation. Unpublished report draft manuscript. Melbourne, 183.

Walker, D. H. T. (2008). Reflections on developing a project management doctorate. *International Journal of Project Management*, *26*(3), 316–325.

Walker, D. H. T. (2012). Innovation and value delivery through supply chain management. In Akintoye A., Goulding, J., & Zoudi, G., *Construction Innovation and Process Improvement* (pp. 125–153). Abingdon, Oxon, UK: Wiley Blackwell.

Walker, D. H. T., Bourne, L., & Rowlinson, S. (2008). Stakeholders and the supply chain. In Walker D. H. T., & Rowlinson, S., *Procurement Systems–A Cross Industry Project Management Perspective* (pp. 246–276). Abingdon, Oxon: Taylor & Francis, (pp. 70-100).

Walker, D. H. T., Cicmil, S., Thomas, J., Anbari, F. T., & Bredillet, C. (2008a). Collaborative academic/practitioner research in project management: Theory and models. *International Journal of Managing Projects in Business*, *1*(1), 17–32.

Walker, D. H. T., & Hampson, K. D. (2003a). Enterprise networks, partnering and alliancing. In Walker D. H. T., & Hampson, K. D., *Procurement Strategies: A Relationship Based Approach* (pp. 30–73). Oxford: Blackwell Publishing.

Walker, D. H. T., & Hampson, K. D. (2003b). Procurement choices. In Walker D. H. T., & Hampson, K. D., *Procurement Strategies: A Relationship Based Approach* (pp. 13–29). Oxford: Blackwell Publishing.

Walker, D. H. T., & Hampson, K. D. (2003c) *Procurement strategies: A relationship based approach*. Oxford, Blackwell Publishing.

Walker, D. H. T., & Hampson, K. D. (2003d). Project Alliance member organisation selection. In Walker D. H. T., & Hampson, K. D., *Procurement Strategies: A Relationship Based Approach* (pp. 74–102). Oxford: Blackwell Publishing.

Walker, D. H. T., Hampson, K. D., & Ashton, S. (2003). Developing in innovation culture. In Walker D. H. T., & Hampson, K. D., *Procurement Strategies: A Relationship Based Approach* (pp. 236–257). Oxford: Blackwell Publishing.

Walker, D. H. T., Hampson, K. D., & Peters, R. J. (2002). Project alliancing vs project partnering: A case study of the Australian National Museum project. *Supply Chain Management: An International Journal*, *7*(2), 83–91.

Walker, D. H. T., Harley, J., & Mills, A. (2013a). Longitudinal study of performance in large australasian public sector infrastructure alliances 2008–2013. Melbourne: RMIT University, Centre for Integrated Project Solutions, 48pp.

Walker, D. H. T., & Johannes, D. S. (2003). Preparing for organisational learning by HK infrastructure project joint ventures organisations. *The Learning Organization, MCB University Press. UK*, *10*(2), 106–117.

Walker, D. H. T., & Lloyd-Walker, B. M. (2011a). Profiling professional excellence in alliance management summary study report. Sydney: Alliancing Association of Australasia, 36.

Walker, D. H. T., & Lloyd-Walker, B. M. (2011b). Profiling professional excellence in alliance management volume one–Findings and results. Sydney: Alliancing Association of Australasia, 76pp.

Walker, D. H. T., & Lloyd-Walker, B. M. (2011c). profiling professional excellence in alliance management volume two–Appendices. Sydney: Alliancing Association of Australasia, 98pp.

Walker, D. H. T., & Lloyd-Walker, B. M. (2012a). Client capabilities – An Ethical dilemma example. In Volberda, H. W., *Social Innovatiion for Competitiveness, Organisational Performance and Human Exellence*. Rotterdam: EURAM, 40pp.

Walker, D. H. T., & Lloyd-Walker, B. M. (2012b). *Understanding early contractor involvement (ECI) procurement forms.* Twenty-Eighth ARCOM Annual Conference, Edinburgh, 5–7 September, Smith S., Association of Researchers in Construction Management, *2*, 877–887.

Walker, D. H. T., & Lloyd-Walker, B. M. (2013). *Making sense of collaborative forms of relationship based construction procurement.* in Carrillo P., & Chinowsky, P., eds, Proceedings of Engineering Project Organization Conference, Devil's Thumb Ranch, Colorado July 9–11, 2013, 15pp.

Walker, D. H. T., & Lloyd-Walker, B. M. (2014). The ambience of a project alliance in Australia. *Engineering Project Organization Journal*, *4*(1), 1–15.

Walker, D. H. T., Lloyd-Walker, B. M., & Mills, A. (2013b). *Innovation through alliancing in a no-blame culture.* 19th CIB World Building Congress, Brisbane, May 6–9, Kajewski S., Manley, K., and Hampson, K. D. CIB, 12pp.

Walker, D. H. T., & Maqsood, T. (2008). Procurement innovation and organisational learning. In Walker D. H. T., & Rowlinson, S., *Procurement Systems–A Cross Industry Project Management Perspective* (pp. 246–276). Abingdon, Oxon: Taylor & Francis.

Walker, D. H. T., & Nogeste, K. (2008). Performance measures and project procurement. In Walker D. H. T., & Rowlinson, S., *Procurement Systems–A Cross Industry Project Management Perspective* (pp. 177–210). Abingdon, Oxon: Taylor & Francis.

Walker, D. H. T., & Rowlinson, S., Eds. (2008a). *Procurement systems–A cross industry project management perspective.* Series Procurement Systems–A Cross Industry Project Management Perspective. Abingdon, Oxon: Taylor & Francis.

Walker, D. H. T., & Rowlinson, S. (2008b). Project types and their procurement needs. In Walker D. H. T., & Rowlinson, S., *Procurement Systems–A Cross Industry Project Management Perspective* (pp. 32–69). Abingdon, Oxon: Taylor & Francis.

Walker, D. H. T., Segon, M., & Rowlinson, S. (2008b). Business ethics and corporate citizenship. In Walker D. H. T., & Rowlinson, S., *Procurement Systems–A Cross Industry Project Management Perspective* (pp. 101–139). Abingdon, Oxon: Taylor & Francis.

Ward, S. C. (1997) *Project risk management: Processes, techniques, and insights.* New York: Wiley.

Ward, S. C. (1999). Assessing and managing important risks. *International Journal of Project Management*, *17*(6), 331–336.

Ward, S. C., & Chapman, C. (2003). Transforming project risk management into project uncertainty management. *International Journal of Project Management*, *21*(2), 97–105.

Wenger, E. C., McDermott, R., & Snyder, W. M. (2002) *Cultivating communities of practice.* Boston, MA: Harvard Business School Press.

Wenger, E. C., & Snyder, W. M. (2000). Communities of practice: The organizational frontier. *Harvard Business Review*, *78*(1), 139–145.

Wheelwright, S. C., & Sasser Jr, W. E. (1989). The new product development map. *Harvard Business Review*, *67*(3), 112–125.

Whitty, J. (2011). How to train tour manager: A Darwinian perspective. In Bourne, L. M., *Advising Upwards–A Framework for Understanding and Engaging Senior Management Stakeholders* (pp. 243–270). Farnham, Surrey, UK: Gower.

Whitty, S. J. (2005). A memetic paradigm of project management. *International Journal of Project Management*, *23*(8), 575–583.

Whitty, S. J. (2009). New philosophy of project management: An investigation into the prevalence of modern project management by means of an evolutionary framework. Doctor of Philosophy, School of Information Technology and Electrical Engineering. Brisbane, Queensland: The University of Queensland.

Whitty, S. J., & Maylor, H. (2007). *And then came complex project management*. 21th IPMA World Congress on Project Management, Cracow, Poland, 18–20 June, International Project Management Association, 7.

Williams, T. (2010). *Analysis of the London underground PPP failure*. Engineering Project Organizations Conference, South Lake Tahoe, CA, Taylor J. E., & P. Chinowsky, Engineering Project Organization Society (EPOS), 15.

Williams, T. M. (1999). The need for new paradigms for complex projects. *International Journal of Project Management*, *17*(5), 269–273.

Williams, T. M., Samset, K., & Sunnevåg, K. J., Eds. (2009). *Making Essential choices with scant information–Front-end decision making in major projects*. Series Making Essential Choices with Scant Information–Front-end decision Making in Major Projects. Basingstoke, UK: Palgrave Macmillan.

Williamson, O. E. (1975) *Markets and hierarchies, analysis and antitrust implications: A study in the economics of internal organization*. New York: Free Press.

Williamson, O. E. (1985) *The economic institutions of capitalism: Firms, markets, relational contracting*. New York: The Free Press.

Williamson, O. E. (1991). Strategizing, economizing, and economic organization. *Strategic Management Journal*, *12* [Special Issue], 75–94.

Winch, G. M. (2003) *Managing construction projects*. Oxford: Blackwell Publishing.

Winter, M., & Smith, C. (2006). EPSRC Network 2004–2006 Rethinking Project Management Final Report, Final report. Manchester, EPSRC, 15.

Winter, M., Smith, C., Morris, P. W. G., & Cicmil, S. (2006). Directions for future research in project management: The main findings of a UK government-funded research network. *International Journal of Project Management*, *24*(8), 638–649.

Winter, M., & Szczepanek, T. (2009) *Images of projects*. Farnham: Gower

Wolff, M. F. (1987). To Innovate faster, try the skunk works. *Research Technology Management*, *30*(5), 7–9.

Wolstenholme, A. (2009). Never waste a good crisis–A review of progress since rethinking construction and thoughts for our future, London, Constructing Excellence, 32pp.

Womack, J. P., Jones, D. T., & Roos, D. (1990) *The machine that changed the world–The story of lean production*. New York: Harper Collins.

Wood, G. D., & Ellis, R. C. T. (2005). An empirical study of the benefits of construction partnering in Hong Kong. *Construction Management & Economics*, *23*(3), 317–325.

Wood, P., & Duffield, C. (2009). In pursuit of additional value: A benchmarking study into alliancing in the Australian Public Sector. Melbourne: Department of Treasury and Finance, Victoria, 191.

Wu, H. J., & Dunn, S. C. (1995). Environmentally responsible logistics systems. *International Journal of Physical Distribution & Logistics Management*, *25*(2), 20–38.

Xu, T., Bower, D. A., & Smith, N. J. (2005). Types of collaboration between foreign contractors and their Chinese partners. *International Journal of Project Management*, *23*(1), 45–53.

Yeung, J. F. Y., Chan, A. P. C., & Chan, D. W. M. (2007). The definition of alliancing in construction as a Wittgenstein family-resemblance concept. *International Journal of Project Management*, *25*(3), 219–231.

Yin, R. (1994) *Case Study Research*. Thousand Oaks, CA: Sage.

Younger, J., Smallwood, N., & Ulrich, D. (2007). Developing Your organization's brand as a talent developer. *Human Resource Planning*, *30*(2), 21–29.

Zahra, S. A., & George, G. (2002). Absorptive capacity: A review, reconceptualisation, and extension. *Academy of Management Review*, *27*(2), 185–203.

Zhang, Y., & Gregory, M. (2011). Managing global network operations along the engineering value chain. *International Journal of Operations & Production Management*, *31*(7), 736–764.

Contributors

Dr. Derek Walker is Professor of project management at the School of Property, Construction and Project Management, RMIT University. He worked in various project management roles in the U.K., Canada, and Australia for 16 years before commencing his academic career in 1986. He obtained a Master of Science from the University of Aston (Birmingham) in 1978, and a PhD in 1995 from RMIT University (Melbourne). He has written over 200 peer-reviewed papers and book chapters. His current research interests include procurement forms, particularly evolving collaborative procurement arrangements, and organizational learning.

Dr. Beverley Lloyd-Walker is based in the Centre for Integrated Project Solutions at RMIT University, Melbourne, and is an Adjunct Professor in the College of Business, Victoria University, Melbourne, Australia. After several years in industry, she commenced her career in academia in 1990. She has a Bachelor of Business degree, Graduate Diploma of Post-secondary Education, Graduate Diploma of Applied Science, and Graduate Certificate of Change Management. She obtained her PhD from Monash University (Melbourne) in 1999. She has published over 40 refereed articles, 10 refereed chapters, and co-authored three editions of the book *Human Resource Management* in Australia. Her current major area of research relates to people in temporary organizations, or project teams, and forms of collaborative procurement.